THE NORMANS

The Normans

The History of a Dynasty

David Crouch

Hambledon and London
London and New York

Hambledon and London
102 Gloucester Avenue
London, NW1 8HX

838 Broadway
New York
NY 10003–4812

First Published 2002

ISBN 1 85285 387 5

A description of this book is available from the
British Library and from the Library of Congress.

Typeset by Carnegie Publishing, Lancaster.

Printed on woodfree paper and bound in
Great Britain by Bath Press, Bath

Contents

Illustrations

Between Pages 176 and 177

Family Trees

Introduction

One of the more curious stories to come out of medieval Europe is that of the Norman dynasty and people. The Norman phenomenon began in an almost inconspicuous way: a small fleet of Scandinavian ships and their miscellaneous crews cruised into the Seine estuary at the beginning of the second decade of the tenth century. Those particular ships were not the first of their sort to sail up that particular river. Their crews were not the first to take possession of the battered Frankish city of Rouen on the third great meander of the Seine. What was different about them? They had a leader of some ability; so much is clear. His name was Hrólfr, but he was not a Viking of any great lineage or royal connections. He was one of many ambitious warriors adrift on the northern Atlantic in those days, a man whose ship had ploughed the grey seas from Norway to the Hebrides and down into the English Channel. He may well have led his men as a breakaway group from the bigger Viking army at that time pillaging and settling the estuary of the Loire and Brittany.

Hrólfr, however, was more accomplished than his fellow jarls. He was able to impose himself on his men and get them to accept his unqualified leadership. He was also astute enough to be able to come to terms with the ecclesiastical authorities of Rouen and use them to make contact with the Frankish king and his counts further upriver. Playing on the political circumstances of the decrepit Frankish kingdom, he got the king to sanction his possession of Rouen and was prompt in accepting Christianity, which allowed the Frankish lords and peasants of the region to associate with him as a respectable man. Soon he and his son were posing as Christian 'counts of Rouen' and claiming equality with the Frankish rulers who surrounded them. But the Franks did not forget that this new lord in the old province of Neustria was an outsider or that his people were northerners: they were the 'Northmen' (*Northmanni*).

Other such Scandinavian colonies in France and England rapidly lost their identity and failed to establish themselves. The Vikings on the Loire were driven out and forgotten within a generation, but this was not to be the fate of the Vikings of the Seine. Hrólfr and his men were assimilated with astonishing rapidity into the Christian Frankish culture that surrounded them. In two generations, the Normans were in fact little different in aspirations and language from the Franks still living in the lands they had settled. In that embracing of Frankishness lay their claim to legitimate possession of their land. Yet they were still called 'Normans'. Why? A succession of talented rulers in succession to Hrólfr realised that, much as they wished to be considered Franks and Christians, their growing principality needed an identity to mark them out from their neighbours. Their unusual origins provided what they needed, and on their colonial identity they built their own distinctiveness. Within three generations of Hrólfr his descendants were secretly rather proud of their free-spirited, swashbuckling and bloodthirsty forebears, even if they did not resemble them much. So grew up the idea of a Norman people and a Norman dynasty.

The Normans went a long way, although it would be anachronistic of us to suggest that it was their Viking ancestry that made them keen to roam Europe and the Middle East. It just so happened that opportunities for travel and adventure were there to be had in the eleventh century. So they joined the pilgrim movements that made Normans princes of Tarragona in Spain and Antioch in Syria. The collapse of Lombard and Byzantine rule in Italy attracted obscure Norman mercenaries, who colonised and assumed control of Apulia and Sicily. Most famously, of course, the long-term involvement of Normandy with the kingdom of England across the Channel led to the descent of a Norman army on English soil in October 1066. Its success raised the Norman ducal dynasty to an immortality comparable to that of the Caesars and Ptolemys.

Such a reputation has attracted many writers to look at the Normans down the centuries, and this book is but the latest of dozens which have examined the Norman phenomenon, their ultimate ancestor being Sir John Hayward's *The Lives of the Three Normans, Kings of England* (1613). Hayward talked of three Norman kings, but in this book you will find four kings reckoned as Normans, adding Stephen to the two

Williams and Henry I. King Stephen was in fact called by a contemporary chronicler, the Anglo-Norman monk Orderic Vitalis, the 'fourth king of Norman stock'. Orderic's purpose was to promote the legitimacy of Stephen, who was a grandson of the Conqueror, but a Frenchman born and raised in Chartres. Yet there are other reasons to consider Stephen along with his three Norman predecessors on the throne. The principal one is that contemporaries decided that the succession of Henry II to Stephen in 1154 marked the end of the Norman story; with him they no longer saw the royal line originating in Hrólfr or Rollo the Viking; instead they saw him as the latest representative of a lineage stretching back through his grandmother Edith-Mathilda to Alfred the Great. Henry II's reign inaugurated an entirely new concept of dynasty and legitimacy.

Now is a good time to re-examine what the past three centuries have made of the Normans. At last the complete body source material for the Normans, their rulers' charters and their chronicles, is readily available in handsome and scientific editions incomparably superior to what was available to Sir John Hayward, or even to Edward Augustus Freeman, the nineteenth-century arch-historian of the Norman Conquest. The historical profession has also been active on a broad front over the past few decades, formulating daring new models of medieval ethnicity, aristocracy and family formation. This book reconciles all that scholarship into what is a new narrative of the Norman dynasty and its achievements, one that is only possible because of the unstinting dedication of generations of other scholars and writers.

To David Bates

Acknowledgements

The idea of writing a book on a dynasty is an appealing one at several levels. When Nigel Saul suggested it, I jumped at the opportunity of writing about the Normans. It took me some months to work out why the idea was so immediately attractive. It was partly because biographies are not entirely satisfying as projects. I have written a number of them, and enjoyed constructing them, but I had come to realise their limitations. A biography spans one life, but the developments that one life illuminates often have long and fascinating histories behind them, and there is not the space or justification to go into depth about them. If you do – and Professor Barlow's *William Rufus* is a good example of this – the book loses in coherence what it gains in general interest. A book on dynasties is a serial biography, so you have the possibility of combining the fascinations of exploring character and motivation with a span of *la longue durée* respectable enough to impress an *Annaliste*. Another reason for writing this book is that it gave me the opportunity to construct a strong historical narrative. To paraphrase Umberto Eco, historians nowadays have a licence to write for 'sheer narrative pleasure' rather than out of a commitment to the present, to explain the world to itself. I'm not entirely sure when this happened, although I have a feeling it had something to do with Simon Schama.

Twentieth-century medieval historiography in Britain as much as France – with some brilliant exceptions – was not dominated by narrative. At its best, it darted upwards with enthusiasm and clarity to follow the questions let loose by Stubbs at Oxford in the 1860s, and by Tout at Manchester and Durkheim at the ENS in the 1900s. At its frequent worst it floundered in muddy pools where dogmatic schemes trapped and hampered bathers like weeds. It encouraged congested and short-lived doctoral monographs and discouraged the interested but unspecialised reader. But in fact, there never was any real reason why historical prose had to abdicate human interest and colour in order to address serious questions; something that French historians remembered but some Anglo-American historians forgot. You cannot penetrate the human condition without taking humanity into consideration. The overriding concern in this book is to provide just such a focused and lucid narrative, with a minimum of footnotes and apparatus. I am rather proud that I have reduced anything resembling the monographic to one short chapter at the end, when I sum up what the story of the Normans tells us about dynasties. I have also tried to avoid telling the story of 'England' and 'Normandy', which is why some readers may feel that I have missed out large chunks of the story. I haven't. National, ethnic and regional stories are not what I am telling here.

Words or concepts useful in understanding the Norman world are explained in the Glossary (pp. 303–9) at the end of the book. Also at the end of the book is a list of Medieval Sources and Authors (pp. 311–20), giving details of the contemporary writers and sources on which much of this book is based.

I have quite a few debts to acknowledge here, not least to my long-suffering wife, Linda, and my less tolerant – but still supportive – sons, Simon and Timmy. Linda's advice was as valuable as ever in making the text readable. This book would have been much harder to write if it had not been done in something of a golden age for the edition and translation of contemporary medieval texts. The debt of present and future historians of the Norman and Anglo-Norman world to Marjorie Chibnall, Ralph Davis, John France, Diana Greenway, Tony Holden, Elisabeth van Houts, Edmund King and Patrick McGurk is a heavy one. I sincerely thank Professor Nigel Saul of Royal Holloway, University of London, and Tony Morris and Martin Sheppard of Hambledon and London for encouraging me to take up the commission, and for channelling the resulting flow of words. Dr Martin Arnold of the University of Hull was generous beyond the call of duty with his advice on Scandinavian literature, names and genealogy, and the first appendix relies heavily on his scholarship. Dr Graham Loud of the University of Leeds, Dr Christopher Lewis of the University of Liverpool, Professor Martha Carlin of the University of Wisconsin,

Professor Lois Hunneycutt of the University of Missouri, Professor Judith Green of the Queen's University, Belfast, Professor Robin Fleming of Boston College and Professor Derek Keene of the University of London assisted by making telling and provocative observations that they probably have now forgotten that they ever made: I hope they don't get too frustrated working out precisely what it was that they did say. They only have to ask. I had the good fortune to enjoy the conversation of Professor Ralph Davis on King Stephen and Professor Warren Hollister on King Henry I. Lastly I need to acknowledge the years of inspiration and support of Professor David Bates of the University of Glasgow, who was once Dr David Bates of the University College of South Wales and Monmouthshire at Cardiff, and who in 1978 took on a secondary school teacher from Mountain Ash as a part-time MA student, without quite realising where these things can lead. It is to him that I dedicate this book, which is in part a consequence of his love of Normandy and Anglo-French history.

Scarborough   January 2002

1

The Counts of Rouen

Beginning the story of the Normans is not easy. What facts there are resemble dinosaur bones in a desert. A huge amount is missing, and you can put what survives together in any number of ways to make a variety of bizarre animals. So what follows is one possible reconstruction, the best that I can make out of what is known. It is the story of one man's opportunism in a time of violence and instability. It is not the story of the conscious building of a realm and a people: the man involved was not a visionary or a military genius, and his followers were ships' crews scraped together from all the northern shores of the Atlantic. But because of his opportunism and their greed for land, a new realm and a new people were nonetheless created within three generations. Another thing that our hero commenced was a dynasty of princes and kings, one of the greatest and most distinguished that has ever been. We can at least be sure that – like any dominant medieval male – it was his intention to create a line of distinguished descendants. Perhaps the extent of his success might have surprised him.

His name was Hrólfr, and you will gather how we know that from a detailed appendix at the end of this book (pp. 297–300). His full name is quite likely to have been Hrólfr Ketilsson. He was born in the second half of the ninth century somewhere in the Norwegian settlements on the fringes of the Atlantic and he became a Viking. He was a man of noble warrior descent, otherwise he would never have been accepted as the jarl* of a Viking fleet, however small it was. Later and quite unreliable traditions linked him to the royal house of Norway or to the powerful rulers of Orkney. He was a commander of the one of the divisions of a great Viking army that arrived on the Atlantic coast

---

* For a glossary of unusual and relevant terms use throughout the book, see the Glossary, below pp. 303–9.

of France at the very end of the ninth century.[1] The army encamped in
the estuary of the Loire valley and began to spread out in all directions.
In savage warfare it destroyed the power of the kings of the Bretons to
the west, and it moved up the Loire eastwards towards Paris. But as the
Vikings moved up the river they encountered the powerful castles that
still make the Loire valley famous. They found that the Frankish counts
and marquises who were established there, backed up by squadrons of
armoured cavalry, were too powerful to overcome.[2]

So the Vikings of the Loire did what Vikings always did when confronted with difficult foes, they moved elsewhere to find easier targets.
In 915 some moved to south Wales and tried to raid the Severn estuary,
but the military power and organisation of the English kings was too
much for them and they were driven across the Irish Sea. Other groups
took to their ships and felt their way up the Channel coast, looking for
unprotected coasts to raid. One group landed in force on the Cotentin
peninsula around the Roman town of Cherbourg, and carved out a
Scandinavian colony. Another group, in which Hrólfr was a dominant
leader, sailed further east, across the bay of the Seine, and came to the
estuary of the great river. They landed there at the beginning of the
second decade of the tenth century and found that the countryside was
exposed and undefended. They marched upriver and seized the city of
Rouen without too much trouble, and Hrólfr established his camp there
on the river bank within the Roman walls of the great city.

Hrólfr was not the first Viking jarl or king to make Rouen his
headquarters; the city was already dilapidated from generations of Viking
attacks. But, like York in Northumbria, Rouen in Neustria was a city
too valuable as a trading centre ever to be entirely abandoned.[3] Hrólfr
probably found the city already closely tied to the northern world and
inhabited by a mixed and hardened population. Serious assaults on the
coastal Frankish lands had begun as long ago as 845, when the Seine
was used as a raiding route to attack Paris. The Viking raids had been
assisted by the fact that the Frankish empire had fallen apart after the
death of Louis the Pious, and his inheritance was squabbled over for
decades. The raids reached something of a crescendo when Paris was
besieged in 885–86, and Charles the Fat (d. 888) had to buy the raiders
off by giving them free rein to plunder Burgundy. Then the external
threat was complicated by internal collapse. A powerful family called

by historians the Robertians rose to power in the region of Paris.[4] The Robertians accumulated estates and dependents westward as far as Brittany and the ocean, including what later became Normandy. In the unsettled times caused by the Viking raids they moved into competition with the descendants of Charlemagne for the throne of West Francia. Eudes, a Robertian, was elected king of the Western Franks in 888 but after 893 was in rivalry with a Carolingian,[5] Charles the Simple, a grandson of Charles the Bald, elected as an anti-king. After Eudes's death in 898, Charles ruled alone, and it was he who was the king who had to deal with the threat represented by Hrólfr the Viking, whom Frankish clerks called by the Latinised name of 'Rollo'.

We assume that Hrólfr was a threat, but in fact we know too little about him to assume anything much. Setting aside the evidence of Dudo of St-Quentin,† who wrote over a century later, there are only one or two contemporary mentions of him.[6] The earliest comes in 918 when an act of Charles the Simple in favour of the Parisian abbey of St-Germain-des-Prés recites that: 'we have granted ... that abbey ... apart from those of its properties which we have given for the protection of the kingdom to the Northmen on the Seine, that is, to Rollo and his associates'. Flodoard,[7] the near-contemporary annalist of Reims, adds a little more to this. In his *History of the Church of Reims* – without mentioning Rollo – he describes what seems to be this earlier grant to the 'Northmen on the Seine' in this way:

> after the campaign that Count Robert [of the Breton March] waged against [the Northmen] in the region of Chartres, they began to accept Christianity. They had been conceded certain coastal provinces along with the city of Rouen, which they had nearly levelled, and other cities dependent on it.

Unfortunately he gives no dates, but Flodoard does at least give us two other contemporary mentions of Rollo, when, in his annal for 925, he records Rollo at Eu leading the Northmen resisting Frankish retaliation against his earlier aggression in the Beauvaisis. Lastly, in 927, he records that 'the son of Rollo' swore faith to King Charles the Simple. That is all that the contemporary historical record tells us of the originator of

† See List of Medieval Sources and Writers, below pp. 311–20, for details of writers and their works throughout the book.

the Norman dynasty, with the exception that a generation later the historian Richer of Reims picked up from somewhere the fact that Rollo's father bore the name Ketil (*Catillus*).[8]

When did Rollo and his associates settle in the lower Seine valley? Dudo tells us that it was in 911 that King Charles met Rollo at St-Clair on the River Epte, the boundary between the two provinces of the Vexin and the Roumois (of which Rouen was the capital). The king conceded to Rollo the city of Rouen and the provinces as far west as Brittany. In view of the retrospective charter reference of 918 which we have already looked at, this date of 911 for the arrival of the Normans is as good as any. Although the only authority for it is Dudo, it does match the date of the well-known military defeat of the Vikings south of Normandy at Chartres. The year 911 would have been one in which the Vikings might have been willing to negotiate. But it could equally well be that Rollo and his people arrived on the Seine later, at the time that other Viking raiders were active in England; we simply do not know. Nor do we know who the *comites* (associates) of Rollo were. Rollo might in fact have been one jarl amongst many in the army of the 'Northmen on the Seine', first amongst military equals. He may have been the Viking leader who – after the surrender of Rouen – succeeded in basing himself in the city, and fought and negotiated his way to dominance over the others. If so, it is not unlikely that his overlordship of the Seine Vikings was a fragile thing, and that he had to contend daily with the ambitions of other jarls and perhaps even surviving local Frankish magnates. Within the silence of the historical record may be contained the lost story of a man who was the greatest, as well as the first, of his line.

The other lost story of Rollo's time is that of the settlement and definition of what became his family's principality. Some things we do know. After decades of debate, historians have come to appreciate that the pre-existing landscape of Normandy, political as well as agricultural, was not erased by the Vikings and built over. There is no doubt that there was Scandinavian settlement around Rouen, and indeed in Rouen (the principal stream to the east of the old city still carries the Scandinavian name 'Robec' and a writer at Soissons in the mid tenth century called it a 'Danish city'). But the Viking settlement was nowhere in Normandy as dense as it was in places like, for instance, East Anglia and

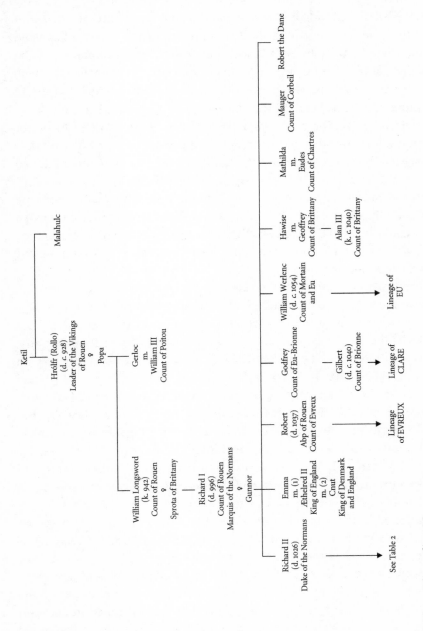

Table 1. The earliest Normans.

East Yorkshire, where field and stream names remain heavily Scandinavian to this day. Place-name evidence shows that in some areas (notably the Pays de Caux, north of the Seine, the southern shore of the bay of the Seine and the north of the Cotentin peninsula) many village and hamlet names refer to Scandinavian owners. Generally they are along the lines of names of villages like 'Borneville', that is 'the *villa* of Bjorn'. The first element of the name recalls a Scandinavian lord who had acquired it in (presumably) the tenth century; the second element however is the '*villa*', the universal and continuing Gallo-Roman name for a rural estate. In other words, much of the place name evidence refers to aristocratic Scandinavian settlement; in many cases it must refer to new lords taking over the management of existing older settlements. There are indicators of some new Scandinavian settlements: there are about a hundred Norman place-names containing the Scandinavian element 'toft', as in Criquetot or Yvetot, but there is no part of Normandy where Scandinavian name elements even come near to swamping the Frankish and Celtic ones.

The distribution of Scandinavian place-names confirms what the historical record has to say. Rollo and his associates settled in Rouen as a sort of forward base towards Paris, and colonised the Seine valley back towards the sea. They were also much in evidence in the Pays de Caux, between the Seine and the Channel coast as far east as the country around Dieppe. These match nicely the 'coastal provinces along with Rouen' referred to by Flodoard's account of King Charles the Simple's territorial concession to the Vikings. It is here that we may locate the heartland of Rollo's lordship. How much further it extended is a matter of guesswork. Rollo had been given Rouen and its hinterland in return for his alliance with the Franks. It was in both his and his Frankish allies' interest to extend his authority over other Viking settlers. This would seem to be the motive for later concessions to the Vikings of the Seine which are mentioned in the records of the time. The need was particularly strong when Robert of Neustria, who briefly succeeded Charles the Simple as king, was killed by the Viking army in Brittany in 924. His son-in-law and successor, King Ralph, is recorded as sponsoring a new agreement by which a group of Northmen were conceded the provinces of the Bessin and Maine: it is logical to assume that the Northmen in question were Rollo and his associates, moving their authority westward from the

Seine valley. What is less clear is whether Rollo was being given lordship over Vikings already settling the area in order to domesticate and restrain them, or whether he was being given lordship over the Franks around Bayeux in order to protect them from other Viking leaders settled in the Cotentin peninsula and eastern Brittany.

By 924, however, 'Normandy' was clearly in the making. The process was assisted by the fact that there was an underlying template on which to build a principality. West Francia in the Carolingian empire of the early ninth century had been administered from the same cities as the Romans had administered Gaul. Each city had a bishop and a count, and also a subordinate civil province or *pagus*, in modern French *pays*.[9] Rouen was also the seat of a metropolitan archbishop who ruled over an ecclesiastical province, the surviving spiritual twin sister of the long-defunct Roman imperial province of Lugdunensis Secunda. It was on that ancient Roman foundation that Normandy was in the end erected. There were still many living memorials to the Roman past in Rollo's time. The fourth-century AD Roman episcopal basilica of St Mary stood, battered but intact, in the city (next to the eighth-century basilica and clerical community of St Stephen). Rollo was perhaps baptised in one or other of these dilapidated ancient basilicas; although the monastery of St-Ouen just to the east of the city might also have had that honour. One of the few things we know about Rollo is that he came into immediate and friendly relations with the archbishop of Rouen, and the relationship may have been of more benefit than just spiritual. It seems that few if any Frankish civil officers survived the Viking incursions, but in the years of crisis some of the bishops stayed with their flocks. 'Normandy' was a new entity, but it depended on older ideas. Just as the idea of a kingdom of 'England' was partly a product of the papacy's decision that there was one English people and an English Church, so the duchy of Normandy was constructed within the boundaries of the province of Rouen, which became the 'Norman Church' of the next century.

We do not know when Rollo died. He was probably alive, but perhaps ailing, in 927, when his son did homage to King Ralph of France. He was clearly dead by 933. Therefore most historians assume that he died around 928; his place of burial is said to have been the cathedral of Rouen. Hopefully he died a Christian, although the historical record leaves some doubt over this. Dudo said that Rollo had been baptised in 912, and his great-grandson records a century later generous restorations and grants of estates that Rollo is said to have made to the church of St-Ouen just outside the walls of Rouen (it is possible that his baptism might have been performed there in view of the known devastation of the basilicas within the city). If we are to believe Dudo, Rollo's godfather was Robert of Neustria, who would have received him as sponsor after his immersion in the font, and given him a new Christian name. The usual, although not invariable, practice would have been that Rollo would have taken the name Robert, in compliment to his godfather. Dudo in fact makes a practice of calling Rollo 'Robert' after his baptism. There is supporting evidence for Dudo in the records of the abbey of St-Denis, which in 968 recalls Duke Richard I's grandfather as 'Robert', not 'Rollo'. But Rollo-Robert and his men may not have been model converts, for the archbishop of Reims sent a handbook on the conversion of errant pagans to his colleague of Rouen around 914. Generations later, the Limousin chronicler, Adhémar of Chabannes,[10] tells a scurrilous story indicating that Rollo might not have got the spiritual point about his baptism. He is supposed to have celebrated it by offering gifts to the churches of the Christian God, and by decapitating (presumably pagan) prisoners in honour of his ancestral northern pantheon. This is a late story from an ill-placed source, but it finds some ominous confirmation around 943, when the elegaist of Rollo's son noted how William had been assailed by enemies 'while his heathen father was dying'.

William Longsword, Count of Rouen

There is a good argument that the most important member of any dynasty is the second one. It is he who establishes the founder's power, redefines it if necessary, and gives it continuity. William son of Rollo did all of this. He was not born in France: the Latin lament (*planctus*) composed soon after his death talks of his being born 'beyond the seas to a father dwelling in heathen lands'.[11] If we accept this, then William was born well before his father's embarkation on his Viking enterprises, somewhere in the Scandinavian-ruled lands. His first language would not have been French, and his education would have been among pagan Vikings. It was in France, we are told, that he was baptised, presumably alongside his father in Rouen. He would not have been 'William' as a child. He took a Christian name on baptism, for William must have been the name of his godfather; William was no Viking name, it was Frankish. It is interesting and worthwhile to speculate who that godfather may have been. One possible candidate would be King Charles the Simple's courtier, William the Pious, duke of Aquitaine, who might well have consented to act as sponsor if only by proxy. More likely might have been William, son of Eblé Manzer, count of Poitiers, who was one of the younger magnates in the front line fighting the Vikings on the Loire, and who actually married Rollo's daughter, and William Long-sword's sister, Gerloc.

William was known to later generations as 'Longsword'. The name first appears in later eleventh-century sources (Dudo does not use it) but it must depend on a solid family tradition. 'Longsword' was a warrior's name, and could very well have been a Viking cognomen. Since William must have been involved in the brutal campaigning of 924–25 around Beauvais, Ponthieu and Amiens, there had been plenty of opportunities for him to earn it bloodily. William was therefore a bridge between the old Viking ways of the Scandinavian settlers, amongst whom he had grown to manhood, and the new world of the competing Frankish principalities in which he had assumed power. By 927 he was a mature adult, and swore faith to the then Robertian king, Ralph, who recognised him as ruler over the areas conceded to Rollo and his associates. The Seine Vikings' expansion to the east had been halted in the valley of the Bresle, at Eu, by the counts of Flanders and Vermandois.[12] It may be that this reverse had decided the Northmen of Rouen to drop Rollo as leader, and rivals amongst the community certainly contended with his son for control. There is an ominous passage in the lament at his death which says that, while his father was dying, 'warfare arose against him, but ever trusting in God, he mastered every enemy by the strength of his right hand'. Dudo too says that William took power before his father died, although he describes an ailing Rollo bestowing his authority on his son and heir in the presence of a regular ducal council. The truth may be that Rollo was seen as a failure by his men, for whatever reason, and William had to fight to reassert the control over the Vikings that his father had lost.

By 927 William seems to have secured the acquiescence of the Seine

Vikings to his overlordship. Alliance with King Ralph brought benefits to the nascent Norman principality. By the 930s the Vikings of Rouen were being seen as domesticated Vikings, and safe to use against their wilder brethren. In 933 King Ralph and William met and, in Flodoard's words, 'William, leader (*princeps*) of the Northmen swore faith to that same king; to whom the king gave the land of the Bretons lying along the sea coast'. The great Viking army on the Loire and in Brittany had continued to hold together through the 920s, but – perhaps because there were so many more of them – had not thrown up a stabilising leader as the Seine Vikings had in Rollo. The Vikings had broken the power of the once considerable Breton kingdom and driven its leaders abroad to shelter in England. There had been a time in the 860s when Charles the Bald had been forced to cede royal regalia to Salomon, the Breton leader, and also make territorial concessions, perhaps the Cotentin peninsula. But the Vikings had occupied Nantes and eastern Brittany, and from place-name evidence, had also moved eastward into the Cotentin.

The native Bretons, long suppressed, began at last to move against their Viking oppressors in 931. This left the Cotentin Vikings exposed and isolated. These settlers may not originally have had any connection with Rollo's group further east, but that was to change. What we see perhaps, in King Ralph's grant of 933, is the king's encouragement of William Longsword to take over lordship of this now-isolated Viking colony to the west of Bayeux, and see what else he might do in the direction of Brittany, which was once again coming under the rule of native counts at Rennes and Nantes. William was clearly enthusiastic about the opportunity. He did secure lordship over the Cotentin (perhaps peacefully) and coins issued in his name have been found further south at Mont St-Michel, on one of which he describes himself exuberantly as 'duke of the Bretons'. How far he managed to give that title any reality is an open question. At the time the coins were issued, William may have been encouraging the remnants of the Vikings in Brittany to rally to his lordship, and assumed the title to imply that under King Ralph he was the lawful prince in the region. One souvenir of his campaigns in Brittany was a concubine, a Breton woman, with whom he had a son, baptised by the Frankish name of Richard, and whom he established in a household at Bayeux, as Flodoard tells us.

Coins and ducal styles tell us that William actively took up the role of a Christian Frankish prince. He issued coins at Rouen from a restored mint; thus taking over one of the royal prerogatives, as he had also taken over the considerable royal fisc (landed estates) and forests within his growing realm. Some of his older subjects may not have liked this transformation of a charismatic Viking war-leader into a rather more mundane Frankish magnate. Dudo tells the story of the outbreak of a revolt in 934 amongst William's Scandinavian subjects, led by a rival leader, Riulf. Riulf and his faction cornered William in Rouen, and William – Longsword the Viking once more – was forced to lead his personal guard out to do battle and assert his leadership. Although he succeeded, and Riulf was forced to flee for his life, this incident – if it indeed happened – tells us that there may have been many sharp pangs in the birth of Normandy.

In the later 930s, the process of transformation continued. William and his intimates, amongst whom would have been churchmen, began crafting a new identity for him. Flodoard calls William in 933 by the neutral Latin title *princeps*, meaning no more than 'leader' of the Northmen. But the Vikings themselves were now being asked to recognise William, Rollo's son, as the *comes Rothomensis*, or 'count of Rouen', and elsewhere – as we have seen – he was asserting his right to the title 'duke of the Bretons'. Count and duke were styles customarily awarded at the discretion of the Carolingian king, but in the 930s there were plenty of other powerful Frankish magnates who were assuming such titles on their own initiative. With the titles went an ideology of Christian rulership, with which the Church was happy to provide him: 'O William! Maker and lover of peace; comforter and defender of the poor; maintainer of widows and orphans!' sobbed the cleric who composed the lament on his death. All were qualities once expected of Christian kings, but now expected of all Christian princes. If a Christian ruler kept to these biblical virtues then his rule was rightful, and it was a sin to resist him. Witgar, the panegyrist of the very Count Arnulf of Flanders who had conspired to kill William, flattered Arnulf by attributing to him exactly the same qualities. With his need to assert legitimacy amongst the other counts and dukes, it may well be that William took the ideology seriously, and perhaps Dudo's picture of both Rollo and William as lawgivers and law enforcers in their realm may not be wholly exaggerated.

William made another step towards legitimacy in the latter years of his reign when he welcomed back into his province and supported the exiled monks of the Merovingian abbey of Jumièges, on the Seine. Some or all of the monks had retreated for a number of decades to an estate at Haspres, near Cambrai, a hundred miles away, but under the leadership of Martin, a reforming abbot sent from Poitiers by Gerloc, William's sister, they returned and revitalised Benedictine life and liturgy on the Seine: the lament on his death credited William with 'founding' Jumièges. If he could found monasteries, then he was truly a lawful Christian prince, especially, perhaps, in the eyes of his Frankish Christian subjects. Later sources go further and say it had been William's intention to retire to the monastery as soon as he possibly could, but this may be no more than an attempt to credit him retrospectively with sanctity, since he met the end of a martyr for peace. Richer of Reims tells the unusually complimentary story (for him) of William's treasure box, which, when opened after his death, contained only a hair shirt which he wore in seasons of penance.

Another significant step in the naturalisation of William Longsword in his adopted land was his marriage. This was arranged c. 936–37 between him and Leutgarde, daughter of Count Herbert II of Vermandois, a direct descendant of Charlemagne in the male line. We know of the marriage gift that 'Count William of the city of Rouen' made to Leutgarde: the substantial estate of Longueville in the Pays de Caux. It was a good investment. Any children of the marriage would share their mother's imperial lineage, and the marriage introduced William as a member of the elite club of princes which was beginning to divide up West Francia amongst its members. Endogamy (or intermarriage) meant acceptance in this, as in other ages. William's sister had married the count of Poitiers, another leading member of the Frankish princely cabal. What sort of game William played amongst this coterie of princes in the decade between 933 and his death in 942 is not clear. The Frankish princes were exploiting to their own advantage the continuing rivalry between the Robertian dynasty, with a power base around Paris, and the descendants of Charlemagne, limited to the vicinity of the old imperial palace of Laon, who had few resources other than moral. Later (Norman) tradition portrays William as the arbiter in the succession of the Carolingian exile, Louis IV, in 936. But this political pre-eminence amongst the other princes is an idea which has little contemporary support, although it is true that William's elegaist says that his enemies resented his closeness to the new king.

In the end, William Longsword was a victim of the power-play of the other Frankish princes, rather than of internal plotting amongst his fellow Scandinavian warlords. The Northmen of the Seine had early fallen foul of the emerging principality of Flanders, under its vigorous marcher counts. Flanders had appeared as a political entity in the reign of Charles the Bald, partly through policy and partly through the enterprise of its founder, Baldwin 'Iron-Arm', count of Ghent. It developed as an important and formidable bulwark against Viking penetration of the Rhineland and the north of France. The Vikings who settled on the Seine had outflanked the Flemings, and were a threat that they did not appreciate. So it is no surprise to find that in 925 Count Arnulf deployed his forces and connections to curb the Northmen of the Seine and contain them at the River Bresle, which was to become the permanent northern frontier of Normandy.

Tension continued between the Northmen and the Flemings. In 939 Count William antagonised Arnulf by his involvement in reinstating a certain Herluin as count over the region of Montreuil, which he himself had attempted to annex. This appears to have decided Arnulf that the Northmen were getting restless and becoming a threat once again. His method of dealing with them was as ruthless as you might expect from a tenth-century marcher count used to dealing with pagan outlanders. He enticed William to a marcher conference on the River Somme at Picquigny, west of Amiens. The two counts met on an island in the river on the afternoon of Saturday 17 December 942 to arrange a peace settlement, William went trustingly, having asked for no hostages from Arnulf. Some of the details of what happened next are given by the lament composed soon after his death, perhaps by a member of the community at Jumièges. After a long and amicable discussion, which the crafty Arnulf protracted until the winter sun was beginning to set behind the black alder thickets on the river bank, William returned to his boat while Arnulf went to his. As he was pulled away across the waters of the river, which was in spate, several of Arnulf's household called him back saying that their lord wanted to tell him some more important information. William obligingly returned in the dusk, only to be met on shore by the swords of as many as six assassins, and he was hacked down, being killed by a savage cut to the head. William himself was unarmed and defenceless, as were his men; nevertheless two of his household, indifferent to wounds, recovered his dead body and hauled it to the boat and back across the river.

Richard I and the Assimilation of the Northmen

If Count Arnulf's intention had been to destabilise and neutralise the principality that William Longsword had built up in the 930s, he may have been quite pleased with himself for a while. William left a young son, Richard, whose mother was his Breton concubine. If he was conceived during the Breton campaigns of 933–34, Richard cannot have been more than nine years old when his father died. The enemies of the Northmen might then have every expectation that the principality would collapse into chaos as internal squabbles for leadership broke out, and war-chief set himself up against war-chief. Troubles certainly came, but surprisingly for such a new political entity the principality of William Longsword survived him. In part that may have had much to do with William's own action in embracing Frankish and Christian models of legitimate rulership. He had established himself at home, at the royal court, and among his Frankish peers as 'the count of Rouen'. Naturally when one count died another must succeed him. As William had but one son, that must be Richard: this was dynastic thinking.

At the end of his poetic account of the death of William Longsword the elegaist burst out patriotically: 'Hail to you, O Richard, count of Rouen! Our prayers for the count and for the salvation of his father! So may Christ grant you [Richard] his protection all the days of your life, that you may be with him at the end forever!' We seem to catch here the spirit of the immediate aftermath of Count William's murder: the dead count laid to rest in the cathedral of Rouen; the boy-heir brought from Bayeux under military escort; the people of the city alarmed and apprehensive, and the nobility in intense conclave, as news filtered in from Laon of the king's army approaching. For the Franks and half-Franks amongst the provincial nobility, the logic of embracing the boy Richard as sole male heir would have been obvious. Over the past century, the Franks had seen the former public office of count become a family 'honor' (as they called it), and the hereditary succession of son to father was becoming the norm. For the senior former-Viking nobles – the original settlers of 911 would be now at least in their fifties – the logic would not have been so obvious: it was their custom to elect the fittest male of suitable lineage to lead the army or fleet. The arrival of King Louis IV in Rouen further complicated matters and may have precipitated a division.

The Church, the Frankish-dominated city of Rouen and a party amongst the Scandinavian nobility clearly supported Richard. The boy had been brought to Rouen by his father's trusted officer and captain, Bernard the Dane, who remained a prominent and stalwart pillar of Richard's cause. But the Scandinavian leaders were not unanimous in accepting the boy. We hear of one Harald, who (perhaps with foreign Viking support) took control of parts of the former lands of Count William in the Cotentin and had extended his control by 944 to Bayeux. As a result Rollo's dynasty's principality apparently shrank back to Rouen and the Seine valley for a while. King Louis's arrival at Rouen some months after Count William's death may have been a mixed blessing. Flodoard tells us: 'King Louis gave the land of the Northmen to the son born of William from his Breton concubine, and some of his nobles swore faith to the king, others to Duke Hugh.' The name 'Normandy' does not yet appear, but there is a vague entity here recognised as 'the land of the Northmen' which is a step towards a new geopolitical term for the lands formerly held by Count William.

King Louis had recognised Richard's legitimate claims, and had taken him under his protection, but Flodoard more than hints at some opportunism. We know from Dudo that Duke Hugh 'the Great', the latest head of the Robertian family, was beginning to be closely interested in the county of Rouen. The fact that the king asked certain of Richard's subjects to swear faith to the duke indicates that some sort of partition in his own interest was contemplated in 943. The next year, with the assistance of the perfidious Flemings, the king marched into the county of Rouen and occupied the city, while Duke Hugh invaded the Bessin, intending to seize Bayeux. Fortunately for the Normans, the king and duke fell out in the course of the campaign, and Hugh was asked to withdraw to his own lands, while Richard's inheritance was now confided by the king to a local Frankish aristocrat, Ralph Torta, who was to administer the principality from Rouen in the king's interest. Richard in the meantime was under tutelage, first at the royal court at Laon, and later with his father's friend, Count Bernard of Senlis. In the meantime, the Viking leader called Harald, who appears to have taken control of Cherbourg and the Cotentin as early as 943, seized Bayeux and began to move against Rouen in 945, forcing the king to return to the city. A botched peace conference between this Harald, Bernard the Dane and the king led to Louis's seizure by the Northmen, much to everyone's satisfaction, especially that of Duke Hugh the Great. With the king in their hands, the Northmen agreed to his release in exchange for young Count Richard. Richard was returned and, at the age of only thirteen at most, took control of his inheritance. His western rival, the Viking Harald, was somehow persuaded to retire or to depart, and the Frankish governor of Rouen, Ralph Torta, was exiled to Paris, where his son was bishop.

Richard in 945 entered on a long reign as count of the Northmen of Rouen; it was to last for fifty-one years. Such lengthy tenures of principalities have major effects on the people that the ruler governs. When Richard began his rule, Scandinavian languages were still spoken at Bayeux – which is where he himself learned his father's native language – and many of Rollo's original associates must still have been active. For them, their Christianity was an acquired and possibly uncomfortable religious practice. There would even in 945 have been quite a few Franks living who remembered a different world, when Rouen and its neighbouring provinces were Neustrian, ruled by counts appointed by the Robertian dynasty (one is mentioned as late as 905), and when numerous ancient Benedictine monasteries and collegiate minsters distinguished the countryside. When Richard died in 996 Neustria was long forgotten and the land he ruled was beginning to be called 'Northmannia', 'Normannia' or 'Normandy' (although the first occurrences of the name in written sources belong to the second decade of the eleventh century). His people, Frankish or Scandinavian in origin, all spoke French and were indistinguishable in most of their customs and their way of life from their Angevin, Parisian or Picard neighbours. Their rapid linguistic and cultural assimilation was commented on by Adhémar of Chabannes in the next generation. Normandy was by 1000 once again a land of distinguished churches and monasteries, and it was accepted as one of the integral principalities which made up the greater realm of France. Richard survived long enough to outlive his first enemies and to inhabit a world with new and different problems and complexities.

Richard's principal concerns must have been the very identity of Normandy, and his own position as ruler. This latter concern had two dimensions. In common with the other Frankish princes, Richard had to come to some accommodation with the continuing, though much decayed, power of the king. Since he, like them, accepted that there must be a king, he had to define his own power in relation to the kingship. At another level, Richard had to come to terms with the power of other men within his principality. The local magnates had to be brought into a formal relationship with his own rulership; and they must accept the role of being his subordinate nobility. The way in which Richard handled these questions is obscure. We know they were on his agenda, though, because we see his son and grandsons continuing to grapple with them, each in their own way. It is likely, however, that Richard was the first ruler seated in Rouen who had to deal with such questions. His father and grandfather had depended on a different mechanism of lordship, and can only have imposed their rule on their lands by a mixture of warrior charisma and the fear of the swords and axes of their personal guards. The authority wielded by Rollo and William Longsword was highly unstable, and we see that instability reflected even in the patchy historical record that has come down to us. But right from the beginning, Count Richard lived in a different world. His succession was regular in Frankish terms, even if contested, and he became a legitimate civil ruler with the blessing of the anointed king of the Western Franks. His task must therefore have been to convince his Scandinavian subjects of the necessity of recognising what legitimate rule was, and the importance of deference to it, even without military threat.

Richard's relationship with his king was as uneven as that of any other Frankish prince. Between 961 and 962, when he was still a young ruler in his late twenties, Richard had to contend with a dangerous alliance between the Carolingian King Lothar (d. 985), son of Louis IV, and his southern neighbour the count of Blois-Chartres, which led to damaging invasions of his lands. Dudo's later explanation for the differences between Richard and the king was the king's unhappiness with Richard's level of acknowedgement of his lordship. This may be so, but part of the difficulty may have been Richard's marriage alliance with Hugh Capet's sister Emma, made as early as the late 950s. This tied the Normans and Capetians into an alliance which naturally threatened the Carolingians and any other Frankish dynasty working to extend itself in central France. Richard felt sufficiently threatened by the hostile incursions in the 960s to end them by the recruitment of Danish mercenaries, who pillaged the upper Seine valley and frightened King Lothar into making peace. Thereafter, at some time in late 963 or 964, Richard is found peacefully at the court of Lothar, and the two seem to have maintained tranquil relations till the king's death. On 18 March 968 Richard was to be found at a meeting at Berneval in company with his brother-in-law, Hugh Capet, duke of the Franks and head of the Robertian dynasty, a man whom he called on that occasion his 'lord' (*senior*), although Hugh was much the younger man. This Hugh ultimately succeeded Lothar as king in 987, and Richard seems to have been happy to assist his brother-in-law to take up the kingship. Richard was involved with fighting against Hugh's enemies in 991, so it would seem that he made support of his powerful Robertian neighbours the keystone of his policy in dealing with his neighbours: a simple strategy followed by all his successors until the 1050s.

The historical record has little else to say of the diplomacy, campaigns and warfare conducted by Count Richard, and historians are doubtless right to deduce that his main enterprises were domestic ones. Being domestic, they were mainly out of sight of the French chroniclers. We can say some things. The idea of 'Normandy' and the status of its ruler received some definition in his lifetime. Although both he and his father undoubtedly used the style 'count of Rouen' to describe themselves from the 930s through to the 960s, Richard began to look for more prestigious titles as his reign progressed. Part of the reason for this was that other counts began to appear within his realm with his blessing. Richard's mother, Sprota, took another partner after the murder of his father, and this produced a half-brother, called Rodulf, whom Richard made lord of Ivry on the southern border of his realm, with the title of count. This may have happened as early as the mid 960s. Richard also awarded the comital title to three of his younger sons, Godfrey, Robert and William (the latter being progenitor of the lineage of the counts of Eu), perhaps as early as the 970s. Part of the reason why Richard spread the title amongst his nearest family may have been a desire to exalt his lineage; part may have been a belief – seen elsewhere in France – that great princely families shared the dignity of countship amongst its male members (Baldwin III of Flanders was called count *c.* 955 in his father's lifetime). There may also have been the need to create a dependable and prestigious group within the emerging nobility of Richard's principality, a group which could help control and shepherd the others.

In exalting others, Richard also needed to exalt himself. In so doing, he could not easily go to the king. The Carolingian king Louis IV had raised Hugh the Great of Neustria to the rank of 'duke of the Franks' in either 937 or 943 as a reward for helping him to the throne. But the ducal 'style' given Hugh was thought at the time to be exceptional, a way of making him first of the Franks after the king.[13] We have seen that William Longsword experimented with the title 'duke of the Bretons' in the 930s, when King Ralph had given him some mandate to extend his control west. It is conceivable that he took the title with royal licence, and the earlier rulers of the Bretons had used a number of exalted titles, including that of king. But we hear no more of Brittany in the reign of Richard. Richard's choice of a new title becomes clear in the later 960s, when he is referred to as 'marquis' (*marchio*) in the solemn diploma of King Lothar which re-established the community of Mont St-Michel in 966. This choice of title was a long-established option for senior counts ruling border regions; marquises were counts who controlled other lesser counts. Richard used the same title again in 968, in an act where he is referred to also by the Roman imperial formula of *inclitus comes* ('distinguished count'). In 990, Richard was awarded by a clerk the Roman style 'consul', which in the central middle ages was becoming a distinguished synonym for 'count'. So we see the first Richard pressing hard the matter of his own prestige as a ruler, and seeking to evoke a status beyond that of count of Rouen which he had inherited.

Of what was Richard 'marquis'? The idea of a 'land of the Normans' was becoming established already in the 960s. The act of 968 in which Richard joined with Duke Hugh of the Franks in restoring the lands of the abbey of St-Denis within his realm referred to the 'people' (*gens*) of the Normans (*Normanni*) and of the Franks whose joint duty it was to support the monks. What precisely the author of this phrase meant is open to debate, but, since the transaction was being carried out on the Norman border near Gisors, it is likely enough that the 'Normans' were meant to be the people who lived on one side of the border under the rule of Richard 'marquis of the Normans'; the 'Franks' were Duke Hugh's people on the other side. The implication in this document of 968 is that the Normans were a recognisable people within recognised bounds under a lawful prince; no longer the 'Northmen of the Seine', but a people of a variety of descents gathered into one political unit within specific borders. This 'greater Normanness' was recognised by Dudo some decades later, when he portrayed Rollo in a vision seeing his future people as a flock of birds gathered from every direction, representing immigrants of a variety of peoples who would all one day be Normans. The 'Normans' had in fact as early as the 960s become one of the sub-divisions of the kingdom of the West Franks, like the Bretons and Aquitanians. Since these folk were regarded as having a distinct regional identity, their ruler was distinguished by greater titles: the Bretons had their prince or king, and the Aquitanians their duke. So naturally the Normans too had a claim to a ruler of more than usual prestige, and Richer of Reims in the 990s was clear enough that their ruler should be a 'duke', although he made his distaste for the Normans clear by calling Richard 'duke of the pirates'. Other writers made their indifference to Norman pretensions plain by continuing to refer to their ruler – as Adhémar of Chabannes was still doing late in the 1020s – as the 'count of Rouen'. Not surprisingly in this context, it was as 'Count Richard' not 'Duke Richard' that Richard II appears in a letter of his enemy, Odo II of Blois, to King Robert in *c.* 1023.

Richard I furthered this understanding of a Norman prince and a Norman people by other subtle means. His re-foundation at Mont St-Michel of a community of monks in 966, for instance, was a clear indication to everyone that he had recovered the authority over the Breton march that his father had exerted. Here he was following his father, who had commenced the good work by his restoration of Jumièges just before his death. There is little doubt that the ecclesiastical organisation of Richard's realm was in need of revitalisation, although there had never been any serious danger of Christianity being eliminated there. A few major churches continued to operate throughout the invasion period, with greater or lesser degrees of prosperity. At the cathedral of Rouen, at the church of St-Ouen in the town, and in communities of some sort or other at Mont St-Michel, Jumièges, Fécamp, and perhaps elsewhere, organised religious life survived into the time of William Longsword. But dislocation continued into the 940s, not least amongst the episcopal communities: Coutances remained abandoned by its bishop till 1025. Ironically, a community of canons is believed to have survived the Viking invasions at St-Evroult, but to have succumbed after they were handed over to the pillaging of the army of Duke Hugh of the Franks in 944.

When William reformed and enlarged the community at Jumièges and Richard restored monastic life at Mont St-Michel, they were not so much restoring Christian observance to their realm as staking a claim to supervise it, as Christian princes did. The fact that many of the reformers had to come from outside their lands rather enhanced their part in the process. As Jumièges depended on an imported abbot from Poitiers for the expertise and enthusiasm to restore Benedictinism there, so Mont St-Michel depended on an abbot and a colony of monks from Ghent to reintroduce regular life there. These, led by one Mainier, had first attempted the restoration of an abandoned Merovingian house at Fontenelle, which they renamed St-Wandrille, from its one-time patron (whose bones had been taken to Ghent during the invasion period). Outside the city walls of Evreux, Richard revived (or refounded, the sources are not in agreement) a community at the earlier church of St-Taurin. At Fécamp, Richard developed further a palace chapel built on the ruins of an old nunnery by his father, introducing first a community of secular priests, and then seeking an abbot and monks from outside his realm to commence regular life. The project failed to win favour at Cluny, but it does confirm a pattern. Richard wanted to create respectable and prestigious abbeys acknowledging him as their patron, even if it meant getting outsiders to do it. In this way he would have both the benefit of their prayers and the status attached to being a protector of Benedictine abbeys. As spiritual heirs of the Emperor Constantine, true Christian princes and kings needed to be seen to appoint and promote bishops and abbots. Richard could now do so. Certainly it was he who appointed his younger son, Robert, to the see of Rouen in c. 990. By 990 he had restored the ecclesiastical hierarchy of the Carolingian province, for alongside Archbishop Robert in that year stood six suffragan bishops.

The other thing that abbeys and religious communities could give Richard was memory. It was almost certainly a member of the community of Jumièges who composed the lament on his father's death; it was in the cathedral of Rouen that the first two Norman counts of Rouen were buried, and presumably commemorated liturgically on their obituary (the anniversary of their death). It was at Fécamp that Richard was buried and commemorated, and it is from Fécamp that we derive the earliest annals of Normandy and an in-house catalogue of the Norman dynasty, with notes on their burial places, which had been compiled before the death of William the Conqueror. It was these Norman religious houses and their writers which developed and sustained the view of the Norman dynasty which we are discovering and analysing here. To give just one example, at the eleventh-century abbey of St-Ouen-de-Rouen, the founder of the dynasty was scrupulously remembered as 'Robert' the Christianised pagan; as the generous benefactor who restored its great estate of Gasny; and as the pious count who walked with bare feet in humility to receive back the relics the sainted archbishop Ouen on their return from the Ile-de-France to Rouen, and who put his own shoulders to the shrine for the last mile into the city. It was as much the Church as the ducal family itself which devised an appropriate texture for the trunk of its family tree.

Richard became ill during the course of the autumn of 996, and moved from Bayeux to his favourite residence of Fécamp, where he wished to die and be buried. The eyewitness account of his end given to Dudo by Richard's half-brother talks of an assembly of nobles gathered at which Richard formally nominated his successor. He piously and laboriously walked barefoot to receive a last communion in the nearby abbey, and, while in the church, selected a burial place in the portico, at the door. The following night, 21 November 996, a sudden seizure carried him off in his early sixties, struggling to get out the words of commendation drawn from Luke's gospel: 'Into thy hands, O Christ, I commend my spirit.' We have an account of his appearance in his latter days, given by Dudo, who met him on a mission to the Norman court in 987. The old man was tall, straight-backed and distinguished in appearance, with alert and clear eyes, thick eyebrows and a long and white patriarchal beard. Like the clerk of Jumièges who commemorated William Long-sword, Dudo commemorated Richard I as a sustainer of the poor, a guardian of orphans, a defender of widows and a redeemer of captives; in other words as a pious Christian prince. But Richard was commem-orated in other ways too; he graduated into legend. The twelfth-century Norman writer, Master Wace, recorded earlier tales of Richard's peculiar practice of fearlessly wandering the streets of Rouen at night, and encountering and defeating phantoms in deserted and dark city churches. Outside Normandy, Richard was not so well-treated in legend. Another contemporary twelfth-century writer, the Picard author of the William of Orange epic cycle, remembered him as a vengeful and ruthlessly ambitious prince: commemorating him variously as 'Richard the Bear-ded', 'Richard the Old' and 'Richard the Red', allotting to him the colour of hair which medieval writers gave to their supernatural, weird or treacherous characters; heroes were blondes. It is a historical fact that several members of the dynasty had reddish hair.

Richard, in his longevity and acknowledged wisdom, became a focus for later French legend, as a prince with uncanny foresight and unnatural bravery. Outside Normandy, Richard managed to identify himself in-extricably with the foundation of the duchy. The earliest romance epics, when they dealt with the times of Roland, Oliver and Charlemagne, found it inconceivable to picture a France without a Normandy – despite the anachronism – and the name they gave its duke, for duke it had to have, was 'Richard the Old', whose historical prototype was Richard I. This romance Richard appears in the 'Song of Roland' (c. 1100) and the 'Coronation of Louis' (c. 1130). With the death and apotheosis of Richard I we come to a new phase in the history of his dynasty: historical sources suddenly multiply and legend retreats. But it is as well to have looked first at the misty lands from which Normandy and the Norman dynasty emerge into hard-edged reality, for it was out of that mist that the later Norman rulers moulded their own image of themselves.

The Women of the Early Norman Dynasty

Women played a very important role in the early days of the Norman dynasty, but we have to be careful what sort of male-female relationships we are talking about here. In the tenth century, marriage was not yet what it would become two centuries later. 'Christian marriage' did not as yet exist. By that, I mean exclusive monogamy based on a contractual relationship between man and woman freely entered into within a church and with the blessing of a priest. In the tenth century marriage was still largely a relationship contracted between families, not individuals. The presiding figures in the contract were usually the fathers of the pair. The key moment in a tenth-century marriage was not the exchange of promises between the couple, but the conferment on the couple of the properties that were the gifts of either family on their marriage. The celebrations of the marriage might involve attending a mass said by a priest, but that was not an essential part of the process. The tenth-century marital bond created husband and wife, but it was not always an exclusive bond. The husband might well already have a sexual partner before his marriage, and he would not always put her away simply because he now had an 'official' wife. Similarly, the existence of an official wife did not stop a wealthy man from forming new sexual and emotional relationships. When it suited him he would live openly with another woman, his 'concubine' as she was often called by Latin writers. He would not form a ménage-à-trois with wife and concubine: his women would have their own homes and households. But the concubine might well be the mother of his children, and those children would have a claim on his estate after his death.

All the earlier male members of the Norman dynasty were born to concubines, not in arranged dynastic marriages. Later Norman writers, like William de Jumièges and Gilbert Crispin, living in an atmosphere of growing and aggressive church control over marriage, were embarrassed by concubinage. William called these concubines wives 'according to Danish custom' (*more Danico*), as if what the early Norman rulers were doing was continuing an irregular Viking marriage practice because they knew no better. Gilbert Crispin in the 1090s blamed 'old Danish ways' for the fact that in the early eleventh century Norman priests and bishops married, had children, carried arms and had a tendency towards fisticuffs to settle arguments. In fact, they were all doing no other than their Frankish contemporaries, such as King Charles the Simple, who had a wife, but who also a concubine by whom he had four sons. The concubine became an embarrassing fact of medieval family life only in the later eleventh century, when ideas about marriage had changed.

Norman historians craftily excused their ancestors on the grounds that they knew no better. More seriously, for writers of William de Jumièges' time there was a question over the legitimacy of children born to concubines, a question which was troubling to their ideas about the legitimacy of the Norman dynasty. Children born outside marriage were beginning to be called 'bastards', and by 1100, because they were bastards, they were being excluded from rights over their parents' property.

The first concubine we hear of is Popa, Rollo's partner *more Danico*, according to William de Jumièges. Dudo – who lived before the days when such irregular relationships were frowned on – only tells us that Rollo and Popa were sexual partners, without comment. According to Dudo, she was the beautiful daughter of a Frankish count, who fell into Rollo's hands when he sacked the city of Bayeux. We are in no position to comment on the truth of this. There may or may not have been a Popa; we can only say that it suited Dudo's purposes that the mother of William Longsword should be both a Christian and a woman of high birth. It also suited Dudo's purposes that Rollo should after his baptism contract a dynastic marriage with a daughter of King Charles the Simple, whom Dudo says was childless and fell into disgrace for insulting her husband and entertaining Frankish male visitors secretly. William de Jumièges discreetly made out that Rollo had put aside Popa while he was married to Gisla, and took up with her again only when Gisla died, but this sort of tactfulness had not occured to Dudo two generations earlier.[14]

As we have already seen, Count William Longsword followed his father's supposed example in taking to bed and forming a long-term relationship with a captive, in this case a Breton woman, whom William de Jumièges calls Sprota, on unknown authority.[15] Dudo does not mention her name, only her existence, and talks of their relationship as one of 'marriage'. Dudo in fact – determined to prove his martyr-hero was a monk in embryo – made out that Count William was very reluctant to engage in sex at all. The only reason he did so was to produce an heir, after his nobles begged and begged him for the sake of the political stability of the realm. We may doubt this. After all, as well as bedding Sprota, Count William also contracted a dynastic marriage with Leutgarde, daughter of the count of Vermandois. Since the marriage was dynastic, Leutgarde was given a substantial landed estate, focused on Longueville in the Pays de Caux. After his death, she married Count Theobald of Blois and had several more children. Sprota, in the meantime, lived under William's protection in her own household at Bayeux, where her son Richard was born. No doubt William hoped for children from the liaison with Leutgarde; and, in view of her Carolingian blood, those children would probably have been preferred over Richard when it came to succession. But the marriage with Leutgarde remained childless. Later sources tell us that Sprota remarried too after Count William's death, taking as husband one Esperleng, presumably a wealthy landowner, of whom it is only known that he managed the mills at Pîtres, upriver from Rouen. Sprota and Esperleng produced several daughters and one son, Rodulf, who was made count of Ivry by his half-brother, Richard I. Rodulf failed to found a male lineage – his children were all girls, or boys who became bishops – but his sisters and daughters married some of the more powerful of the emerging Norman aristocrats, and he was grandfather of arguably the most famous of them all, William fitz Osbern.

Richard I of Rouen duplicated the pattern of his father (and possibly grandfather) in making a dynastic marriage outside Normandy, and seeking emotional and sexual satisfaction in other relationships. He was clearly enthusiastic about women and produced numerous offspring from several liaisons; all the children were acknowledged and provided for out of Count Richard's great wealth. Dudo implies that the marriage to Emma Capet lasted only into the later 960s, no more than a decade, and it was only after her premature death that Count Richard began his principal sexual partnership. This was with Gunnor, a woman of Danish descent from within his realm, whom he formally married after a period of concubinage, but when he married her the count may have had other reasons than sexual and emotional. The union with Gunnor seems to have had a political purpose. Her family was great in western Normandy, and she was herself reputed to be very wealthy. In taking her to wife, he may have been creating a link with one of those putative rival Viking dynasties within his principality at whose existence we may guess, and by allying with her enhancing his own power. We know of her brother, Arfast, who was the progenitor of one of the great noble lineages of Normandy, and grandfather in the male line of William fitz Osbern. To emphasise the importance of her lineage, a number of

Gunnor's sisters made great marriages to some of the most significant nobles of Normandy at the beginning of the eleventh century. It is a startling fact that in the year 1110 seven of the counts and earls of the aristocracy of the Anglo-Norman realm, and numerous high barons, were great-grandchildren of Gunnor and her sisters, as also was the then king, Henry I of England.

On the authority of William de Jumièges, we learn that Gunnor and Count Richard had the count's heir Richard II; Robert, archbishop of Rouen and count of Evreux (989–1037); and also Mauger, count of Corbeil; and two other boys, one of whom was called Robert 'the Dane' and died young in the 980s. Dudo mentions two other sons from different mothers, Godfrey and William, successively counts of Eu. A further son, yet again called Robert, is known, who was created count of Mortain. As well as fathering the highest echelon of a new aristocracy, Richard I also had numerous daughters with Gunnor and other partners. With Gunnor he had Emma, Hawise and Mathilda, whom he used to enhance his marital connections with his neighbours. Emma became queen of England, marrying successively King Æthelred II and King Cnut, Hawise married the count of Nantes in Brittany, and Mathilda married Count Odo II of Blois.

So we find that by the third generation of the Norman dynasty it had already embedded itself deeply into the network of princely families that ruled north-western Europe, including the Capetian and West Saxon royal dynasties. This brought high status, diplomatic advantage and the security that intermarriage brought to new families within older societies. On a lower level, the dynasty had produced male and female cadet members who had begun to found lesser lineages within the principality, who secured clerical high office and who tied other magnates to the ruling dynasty by intermarriage. As well as inventing a duchy, the first counts of Rouen also originated much of its aristocracy. We can see from the Norman lineage how quickly complete outsiders could take possession of and transform the structures of power within a region.

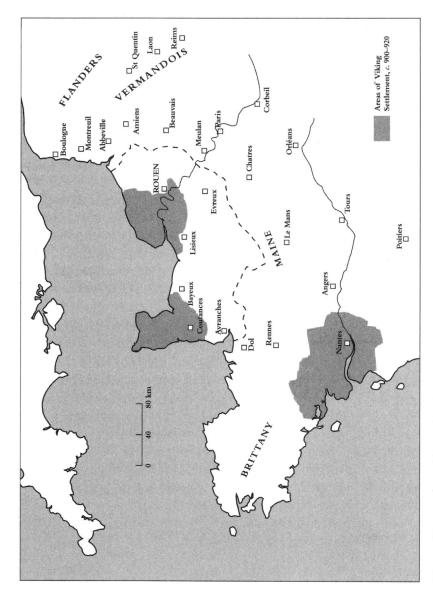

Map 1. Normandy and its environs, c. 950.

2

Richard II and his Sons

There is a good argument that the successful and aggressive West Saxon dynasty of the early tenth century played a part in creating Normandy. In the 890s England had diverted part of the energy of Viking activity south towards Brittany and Neustria; forcing Hrólfr and his colleagues away from its own coasts. It would be just as true to say that the decline of the West Saxon dynasty under Æthelred II (979–1016) at the end of the tenth century played just as important a part in shaping the emerging identity of the Norman people and its princely family. With the growing weakness of England, the possibilities for profitable Viking activity across the North Sea returned. There seemed to have been no shortage of Viking entrepreneurs in the 980s willing to take advantage of a wealthy and politically weak England, an enterprise which eventually attracted even the Danish royal family. The renewed Viking activity across the Channel was bound to influence the Normans, to challenge their new relationship with the rest of the French, and to involve them in the affairs of England.

Over the past fifty years, one of the most absorbing parts of the debate on the emergence of Normandy has been the pace of the process by which it lost its Viking identity. How big a proportion of the population of the tenth-century duchy was of Scandinavian extraction? How Scandinavian was its language and social structure? How much had the duchy we see in 1000 preserved a Frankish social and institutional legacy despite the Vikings? How far was Normandy in 1000 still connected to a wider Viking cultural and mercantile world? The state of the evidence means that most of these questions can never be answered firmly and finally. Historians tend to keep their own counsel in such circumstances, but some things now seem established. By 1000 the overwhelming bulk of the Norman population was both Christian and French-speaking; parents had ceased or were ceasing to give their children names that were

obviously and exotically Scandinavian. Frankish forms of relationships
and Frankish customs were being embraced and becoming accepted as
the norm. The ruling dynasty had been looking to its Frankish and
Breton neighbours for three generations for marriage alliances, and native
Franks were identifiable and important in both Norman Church and
lay society. One of the newly dominant aristocratic families of central
Normandy – that of the Tosny – was Frankish. The first Tosnys were
Franks who were established on their extensive lands by the former
monk of St-Denis, Archbishop Hugh of Rouen (d. 989). Although later
Tosny family tradition balances this Frankishness by including in the
lineage an otherwise unknown uncle of Rollo, called 'Malahulc', this
may only be a remote link by marriage, or may even be a total fabrication
in order to provide the Tosny family with some trace of Norman identity.
There was as much an influx of Frankish immigrants into the duchy as
there was of Northerners. Known aristocratic incomers in about 1000
included the Taisson family (from Anjou) and the Giroie (from Brittany
via the Perche), who somehow found a patron willing to give them large
estates in central Normandy on which to settle.

Nonetheless, historians have found reasons to think that the Normandy of 1000 had by no means severed its links with the North, nor
had its people turned their collective and metaphorical back on their
Viking origins. The city of Rouen is the key to this continuing feeling
of northernness. It was one of the principal entry points of northern
trade into France. There is an argument that the Viking invaders of the
late ninth century had secured the city well before the time of Rollo so
as to use it as a market for selling on the slaves and plunder of France,
England and Ireland. By this argument, the Vikings were not so much
a setback to Rouen's commercial fortune but the creators of it, as Rouen
would by this argument have been a city exempt from the devastation
that surrounded it. The argument perhaps assumes too much central
economic direction within the undisciplined Scandinavian warbands.
Towns were tempting targets for plundering; but, even if looted, they
were resilient institutions capable of rapid recovery when profit was still
to be had from them. The persistence of trade is itself reason enough
to explain why Rouen prospered and grew in the tenth century, and a
good part of that trade was with the north. Coins from Rouen continue
to be found in numbers in Scandinavian hoards well into the eleventh

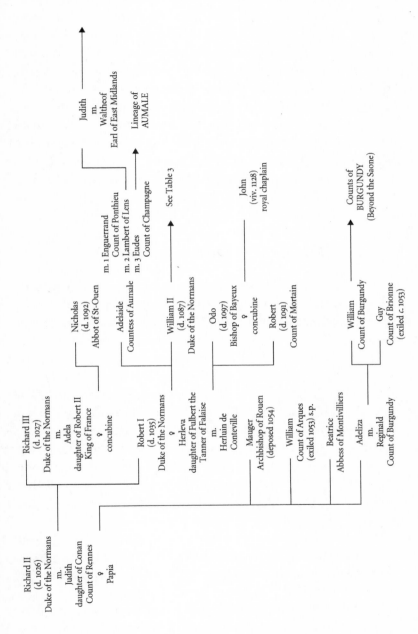

Table 2. Descent from Richard II.

century. There is also the evidence of the often-quoted and often obscene satire by a Frankish clerk, Garnier of Rouen,[1] on an Irish enemy of his, called Moriuht. This Moriuht and his wife had been captured by Vikings and sold separately as slaves. Moriuht eventually freed himself and found his way to Normandy in his search for his wife. He found her working as a slave in a mill at Vaudreuil, south of Rouen. He secured her release, and they both settled in the city, where Moriuht made an enemy of Garnier, who in his irritation with the man inadvertently immortalised Moriuht's adventures. Garnier showed himself not only familiar with a Viking slave trade which unloaded victims in Normandy, but also well-informed on Scandinavian culture and pagan practices, and he gives us good evidence that Normandy – like England in the 990s – had not yet turned away from the north culturally or commercially.

Duke Richard II, Denmark and England

The reign of Richard II of Normandy (996–1026) was characterised by a new crisis of identity in the former Viking colony that was his realm. We know this because the duke himself took measures to intervene in the way Normandy and his dynasty were perceived by both his subjects and his neighbours. It was Richard II who in his last years commissioned Dudo of St-Quentin,[2] his confidant and clerk, to craft an image of his Norman realm as a Viking colony which had rapidly transformed itself into a Frankish principality. Duke Richard wanted Normandy to be seen not just as conventional in its organisation, but as a particular abode of Christian virtue. Dudo portrayed Richard's ancestors as a succession of Christian dukes and lawgivers of great moral integrity, succeeding each other regularly with the consent of their people, despite all that their treacherous neighbours and overlords could do. This was the historical fiction that Richard II wanted to present as fact to the literate world. He was perhaps the more anxious to do this because his own reign as duke seemed at times to be drawing his principality away from the Frankish customs and orientation that his father had laboured so hard to impress upon it.

The last years of the reign of Richard I had seen Viking activity resuming and intensifying in the Channel. Throughout the 980s the English coast was raided by Viking bands, and we know that the Vikings crossed over to the Norman side of the Channel to find a ready market for their plunder. It may be that Richard was willing to allow this rather than find his own coasts being plundered, or it may be that the Vikings knew that the Normans would open their ports to them for historical and cultural reasons. Viking mercenaries had been freely employed by Richard in the 960s when he was under severe threat from a coalition of Frankish rivals, and this had not been forgotten. The free hospitality offered to the pagan raiders by a Christian principality caused scandal, and English agitation as far away as Rome was sufficient for the pope himself to intervene to condemn what was going on. On Christmas Day 990 a papal envoy reached Æthelred's court with authority to negotiate a treaty between the king and Count Richard. On 1 March 991 the bishop of Sherborne led a party of English envoys who concluded a formal treaty at Rouen by which Richard (amongst other things) promised not to harbour Æthelred's enemies any more.

Richard II succeeded his father in 996, and the first years of his reign saw a worsening of conditions across the Channel. A great army of Vikings descended on Wessex and systematically pillaged it, province by province, from 997 to 1000. The treaty between Æthelred and Richard II's father was plainly forgotten, since in the summer of 1000 the Viking army plundering England decamped to Normandy, or 'Richard's realm', as the Anglo-Saxon Chronicle called it.[3] The army was allowed peacefully to land, even if it was not welcomed. It was in 1002, in the aftermath of Æthelred's huge bribe to the army to depart from England, that the king sent ambassadors to Normandy to negotiate a marriage alliance with Duke Richard. In the late spring Æthelred married Emma, the duke's sister, and gave her the city of Exeter as a dowry. The marriage alliance at that particular time looks like an attempt to close off future support for Viking armies and prolong the peace the king had so expensively bought. The failure of the diplomacy it represents can be put down to Æthelred's fatal mistake in instigating the massacre of the Danes settled in the south east of England that November. The result was to bring King Swein of Denmark himself into England, and the power of the aggressive and expansionist Danish kingdom was therefore directed away from the Baltic and towards the shores of England. A further danger in this was the fact that Swein was no pagan but an established Christian king, and could therefore freely indulge in diplomatic manoeuvres of his own, without having to contend with the automatic fear and suspicion with which his pagan ancestors would have been met.

Richard's brief alliance with Æthelred probably did not survive the new Danish assault on England. William de Jumièges records an (unsuccessful) English raid on the Cotentin at some unspecified time after the marriage. By his account the raid had been meant by Æthelred to devastate Lower Normandy, but the English soldiers were taken unawares by the rapid response of the cavalry of the viscount of the Cotentin, and destroyed. William does not date this first episode of Anglo-Norman warfare, but a possible period might well be the years 1008–9 when for the last time Æthelred mobilised a great English fleet in the Channel. Although the fleet was meant to deter King Swein, there was opportunity for it to accomplish other missions, such as to take vengeance on Duke Richard for his lukewarm support for his brother-in-law. Internal quarrels amongst the thegns commanding this great fleet are recorded by the Anglo-Saxon Chronicle as the cause of its destruction; a military failure by a squadron detached to harry the Norman coast would seem to be fully in accord with what else we know of this great naval disaster. By 1013, Richard had gone so far (and Æthelred's prestige was so low) that the duke was quick to welcome King Swein himself to Rouen. A formal alliance was concluded by which the duke firstly offered aid and shelter to Danish crews seeking his ports, and secondly offered his markets for the sale of Viking plunder. Both parties swore a perpetual dynastic peace. Richard may have been recognising in this that the fall of England to Swein was inevitable, and an unstated intention of the treaty may have been to clear the way for his sister and his young Anglo-Norman nephews to take refuge in Normandy. By the end of the year, Queen Emma and her sons had indeed crossed the Channel as refugees and England was Swein's.

Between 990 and 1014 the rulers of Normandy were continually and forcefully reminded that the Viking world included their coasts. During this period, they could not but have been aware that, in the eyes of the kings of England, Norway and Denmark, the Normans were still a political part of the northern world, not just a cultural and mercantile part of it. For all the opportunities this liminal position brought the Normans, it also brought dangers. The Normans could conceivably have closed their ports to the Vikings, as the English had wanted, but the retaliation might have been dreadful. If the Normans had refused to be Viking collaborators, they would then have been potential victims. This fear alone guaranteed a reception for Viking ships in Normandy. The unwelcome consequence was that there was a renewed ambiguity in Norman identity: other French people would have been reminded of the Viking within them. While the Normans were being forced to look towards England and Denmark, they became less obviously French, and the ambition of the duke to maintain a place amongst the other French princes became compromised.

Richard II and the Identity of Normandy

The identity of Normandy was a matter of concern for its duke in the early eleventh century. It is no coincidence that Richer of Reims was so determined an abuser of the Normans in the 990s as 'pirates' and their ruler as a 'duke of pirates'. The Normans in that decade were compromising their identity as would-be Franks. Duke Richard himself must have compounded this problem when he could not resist exploiting the advantages of his northern links. In 1013–14, at the same time as Æthelred was losing England to Swein of Denmark and Swein himself travelled to Rouen, Richard II followed his father's example and hired Viking mercenaries in his border war with Odo II, count of Blois (d. 1037). He secured the support of a nominally Christian Viking leader, Olaf Haraldsson (later to be king of Norway), and another Atlantic Viking by name of Lacman, a king of the Isles, and with them came a miscellaneous horde which would have been mostly pagan. Their arrival, by way of Brittany, shocked the French, and King Robert II himself promptly arranged a peace conference to settle the difficulties between Duke Richard and Count Odo, while the Vikings camped menacingly on the River Avre. Duke Richard paid off his northern army lavishly, as well he might. The duke's identification with the Vikings must have been underlined a few years later when his by now widowed sister, Emma, remarried to the new king of England, Cnut of Denmark. The effect of all this can be found in the remark of Ralph Glaber thirty or so years later that it was the ability of the 'duke of Rouen' to summon military aid from beyond the seas that explained the immunity of the Normans from attack: 'far from the other nations terrorising them, the fear they inspired terrified foreign peoples'.⁴ Ralph tellingly comprehended he inhabitants of Normandy and their Viking brethren in one phrase.

Richard's main endeavours, like those of his father, had still to be carried out at home in France, despite the renewed problems across the Channel. For all the clogging of his harbours with Viking ships unloading the plunder of England, and the infection of his market places with Hiberno-Norse slave traders, Richard II was in all his aspirations and upbringing a Frankish prince, and a loyal vassal of the Capetian king. He continued his father's long-standing alliance with Paris as the lode-stone of his policy. As late as 991, his aged father had contributed a large military force to assist King Hugh against Odo of Blois, who had seized Melun, thirty miles upriver from Paris on the Seine. Richard II was equally ready to commit troops far from Normandy to assist the king of his day, Robert II, who had succeeded his father in the same year (996) as Richard had succeeded his. In 1003, a large Norman force joined King Robert's invasion of Burgundy in pursuit of his claim to succeed as duke, and many Norman soldiers fell in the assault on Auxerre. Richard seems to have maintained his support for the king in Burgundy until the king finally secured the duchy in 1005. The unin-terrupted harmony in Capetian and Norman interests is clear in the way that King Robert hastened to make peace between Duke Richard and Odo of Blois in 1014, and in a remark by Bishop Fulbert of Chartres c. 1025 that he could count on the king and the duke to act jointly to help him in his difficulties with the viscount of Châteaudun.

One consequence of this Norman military activity within France was a far-flung dynastic marriage when Richard II in about 1006 married his daughter Adelaide, still then a child, to Count Reginald of Burgundy (who ruled the part of Burgundy across the Saone, including the Jura mountains). In due course, in the latter years of his reign, Duke Richard was once again drawn into a campaign in Burgundy, when he sent his son Richard III with an army to liberate Reginald from captivity by his rival, the count-bishop of Chalon. Richard looked to his own borders also. His choice of wife fell on Judith, sister of Count Geoffrey of Brittany, who was married to his own sister Hawise. Richard II married Judith (as William of Jumièges insists) in a church ceremony at the abbey of Mont St-Michel on the Norman-Breton border. The marriage seems to have occurred by 1003, although it might conceivably have been earlier still, and was very successful. It produced children and led to Richard's intervention in Brittany during the minority of Count Geoffrey's heirs. We can also glimpse Richard II as the first to pursue a border policy which became a common tactic amongst his descendants for the next century and more. He looked to make alliances with the lesser counts around his southern and eastern borders, would-be princelings who were asserting their independence from the control of the king. In this way he created a buffer zone towards his powerful enemies the counts of Blois-Chartres and (a newly emerging force) the counts of Anjou. One such target seems to have been Count Drogo of Amiens and the Vexin (d. 1035), who obtained from Richard a grant out of the ducal fisc of the castle and town of Elbeuf,[5] upriver on the Seine from Rouen. The lands of counts of the Vexin lay outside Normandy, north eastwards towards Paris and Vermandois, and they were very well-placed and desirable allies. Alongside Drogo, the duke attracted the friendship of another count from the Seine valley, Waleran I of Meulan, whose fortified island in the Seine commanded the river trade towards Paris. Waleran appears with the duke at Rouen in 1023 when he made a grant of free movement on the Seine to Richard's favoured abbey of Fécamp.

Whatever the outside perceptions of the Norman duchy and its inhabitants, sources from within the duchy show it in Richard II's days to have been a Frankish principality organised much like any other, indeed, to have been a little more conservative than some. Around four dozen written acts survive from the reign of Richard II, a tribute to the growing number of monastic foundations in his duchy, institutions which generated records and sought written ducal privileges. These records show that, by the 1010s at least, Duke Richard was operating a system of local administration based on the traditional Carolingian divisions of his duchy: called the *pagi* or *comitatus*. Each of these divisions had a ducal officer operating within it, a 'viscount'. The office of viscount (*vicecomes*) had first appeared in the ninth century as the judicial deputy of the former Carolingian provincial count. We see the title being revived in Normandy in the time of Richard II and attached to his regional officers. It is difficult to say what their duties were in eleventh-century Normandy, although we know from the defence of the Cotentin against English raiders by Viscount Nigel in about 1008, and from his control of the ducal fortress of Le Homme, that he at least had a military command and access to local levies. In 1025 a solemn ducal act at Fécamp was attested by twelve of these viscounts, which corresponds to the number of Norman *pays* or *pagi* available for them to officiate in,[6] although, since half of these men do not appear again in any source, it would not do to make too much of this fact. We know that some of Richard II's viscounts commanded substantial resources of their own. Viscount Rainald of Arques had considerable property in the vicinity of the ducal fortress from which he took his title, and Viscount Nigel of the Cotentin controlled the fortress of St-Sauveur and its associated lands within his bailiwick. Thurstin Goz, viscount of the Hièmois, also gave rise to a landed family of hereditary viscounts with great estates at Creully and St-Jacques-de-Beuvron. These vicecomital families were all later to give rise to great Norman aristocratic houses.

The charters of Richard II also reveal that the duke was finding new ways of stressing his princely dignity. On several occasions in his reign the clerks drawing up his written instruments decided to dignify him with the title duke 'by the generous mercy of God's grace' or 'by the decision of divine mercy' or 'by the concession of God's grace'. These were phrases that might appear in royal titles, and directly attributed Richard II's position and power to God's favour and protection. They were the logical development of the attribution of the biblical princely virtues to the Norman rulers, which we find being made as early as the time of William Longsword. Another borrowing Duke Richard made from the royal dignity was the use of titled court officials. These grandees first appear in history as accessories to the imperial majesty of the Carolingians, and there had even been a long and learned treatise published in 880 on the proper way to organise them. Chamberlains, an usher, clerks, a notary, chancellor and chaplains (one being the ubiquitous Dudo of St-Quentin) dignified the retinue of Richard II before 1026. Since his son, Duke Robert (1027–35) was to deploy the greater titles of seneschal and constable in his household, and since Robert's seneschal,[7] Osbern fitz Arfast, was a first cousin and courtier of Richard II, it is likely that Richard II had instituted that office and Robert had continued it. Court officers gave the subtle message that the dukes of Normandy were to be treated as among the great of the earth, with a majesty approaching that of kings, even if they were not crowned. The deployment of seneschals, chamberlains and constables in the Norman court has even more point when we note that the Capetian kings were doing without such regal accessories in the early eleventh century.

Dudo of St-Quentin provided for his master, Richard II, the gilded finials to place on the top of the turrets of his pretensions, with the pointed rhetoric of his paean of praise to the ducal house. Aware of the way that his master wished to be seen – as a distinguished French prince and major prop to the Capetian monarchy – Dudo deployed his pen in the early 1020s to counter doubts about Norman legitimacy and the shady associations of the duke with Northern plunderers. Dudo met the critics head on. He wrote lavishly of the Viking Rollo's innate nobility and implied his high birth. He dwelt on his sincere Christianity and rapid transformation into a regular Frankish count, with councillors, nobles and clerical entourage. Rollo's equally Viking son was given a hagiographical whitewash: William was at heart a true monk, a lover of clergy and of peace, and in the end died the death of a Christian martyr. A portrayal of such predecessors naturally reflected on Dudo's current patron; these were the ancestors one of the greatest amongst French dukes of his day required, especially at a time when the inconvenient Viking past of his dynasty was getting in the way of his pretensions to post-Carolingian splendour.

Richard III (1026–27), Robert I (1027–35) and the Norman Aristocracy

The genealogical compilation on the Norman ducal house drawn up at Fécamp and copied at Battle abbey in the early twelfth century (the 'Brevis Relatio') describes a touching custom of Duke Richard II.[8] The duke had completed his father's work at Fécamp and erected an appropriate Romanesque abbey church and claustral buildings for the monks opposite his ducal palace, which stood below the abbey's west front.[9]

> The duke was in the habit of holding his Easter court almost every year at Fécamp, and, at a time of his choosing, he and his wife would carry a box full of books, thuribles, candlesticks and other ornaments, covered with a beautiful cloth, up to the altar of the Holy Trinity, and she and he would offer it there to God for their sins. On Easter Day itself, after mass and

before he would go to his palace and eat with his men, he came with his two sons, Richard and Robert, to the monks' refectory. The two sons would carry the dishes from the kitchen hatch, as the monks usually did, and give them to their father. He would himself place the first course before the abbot and afterwards served the monks. When this was done, he would approach the abbot with great humility and when he had his permission would go happily and cheerily to his palace.[10]

This eleventh-century recollection is touching because it depicts a pious Christian prince amongst his monks, rejoicing in not one but two male heirs, who were joining with him in an act of humility before God. But it is suspicious in the way it stresses the harmony and peace within the ducal family: why is it so insistent? At Fécamp in 1025, a ducal act referred to both boys as Richard's 'heirs'. This may simply indicate that Robert was the presumed heir of his brother Richard; but, since the younger Richard had by then a male child, this assumption may not be correct. Richard and Robert may have been jointly called 'heirs' because the Fécamp clerk did not dare to prefer one son over the other at that time. It may be that the Fécamp tradition and the Fécamp charter both hint at tension between the brothers in their father's last years, as he grew old and sickened. Dudo too may hint at this. He is very concerned to portray the successions of William Longsword, Richard I and Richard II as regular ceremonies presided over by their fathers. This is a particularly strained literary device on Dudo's part as William Longsword could not reasonably have expected to go off to die at Picquigny in 943. But in each case, Dudo has the old duke designate his successor in the presence of his assembled counsellors, to make clear to everyone that the duchy will pass regularly to one heir. In the case of the designation of William Longsword, Rollo's nobles pledge their faith to him. Some modern writers have pointed out that there was no real reason why Normandy had to pass intact from one prince to the next: other Frankish principalities were on occasion divided up between sons. It could be that Dudo feared just this eventuality when he wrote his book for Richard II, and he wrote it with a fearful side glance at the known tensions within the ducal family.

Richard III and Robert were both adults when their father died. Richard was already a tried and successful warrior, with several children of his own from a concubine. There was no doubt that he was to succeed

his father, an event which came about on 23 August 1026 at the elder
Richard's beloved Fécamp, after the old duke's extended and painful
illness. But his younger brother, Robert, did not accept Richard III's
ascendancy. The fraternal animosity of the 1020s seems to have been
personal and longstanding, but for all that was something new in the
ducal house. When Richard II had succeeded his father in 996, he had
been the eldest of several brothers, but his younger brothers had been
mostly far younger than he was. The one who was closest to him in
age, Robert, was neutralised (if that was indeed the purpose) by being
made archbishop of Rouen around 990, and by being given the secular
dignity of count of Evreux. The fact that Robert was intended for the
church must have been long made clear to him, although it did not
prevent the future archbishop from taking a concubine and producing
children. It has been suggested that Richard I (always conscious of the
fragility of his realm) had taken especial care to neutralise any possible
damage to it by sibling rivalry. The siblings themselves may even have
shared his anxiety and rallied to the nominated heir. Richard II succeeded as a mature man to a long-expected dignity, but he was unable
to duplicate his father's success in managing his own succession. We
can only suggest that this was because the nature of the relationship
between his sons was more antagonistic; antagonistic enough to put the
integrity of the duchy at risk. Also, by 1026, if there had once been rival
dynasties to Rollo's, they had been neutralised and had melted into a
regional aristocracy, so the need for dynastic solidarity was less obvious.

A reason why the dynastic situation in 1026 became so serious must
have been the developing social structure of Normandy. Somewhere
between the death of Rollo and the death of his great-grandson, Richard
II, Normandy had acquired an aristocracy. It is an unstated assumption
in Dudo's work that Normandy had a group of leading landowners who
were the duke's close counsellors and who gave consent to ducal elec-
tions. It is unstated because by Dudo's time it was so obvious that there
should be a dominant group of landowners close to the duke that it
never occurred to him that things might have been otherwise. Other,
later Norman historians also naturally assumed that this had always
been the case. When Wace in his *Roman de Rou* wrote in the 1160s
about Rollo's settlement of Neustria,[11] he imagined Rollo first having
his 'men' instructed in Christianity and baptised, then dividing amongst

them the towns, castles, cities, revenues, mills, meadows, forests and 'ample inheritances' of the empty province, to each man according to his lineage, noble service, age and repute.[12] In this way, for Wace writing in the mid twelfth century, Normandy and its aristocracy appeared at one and the same time. But it is unlikely that anything at all like that happened.

What actually happened will never be clear; it is, as one of the foremost Norman historians has said, a 'desperate problem', desperate both because of its importance and its insolubility.[13] We have seen how in the 920s and the 940s the succession to the countship of Rouen was complicated by the intervention of powerful local Scandinavian leaders: William Longsword had to fight and defeat rivals to establish himself in Rouen, and, as a young count, Richard I found himself contending with a certain Harald, a Viking rival who had seized the Cotentin and Bayeux. We hear also how the boy count could rely on the support of Bernard, a powerful but friendly leader of Danish extraction. Such sources as there are indicate the existence of rivals and allies, rather than nobles, in Normandy's early days. This state of affairs may have continued well into Richard I's time. It has been suggested that when Richard married Gunnor, in the 970s, he was marrying into a rival, powerful Scandinavian dynasty and so neutralising the danger they represented. The influential and dangerous viscount of the Hièmois, Thurstin Goz, was the product of just such another Viking dynasty. He had as father a man called Ansfrid the Dane, who would have been active in Richard I's reign. Lurking in the misty reaches of the mid tenth century must have been a number of obscure but powerful former Viking families, already rich in land, who had settled the region alongside Rollo and his family but who only emerge into history with the eleventh century. What descent other than Viking could Stigandr, mentioned as lord of Mézidon in the 1020s, have had with a Norse name like that? A major step in the formation of Normandy must have been when these powerful families decided to submit themselves to the 'ban', the lordship and jurisdiction of Rollo's dynasty, and no longer compete with it – but we will never know precisely when that happened.

When such people (along with Frankish survivors and immigrants) became a Norman nobility is not a question that will ever be settled, although there is no doubt that an elite and noble social group was a political reality by the reign of Richard II. Plotting back the great complexes of estates and forests (or 'honors') held by the great Norman noble families of the twelfth century, investigators have found that a good number can be traced back to the time of Richard II, not just those estates held by his siblings, the counts of Brionne, Evreux, Mortain and Eu. An excellent example is Humphrey, the ancestor of the powerful family that later provided the Anglo-Norman realm with the earls of Leicester and Warwick. He was already established in the 1020s on the core of the family's Norman estates, the honor of Pont Audemer, south of the Seine estuary. Robert de Torigny says that Humphrey had succeeded a father with the very Scandinavian name of Turulf, who would have been active in the time of Richard I, and who is said to have married another sister of Duchess Gunnor. This Turulf is further said to have been son of one Torf, who, if he ever really had existed, would have been of the generation of William Longsword. We can project back this particular family an unusually long way into the tenth century, and we can assume that it settled in the Seine estuary with the primary wave of Scandinavian immigration. Humphrey, son of Turulf son of Torf, the lord of Pont Audemer, is found keeping company with Duke Richard II and the widowed Gunnor (his aunt) as early as 1010, and he was probably later a seneschal of Duke Robert. Humphrey undoubtedly saw himself as an aristocrat: he was one of the first Normans to follow the lead of the ducal family and (with ducal permission) refound a former Carolingian monastery on his estates, at Les Préaux, south of Pont Audemer. The irony may be that it would have been the earlier generations of his family that had originally terminated the monastery's life.

Such men – with the wealth they had, the soldiers they could hire, and the lesser men they controlled – were essential to the dukes. Richard II of Normandy was certainly a powerful and enviably rich prince, with enormous resources in land and revenue, but even he needed men like Humphrey of Pont Audemer, Thurstin Goz, Nigel of St-Sauveur, Ralph de Tosny, and Osbern fitz Arfast. Their attendance on him gave him the dignity of a distinguished court, in which some of them took offices; their allegiance gave him strengthened control over the people of his duchy; and their military support helped him to field and command armies, like the one he sent under the leadership of Richard, his son, far away into Burgundy around 1020. The nature of the formal bonds between the duke and his aristocracy is unknown at this time. We can assume that the duke insisted on some ritual of subordination when these men entered his service. Dudo knew about such things and their importance. He imagined Rollo's embarrassment on realising that he must formally submit to King Charles by kissing his foot. Yet, Viking disdain apart, kneeling and at least clasping his legs was one way a nobleman acknowledged a greater lord in western society well into the thirteenth century. Another ceremony which expressed dependance was when a lord bestowed military equipment on a lesser man. Although usually done when a young adult was commencing public life, this ceremony, called in French *adoubement*, might be performed later,[14] when a warrior took service with a lord, as when Duke William II took Harold of Wessex under his formal protection in around 1064.

Whether the subordination of a Norman aristocrat in the early eleventh century involved contracting with the duke for a quota of mounted warriors is entirely unknown. That there was an early link between land and military service is at least clear from the finding of a reference from before 1033 to a man holding an estate from the abbey of St-Ouen of Rouen as a *miles*, a 'knight' (or, more loosely, 'soldier'), which land he was allowed to pass on to his sons, for the same service.[15] In view of the central place that military organisation plays in our understanding of what it was to be a conquering Norman, it would be good to know more about early Norman military practices than this. All we have are hints. The exploits of the military retinue of Viscount Nigel of the Cotentin in defence of his province against English raiders in about 1008 have already been mentioned. The plains of the Ouche, in the centre of Normandy, were breeding the great war horses necessary to support this horseback culture by at least the middle of the eleventh century, when we hear of studs owned there by the wealthy Grandmesnil family. We know quite a bit about one early Norman warrior, Herluin son of Ansgot, who was born around the time Richard I died (996). His father was said to be of Danish extraction but his mother was from Flanders, and Herluin and his brothers were all provided with land from Ansgot's inheritance. He grew up to be a retained warrior in the household of Godfrey, count of Eu and Brionne, and was an especial favourite of Gilbert, son of Count Godfrey. He was very likely to have been brought up and educated with Gilbert in the reign of Richard II, and naturally became one of his military household.

Herluin son of Ansgot was a renowned warrior and horseman, and (according to his biographer) also a man of affairs with a high moral reputation. In the course of a varied military career, Herluin was able to acquire further land and tenants of his own from his lord, and formed political contacts with other magnates sufficiently strong to get him in trouble with Count Gilbert. He was able to use both his land and those contacts in the end to invest in the foundation of a great abbey in 1034, at Le Bec-Hellouin, near the fortress of Brionne, where he became the first abbot. His eventual elevation to sainthood means that we know something both of him and his secular career. What his career tells us is that the Norman duke and his aristocrats were by 1000 retaining horseback military households, and had adopted with enthusiasm the military lifestyle which had been a characteristic of late Frankish noble society. We can use the later English word 'knight' to describe these men, because the social structure, training, and exclusive military culture and equipment to support such professionals already then existed. They would have called themselves *chivalers*; they would have called their way of life the pursuit of deeds of arms (*chivalerie*) and the purpose of existence was for them a competition to be recognised and applauded as tried and mature men-at-arms (*preux* or *ber*).

A military aristocracy was useful, and even necessary, to the duke of the Normans, but it had some disadvantages. When a duke was powerful such men magnified his power, but when a duke was weak they sapped further what little power he had. A strong and unchallengeable prince would find that his aristocracy eagerly competed for his favour and enthusiastically took up his service, and so things would go well with him. A prince who was compromised by a poor reputation or by a dangerous rival would find the selfsame aristocracy dividing into factions against him, giving hope and support to pretenders to his authority. The aristocracy was to its prince like a sheepdog to a shepherd, an indispensable help – unless it got the taste of blood, at which point it became an uncontrollable predator and a desperate liability. The brief reigns of Duke Richard III (1026–27) and Duke Robert I (1027–35) prove how the aristocracy could be a potentially destabilising force in the duchy.

Richard III succeeded his father in August 1026, and was faced almost immediately by the armed revolt of his younger brother. Their father had attempted to provide for Robert in the same way his own father had provided for his siblings, by settling on him the town of Exmes and its dependant pays, the Hiémois. Whether or not, as some dispute, he was intended to found there a cadet comital dynasty, like the developing lines of Eu and Evreux, the inheritance strategy was well-tried within the princely dynasty by 1026. But, unlike most of his uncles,[16] Robert would not be satisfied. He assembled a military force and, for whatever purpose, defied his brother's authority, causing considerable damage and dislocation in the diocese of Bayeux, as its bishop, his cousin, complained. One possible bone of contention between the brothers may have been Robert's desire to control the powerful fortress of Falaise, within the Hiémois, which his brother the duke had retained and which he had therefore seized. The revolt was focused here, but Robert discovered that his brother was more than his equal in energy and resources. Falaise was besieged and remorselessly and scientifically reduced with the use of siege engines. The end result was that Robert was forced to acknowledge Richard's authority, as William de Jumièges says, by kneeling before him and placing his hands in his. Richard is known to have consolidated his power by an immediate arranged marriage in January 1027 with Adela, infant daughter of King Robert, who was dowered with a handsome settlement, including the city and county of Coutances. Early that summer, Richard met his father-in-law, the king, at Senlis, so advertising the continuation and intensification of his father's relationship with the Capetian king.

Duke Richard III, an eminent young soldier, newly married to a king's daughter, but already father by a concubine of a male heir and two daughters, was clearly embarked on a career to match those of his predecessors, but he had only a year to create expectations. He died at Rouen less than twelve months after his father. Contemporaries like Adhémar of Chabannes and William de Jumièges repeat the usual medieval suspicion associated with sudden and unexpected death, that Richard was poisoned. By the early twelfth century, it was indeed being alleged that the perpetrator of the poisoning was his own brother, Robert (*cui bono*). A century after the event William of Malmesbury was even willing to identify Robert's agent in the murder, one Ralph Mowin (probably a garbled version of Ralph le Moine, appointed tutor by Duke Robert to his son, William). It was later explained that Robert's subsequent pilgrimage to the Holy Land was in order to clear the guilt of his fratricide. We may doubt all this. Medieval society was occasionally swept with dysentery and ferocious internal diseases, leading to abrupt and unexpected deaths (a dreadful outbreak in 1151–53 carried off King Stephen's heir and a number of his aristocracy). People were unsettled by sudden death, which left no time for preparation, confession and the ritual of separation, indeed 'May you die without warning!' was a particularly vicious medieval curse against an enemy. Such deaths led to suspicions that God had a hand in them, as was assumed when Earl Godwin of Wessex died of a seizure at Lambeth in 1052. So it was preferable for some medieval people that a prince's sudden and unshriven death should be attributed to human malice and agency, rather than to God's doom and displeasure.

The Reign of Duke Robert I (1028–35)

Richard III's death was immediately followed by the assumption of the duchy by his brother, Robert. Had Richard lived another ten years, Robert would not have succeeded him, for by then the expectation would have been that Richard's son, Nicholas, would have been duke after his father. But in 1027 Nicholas was at most an adolescent boy, and his uncle Robert promptly placed him safely out of the way within the walls of the abbey of Fécamp. In 1027 there was no question but that Robert, the mature if impetuous warrior, would succeed his brother. William de Jumièges writes blandly and without comment that Robert was in 1027 'heir to the duchy'. The official version is given in an act of Duke Robert for the abbey of Jumièges: it says that the 'rule over the realm of the Normans was manfully wielded by the great Duke Richard [II]' and when he died he was succeeded by his son of the same name, but then 'surprised by sudden death he relinquished his realm to his brother Robert, *by hereditary right*'.[17] Nicholas entered the religious life at Fécamp with no apparent regrets. He was appointed abbot of St-Ouen by his uncle in 1034, and ruled the great abbey outside Rouen with distinction till his death in 1092, having outlived by several years his younger first cousin, the conqueror of England.

Quick though he was to lay claim to his brother's inheritance, the new Duke Robert did not possess it in quite the tranquillity that his father had apparently enjoyed. His brief reign was packed with incident, and left its mark on Norman historiography. Contemporary monastic chroniclers did not wholly approve of him: sources from the established abbeys of Jumièges and St-Wandrille talk of difficulties experienced in his reign, which they attribute to his unwillingness to restrain his 'perverse' aristocratic associates. We find him *c.* 1033 restoring possessions he had taken for the benefit of his military household from his father's favoured abbey of Fécamp, blaming his heedless youth and 'certain councillors' for misleading him in the matter. These sources talk of a reputation for poor judgement and lack of restraint which he had acquired as a youth: which may be a reference to his rivalry with his elder brother which broke out into violence between them in 1026. The later French chronicler, Hugh de Flavigny, who travelled through Normandy in the 1090s researching the history of the Capetian kings, picked up stories of Duke Robert's conflict with a party amongst his nobility. All in all – bearing in mind the reluctance of Norman historians to criticise a duke who died a pilgrim in a foreign land – sufficient negative comment sifts past their discretion to hint at a wilful and uncontrolled personality, who was plagued by conflict amongst the aristocracy, which he himself had actively promoted in his brother's reign. Duke Robert I was the first of his lineage who was not admitted to be an unqualified success as a ruler since Rollo-Robert, his great-great-grandfather, after whom he was named.

Within a short time of becoming duke, Robert began to find scores to settle. One of his first actions was to lead an army against his distinguished uncle, Archbishop Robert of Rouen, and beseige him in his city of Evreux, where he was count. William de Jumièges blames this aggression on the duke's evil advisers, the usual resort of a writer who did not wish to criticise a prince openly. In fact, Duke Robert may have been punishing his uncle for his support of his brother during the previous year. The archbishop resisted the duke long enough within the Roman walls of Evreux for him to secure a truce by which he could leave Normandy for exile at the Capetian court. But he also left the duchy under anathema, which was only lifted when his nephew restored Evreux to him and lifted the banishment. This was not Duke Robert's only violent assault on an episcopal relative. At some time around 1028 he attacked his cousin Bishop Hugh of Bayeux, son of his great-uncle, Count Rodulf of Ivry. Like the archbishop, Hugh too held great secular possessions, notably the castle and honor of Ivry, on the Norman border. This was seized after a close siege and surrender, and not returned to the bishop, who remained in exile till 1032.

Robert's relations with the secular aristocracy seem to have been less aggressive than his moves against the Church. Indeed he seems to have been negligent in his attitude to his magnates at times. One of the best insights into his relationship with his nobles comes curiously late, when the monk-historian of St-Evroult, Orderic Vitalis,[18] wrote up the result of his intensive research into the local and family history of the region around his abbey in the 1110s. This is nonetheless a good source because Orderic compiled memoirs of the 1030s from the older residents of his neighbourhood, and wove them into a carefully factual and understated study of what was clearly a dangerous age. We hear of the duke's cousin, Count Gilbert of Brionne, 'chafing to enlarge his estates' and beginning a local war with the young sons of Giroie fitz Arnold of Montreuil and Echauffour. The count expected to dispossess them, but was driven back instead on his own estate of Le Sap, and lost it. Duke Robert appears in this story only as a distant referee who is called in to persuade the count to surrender Le Sap as a pledge for his continued good behaviour. He does not appear as a duke outraged that private war is being levied within his realm. Orderic has another tale which shows him as more severe; it is of an assassination carried out in a hunting party in the duke's presence, by an outraged father avenging a deflowered daughter. Robert in this case outlawed the murderer and exiled him to Brittany, but in this case the incident had compromised his personal dignity, by affronting the peace of his court.[19]

William de Jumièges, who lived through the reign, was more keen to discuss Duke Robert's foreign wars than his domestic troubles. This may have been because he wished to avoid the subject, as his abbey suffered under the duke's rule and he was writing a book addressed to the duke's son. Robert's foreign adventures were more varied and aggressive than his father's and made respectable telling in the 1070s. His first major enterprise was to take advantage of a civil war in Flanders, where Count Baldwin IV had been driven out of his realm by his son,

Baldwin V, in alliance with King Robert II, his father-in-law. Duke
Robert offered military support sufficient to intimidate the younger
Baldwin into making peace with his father at Oudenarde in 1030. On
the western side of his duchy, Robert indulged in a major campaign
against his first cousin, Alan III. The counts of Brittany were successfully
extending their influence from Rennes, and the young Count Alan seems
to have caused some concern by his ambitions in the region around
Mont St-Michel. Duke Robert sacked Dol at some time in the early
1030s, and Alan's attempted retaliation on Avranches was vigorously
repulsed. In 1033, after further raiding, Alan and Robert were reconciled
in a peace coordinated by a returned Archbishop Robert of Rouen, their
mutual uncle. If these border campaigns had not been enough, the duke
was also engaged in asserting his authority along his southern frontier
towards Chartres and Maine. His principal efforts were expended in
curbing the powerful Bellême clan, which had erected a marcher lordship
in the space where the rulers of Maine, Chartres and Normandy were
in competition. It seems to have been Robert's particular concern to
secure recognition of his authority in the frontier towns of Alençon and
Séez, where the Bellême had established themselves.

Duke Robert's most spectacular venture in his brief reign was his part
in the Capetian succession following the death of King Robert II in
1031. There are signs of something like a breach in the longstanding
Norman-Capetian alliance in the king's last years, but this was abruptly
reversed when, in 1033, the young king, Henry I of France, was ousted
by his stepmother Queen Constance. The queen had allied with Odo II
of Blois to try to establish her own son and Henry's younger brother,
Robert, on the throne. King Henry fled with a small escort to Fécamp,
where he sought the help of the duke of Normandy. A ducal act of 1033
for the benefit of the abbey of St-Wandrille indicates by its witness list
something of Duke Robert's response to this crisis. There with him was
the king 'who at this time was a fugitive maintained in this land' and
also those allies who could help the duke to restore the king: the duke's
uncle, Mauger, count of Corbeil, a city on the Seine upriver from Paris;
the count of Meulan; and a number of prominent nobles and viscounts.
William de Jumièges tells us that Duke Robert mobilised his army and
border allies on the Seine towards Paris, and gave the king money and
troops to carry on a campaign in the Ile de France with the help of

Count Mauger (who had perhaps been ousted from the Ile de France with the king). The assistance of the Normans – and also Odo of Blois' other enemy, the count of Anjou – was enough to enable King Henry to force his mother and brother to a settlement, and reclaim his weakened throne. Duke Robert's exorbitant reward was, it seems, the gift of the overlordship of the whole of the Vexin from the king. It secured the Norman border towards Paris as far as Pontoise, but also created a fertile source of future dispute between Normans and Capetians.

Duke Robert, as much as his father before him, was involved with the affairs of his other neighbouring royal dynasty, that of England. There were some moves to arrange a dynastic marriage between him and Cnut's sister, Estrith, although the scheme did not proceed as far as a contract. Ralph Glaber thought that Robert took a dislike to the woman and refused to go through with the arrangement. The duke's cousins, Edward and Alfred, sons of Emma and King Æthelred, were still in exile in the duchy, while their mother, the duke's aunt, was in England as Cnut's queen. William de Jumièges is the sole source – but nonetheless a good source – for Duke Robert's attempt to intervene in English affairs. He made representations to Cnut's court that something be done for the two athelings, or princes,[20] who had been living in Normandy now since 1016 and who were in 1033 both now mature men in their late twenties. Their sister, Godgifu, had long been married by then to Drogo, count of the Vexin, Duke Richard II's friend. When Drogo was given the duke's town and honor of Elbeuf, it can only have been as a marriage gift by the duke, Godgifu's uncle. This tells us that William de Jumièges may not have been exaggerating when he said that the English princes were treated by the dukes as members of their own family. There is cumulative but strong evidence that Edward was being accorded the title of 'king of the English' by the Normans in the early 1030s. Therefore when William de Jumièges said that Duke Robert followed up his threats to Cnut in 1033 with the preparation of an invasion fleet, we may well believe him. The fleet was driven down the Channel by a gale and took refuge in the harbours of Jersey, and the expedition was called off. Still, it attests to a continuing willingness amongst the Normans in the 1030s to look for opportunities north across the Channel, as well as eastward up the Seine.

It was probably at Fécamp in his Christmas court of 1034 that Duke

Robert astonished his magnates with his announcement that he would undertake a pilgrimage to the Holy Land. It was not unprecedented for pious kings and princes to wish to pay homage to the heavenly king at His empty tomb under the great rotunda of the Holy Sepulchre in Jerusalem. Fulk of Anjou died in 1040 at Metz returning from his third trip to the Sepulchre. In the century before the First Crusade, it was not unusual for counts, bishops and commoners to take the road there on pilgrimage. Some (like Swein, son of Earl Godwin of Wessex) went barefoot all the way. Ralph Glaber reflected on the unprecedented number of pilgrims going to Jerusalem in the 1030s, and had pious hopes that it might herald the Second Coming. Norman writers gave their own reasons why the duke chose to leave his realm on a hazardous journey. William de Jumièges believed that it was simple piety and the product of a resolve taken when the duke was younger. Certainly, Robert's conversion of a minster church at Cerisy in western Normandy into a Benedictine abbey in 1032, 'aware of the impermanence of this world's prosperity', is some evidence that he did think seriously on serious things. There is reason to believe that the resolve to go eventually to Jerusalem had been in fact made as early as 1031.[21] A monk of St-Wandrille, writing in the 1050s, believed that the duke, in his natural piety and respect for what was godly, wished to find absolution for deeds done under the influence of bad counsellors. All of this may well be true, although a modern commentator might see, in the sudden act of the surrender of power, the need for an exhausted man to escape for a while a life he found increasingly burdensome and stressful. It was not the right time in his reign or in the course of his life for a great prince to take the pilgrim road.

Although still unmarried, Duke Robert was all the more able to go in that he had, like his brother before him, entered into a relationship with a concubine, with whom he had had a son. She was Herleva, a young woman of the town of Falaise, daughter of one Fulbert, a ducal chamberlain. A chamberlain was not necessarily a high officer of the court, and Fulbert is called by other accounts a *pollinctor* ('skinner'), from which it has been argued that Fulbert might have made the care of the dead part of his profession, which would account for some of the odium that came the way of his daughter (in ancient Roman society a *pollinctor* had been a professional funeral arranger).[22] Robert acquired the Hièmois – in which Falaise was located – from his father before he died, so it is likely enough that he and Herleva had already entered on their relationship before 1026. Their son William was born in or around 1028, and as an infant was living in or near his father's household. He appears in several of his father's written acts, most notably together with him at Rouen at some indeterminate time before 1034 when they are described as 'Robert, the noble prince and duke of the Normans and his son William his heir (*successor*)'.[23] At the Christmas court of 1034, when William was about seven years of age, he was presented to the court as his father's heir, should the duke not return from his pilgrimage. Preparations must have continued over several months. We glimpse some of them. We find the duke at Fécamp still on 15 January 1035 with his aunt Beatrice, who had decided to profess herself as a nun at the abbey of Montivilliers, refounded by her brother Richard II, and had asked Robert to confirm its properties and privileges. He did so telling everyone that he too had made a life-changing decision: this was the year of his reign in which he had sought the 'licence' of God and his saints to go to Jerusalem. Another such glimpse is when his courtier, Humphrey de Vieilles, sought him out and purchased a privilege for his newly founded abbey of Les Préaux. The price was twelve pounds of gold, two great silk cloths and two exceedingly valuable warhorses; all treasures which would enhance the ducal pilgrim's equipage.

Guardians and tutors were appointed to mind both William and Normandy while his father was abroad, and the duke set off towards Jerusalem with a noble retinue (including Drogo, count of the Vexin) and a great supply of portable wealth, no doubt much of it contributed by Humphrey de Vieilles and others. His prodigality with gifts on his journey guaranteed him the posthumous title of Robert 'the Magnificent'. The duke left Normandy in the springtime of 1035, and probably travelled overland by way of Metz and the Danube basin to Constantinople, then the favoured route. There he and his retinue apparently impressed the imperial court with the amount of wealth he had brought with him, and received permission to continue across the Christian Asian provinces, through the Armenian kingdoms and into Muslim-controlled Palestine. Although this pilgrimage was not intended to secure the duke's future reputation, its outcome made him something of a sanctified figure. A later eleventh-century Fécamp source had a pious story or two to tell of the pilgrim's progress. One of the best is what happened when the duke paid *mussella* (pilgrim tax) at a Turkish city on the route. He let the poor folk in his caravan go past the collection point first, wishing to pay for them, but as he held back, the Muslim toll keeper got annoyed that he and his entourage were blocking the gate and set about the duke with a stick. The duke restrained his knights from cutting the man down. Likening his sufferings to Christ's, he supposedly said: 'Leave the fellow alone. The depths of my soul are more flooded with joy by his beating than if he had given me a pile of money!'

He reached Jerusalem, doubtless wishing to witness the Easter and Pentecost festivities on the very site of their happening. William de Jumièges implies that the duke saw out Holy Week and the Triduum [24] in the church of the Holy Sepulchre. On his return through Asia Minor, Robert was staying at the city of Nicaea, south of the Bosphorus, when he suddenly fell ill, died on 2 July or thereabouts, and was buried in the basilica of the Virgin in the city. As usual there were accusations of poison. The author of the 'Discovery and Translation of St Wulfrann',[25] a monk of St-Wandrille writing in the 1050s, notes the allegations, but says that he thought it more likely that God had taken the duke, as otherwise being too good for the world. The monastery of St-Wandrille benefited from his death, for the duke on his deathbed confided to a noble companion, Gerard Flaitel, a finger-bone of St Stephen (which he must have acquired in Jerusalem where Stephen was martyred) and urged him when he got home to give it to a monastery worthy of such a relic. Gerard, 'a most powerful lord in Normandy in the time of the Richards' (according to Orderic), entered St-Wandrille as a monk after his safe return, taking the finger with him. In this way, the duke's temporary arrangements for the custody of his son and his duchy until his return became permanent.

Marriage and Lineage in the Norman Dynasty, 996–1035

The marriage of Richard II of Normandy had occurred at some time on either side of 1000, certainly well before 1008 when Count Geoffrey of Brittany, one of the contracting parties, died, and probably soon after his father's death in 996. It was the first ducal marriage in which we can find the involvement of the Church. According to William of Jumièges, the marriage occurred on the holy island of Mont St-Michel. This would indicate that the ceremonies involved at least a mass said at the abbey church. Another new thing is the survival of a text of the marriage contract by which Duke Richard bestowed a dower portion on his wife, a copy of which was kept at the abbey of Fécamp and survived until the French Revolution (and which we know of as it was copied and published in 1717). The contract sets out an early summary of a Christian theology of marriage, the product of centuries of reflection on Scripture. It states that marriage was instituted by God in the Garden of Eden; that Jesus Christ had chosen to commence his ministry by sanctifying a marriage at Cana with his presence and his first miracle; that the marriage of man and woman must duplicate the faithful relationship between Christ and his Church; and all these assertions were supported by appropriate texts. The contract then makes its point. It addresses Judith in the first person, the person of Duke Richard himself:

> Instructed by the compilation of such examples and authorities, I Richard (filled in God's name with a desire for God-fearing children, so to have them down the course of years, if such should be the Creator's merciful will) have taken you, O Judith, sweetest of spouses and most tender of wives, in love. I have sought you from your kinsfolk and relations, and I have espoused you with bridal ornaments.

He goes on to declare that they had consummated their lawful marriage, and he now bestowed over fifty villages in Normandy on her, with their churches, mills and livestock: a princely endowment which confirmed the great landed wealth of the duke.[26]

The contract is in its way traditional, and comparable with what else we know of Frankish marriage customs. The duke had sought Judith from her family, and they pledged themselves to each other in a ceremony involving gifts (jewels, plate and luxury fabrics, perhaps, but also no doubt some land or treasure from her own family). The arrangements were secular, and not the least secular thing about them was the bestowal of dower on Judith after the couple had first had sexual intercourse; the main point after all was to seek children to perpetuate the dynasty, and God's aid was discreetly solicited for this. What is new in this document is the pointed citation of scripture to imply that the new relationship was to be faithful and monogamous. We know that Duke Richard thought much about things religious. Exactly the same considerations and much the same language appear in Richard III's marriage contract of January 1027 with Adela, whose lineage is not given, but who is assumed by some to have been the daughter of King Robert II (and who after Richard's death returned to her father and was later remarried to Baldwin V of Flanders). The introduction to this contract shows a further intensification of theological language, drawing on St Augustine: the monogamous nature of marriage is firmly laid down, and an ascetic element is added when the young duke tells his wife that 'I Richard, duke of the Normans – striving to submit to these sentiments – accept you Lady Adela in marriage by the ring of lawful espousal, joining to me in one flesh, not for the sake of sexual pleasure but for the cause of procreating'. This was perhaps appropriate language for the occasion, as Adela was still a child at the time.[27] The price of this decorous royal match was the city and province of Coutances and numerous other ample provisions, including the towns of Caen and Cherbourg.

With such wealth conferred on them, it is no wonder that women played a considerable part in the ducal family and its politics. This is clearest in the reign of Richard II. Gunnor, widow of Richard I, was the most regular witness in the written acts of her son, until her death after 1017. In such documents she always preceded her daughters-in-law, the duchesses Judith and (after 1017) Papia. Dudo recognised her influence, saying how much of her son's business depended on her advice and memory. She was wealthy in land and in dynastic connections. The prominent appearance at court of her nephews, Osbern fitz Arfast, the ducal seneschal, and Humphrey de Vieilles, may have had as much to do with her as with Richard II, their cousin. It was never quite accepted in medieval society that gender roles excluded women from any exercise of power, although it was usual for them to use their influence in interceding and encouraging. But if women controlled estates and independent wealth, nothing disabled them from a more active part in affairs if they so chose. Gunnor, being a very wealthy widow after 996, naturally became a powerful force at the court of her son, as Dudo recognised.

There were other forms of political relationships and problems that women created. Duchess Judith did not, it seems, suckle her own children; she put them out to a wet nurse. The young Duke Robert spent his first years, around the year 1000, in the household of a foster mother in Rouen. He seems to have been happy there, for in the 1030s Achard, one of the children of his nurse and obviously a childhood companion, was high in ducal favour and acknowledged as 'Achard my foster brother (*nutricius*)'. He had been, up till about 1033, in enjoyment of a sum due from the ducal rents of the city.[28] Duchess Judith's great landed wealth shows yet another sort of influence that she might exert. She attempted to devote much of her land to the foundation of an abbey. This decision of hers occurred on her deathbed in 1017, as appears from the remark of her widower, Duke Richard II, that 'she sought to make Christ her heir for that which I had given her from my estates according to the custom of dower'. Seven years later the duke finally agreed, although he turned the huge grant partly to his own spiritual benefit by making the new abbey of Bernay a dependency of his own dynastic house of Fécamp.[29] The transfer of such a major landed endowment away from the family must have caused major problems, and may partly explain Duke Robert's animus against the established monasteries of his principality, including the previously favoured house of Fécamp: a younger son might reasonably expect to inherit his mother's dower lands, and he had been robbed. It was through Robert's agency that several of the former manors associated with Judith and Bernay were transferred to the duke's confidant, Humphrey lord of Pont Audemer, including the estate of Beaumont, which later became the family centre. Another associate of Duke Robert, Roger de Montgomery, enriched himself not just at the expense of the estates of Bernay, but also at that of the outlying estates of the mother house of Fécamp. This upheaval was in part due to the miscalculated overgenerosity of his father's marriage settlement.

Duke Richard III and Duke Robert both continued the established family practice of taking concubines and producing children outside formal marriage. Richard at least intended to take a formal partner. Although only briefly duke, he arranged the most exalted possible marriage, to a Capetian princess. Robert did not follow his elder brother's dynastic strategy, so far as we know. Apart from a half-hearted scheme to marry Cnut's sister, he did not contract a dynastic marriage. It may be that he was put off by the huge cost in dower lands involved in the marriages of his father and brother. His son and heir was therefore economically engendered in an informal sexual partnership with a woman of low social status. Even in the 1030s, this does not seem to have caused much trouble or scandal; Ralph Glaber noted the fact that the Norman dukes were given to producing heirs with concubines, and shrugged his literary shoulders by comparing them with the biblical patriarchs of the Israelites. Such children were not yet at this time branded with any social stigma; all that was important in 1035 was that William II was his father's son. Herleva was decently put aside (perhaps before Duke Robert's pilgrimage) and married to a minor landowner of the Lieuvin, Herluin de Conteville, by whom she was to have two other sons, Robert and Odo, both later famous in the affairs of England and Normandy.

3

William of Normandy

In the story of dynasties it is customary to look for the man who is 'greatest of his line'. By most reckonings, that distinction would lie with William, son of Duke Robert II. The fact that he was the conqueror of England, and the even more remarkable fact that he maintained his hold on it, has guaranteed his historical eminence. As we have seen, he was not necessarily the greatest duke Normandy ever had; his great-grandfather, Richard I, did far more to preserve and mould the duchy. What cannot be denied to William is his place as a world figure in history. His decision to pursue his claims to England in 1066 irreversibly changed the course of European history. He may not perhaps have been such a radical reformer and engineer of realms as was once thought, but his military reputation remains resistant to criticism. Other claims to distinction he has – particularly in the ideal he gave his own time in lay spirituality – have been overlooked. One chapter is insufficient to contain William, and so the following two have been set aside to give an assessment of the man who can properly be said to have changed the course of Norman history, and exalted his dynasty – as his own court flatterers said he did – to an equality with the Caesars.

Succession and Minority, 1035–44

Between Christmas 1034 and August 1035, while Duke Robert was preparing for his pilgrimage, while he was travelling in the East, and before news of his death reached Normandy, his realm had time to get used to the idea of the boy William as his nominated heir. If Robert had died suddenly at home, it is less likely that William would have succeeded him. But in the autumn of 1035 his many powerful cousins, uncles and great uncles had long publicly accepted that William would be duke and had all sworn to support his succession, even if they had

not expected him to be duke so soon. Duke Robert's arrangements for
the government of Normandy, while he was away, acknowledged that
there was a family problem to contend with. The list of guardians that
he left can be reconstructed from those we find in authority after 1035.
In associating his first cousin, Alan III of Brittany, with the guardians,
Duke Robert was involving a close family member who would be
unlikely to compete with his heir. It is probable that the duke expected
another cousin, Count Gilbert of Eu-Brionne, son of Count Godfrey of
Eu and grandson of Richard I, to rally the male kin of young William
and provide the military strength to defend the boy. The existence
and protection of his aged great-uncle, the tried-and-tested Archbishop
Robert of Rouen, associated the greatest and most senior of his male
relatives behind the boy heir. Robert's further selection of his cousin
and steward, Osbern fitz Arfast, as a guardian shows how Duke Robert
was attempting to unite family and court in a common cause.

Duke William's subsequent problems did not stem from the fact that
his father and mother were not contractually married; voices that say
as much come from the later eleventh century, when there were beginning to be serious social consequences in being a bastard. But this was
not the case in the 1030s, and the contemporary historian Ralph Glaber
certainly thought it was not. In any case, many of William's potential
dynastic rivals shared the same disability. The alleged unacceptability of
'William the Bastard' is an anachronistic social comment from later
generations.[1] What made the years of William's minority so fraught and
– on occasion – tragic, was his father's indecisive handling of his Norman
aristocracy while he was duke. By 1035 the cadet males of the ducal
family had expanded to form a formidable cadre at the head of the
nobility. William's older male relatives controlled impressive and concentrated honors such as Mortain-Avranchin, Eu-Brionne, Exmes,
Evreux, and soon also Arques-Talou and Gacé. All these men controlled
castles and cities and most carried the title of 'count', the title which
William himself was to use in the majority of his official written acts.
In later life, William harshly rationed the comital dignity in England,
which is some evidence that he had learned the danger of such inflated
honours in his youth. But these were only the most dangerous of his
aristocracy: the men who could conceivably challenge his right to be
duke. His father had encountered but failed to master the scores of

families who were busy establishing themselves around castles and smaller honors across the duchy, employing troops of mounted warriors to bolster their local power. The fault was entirely Duke Robert's. There is every reason to think that Richard II had exerted a much tighter control over these same families, and Richard III's determination and energy in the face of the threat posed by his brother in 1027 shows that he too knew what to do to maintain civic order. Most of William II's Norman reign was a slow and painful climb back to the level of ducal control that his grandfather had plainly exerted and his father had frittered away.

Duke William would have come of age around 1044; until then he was in tutelage. William seems to have lived in the household of whichever of his guardians was dominant at a particular time, and his entourage moved around the ducal residences. The rule of Normandy was committed to guardians, and the person of the boy-duke to tutors: these were named by later writers as the laymen Turold and Ralph le Moine, and the clerk Master William. Ralph Glaber says that King Henry of France (perhaps remembering that he owed his throne to Duke Robert) made it known that William's succession had his support. So the first two years of William's minority seem to have been relatively safe for him, but the death of Archbishop Robert in 1037 began a period of serious instability in Normandy. Count Gilbert and Count Alan were left to try to hold the duchy together. They seem to have attempted to reinforce the power of the loyal ducal family by furthering the fortunes of the two youngest brothers of Duke Robert: Mauger was promoted to the see of Rouen, and the younger, William, to be count over the pays de Talou, north of Rouen towards the Channel coast. This new dominant dynastic clique held things together at least until Count Alan died at Vimoutiers on 1 October 1040, while beseiging a rebel castle. Count Gilbert did not long survive him. He had acquired enemies in central Normandy: the Giroie brothers were his rivals for control over his castle of Le Sap, and Ralph de Gacé, the younger son of the late Archbishop Robert, did not see why he should be kept out of a dominant place in the duchy's affairs. Count Gilbert was assassinated by these enemies in the spring of 1041 while out riding with some friends, not suspecting any attack. Turold, the boy William's tutor, was killed soon after. The murders continued. The most experienced of the original guardians, Osbern fitz Arfast, was sheltering with Duke William in the town of Vaudreuil, south of Rouen. William de Montgomery, whose father the guardians had ousted from the duchy, fought his way into the duke's bedchamber where Osbern too was sleeping, and cut the throat of the old man in the boy's presence. There was something appallingly symbolic in this: Osbern had been known as the 'Peacemaker' in his lifetime, but now Montgomery had murdered peace.

By the end of 1041, the arrangements for the custody of the boy-duke had collapsed, and he was clearly in personal danger from an aristocracy which was at war with itself. Between 1041 and 1043 the castellans of Normandy ceased to respect any greater power. Humphrey de Vieilles and his son, Roger de Beaumont, disturbed the southern Roumois with a war for control of the Risle valley against Roger de Tosny. In a pitched battle, probably in June 1041, Roger de Beaumont annihilated the Tosny household, including two of Roger de Tosny's sons. In the meantime, the murder of Osbern fitz Arfast was avenged by a surprise night attack on some of the Montgomery family by Osbern's bereaved household, led by Bjarni de Glos, his steward. External troubles also fell on the duchy. Duke Robert's former friend, Count Waleran I of Meulan, was chased into Normandy by his overlord, King Henry, in a small war to gain control of the Seine valley. When the king realised that Waleran's friends amongst the local Norman aristocracy were supporting the exile, he found he had no choice but to seize the border fortress of Tillières as a forward base for a protracted campaign. Several amongst the Norman aristocracy joined Henry, perhaps hoping that the king would be a more effective lord than their adolescent duke and his rapacious relatives. One of the most prominent of these defectors was the veteran viscount of the Hièmois, Thurstin Goz. He fortified Falaise in alliance with the king, and it was doubtless in support of him that the king campaigned the next year across the Hièmois, seizing and looting Argentan.

It was at this point, around 1043, that the personality of the boy William first caused tremors in his world. He was now around fifteen, a year away from the earlier of the ages when a boy might customarily be proclaimed a man. We know that in one respect his tutors had done their job well. They had trained him up to have the makings of a superb soldier; indeed, they had infected him with his principal interest in life: war and arms. Not all medieval aristocrats were good or keen soldiers, although all were given military training and all talked horses, dogs, weapons and war. But a number were extremely good at it, and Duke William was destined to be an acknowledged master of the art. As duke, the image on the seal he would have pressed on to documents was of him riding to war in armour, with shield and spear.[2] This was how he saw himself as prince and ruler; his power founded on military might, and rooted in the horseback military culture of the camp. The artistic image was based on what had become a universal pattern of battledress. By the 1040s the military equipment so familiar from the cartoons of the Bayeux Tapestry had already evolved from earlier Carolingian styles. For defence, French warriors wore a conical helmet made of iron bands and plates. The body was protected by leather or quilted tunic covered by a knee-length hauberk of mail, which had been known to Rollo's generation. The warrior carried a narrow, body-length kite-shaped shield of wood and leather. For attack Normans deployed ashwood spears and highly-polished steel blades marked with their makers' names, so expensive they passed from father to son: some may have come south from the Northlands with their Viking ancestors. Eleventh-century harness was flexible, light and well-designed for cavalry and foot combat. Its silvery elegance earned it the name of 'white harness' in the next century, when more colourful and elaborate styles began to supplant it.

The young duke combined his warlike enthusiasms with the skills of an adroit politician. He had a survivor's ability to spot potential allies and opportunities: an ability which we may suspect was won at a heavy personal cost. Young Duke William is given credit by later commentators for rallying his advisers, who in 1043 were his uncles, Count William of Arques and Archbishop Mauger. Together they agreed to recruit Ralph de Gacé, the warlike and ruthless son of the late Archbishop Robert to their council. In 1041 Ralph had masterminded the murder of his own cousin, Count Gilbert, the former ducal guardian, presumably because he saw the count as an obstacle to his ambitions to succeed to some measure of his father's influence. Once he had been given command of the Norman army, Ralph did what was expected of such a remorseless man at arms. He waged an energetic and successful campaign against Thurstin Goz. He recaptured Falaise, driving Thurstin into exile. King Henry himself withdrew, leaving the cause of war, Waleran of Meulan, in exile but at least sheltering with his friends. The king may perhaps have been satisfied that his power had been sufficiently acknowledged by his incursion across the Norman frontier, for the next we hear of him he was, a year or two later, in alliance again with the young duke.

The historian William de Poitiers tells us that the king and duke were friends by the time that William came of age, for King Henry was the man who delivered arms to the young duke.[3] We do not know when that ceremony was, although the description of the events attributable to the early 1040s gives the impression that William was already then grasping for control of his inheritance. He would have been sixteen by the end of 1044, and that may have been the time he was admitted to be a man. By the mid 1040s significant new names begin to appear around the duke, as he moved to select a younger group of military courtiers on whom he felt he could rely: Roger de Beaumont and Robert fitz Humphrey his brother; Roger de Montgomery, brother of that William who had murdered Osbern fitz Arfast; Walter Giffard and William fitz Osbern fitz Arfast, the man who became closest to his master.[4] It was on the talents and loyalty of this carefully selected group of men – most of them a little older than himself – that all Duke William's later achievements rested.

Mastering Normandy, 1047–54

Two key successes transformed the young and dynastically insecure Duke William into one of the dominant princes of northern France. The first of these was his suppression of a dangerous revolt amongst his younger cousins in the ducal family in alliance with his viscounts. Presumably neither group liked the way that William was furthering a new cadre of courtiers, or the way that he was enforcing his peace. They might not also have been happy at the way that the highest level of political power was still monopolised by the older dynastic clique of Count William of Arques, Ralph de Gacé and Archbishop Mauger. The archbishop, the duke's uncle, was not a popular man and his reputation amongst later Normans was particularly shady. Apart from reporting charges by earlier historians of Mauger's plundering of his diocese's assets and his irregular life, Wace of Bayeux also talks of his reputation as a necromancer. The people of the Channel Islands, where he retired when he was later deposed from Rouen, still talked in Wace's day of Mauger's invisible, familiar demon, with which he openly conversed, and of his sinister gifts of malign prophecy.

One of the magnates most openly frustrated by the state of affairs in Normandy in the mid 1040s was a newcomer to the duchy, Guy of Burgundy. Guy was a younger son of Adeliza, Duke William's aunt, who had been married to Count Reginald of Burgundy.[5] Guy was a younger son of the marriage, who had been sent to Normandy in the early 1040s in the hope of having his fortunes advanced by his young cousin's guardians. Guy was not disappointed: after a period as his cousin's household companion, he was given possession of the towers of Brionne and Vernon. This success seems, however, to have been insufficient for him. Around 1047, Guy put himself forward as the leader of a faction of Norman magnates in opposition to the duke and his advisers. Their demands are not known, but the presence of the veteran viscount, Nigel de Saint-Sauveur, along with the viscount of the Bessin and several other great barons of western Normandy, is witness to the seriousness of the rising. It is unlikely that either Guy or his cousin, the count of Eu (who apparently joined him in revolt), were attempting to seize the duchy in a family coup – although William de Poitiers and Orderic Vitalis allege that was the young counts' intention – but both of them may well have been demonstrating their unhappiness at not being included in the ruling clique headed by William of Arques.

Duke William appealed to King Henry in this dynastic crisis, and the king arrived promptly in Normandy with a large force of warriors. A pitched battle was fought between the armies at Val-ès-Dunes, east of the Orne between Caen and Falaise. There, although the duke was supported by the minority party amongst the Norman aristocracy, the military experience and the support of the remorseless king (called the 'Henry the Castle-Grabber' by his friends) were enough to rout the rebels – although Henry had a narrow escape from death, when one of the rebel barons knocked him from his horse. Guy fled to his castle of Brionne, and maintained himself there under the duke's patient blockade until 1049, when he finally surrendered, was forgiven, but soon left the realm and went back to Burgundy. The other rebel member of the dynasty, William Busac of Eu, was driven out of his fortress and county and into exile. He never returned to Normandy, but was eventually

given by the king the marriage of Adelaide, heiress of the county of
Soissons, and founded a short-lived offshoot of the Norman dynasty in
the north of the Capetian lands. It survived until 1148, with the death
of Count Reginald II.

Commentators of the next generation date the effective beginning of
William II's reign from the battle of Val-ès-Dunes, and they attribute
William's emerging reputation as a masterful warrior to the victory.
Until 1047 he was very much treated by the sources as a cipher; magnates
sought to control him, and the duchy through him. After 1047, William
appears as his own man, and a ruler increasingly dominant in his duchy
and in northern France. The proclamation of the Truce of God at the
council of Caen in October 1047 is good evidence that the uncertainty
and civil disruption was being mastered, rather than that it was out of
control.[6] By imposing ecclesiastical sanctions against private war and
violence, Archbishop Mauger was simply taking the opportunity to
buttress his nephew's growing power. It is perhaps one of the most
telling symptoms of emerging domestic peace in the duchy that the
duke's involvement with external conflicts begins to be mentioned.
William would not have led his forces out of the duchy if his aristocracy
had not been properly chastised and pacified. Like his father, William
perhaps realised that those of his subjects who did not like a quiet life
would be happy to join border campaigns where they could practise
their military skills and pick up ransoms and plunder. Between 1047
and 1052, William sharpened his reputation as a prince along with his
sword.

External conflict was certainly there to be had. The years 1051–52 saw
Normandy's first major confrontation with another growing power in
northern France. The county of Anjou had grown up out of the ruins
of the Robertian march of Neustria. Its dynasty – which would ultimately succeed that of the Normans on the throne of England – had
most likely been planted at Angers in the late ninth century to help
defend the Loire valley from the Vikings and Bretons, who were attempting to use the river as a high road deep into central France. The
house of Anjou prospered, and in the 1040s, while William was busy
surviving his boyhood, Count Geoffrey Martel (1040–60) had maintained in alliance with King Henry a damaging and profitable war
against the power of the counts of Blois-Chartres. Geoffrey was able

to conquer the city and county of Tours and much magnify his own power as well as cripple the power and reputation of Count Theobald I (1034–89). As the power of Blois-Chartres declined in the 1040s, so that of Anjou increased. If it was to increase further, then Normandy and its satellite statelets would be next in line to experience Angevin aggression. Duke William himself may have helped to precipitate the crisis. When King Henry turned against Geoffrey in the late 1040s – for he was now too dangerous an ally – the duke dutifully joined the royal army when it sallied into Anjou itself. William and the Norman contingent distinguished themselves at the seizure of the castle of Mouliherne in the autumn of 1049. The young duke demonstrated an unheard of mastery of the art of horseback combat, as later flatterers are keen to tell us. Apparently, even Count Geoffrey applauded William's expertise as he led spirited raids around Mouliherne with small mounted squadrons, taking captives and outflanking much superior columns of knights. King Henry, an old lion of the duke's father's generation, was said by William of Poitiers to have become envious of the young warrior's effortless prowess, to the extent of conceiving a particular hatred for him from then onwards.

Geoffrey Martel made mastery of the county of Maine – between Anjou and Normandy – his objective, and had achieved it by 1051. Duke William could not do much about this, yet he could not ignore Geoffrey's moves into the south of the long-established Norman frontier zone, where minor counts and castellans were expected to respect the duke's authority, even if in practice they ignored it. The Angevin advance was even harder to ignore when it surged through the lands of the border castellans and into territory the duke considered part of his principality. Making as little of the Norman frontier as he and his father had of the borders of the Touraine, Count Geoffrey took over the castle of Domfront, on the borders of Maine. It was perhaps no more than a move by the Bellême family, who are credited with building it, to seek Geoffrey's support against the duke – who maintained a claim on the castle. Whatever the purpose, the duke could not ignore it, and he arrived promptly. He set up a carefully constructed siege camp and perimeter forts, and settled down to wait for the garrison to lose heart. In the meantime, informers reached him saying that the border town of Alençon, towards Maine, could be taken from the Bellême family.

Although the town had a mind to resist, the duke led his men in storming an outlying fort. Since the garrison there had dared to mock him with the origins of his mother's family – calling them tanners, and beating animal skins hung over the rampart – William made a terrible example of those he captured: having the hands and feet of thirty-two of them severed before the eyes of the horrified townsfolk. Bloody brutality of this severity persuaded the people of Alençon that it was in their interest to surrender promptly. When news of it reached Domfront, the castle garrison too trembled, and surrendered.

Count Geoffrey's first attempt on Normandy produced no benefit for him; but if it was Maine that had been his real objective, then the loss of Domfront and Alençon may not have been too distressful. Indeed the incursion into the Norman March may not have been more than opportunism, as the sources imply. But the hostile activity of the counts of Anjou was not something that was going to go away of its own accord, and the Angevins were by no means finished with Normandy. While Geoffrey and the king were mutual enemies – as they were in the late 1040s when the king realised that Blois-Chartres had been weakened too much – things had not been too dangerous for Duke William. But in 1052 the situation changed once more, as the king, now that he had demonstrated that he could lead an army into Anjou to punish the count, became once again friendly to Geoffrey – and hostile to William. The significance of this decision needs to be underlined. Since the time of William Longsword, the Capetians and Normans had maintained a solid alliance. It had given both parties advantages. The Capetian dukes and kings of France had protection from Viking raids and heavy military backup in their relations with powers to east and south of Paris. The Norman dukes for a full century had mutual aid likewise against southern and western rivals, but also a certain respectability and accept-ability they might not otherwise have had. The alliance was good for both parties. In breaking it, Paris was casting Rouen adrift and much weakening itself, for William would not forget what King Henry had done. King Henry's dubious decision began a century and a half of fitful warfare between Rouen and Paris that did not end until Normandy was extinguished as an independent principality in 1204.

If this was not serious enough, the family coalition which had helped contain internal problems since 1047 broke down. We might reasonably look, for one obvious cause of the problem, to the fact that William had by now raised his own crop of henchmen, and was by 1052 furthering them, rather than cultivating his uncles. But there may well have been other contributory grievances. The period from 1034 to 1052 was one when the ducal family had operated as a coalition of senior males (and also, for a time, senior females) protecting and directing the boy heir. Families – as has been observed by historians in recent years – change to meet circumstances, and the need to protect the principality which it had created led to a temporary investiture of an entire generation of elder males with the task of leadership. This defined the ducal family as a cooperative generation of brothers (a *frèreche*, as the French call it) holding the balance of power. Now the ducal family was changing once again. The boy-duke was by 1049 a man, and his subsequent marriage would redefine the family for him as the basic nuclear unit of husband, wife and (soon) children. This redefinition was likely to have been all the more abrupt as there is no doubt that the couple entered into a close emotional relationship. Their marriage was never merely a political union. The uncles and senior cousins whom William would previously have relied on for advice and support were now removed from him emotionally and politically by a step. For military supporters, William turned instead to his chosen intimates, and to his younger half-brothers, Robert and Odo. The resentful uncles would not have seen the necessity of this, and resented the exclusion from patronage that it represented.

Archbishop Mauger and Count William of Arques began publicly to oppose their nephew as early as 1052, and William of Arques was in full rebellion during 1053, with the support of his brother-in-law, Count Enguerrand of Ponthieu. Duke William retaliated – as he had to do if he were to maintain his credibility as duke – and closely blockaded Arques with siege works, but the great promontory fortress above Dieppe was no easy victim for his military skills. Matters were only resolved in October when a relief column for Arques was led brazenly into the duchy by King Henry himself. The duke rose to the occasion with a stratagem of Napoleonic resourcefulness. Outnumbered, he nonetheless succeeded in separating his enemies' forces and led the Ponthevins into an ambush, crushing them and killing their count, Enguerrand. The king, seeing that the balance of forces had unexpectedly shifted to

the duke, withdrew after the token victory of successfully moving provisions into Arques. Since, however, the king did not return, the castle
was obliged to surrender on terms, and Count William entered into an
exile across the frontier at the court of the count of Boulogne, where
he later died. He was, however, given an ample allowance out of his
Norman estates by his nephew so that he could live in the state appropriate to a duke's son. Archbishop Mauger was also treated leniently.
With the assistance of a papal legate, he was forced into early retirement
by a church council at Lisieux in 1054. He retreated to his estates in
Guernsey, where he lived in peace – if not in popularity – for many
years, a disgraced but still feared clergyman, until his death by drowning
near Cherbourg.

King Henry was by no means finished with Normandy, despite failing
to relieve Arques, and despite being unable to prevent the collapse of
Count William's rebellion. The king's intention in Normandy in the
early 1050s was perhaps to do no more than what the Mouliherne
campaign had been intended to do in Anjou in 1049: to assemble
powerful armies under royal leadership and overawe a dangerous neighbour. The king's mistake in this was that Normandy was, and had been
for decades, a fairly secure and undemanding ally. The Normans did
not need to be overawed. The king was not, however, going to give up.
He massed his armies in 1054 with the apparent intention of leading a
host into Normandy to bring William down. Two columns entered the
duchy, one north and one south of the Seine. The king himself, with
Geoffrey of Anjou, assaulted Evreux, to the south. Duke William chose
to face the king, while sending his cousin, Count Robert of Eu, to lead
the main Norman army against the other, northern column, whose
commander was the French king's brother Odo. Count Robert of Eu
encountered the French in the act of pillaging the town of Mortemer
in the Norman Vexin and inflicted a catastrophic defeat on the invaders.
Duke William – not in the least envious of his cousin's fine victory –
gleefully had the king informed by envoy of the massacre. When he
heard the news of Mortemer shouted down into his camp at dawn from
a treetop, King Henry made a rapid withdrawal from the duchy. Duke
William was left a young man in tight control of his lands, held in
cautious fear by his men, and the possessor of a formidable reputation
amongst his neighbours.

Military Consolidation, 1054–63

Over the next five or six years, a fitful brawl was fought across northern France by the king, the duke of the Normans and the count of the Angevins. The principal arena of war between Normandy and Anjou was the county of Maine, which lay between the two principalities. Maine, with its capital of Le Mans, was on the watershed between the Norman plain and the Channel to the north and the Loire valley to the south. It was a hilly land dominated by powerful castellan families, nominally under the rule of a dynasty of autonomous counts, but Geoffrey of Anjou and his father had already destroyed their prestige by the 1050s, as they sought to add Maine to their principality, and extorted the submission of its counts. As the Vexin was the principal theatre of war between the Normans and French, so Maine was the war ground between the Normans and Angevins. William's aggression in these border zones in the later 1050s and 1060s is a measure of his growing strength and ambition.

There are earlier indicators of William's growing importance in northern France. The fact that he was recognised as worthy to be a husband for his daughter by Count Baldwin V of Flanders, at some time around 1050, was just such a sign. The marriage was probably not what the duke would have been happy with ten years later (when both his old rivals at Paris and Angers were dead), for the lady in question brought lineage but no land or claims with her. She did however bring recognition that William was now a great French prince and it also brought the military acquiescence of her powerful father, which translated into border security in the north of the duchy, so William could concentrate on his enemies to south and east. The lady was Mathilda, who was, amongst her other claims to distinction, the niece of King Henry of France. At the time he married, a union with the king's niece would have enhanced his link with his most important political supporter. The marriage was being planned by the end of 1049, and it caused a stir, for objections to the union were raised at a church council in Reims. Orderic Vitalis, writing in the 1120s, believed the objection was on the grounds that she and William were within the prohibited degrees of cousinship, and this is possible. Other grounds may have been that William's uncle, Richard III, had been briefly married, or at least betrothed, to Adela of

France, Mathilda's mother. The marriage could not have been consummated, because of Adela's age in 1028, but such a marital link would
nonetheless raise the theoretical issue of incest in the hypersensitive
papacy of Leo IX. The objections caused a delay in the union, but not
an insuperable one. Mathilda and William were married by the end of
1051, when she was in her late teens and he was around twenty-three.

It was the belief of the two principal contemporary Norman writers,
William de Jumièges and William de Poitiers, that every prince in
northern France, from the king downwards, was out to get Normandy
in the 1050s. Certainly Duke William had few friends amongst his fellow
princes in that decade. As far as these two writers were concerned, his
weathering of this storm of aggression from his neighbours was evidence
of the duke's great virtue and God's great favour. The aggression itself
might also be interpreted as pragmatic evidence of the emerging power
of Normandy in the 1050s: his neighbours were not attacking William
because of his weakness, but because of the threat of his military energy
and resources. They were attempting to get their retaliation in first.

In 1054 William began a long-term campaign to secure Maine as a
border province towards Anjou, which was to occupy the rest of his
life, off and on. His intention was to pursue a mirror image of Count
Geoffrey's strategy against Normandy. Within a year he had built a new
fortress on a strong site at Ambrières, some 20 km south of Domfront
in the northern part of Maine. He now had a forward base which
threatened the lord of Mayenne, one of the principal castellans of the
county and a leading Angevin sympathiser. The new castle also relieved
pressure on the Norman frontier. The lord of Mayenne knew that the
move was directed against him, and urged Count Geoffrey to join him
in overthrowing the fortification. An Angevin expedition was mounted
in force, but was foiled by the duke's prompt arrival with a column
sufficient to deter the Angevins and their allies. Geoffrey de Mayenne,
realising that the balance of power was shifting in his region and
threatened with retaliation, made the decision to seek out the duke and
offer a formal alliance. William of Poitiers says that he went so far as
to make formal homage to Duke William. If so, this was only a gesture
of submission in the context of a political alliance, because for generations afterwards the lords of Mayenne continued to claim that
Ambrières was built on their lands and was by rights their castle; not

something a vassal would claim against an overlord. The duke would not have been much concerned by this; he had made his point and destabilised Maine.

Count Geoffrey certainly thought so too. By 1057 he had put together the resources to mount a final expedition, designed to break Norman power and prestige once and for all. He and King Henry made a concerted campaign to break through the Norman frontier from the south, devastate the duchy and undermine William's troublesome reputation for dash, resourcefulness and military brilliance. The result was in fact to consolidate it. The French column, carefully screening its movements, assembled south of the Norman border in August 1057. It then began the brutal business of laying waste all the countryside as it moved north to the Channel coast. But in the event the sea was to be not so much the end of the French *chevauchée* as its undoing. As the French army began the crossing of the little River Dives at Varaville a few kilometres south of the seacoast, it was taken by surprise by the sudden rise of the tide in the estuary and cut in two. The French advance guard on the eastern shore was ambushed by a Norman force awaiting it under the duke, which proceeded to slaughter the trapped French, while King Henry and Count Geoffrey looked on impotently from the left bank. Varaville inflicted a terrible penalty on William's enemies, not so much in military losses but in lost prestige. It was many years before the frontiers of Normandy were again threatened as they were in the 1050s. But Varaville did not end the long struggle: it was not until King Henry died in August 1060 that 'it was reckoned that the civil war between King Henry and Count William that lasted for some while finally came to an end', as a clerk of Chartres put it.[7]

Being Norman and Being a Duke

Although King Henry died in 1060, leaving an eight-year-old heir, and although Geoffrey Martel of Anjou died the same year, there was not to be peace on the frontiers. Duke William was not a soldier because he had to be, he was a soldier because he was good at it, and intended to bolster and extend his power by military might; a strategy that suited both him and his aristocratic supporters. It is from the 1050s that the Norman reputation for military excellence and ruthlessness comes, and it originated principally in the duke's choice to be the Caesar his flatterers praised him for being. Although it might be argued that William was forced by aggressive and militaristic neighbours into a similar pattern of Norman rulership, the fact that he trounced them so thoroughly at their own game proves that his heart was in the transformation.

There was a feeling in the later 1050s that it was good to be a Norman; and winning is always good for morale. One symptom of this was the way that historians of Normandy and its dukes begin to appear to celebrate the Norman achievement. William de Jumièges was at work compiling his history in the mid 1050s, and very soon William de Poitiers would address the same subject. The intention of both writers was to commemorate the virtues of past Normans and their dukes for the benefit of present Normans and to the glory of Duke William. There is some reference to the deeds of William being likewise celebrated in verse and song by 1060, for a wider and less learned audience. In the church, distinguished immigrants began to wander into Normandy. Lanfranc, a celebrated teacher from Pavia, had sought seclusion and a true monastic vocation in the obscure, remoter regions of Gaul early in the 1040s. By the later 1050s any hopes of seclusion at Bec-Hellouin had been abandoned, and as prior of the abbey he was operating one of the most famous schools in northern Europe, attracting the intellectual comet of the young St Anselm into a Norman orbit in 1059.

Never happy to be entirely identified with France, the Normans were beginning to feel they belonged to an even wider world. Norman adventurers had been travelling south and eastwards for decades, some undoubtedly pushed out by the stern and effective rule of Richard II. Perhaps as early as 1016, they had been drawn to the wealth and opportunity of southern Italy, where Lombards, Greeks and Moslems were in continual conflict. Ranulf, who became ruler of Capua and Aversa around 1030, was a Norman. In 1059, Robert Guiscard – a member of an obscure migrant family from one of the places called Hauteville in the Cotentin – was invested by the pope as duke of Apulia. In the subsequent decade a member of the Norman aristocratic dynasty of Giroie, William de Montreuil, became captain of the papal mercenary cavalry. Although none of these Normans were related to the ducal house, and most were quite obscure in origins, the domestic Normans of the generation of William de Poitiers still took some interest and even pride in their activities. In the 1060s conquering Normans were to be found in Italy, and their brethren in northern France – having survived some dangerous challenges from their neighbours – began to see themselves in a similar way, as military entrepreneurs. So a feeling of Norman euphoria was sparkling in the air.

The Normans of Normandy were by the 1050s more assured and assertive of their own identity as a people than they had been even half a century earlier. They were no longer posturing as latter-day Franks, as their ducal court had been in the days of Dudo. William de Jumièges was quite clear in his mind that the French were – and had been for a long time – the enemy. The break with the long Capetian alliance in 1052 may have had something to do with this. Duke William, unlike his ancestors, was not a loyal dependent and auxiliary of a King Hugh or a King Robert; he was an autonomous prince fighting for survival against most of his neighbours, including the king. This in itself tended to sharpen the sense of there being a Norman prince leading a Norman people in a hostile world. Perhaps it is no surprise to find one of the duke's closest intimates, Roger de Montgomery, declaring himself proudly around 1060, in somewhat blimpish fashion, to be 'a Norman (*Northmannus*) descended from Normans': no feeling here of integration into a greater French polity. And Roger may simply have been echoing the sentiments current in William's court and military household.

The Normans of 1060 found in William II the sort of duke able to unite a threatened and yet vigorous principality. He had inherited a duchy which had for generations been rich in resources; and, despite the vicissitudes of his minority and the inroads of his rivals, William was still probably wealthier than his neighbours. The economy of northern France was expanding during his lifetime, towns were beginning to grow and attract population. Not just Rouen, but Bayeux and William's own urban project of Caen (where he founded an abbey *c.* 1059) were sizeable towns, with new suburban overspill settlements. Major new currents of trade were stirring in central France, most notably the luxury wine trade, which in the early eleventh century began to flow with gathering strength westward down the Seine to reach markets in Britain and further north. Rouen's considerable wealth received a new and powerful boost from this trade. Significantly, it was around 1060 that

an immigrant Jewish community began to settle in the city; at this date
Jews were important as commodity merchants and artisans. Duke William was undoubtedly even wealthier than his wealthy predecessors, and
the prosperity filtered down to his nobility.

Such surplus wealth had to find channels. In part, these were found
in prestige projects, such as the new Benedictine abbeys that were
founded across the duchy in the middle years of the century: the twin
ducal abbeys of St Stephen and Holy Trinity of Caen; Roger de Beaumont's paired abbeys of St Peter and St Leger of Préaux; fitz Osbern's
foundations of Lyre and Cormeilles; the Tosny foundation of Conches;
the Tancarville abbey of St-Georges-de-Boscherville. These abbeys, and
several others, in all their Romanesque grandeur, represented money
to invest, as much as spiritual investment. Duke William can also be
seen deploying a material vocabulary of secular splendour and display,
so that people could understand that he was a prince amongst men.
On the Bayeux tapestry he can be seen as duke surrounded by his
courtiers and officers, sitting on a chair of state – carved with lions,
like the justice seat of King Solomon – holding up in his right hand
a sheathed ceremonial sword. Crowns and coronets were not yet worn
by dukes in the 1060s, but there were trappings and symbols they could
use to advertise their status other than simply flaunting their raw
treasure: their gold plate, jewels, silks and furs. The baggage that accompanied William on the road included items that allowed him a
certain dignity even in informal surroundings, such as the carpet that
was spread out for him in the open air to set his faldstool [8] upon at
Bernouville around 1081 'between the church and forester's house' when
he made a grant to the abbey of St-Sauveur. When he attended the
great churches under his patronage, William may well have experienced
quasi-royal state. At his entry into the mass on feast days, the clergy
would sing formal Latin *laudes* (praises), like those sung also before
the kings of France and Germany, and pray for his health and perpetual
peace. But peace was not the first thing on his mind. For an energetic
and accomplished ruler in his early thirties, unchallenged in war, with
a brimming treasury and prosperous and confident principality at his
back, it may have seemed that almost anything was in his grasp. For
no other reason than this he may well have turned his eyes, like Caesar,
across the Channel.

Duke William and King Edward of England

The self-confidence of Normandy and its people in the 1060s was not of itself the reason why Duke William turned his mind to securing the throne of England, although it may have made the project seem more achievable. The histories of Normandy and England had been entwined for decades, and England would have been as much in the mind of a Norman duke as would have been neighbouring French realms. Under Richard II and Robert I, the association had been particularly close. Richard II had played a significant part in the warfare between Æthelred II of England and Swein of Denmark, and in 1013 he had received into exile his nephews Edward and Alfred, with their mother and his own sister, Queen Emma. In 1016 Æthelred died in England while trying to recover the throne, and his eldest son, Edmund, died too, before being able to secure his inheritance. The queen married Cnut as her second husband in 1017, although opinion is divided as to whether she managed in the meantime to escape from London to Normandy in 1016 to her brother's protection. If she did, she returned to England with her brother's consent to remarry, and prudently left her own children by Æthelred, Edward, Alfred and Godgifu, in his custody in France. There followed many years of exile when the two athelings lived in and around the Norman court, supported by the duke. Duke Richard even provided the marriage portion for his niece, their sister Godgifu, when she married the count of Amiens and the Vexin, his friend and ally.

From 1002, when Emma had married Æthelred, there was not a decade when Norman and English affairs were not entangled. Leaving two of her sons in Normandy, when she went back to resume the queenship with a new partner, meant that the duke their protector was going to continue to monitor English affairs. Since he harboured two potential claimants to the throne, the opportunity to meddle across the Channel was always his. The two young English princes were brought up in Duke Richard's retinue, and were fully adult and in their twenties when he died in 1026. This meant that their outlook was formed in a French environment, and that French would have been their principal language and cultural influence for many years. The fact that the bishop of London had been sent with them to Normandy in 1013 shows no long-term plan to keep them in contact with English culture. Their exile was doubtless expected to be brief, and the bishop may soon have died: his successor was consecrated in 1014. We know only a little about their French lives. The two English princes were brought up by their uncle, and appear at the court of their first cousin, Duke Robert; and Edward even appears once in an act of the boy William II. The nature of the appearances tell us little about Edward's relationship with the dukes his cousins, other than they were willing to associate him with the family and also call him 'king', for he was credited with that title on several occasions (and one such occasion is an unimpeachable and original ducal act). But it may be that the dukes insisted on Edward's royal status because it was rather grand to have in the family a man who claimed to be a king, rather than because they were committed to his restoration to England.

After coming of age it is likely that Edward and Alfred lived in other places as well as the Norman court. We know of no provision of lands for their support where they could form their own establishments, so theirs could only have been a wandering life. It is a fair assumption that Duke Richard did do something for them, at the very least offering them a cash income, and maybe he also provided the use of a ducal estate in the Seine valley. Edward later had a close connection with the abbey of Jumièges, and favoured it after he secured England, so it is probable that he spent time there, or in its vicinity where there were a number of ducal estates. There is good reason to believe that Edward made a tour of northern Europe soon after his father's death in 1016, seeking recognition of his claims by at least the saints. The monks of Ghent latched on to him, and secured an oath from him that, if ever he was restored to his father's kingdom, he would honour grants they claimed at Greenwich and Lewisham.[9] His favour to his sister Godgifu's children hints that Edward also travelled to her first husband's considerable realm, between Amiens and the Seine, but that is all we can surmise about his travels. But Edward's appearance at Ghent in 1016 and his use of the royal title in the early 1030s tells us that the atheling himself did not forget that he had a claim on his late father's realm. And if that was not enough, there is the evidence of a grant he apparently made as 'Edward by God's grace king of the English' before 1035 to the ducal abbey of Mont St-Michel. It was a grant of St Michael's Mount in Cornwall by the exiled king to the abbey, along with several other properties in his lost kingdom.

The dukes did not ignore their obligations to their exiled English relatives in practical support and protection. Dudo and William de Jumièges give some evidence that they were willing also to commit themselves to limited support of the athelings' political claims. Dudo's florid rhetoric, composed in the last years of Richard II, includes some inflated and vague claims to control the fate of the English, and he is also full of the links between Rollo and the good but anachronistic King Athelstan of England (who actually flourished after Rollo's day). Rollo was supposed to have been active and successful in war in England before he came to France. This literary device would seem to be a mythical explanation of the friendship and political alliance between the Norman and West Saxon dynasties in the 1020s. William de Jumièges is rather more circumstantial. When Duke Robert succeeded his father, William says that he interceded with King Cnut on his cousins' behalf, and when his messages were ignored he gathered a fleet and an army to assert forcibly the athelings' claims. Although the expedition failed, due to a storm in the Channel, William gives details of Cnut's supposed deathbed messages to Duke Robert, offering to restore half their father's kingdom to the athelings.

Although we cannot make too much of William's evidence, neither can we ignore it, for William was well-placed to record rumours and memories of ducal posturings with regard to England in the 1030s, as he was at the time a young and literary monk at Jumièges, with access to sources both about the court and the doings of the athelings. So we can be sure that Duke Robert, who was given to grand postures, did strike an aggressive pose towards England in around 1033. The pointless protests of a French duke would not much have concerned the English at the time. Edward and Alfred had remained strangers to England between 1013 and 1036, and the English seemed happy enough to forget them. The debate in 1035, when Cnut died, was over which of his several sons should succeed in England. His preoccupation with the affairs of Denmark meant that Harthacnut – Edward and Alfred's younger half-brother – did not exert himself, and England went by default to his elder brother Harold Harefoot, Cnut's half-English son by Aelfgifu of North-ampton. No one seems to have given the exiles in Normandy serious thought, and, since Normandy was without a duke at the time, the athelings were handicapped in seeking support to assert their own rights.

Yet they were tragically sucked into the succession struggle nonetheless. Queen Emma was not happy at the outcome of events, and she
did her best to put obstacles in the way of Harold's assumption of
kingship. One of the obstacles she attempted to throw before the hated
Harold was her elder sons, whom she summoned to her aid from
Normandy. Although she herself later claimed that Harold had lured
the young men to England by a forged letter in order to do away with
them, modern commentators find it easier to believe that she was
grasping at every straw that would help secure England for Harthacnut,
and so preserve her great power. Edward scraped together a small force
in forty ships – getting little or no support from his embattled Norman
relations – landed in 1036 near Southampton, and was driven off with
ease. Despite the humiliation, he was luckier than his younger brother
Alfred, who slipped across the Channel trying to join his mother, but
was arrested by the soldiers of Earl Godwin of Wessex and hauled off
to Guildford, where his companions were summarily killed. The prince
himself was humiliated and tortured, and packed off to Ely. He died
soon after being blinded there at King Harold's orders.

Edward returned alone to a grim and apparently hopeless future back
in France, the last now of the sons of Æthelred. Harold Harefoot took
power in England in 1037, but after an unexpectedly short reign was
succeeded by Edward's half-brother, Harthacnut in 1040. At this point,
events turned in Edward's favour, for Harthacnut summoned his mother
back from temporary exile in Flanders to attend him. The next year an
invitation was extended by the childless king and his mother to Edward
to join them in England, and so the exile at last returned in peace. His
relatives' motives are unknown, and indeed they may have been mixed,
but Edward returned nonetheless, and his kingship received some apparent endorsement from his mother and younger brother, although
the precise degree of his new power is unknown. Family affection was
absent from the reunion. We know this because when Harthacnut died
unexpectedly in June 1042, and Edward took the throne unopposed, one
of his first acts was to eject his pragmatic and scheming mother from
court, a few months after his coronation in 1043. Ambassadors of many
foreign kings and princes were at his coronation, and it does not take
too much to believe that there were Norman ambassadors present too,
although no source names any. But Normans certainly followed Edward

1. Four Norman kings, three holding churches: (top) William the Conqueror and William Rufus; (bottom) Henry I and Stephen. Rufus holds Westminster Hall. From the thirteenth-century *History Anglorum* by Matthew Paris. British Library, MS 58315. (*British Library*)

2. Rollo (Hrólfr), the founder of the Norman dynasty, landing at Rouen. A fifteenth-century depiction from *Chroniques de Normandie*, *c.* 1475. British Library, MS Yates Thompson 33, fol. 1. (*British Library*)

3. The murder of William Longsword. William is shown twice: first talking to Arnold, count of Flanders, then being murdered. A fifteenth-century impression from *Chroniques de Normandie*, *c.* 1475. British Library, MS Yates Thompson 33, fol. 35v. (*British Library*)

4. William of Jumièges presenting his *History of the Norman Dukes* to William the Conqueror, taken from the historian Orderic Vitalis's autograph copy of William of Jumièges's work. Bibliothèque Municipale, Rouen, MS D.Y. 14, fol. 116. (*Bibliothèque Municipale, Rouen*)

5. The nave of the abbey of Jumièges, dedicated in 1067. (*James Austin*)

6. The keep of Oxford Castle, dating from *c.*1074. The Empress Matilda fled from here across the snow in December 1142. (*A. F. Kersting*)

HIC·WILLELM DVX·IVSSIT NAVES·EDI FICARE·

7. Duke William orders ships to be built. Bayeux Tapestry.

NIT AD PEVENE SÆ·

8. The Norman fleet, with Duke William in his flagship, the *Mora* (with figure of a man as the stern-post), sails across the English Channel to Pevensey. Bayeux Tapestry.

9. The horses disembark from the ships. Bayeux Tapestry.

10. Duke William encourages his knights before the battle of Hastings. Bayeux Tapestry.

11. The height of the battle, with both Anglo-Saxons and Normans being killed. Bayeux Tapestry.

12. King Harold is killed. Bayeux Tapestry.

to England, and he had enough good feeling towards them to offer some of them patronage and support, not least Robert, abbot of Jumièges, made bishop of London (1044) and archbishop of Canterbury (1051–52).

Duke William was first cousin to King Edward of England. He was cousin to several other rulers too. In most cases (such as his kinship to the king of France) the link was inconsequential; but his cousinship to Edward was more of an emotional link. The young duke and the king, some twenty years his senior, had a mutual family history. They had shared hall and table on what must have been numerous occasions, and whether or not there was much affection and confidence between them, they were tied together by the family bond. Norman sources – looking forward to 1066 – are eager to assure us that this was so, because it added weight to the legitimacy of William's succession to England. But the bond was real for all that. Norman sources make much of Edward's childlessness and his alleged adoption of William as heir, but the fact that the principal sources (William de Jumièges and William de Poitiers) published their works after 1066 does open them to the charge of overstating the relationship between Edward and William, for political purposes. The fact that English sources fail to mention William at all in the context of candidacy for the throne simply strengthens the argument that William was only a candidate for the succession in his own head. There is, however, a counter-argument.

William de Poitiers tells us that, at the time when Robert of Jumièges was archbishop, the archbishop himself acted as emissary from King Edward to inform Duke William that the king had selected him as his heir. The archbishop brought more than promises; he also brought noble hostages for the good faith of the king and his nobility – a son and grandson of Godwin of Wessex amongst them – young men who would be brought up at the Norman court. Later rumours also said that the duke received from England a ring and ceremonial sword, items of ducal regalia which were also appropriate to a king-in-waiting. William was stronger that year (1051) than he had been for a while. He was still in alliance with King Henry of France and had routed his internal critics, while his powerful uncles still stood by him. Most importantly, he had established himself as a talented warrior in a warrior society. It is very likely, as has been suggested,[10] that it was the young duke who had first sought out the king and solicited his attention. In his continuing struggles with the Angevins and internal rivals, Duke William would have benefited very much from backing from, and a solid connection with, the looming power of England across the Channel behind him. It was a great benefit to him just that his name was one of those mentioned as a possible future king. Historians are now convinced that the offer to William of a place in the succession in 1051 really did happen. But whether Edward had as yet singled William out as sole heir from among his other close cousins (the Anglo-French children of Godgifu, his sister, and the exiled children of Edmund Ironside) is another matter, and not a question that will ever be resolved.

Although William's candidacy for the throne of England was a real one, its fortunes sank at the same time as his star rose in northern France in the 1050s. The family of Earl Godwin gained an increasing hold on the king and the court after temporary disgrace in 1052, and they were not friendly to Normans. In 1057 Edward the Exile, son of Edmund Ironside and the king's eldest nephew, returned to England; although he died soon afterwards, he left a young son, Edgar, to continue his pressing claims. All these events combined to distance William from the succession. He was never in a position, as were some of his potential rivals (like Ralph of Mantes, son of Godgifu), to go to England and become known in the English court and countryside, although Wace (writing a century later) asserts that William did cross the Channel once, at least, before 1066. Wace's information cannot be relied on, but if William could not go to England in the early 1060s, it so happened that England came to him. In the summer of 1064, Harold son of Godwin, earl of Wessex, by now pre-eminent in England, took leave of the court of the king, his brother-in-law, and took ship from Bosham to Normandy.

We have it on the good authority of Eadmer, monk of Canterbury, that Harold's mission was intended to tie up the loose business of 1051, and secure the release of Wulfnoth, Harold's brother, and Haakon, his nephew, who had been sent to William's court as hostages thirteen years before. Eadmer's authority is good, because he could draw on Archbishop Anselm as his source. Anselm was the new prior of Bec in 1064 and in contact with William's court. The mission did not end quite as straightforwardly as it began. Harold's ship was blown up the Channel by a storm and driven onto the shores of the county of Ponthieu. Count

Guy's officers arrested Harold and his entourage as they landed and imprisoned them in the castle of Beaurain, seeking a ransom. This presented an opportunity for the duke to revive his candidacy for the throne, simply by being gracious and helpful. Harold's pre-eminence in England cannot but have been known to him, and he may have assumed that Harold's lack of any blood link to the royal family excluded him from consideration as future king: Harold could be a very useful ally. So Duke William personally secured Harold's release from prison, and had him escorted in great honour to Rouen, where the earl was showered with gifts and fêted throughout the summer. There is every likelihood that a good time was had by all, even though Harold must have realised that he was being manipulated. But both men were great and recognised warriors; they were of equal status (contemporaries equated a pre-conquest English earl with a continental duke) and they may even have formed a personal friendship, within the bounds of their own political interests.

The duke was ruthless with the opportunity that he had been given. He took advantage of the situation to put Harold in a situation of dependency. The Bayeux tapestry shows William conferring arms and military equipment on the earl: a common French ritual called in the vernacular *adoubement* ('equipping'),[11] by which a lord formally took a man into his service. William also asked the earl to associate himself with the support of his candidacy to the throne of England. In a ceremony at Bonneville-sur-Touque Harold swore (according to William de Poitiers) that he would represent the duke's interests in England and work for his succession to the throne, and offered certain estates (including Dover) as pledges for his conduct. This conditional swearing of faith was a political ritual we have already seen being required of Geoffrey de Mayenne by William in the early 1050s; and it has to be said that Geoffrey was as faithful to his word as Harold was to be. Eleventh-century politicians were as pragmatic in fulfilling their promises as their twenty-first-century descendants.

Perhaps the main difference between political culture in the eleventh century and this one is that people expected public figures to keep their promises, especially those to which God and his saints were witnesses. Failure to honour faith that had been pledged meant that a man was *parjuré* (a forsworn oath-breaker): such a charge did not publicly discredit him and make him unacceptable in respectable society, but it was a charge that people remembered for an inconveniently long time. But in the summer of 1064 everyone was delighted that Harold, the foreign moustachioed grandee from England, was now a useful political ally for Duke William. The ducal retinue went off happily to war on the Breton frontier, with Harold riding alongside them. The frontier city of Dol was secured, by the defection of its Breton lord, Rhiwallon, and the duke's cousin, Count Conan of Rennes, was chastised for failing to acknowledge the traditional ascendancy of the Normans over his principality. Battle was largely avoided, as was usual in medieval French campaigns, but Conan had been disciplined and Harold was given a chance to witness the sophisticated northern French political order in action, with its subtle power relationships of historical dependency and defiance, military feint and shifting alliance. One wonders what lessons the Englishman drew from his experience; he was used to more savage and unrelenting warfare on the Welsh March. The previous summer he had been presented with the head of a defeated Welsh over-king, as a present from the latter's successful rivals. He was fondly sent on his way home from Normandy with handsome gifts and his young nephew, Haakon, the original object of his embassy (his brother Wulfnoth lived on in Normandy as an exile for over two decades after Hastings; kept back, perhaps as a reminder of Harold's new obligations. He only returned to England with William Rufus in 1087, and ended his days in Winchester cathedral priory).

When, about eighteen months later, King Edward died, Earl Harold gave no thought to any theoretical obligations to Duke William. Using or abusing his political ascendancy at court, Harold sidelined the young atheling, Edgar, Æthelred's only grandchild of male descent,[12] and graciously accepted election as king by the English nobility. He was already king before William even heard that Edward was dead. It was at that point, in the first week of January 1066, that William had to decide how much his long-term plans concerning England were worth to him. He had been counting on the English succession now for fifteen years, and perhaps reckoned it to be his right and due (like Harold, also conveniently forgetting Æthelred's surviving grandchildren). He had been for a decade a feared and highly successful power in northern France, and had invested much of his prestige in restoring the civil peace of Normandy to the state it had been in his grandfather's day. He had the wealth and eminence to attempt the conquest of a kingdom, and, in the conquering Normans he heard about in southern Italy, examples to stir his pride and envy to do so. The Norman Conquest of 1066 was not therefore a matter of opportunism, but the product of a long history of cross-channel involvement and careful calculation.

4

The Conqueror of England

William was neither foolhardy nor an opportunist. If he took any decision, it would have been preceded by a long period of calculation. He had enjoyed many chances down the years to learn about England, the English and their internal politics. If Wace is to be trusted, he may even have crossed the Channel himself in the brief period of Earl Godwin's exile in 1051–52. He had spent most of the summer of 1064 with Harold of Wessex, and by the time he had returned to England knew Harold well as soldier and courtier. Norman clergy had attained high office in England and Norman aristocrats had settled there peacefully; there is reason to believe that one, William Malet, lived in Harold's own household for a while. Malet was to act as adviser to the duke in the 1066 campaign. If Harold was expected by Duke William in 1064 to undertake the task of helping to manage his eventual succession, he may have employed other, lowlier English agents in the same task. The English were at the same game; Harold is said to have sent spies to the Continent to monitor William's preparations. William de Poitiers tells us that on his landing in Sussex, in October 1066, the duke immediately got in touch with Robert fitz Wimarc, a Norman who had settled in Essex by 1052 and had filled a court office under Edward. Fitz Wimarc offered him valuable local intelligence and advice, and he and others could well have been doing so covertly for months or even years. It has been customary amongst historians to suggest that the Normans were ignorant of the government and politics of the land they had arrived in and conquered, but it would go against what we know of the methodical nature of their duke to believe that William did not prepare himself carefully in mind as well as in the field for the campaign of 1066.

He put the scheme to his intimates, those same close noble counsellors with whom he had campaigned since Val-ès-Dunes in 1047. Most – but not all – applauded his ambition and set to work with him to execute the scheme.[1] While the spring night sky was being illuminated with the uncanny 'long-haired star' – Halley's comet swinging in towards the sun on its long orbit that year – the duke's emissaries spread out across France and the Empire seeking allies and approval. The Emperor Henry IV and Pope Alexander II both made positive noises. The pope sent a banner from Rome 'to signify the approval of St Peter', as William de Poitiers puts it. What precisely that approval involved is hard to say: the language of banners is ambiguous. A layman would understand the taking up of a banner as a way of declaring rightful assumption of power over a realm, if its bearer was a count or a duke. But a clergyman would see the granting of sacred banners as just a way that the Church could offer approval and support to a favoured son (as when the count of Mortain in the 1060s carried the banner of St Michael on behalf of the abbey of Mont St-Michel). During the summer of 1066 Flemings, Bretons, French, Poitevins and even Aquitanians offered themselves for service in the campaign. Non-Norman Frenchmen were to make up a significant proportion of the invasion force, men like the brothers Garnier le Riche and Simon de Senlis, young and noble knights from the region of France across the western border of Normandy, who in their father's lifetime made a living by hiring out their services to employers. They took service with the duke in expectation of reward if the expedition was a success, and contracted to bring with them a company of forty knights.

The bulk of the army that assembled on the shores of the bay of the Seine was, however, Norman. It was raised by the duke's principal followers among their tenants and connections in response to their obligation to support him in the field. It was in that sense a 'feudal' army, although it would be anachronistic to assume that the Norman barons were summoned to serve the duke with set quotas of knights, since it is not until the 1090s that we have any firm evidence that such quotas existed in Normandy. Before this army assembled, there was a more pressing need to find the boats to ferry men, horses and military supplies to England: a list survives detailing the quotas of vessels to be found by individuals, towns and churches. This – rather than bad weather in the Channel – is the probable reason why the duke was not ready to move until autumn, as a number of vessels would have had to have been hired and built to meet the need for sea transport. The assembly point was an anchorage in the muddy estuary of the Somme off the Ponthevin port of St-Valéry. Duke William was able to persuade Count Guy to allow the great navy and army to assemble in his small realm, which offered a much shorter Channel crossing than a Norman port like Dieppe. William de Poitiers – a military man in his younger days – points out that the duke had made very careful arrangements for the lodging, provisioning and supply of his force, so that local citizens had no cause to complain of the Norman presence. Harold, on the other coast, was not so canny. In September lack of provisions forced him to dismiss the fleet and army he had assembled to defend the south coast.

After a morning mass, and what may have been a solemn devotional procession of the relics of St Valeria around the camp, the Norman army embarked. The fleet, reputed by one account to have been as many as 3000 vessels (but more likely a fifth of that), took advantage of the afternoon breeze of an unseasonably hot day, and sailed out into the Channel at high tide (which was between three and four o'clock) on Thursday 28 September 1066. The fleet gathered in deep water outside the estuary as the sun went down. Taking advantage of what moonlight there was, and managing to keep together in the night by lamps and signals, the ships arrived with the morning off the Sussex coast on 29 September, the feast of Michaelmas, accomplishing a voyage of some 125 km. The duke and his attendants apparently had a cheery breakfast on the deck of his own great ship, the *Mora*, while the fleet reformed around it in the dawn light. The bulk of the fleet then came to shore at Pevensey Bay, which was clearly where they had always intended to land: the long beach was very suitable for the rapid landing of men and horses, and a strong fortification could be raised nearby in the shell of a Roman fort, which was right on the shore line. But the army did not stay encamped there, and some or all of it moved on rapidly to seize the town of Hastings, from where it was possible to move inland easily, whenever the duke chose. Another reason to head east along the coast was that some French ships had become separated and landed their men in St Mary's Bay near Romney, where local troops attacked and killed many of them. Four days before William's landing, King Harold had triumphed over a Norwegian army in Yorkshire, at Stamford Bridge, and news of the impending Norman invasion reached him as he returned south, while news of the English victory in the north had greeted William as he landed.

Far from there being a great rush of the English forces south to confront their new French enemies on the coast, the duke and the king each had a chance to take counsel and size up the chances of the impending campaign. The duke sat tight on the coast and the king halted in London. They found time to exchange emissaries, threats and self-justifications. There was plenty of material for cutting and sardonic invective, and later accounts dwell on Harold's claims that he was rightful king by Edward's deathbed nomination and election, while William talked of his close kinship to King Edward, his earlier nomination as heir, and Harold's despicable perjury. According to William de Poitiers, who claims that he had carefully researched what had actually been said through the mouth of the ducal envoy, William proposed to Harold that they should fight out their quarrel in a duel, man to man. It is possible that he suggested just that, for proposing a judicial battle was one way for a French nobleman to put his enemy in the wrong. To refuse it and seek instead an arbitration was to act as if you were unsure of your claim and unwilling to trust in God. It was all part of the skilful game that was northern French politics. The subtleties went quite over Harold's head, as much as had the lessons of the campaigning he had witnessed in Normandy in 1064. He seems to have come away from Normandy with the idea that French warriors were ineffectual posers, and concluded that a determined front would send them back in disarray across the sea. He perhaps had forgotten that William had established himself in his duchy in a series of pitched battles, and knew when (and when not) to fight them. In Sussex in 1066, with the sea behind him and his fellow princes bound to punish him for failure if he got back after a defeat, William was intending to fight.

Harold was in London on 6 October, and rested there a week, gathering his strength, before marching down across the Weald to approach the Norman base at Hastings. When he did move he moved fast. Harold seems to have hoped to march rapidly enough to catch the duke off guard; but, whether through informants or simply through efficient scouting, his approach was detected and William was able to move his force north from Hastings to confront the oncoming English army. Harold reached what was to be the field of battle soon after the cold

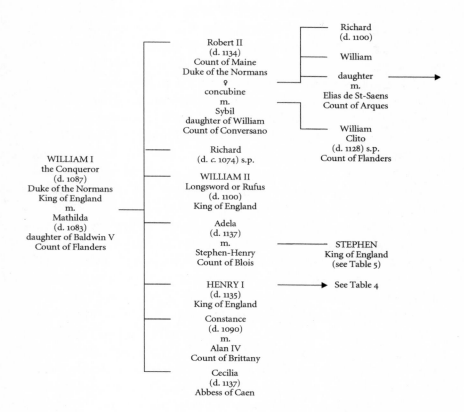

Table 3. Descent from William the Conqueror.

dawn of Saturday 14 October 1066. He had the luck to come up against the Normans on their northward march when his troops were in a strong defensive position: a wooded east-west ridge at the end of a spur of the Weald with a steep southward slope lying across the road northwards out of Hastings. The valley in front of it was wet and rough with sedge, features which were bound to hinder the Normans. Harold's army was probably superior in number to William's, and it was made up of a mixture of his own military household and southern English levies. But it was a tired army, having marched much of the Friday night and maybe the previous day also, in a vain attempt to surprise the French in their camp. It also lacked any support from Mercia and Northumbria, whose earls were not of Harold's family and not friendly to his rule.

William's men, although at a disadvantage in numbers and in situation, were more ready to fight. The duke did not waste time – his only recorded words were a prayer to the effect that: 'I'll found an abbey here if I survive!' On sighting the English spears and armour in the trees, glittering in the morning light, he hastily deployed his men: too hastily, according to the Latin poem called *the Song of the Battle of Hastings*,[2] written within a few years of the event itself. Its knowledgable writer – believed to have been Bishop Guy of Amiens – colourfully depicts the sudden appearance of the massed columns of the English on the ridge. He describes the noble thegns dismounting,[3] sending their horses to the rear and taking up position on foot under their standards. And just as colourfully he depicts the duke at the foot of the ridge caught in the act of marshalling his knights and bowmen. William was unable to deploy his infantry to complete advantage, so that his bowmen could work on the English line under protection of spearmen. There was no time and no space for the 'ordered and well-marshalled companies' thought then to be the mark of a good commander.[4] The duke's cavalry had to be brought forward as soon as possible to deter any possible English charge into the line of the lighter French footsoldiers.

Much, we may guess, to the duke's irritation, the battle of Hastings was not so much planned as experienced. It is one of the best recorded of all medieval battles, and the impression that the records give is of a protracted scramble. Wrong-footed at the beginning, the duke sent his bowmen part way up the slopes to harass the English line, while he sent squadrons of cavalry to search out the edge of the position: Bretons sent to the right and the non-Norman French sent to the left. But the English shields continued to present an unbroken wall along the ridge to the front, and when the Norman knights attempted to break through it by using the weight of their horses they found it a hopeless task. The steepness of the slope all along the front allowed them no chance to charge with any momentum, or even to manoeuvre in front of the English line. Meanwhile the English were able to rout the outflanking Breton squadron and also to drive back the infantry with a sleet of javelins. At this point, William de Poitiers had to admit that the duke's army began to lose heart and fall back, unable to make any headway. A rumour went round that the duke himself had fallen on the hill – perhaps a consequence of the first time that he had his horse killed under him. In places a retreat began. William de Poitiers, the historian, was embarrassed by this, but comforted himself and his readers with the reflection that even Caesar's legions sometimes retreated. The Bayeux Tapestry famously pictures the duke at this point riding the line unhelmeted so his men could see the falsity of the rumour of his death for themselves, while his half-brother, Bishop Odo, equipped as a knight, was one of those who rallied the companies which were falling back. It was then, had the English advanced remorselessly down the hill, that the battle could have ended in victory for them. Why they did not do this is a question that has intrigued many historians, although the question can only be answered by speculation. The best suggestion is that the English actually did get under way, but that the leaders (perhaps Harold's brothers Gyrth and Leofwine) were killed as they moved forward to lead the charge, and their fall threw the general English advance into confusion.

Unfortunately for the English at this point, the Normans were not quite so disorganised as they might have appeared from the hilltop. Unfortunately also the English were pitted against a commander who knew that giving way could be a real opportunity when faced with an entrenched opponent. It was a tactic he had used against King Henry of France at St-Aubin-sur-Scie near Arques twelve years before, in his days of youthful, military exuberance. When William observed a part of Harold's army beginning to follow his fleeing knights, he was able to lead the companies he had rallied in a counter-attack. It utterly destroyed the English who had got to the base of the hill. Once the

English line was weakened, William's task became less desperate, although the English army still remained formidable. It was now mid morning and there was probably a long pause in the fighting. William regrouped his army and returned with more leisure to his original plan: his archers and crossbowmen moved within range of the English once more, with less danger to themselves, and as the noontide and afternoon wore past, the attrition of their fire opened gaps in the line of shields till William judged it was so weakened that even the constraints of the contours could not cancel out the punch of his mounted squadrons.

So it proved. Even if, as William de Poitiers implies, the Normans were repulsed at some parts of the line, they broke through at others. The duke was ever in the thick of the fight, and is said to have lost three mounts under him, replacing one by hurling a retreating knight from Maine to the ground and taking his horse. No one can doubt his energy and valour, but it is unlikely (as the *Song* claims) that he led the troop that overthrew Harold, his brother Earl Gyrth and his household. Had he done so, then he would not have had to send people to search for the body of the dead king later. As the afternoon drew on, he and his knights saw that the English were beginning to flee, in groups and in solitary flight, leaving lines of the dead behind them to mark their former position. Amongst the dead was King Harold, who fell to arrows and the sudden breakthrough of a line of knights. These had swept across his part of the field, in the very centre of the ridge, throwing down the royal banners: the red dragon and the 'Fighting Man', Harold's personal ensign. No one knows at what point in the battle the king fell or how, as all his household fell with him, and his enemies did not recognise him as they killed him; but early accounts (perhaps based on the inspection of his corpse after the battle) say he fell when an arrow pierced his brain through an eye socket. When he died, his kingship died with him, for there were no adults of his family left to continue his ambitions, apart from his brother Earl Wulfnoth, long in custody in Normandy.

Becoming a King

Hastings was a decisive battle, but it was decisive because Harold's bid for the English throne was shallow, based on personal charisma with little in the way of hereditary right or custom to back it up. In both England and France royal blood had been for centuries a man's principal claim for candidacy for the throne. Harold, the descendant of Sussex landholders, could claim only remote kinship with the royal family; it was his wealth and prestige (and perhaps his Englishness) that had been far more persuasive to his colleagues in 1066. The Norman criticism of him as an ambitious man corrupted by a lust for power was a perfectly fair one. Without Harold in person to override them, William's moral and hereditary claims to the throne were strong, especially as he had the military power now in England to back them up. William, encamped on the battlefield in the night of 14 October after organising a fierce pursuit of the fleeing enemy, must have had every hope that England would fall to him now with little opposition. The fact that he took his time about following up his victory is eloquent testimony that he – as much as the English – knew that his claim was no longer easily contestable. He spent the Sunday inspecting the field, and looking for the body of his dead rival; a search he entrusted to a senior Norman in his army, William Malet. Malet had lived in England and had some personal link with Harold, so was able to identify his corpse even though it was badly hacked about. The body was treated respectfully by all accounts, but it is not known for sure where it was buried, or if William allowed its surrender to Harold's family, who petitioned for it, as some texts say. The French who fell were all decently buried, but the remaining English bodies were left to the chances of fate and to the persistence and piety of their relatives.

From the battlefield, the duke returned to his base at Hastings. He was to spend several weeks more on the Sussex and Kentish coast. He first sacked Romney in revenge for the bloody repulse of some of his ships which had landed there, and then at the end of October secured the fortified burh at Dover, which offered no resistance. With the Channel ports garrisoned by his men, he was ready to move inland, and undefended Canterbury submitted without any direct threat, while Winchester received and accepted his summons to recognise his rule. Moving on from Dover and Canterbury – at the end of November – he began a slow approach to London; slow partly through policy and partly due to the fact that he fell seriously ill on the road, somewhere in Kent. The earls and bishops gathered in London proved equally cautious. They were locked in a debate whether to accept William's claims (backed up by force) or to persuade the young Edgar atheling, the late King Edward's nephew, to follow up his superior hereditary claim and put himself forward. When William recovered his health, he had grown impatient with the temporising of the English leaders. He led his army south around London, and menaced the city from the south, burning down Southwark and driving off English soldiers who tried to challenge him. The strategy had some effect, as at least one leading English noble, Ansgar, a court official, stood out and openly advocated to the city assembly that the time had come to accept the Norman duke. William meanwhile passed on up the Thames, giving his army licence to pillage as he went, before circling back through the Chilterns to the city. By the middle of December he was residing at the estate of Berkhamsted, which had belonged to one of Harold's dead thegns. There the leaders of the English finally reached him: the several earls of Mercia and Northumbria with Edgar atheling (who had stood down as a candidate), a number of bishops and nobles, and representatives of the Londoners. They submitted to his claims, gave hostages and swore faith with him, and between them they arranged his coronation for Westminster on Christmas Day, a Monday.

The coronation was a tense affair, and the crowded abbey precincts were heavily policed by French soldiers. The English people and surviving English nobility turned out in force to see their latest foreign king crowned, but it does not seem that they were hostile. The coronation was presided over by Archbishop Ealdred of York, rather than Stigand of Canterbury, who was compromised by his close association with the late Harold, and by irregularities of life; but Stigand was nonetheless present, and supported William's arm in the procession. Geoffrey, bishop of Coutances, stood alongside the archbishop of York so that, when William was presented to the Anglo-French assembly within the abbey as king 'by hereditary right', the presentation could be made in French as well as English. The presentation happened around fifteen minutes into the service in the form of a question put to the people. The shout of acclamation in the abbey church, in reply to the question when it was put in English, sparked off an unfortunate panic amongst the guards outside the abbey when the crowd around them joined in the shout. They laid into the crowd in the way of nervous riot police throughout the ages and in the course of their struggle set fire to houses in the abbey precinct. As the screams and shouts of the crowd outside, and the reek of burning, penetrated the abbey, and as the congregation moved uneasily, the service continued with various anointings, investitures and benedictions. The much later account of Orderic Vitalis talks of members of the congregation slipping out through the doors – some to help in the fire-fighting – and William visibly tense and nervous on his throne as the ceremony was completed.[5]

It would not do to underestimate the significance for William of his elevation to kingship. For all the decay of the kingdom of France, the honour and distinction of its king and kingship were undimmed. In England and in the continental realms, the scholars and prelates of the Church had devoted much thought into explaining, justifying and exalting the idea of Christian kingship. The kings of the eleventh century may have been the physical descendants of the tribal kings who had overthrown and settled the later Roman empire, but their kingship had been thoroughly worked over and Romanised. Like the Emperor Constantine, they summoned church councils, and appointed bishops and abbots. Like the Emperor Justinian, they issued law codes and enforced civil peace. But more than that, their kingship had been morally and theologically reformed to the point where coronation was held to have transformed them as much as consecration transformed a priest into a bishop. The good kings of the Old Testament were held up in the coronation service as models of righteous rulers. When the *Song* wanted to exalt William as king, it had the examples to hand: there had been no such king since David, he was wiser than Solomon, and – as a gratuitous sideswipe – more generous than Charlemagne (the founder of poverty-stricken French kingship). Usurpers of this model were compared to the wilful and disobedient biblical monarchs, to Pharaoh and Saul, and lambasted – like Harold – as 'tyrants'. The royal regalia included the gloves, sandals, dalmatic, tunicle and stole worn by a bishop, but in their hands kings bore the sceptre, rod and orb of the Holy Roman Emperor, the archetype of Christian rulership. For this ideological gift, the Church expected protection and peace in return.

William had been a most noble 'count, marquis and duke of the Normans', all titles with their own unique history and dignity. In banner, ring and sword, he too had his emblems of rulership, but all his titles

recalled delegated authority from a greater ruler. His powers over
Church appointments, coinage and law in Normandy were powers
usurped from the Carolingian king by his ancestors. Occasionally that
subordination was asserted over the duke. Even in William's own day,
the Capetian kings still presumed to issue charters to abbeys in his
duchy; reminders that there was a kingdom of France of which Normandy was a part. King Henry had on more than one occasion
summoned William to the royal army, as one who was his subject. Even
when the *laudes* (solemn prayers and praise) were sung before him in
the churches of his own duchy, William's clerks prayed first for the king
of France before they came to his name in the litany.[6] Now William
was himself by conquest, acclamation and hereditary right the latest
king of one of the oldest lines of monarchs in Christendom. This had
a powerful effect on both him and on those around him. When he
returned to Normandy in 1067, his first act was to hold the most splendid
royal court ever seen in France in recent years; for the French king,
Philip, was only a boy in tutelage. William brought the English regalia
with him amongst other treasures, and he had the royal *laudes* sung
before him by his chapel clerks at Fécamp at Easter (8 April) 1067. The
name of King Philip of France was apparently left out of the litany,
while William was hailed not as duke, but 'the most serene William,
the great and peace-giving king, crowned by God'. So ducal Fécamp,
the heart of the Norman realm and burial place of his forbears, witnessed
the apotheosis of its greatest son.

To have more than one person wielding power within the realm of
France who was called king was not something that had happened since
the days of the independent kings of Provence, the last of whom had
died in 936, at the time when William Longsword was count of Rouen.
It was uncomfortable for the Capetian family to find that William, duke
of Normandy, already formidable in power, wealth and reputation, was
now also lawful king of an ancient and very wealthy realm; rather
wealthier and considerably more powerful than its own decayed estate.
William's own idea of his new status is to be found on his great round
seal, whose silver dies would have been produced by the skilled goldsmiths of Cheapside before he returned across the Channel in March
1067 (we know from the study of the seals of Stephen and Henry II that
it took just over a month for the London shops to design and produce

such an artefact). On one side, William appears in the traditional image of throned king, with orb and sceptre, an image that King Edward had introduced by copying the imperial German seal. Now William was copying Edward, as a way of broadcasting the continuity of his kingship. But where Edward's seal had two sides, both showing him enthroned, the front side of King William's seal shows an image of him riding as a mailed warrior with banner and shield; it proclaimed him in a learned, Latin hexameter to be still 'father (*patronus*) of the Normans'. It seems likely that the London goldsmiths were given his old ducal seal to expand and copy to match the reverse 'majesty' side. It was a striking juxtaposition of images and was commented upon by a Flemish writer of the next generation, who had seen an impression of it and quite understood the message of dual authority it broadcast.[7] William was now both king and duke, but his behaviour demonstrates that he was in his own eyes as much a king when he was in Normandy as when he was in England.

Consolidating the Conquest, 1067–71

There was never to be any single, united 'Anglo-Norman' kingdom, although there was a complex of claims and realms which spanned the Channel held together by the individual who was both king and duke. Nor was there a Norman 'empire' along the Atlantic seaboard, although King William on occasion had his clerks describe him by the imperial Byzantine style of *basileus* rather than the Latin *rex* (king), as his English predecessors had done too. But although there was no single coherent kingdom and empire under William, the realm he ruled was more than the sum of its parts. Like his predecessors, Cnut and Harthacnut, William at Westminster and Winchester sat in the middle of an extended web of political, economic and military interests. These tied together not just Welsh and Scottish kings and English earls, but in his case Normandy with the numerous satellite realms of counts and castellans that he had daunted and subjected: some of them (like the Bellême and Mayenne families) soon to be further tied to him by large English grants.

Like Cnut, William did not necessarily see England as the centre of his activities. This was demonstrated right from the beginning. He stayed only a few months in England after his coronation. The English had accepted him, as it seemed, and William – glad to be off back to France

– accepted the status quo that he had found there. This was nowhere
better demonstrated than in his arrangements for England's government
before he left. He began by issuing writs in the English language as well
as in Latin; he retained Edward's chancellor; and his first appointments
of earls in 1067 duplicated the regional arrangements of the reign of
Edward. In place of Harold as earl of Wessex, King William placed his
old and intimate friend, William fitz Osbern. The king placed a French
former court official of Edward's, Ralph the Staller, and his own brother
Bishop Odo in the earldoms formerly occupied by Harold's dead
brothers, Gyrth and Leofwine, based respectively in East Anglia and
Kent; but in the latter case Odo's authority, like Leofwine's, extended
over most of the home counties. As far as the rest of the kingdom was
concerned, the English earldoms of Mercia, the east midlands and
Northumbria were left as he found them, for he was off to France.

William sailed home with a great company, including returning
French soldiers, some now handsomely paid off with the contents of
the royal and monastic treasuries of south-east England. There were
other debts owing. The king brought with him many gifts for Norman
and other French monasteries. To the pope he sent, by way of exchange
for the banner sent him, the embroidered personal ensign of his fallen
rival, Harold. He was not indifferent to the possibility of trouble in
England in his absence: he brought with him to Normandy Archbishop
Stigand, Edgar atheling, and Edwin, Morcar and Waltheof (respectively
the earls of Mercia, Northumbria and the east midlands), 'so that during
his absence' as William de Poitiers says, 'no revolt instigated by them
might break out'. He also ordered that the commanders he had left
behind should raise suitable castles in London and Winchester, to
overawe the citizens: 'rich, untrustworthy and bold'. But, indifferent to
the danger or not, William still had to be back in Normandy, for the
complex politics of northern France could only be orchestrated by such
a master as he knew himself to be. His people seem to have thought so
too. Glad though they were to have their duke transformed into a king
in great splendour, and to find him in a generous frame of mind, the
fact that the duchy had for several months been denuded of troops and
was surrounded by resentful neighbouring powers must have added
further sincerity to a welcome which turned Lent 1067 into a high feast.

William stayed in Normandy till early December 1067. Though the only recorded deed of his in the duchy during that time was to attend the dedication of the new abbey church of Jumièges on 1 July, it would be unwise to think that he was mistaken in his sense that he was needed there. He had many French enemies who would be discouraged from attacking his lands now that he was in them. Indeed, the count of Boulogne – who had fought for him at Hastings – did move against him. Rather than attempt to cross the borders of the duchy, Count Eustace instead tried the enterprising and cunning tactic of fitting out a fleet to attack the parts of William's realm where he was not. He launched a naval assault on Dover. Eustace might have had hopes – inspired by domestic dissidents – that the English would join him to fight against the conqueror. In this he was proven wrong, for the garrison of the new castle at Dover easily repulsed his force.

With the summer campaigning season over in France, William sailed again to England, bringing troops and fresh energy to confront the problems conquest had thrown up. He was welcomed in London with a gratifying degree of civic festivities, and there he celebrated Christmas. When he conferred with his council, he began to discover what the problems were. There had been fighting in Herefordshire with alienated Mercian landowners raiding into it from the north. In the far south west Exeter, it seems, had never agreed to accept William, and resistance to him openly continued there, where King Harold's mother, Gytha, was living. So King William raised a large sum from those parts of England which would pay, and took an army into the west to which he summoned also the English shire levies, who did not refuse to turn out for him. Exeter surrendered, although not until William had blinded one of the hostages whom a faction of the citizens had offered, and not until he had shown by his energy and aggression that the siege would be prosecuted to the bitter end. Devon and Cornwall were subdued and all seemed well again; so much so that after Easter (which he spent at Winchester) William sent to Normandy for his wife, Mathilda, who had not yet been crowned queen, and on the high feast of Pentecost (11 May 1068) Archbishop Ealdred of York performed the ceremony of anointing and coronation; and, as in 1066, a large number of English earls and thegns were present to acclaim Mathilda as their queen.

May 1068 was perhaps for William a high point of his rule in England. He had secured the acquiescence of London and the south, and his

English subjects – with a few exceptions – respected his kingship. The majority of his earls, and all but a few of his bishops and abbots, were still English, and he perpetuated a structure of government that was recognisably that which he had inherited. But from now on, for several years, rebellion and crisis became endemic in his realm. Whose fault was it? Undoubtedly it was his own and that of his advisers. That euphoric sense of Norman achievement and self-consequence which emerges in the mid 1050s betrayed them. Its apostle, William de Poitiers, tells us how. When dealing with other peoples, the Normans had already become arrogant and even dismissive before 1066. When William de Poitiers (who had been a ducal chaplain) writes of the Bretons in the early 1060s he sinks into crude and quite unmerited abuse: they were polygamous barbarians, addicted to war, bloody feuds and brigandage; they did not live in settlements like decent Christian folk, but lived off the land like nomads. This was not just William's eccentricity: when the rebel earl Ralph de Gael and his Breton knights were defeated in England in 1075 and exiled, Archbishop Lanfranc rejoiced that England 'has been cleansed of its Breton filth'.[8] Over the next century, we find Norman and Anglo-Norman writers again and again dehumanising their opponents and rivals in such terms: the Welsh, Scots and Irish each in their turn experienced the treatment. By effectively putting their neighbours outside the Christian pale, the Normans were able to excuse any barbarity they cared to use against them. In William de Poitiers' account of the English after the Conquest, we find him already insidiously harping on the tune of English treachery, their seething and murderous resentment of the French, and their moral corruption. In other words, everything they were to get they had asked for.

By 1068 the pretence that Normans and English occupied England on anything like equal terms was beginning to be only a pretence. William fitz Osbern and Bishop Odo had started a piecemeal deprivation and demotion of the surviving English aristocrats and their families. The families of the thegns of Wessex and the south who had fallen in battle might perhaps have expected better, but nonetheless they were excluded from their inheritance, and in some areas – notably Sussex and Kent – lands were redistributed and subordinated wholesale to incoming French noblemen as rewards and to promote security. Since this was carried out in King William's name, his new subjects had every reason to be alarmed for the future. William's rhetoric was all about continuity and inheritance; his actions spoke of high-handed superiority and dispossession. He was proving himself to the English both a more hypocritical and a more tyrannical conqueror than Cnut had ever been; and many still remembered Cnut as king and could compare the two as rulers.

The king's 'severity' was beginning to drive abroad those English aristocrats who felt they had something to fear. Just after the queen's coronation, the family of Edgar atheling, his mother and sisters, vanished out of England and took refuge in Scotland with Malcolm III, and several northern thegns retreated into Lothian. Their retreat may only have been due in part to fear of the Normans: the northern earldoms were full of internal rivalries, which had already accounted for the murder of William's nominee as earl of Northumbria, Copsi, in March 1067. In the summer of 1068 William took the significant step of moving for the first time beyond the south east and entering Mercia and the north. He was briefly resisted by the brothers Edwin and Morcar, earls of Mercia and Northumbria, but as the king's army moved slowly north, leaving detachments to fortify Warwick and Nottingham, and closed in on York, the earls once more submitted. William entered York and received the submission of the northern metropolis, and while there entertained envoys from King Malcolm, who sought to make a peace agreement with him. Sending north as earl a French knight, Robert Comin, to secure Durham and Northumberland, the king slowly returned south, planning new castles at Lincoln, Huntingdon and Cambridge on the way. Judging by his decision to return to Normandy with the queen for Christmas 1068, King William was happy that he had settled the problem of the north for the present.

But the north was not finished with William and precipitated the first great crisis of his reign in England. The northern magnates had taken the king's appearance at York as a sign that they must fight or submit, and they chose rebellion. On 28 January 1069 Comin and his knights were taken unawares on their first night at Durham, and were massacred by the insurgent English. The massacre was indiscriminate and only one or two French escaped. The king could not ignore such an insult to his peace, and news of it brought him back rapidly across the Channel. The Northumbrians no doubt did not much care, for the rebellion included leaders with a wider plan in mind. The massacre at Durham was repeated not long afterwards near York, when a Norman force under its castellan was trapped and destroyed, while the castle was closely besieged. The rebels were now led by those northern nobles who had retreated to Scotland the previous year, notably Edgar atheling. King William arrived at York in March and managed to drive off the rebels, leaving a part of his host to refortify the city and strengthen it with a second castle. His view of the seriousness of the situation is clear in that he left Earl William fitz Osbern in charge as he went south to celebrate Easter (12 April) at Winchester. He also wanted to watch the situation in the south west, where the illegitimate sons of the late King Harold had landed with a force of Irish mercenaries. The Normans at York were attacked again once the king had left, but the force at Earl William's disposal was adequate to deal with the situation for the moment.

Over the summer of 1069, with a northern rebel army still threatening York, the situation became a critical one for William as King Swein Estrithson of Denmark responded to English appeals and sent a powerful fleet and army. Swein was a nephew of King Cnut through his sister Estrith, which constituted a better claim on the English throne than Harold had possessed. One reason William stayed in the south must have been the need to guard the southern and eastern coasts against the Danes. The Danish force did indeed appear first off Kent, but moved up the North Sea coast, raiding as it went. Its objective was to join the rebel English army in the north by landing on the banks of the Humber estuary. The Danes and the northern English were able to join forces at the beginning of September – which was itself a mighty blow against William – and all the surviving English earls found the chance to defy William irresistible. Waltheof of the east midlands, Edwin of Mercia, Morcar and Gospatric of Northumbria, all entered the Anglo-Danish camp. York was sadly vulnerable to this host of William's enemies and, on 19 September, with the Anglo-Danish army approaching, the Norman garrisons torched the houses near the castles, so that they could not be used to aid a siege. But the fire spread across the city and burned down the minster. Two days later, after an ill-judged sally, the castle defences were overwhelmed and what was left of the garrisons cut down, with only a few women and children sheltering within spared, and one Norman, William Malet, a man apparently well known to the English aristocracy before 1066.

With local outbreaks erupting across the south west and Welsh marches, with his northern army slaughtered, York smoking in ruins, and Shrewsbury and Exeter besieged, King William was now in deep trouble. It may be significant that he had already recalled to his side William fitz Osbern, getting him away from his exposed command in the north, ready for the final confrontation. Now the worst had happened. Drawing on his experiences in his dark days in Normandy in the 1040s, the king moved to deal with one crisis at a time, willing now to risk the chance of pitched battles. William fitz Osbern and Count Brian of Brittany were sent into the west and successfully destroyed the rebels outside Exeter. The king himself encountered a Welsh and English army pushing east from the March as far into Mercia as Stafford, and in a little-recorded battle, that may indeed have been the decisive victory of his reign, he utterly destroyed them and so suppressed the most dangerous challenge to his rule in the south. William now had to move on to the main challenge to his rule in the north. He was able to deter the Anglo-Danish force from an assault on Lincoln, but as Christmas 1069 approached he found himself unable to penetrate further north than Pontefract, where his route into Yorkshire was barred by a strong English force.

In camp at Pontefract for several weeks in early December, the king attempted cunning. He secretly contacted Earl Osbern, the brother of King Swein, who was in command of the Danish fleet, and offered a huge bribe if he withdrew from York and accepted a truce to last throughout the winter. Agreeable to taking out this sort of insurance against the chances of defeat, Osbern took the money and withdrew into quarters at the mouth of the Humber. This left his English allies weakened, and their army broke up, allowing the king to continue north. So William came again to ruined York, repaired the castles and held Christmas there amongst the ashes. He took advantage of the winter truce with the Danes to ensure – in the most brutal contemporary fashion – that there would be no English resistance to his rule the next year. His knights spread out across the Vale of York, systematically destroying any opposition and laying waste to the land. Houses were burned and all food and stock commandeered. The result was a catastrophic famine in which the bulk of the population of western and southern Yorkshire either starved, died or had to flee the land. After

Christmas, King William moved to the northern borders of Yorkshire, and camped on banks of the Tees. His wretched opponents began to submit, and Earl Waltheof came in person seeking clemency, which he received. The king seems to have marched on up to the Tyne in January, his army suffering in the snow and the cold, so that many (used to warmer weather) threatened mutiny. But he safely returned to York and, not content, crossed the Pennines to secure Chester before at last moving south through a cowed kingdom to Salisbury.

By cool strategy, and by mingled savagery, diplomacy and mercy, and by the military utility of his castle-building, William was still king of England at Easter 1070, a fact which may have surprised many at the time. He had passed the longest period of his life that he was ever to spend in England, arriving early in 1069 and not leaving till the end of 1070. As has been noted by one his principal biographers,[9] the measure of his absorption in the problems of England is that he ignored the collapse of hard-won Norman power over the county of Maine in 1069, so as to concentrate all his resources across the Channel. The cost of his eventual success was heavy in lives and suffering, and William himself was not exempt from having to pay some of it. He had not begun by wishing to reign through terror; he regarded himself as rightful king of England, and for a while had clearly expected himself and the English to take up where King Edward had ended. He may even have hoped to have been merely an occasional and seasonal visitor in England, a royal bird of passage. But he had failed to inspire confidence in the English aristocracy: perhaps simply by not being as Anglo-French as previous French in England had been; he had certainly sanctioned an alarming level of dispossession in southern England in 1067. In 1070 he found himself with an effective but burdensome reputation as a ruthless and brutal conqueror, whom it was death to oppose. He may not have wanted it: the story of his entire military career up to 1070 was of an intelligent and visionary soldier, economical with people's lives and preferring feint and strategy to blood-soaked battlefields. Orderic Vitalis, introducing his personal opinion into the material he had culled from William de Poitiers, puts it frankly and humanely: 'for this act which condemned the innocent and guilty alike to die by slow starvation, I cannot commend him'.[10] The irony is that King William himself might not have disagreed with this Anglo-Norman monk of his children's generation.

Dispossession, and destruction of the pre-conquest power structures, was now William's policy. Within five years there would be no native survivors at the highest levels of English society, other than a few English 'new men' the Conqueror himself had raised to local eminence. The Easter council of 1070 saw significant moves against the order the king had inherited. The first distinguished victim was Archbishop Stigand, whose continued tenure of Canterbury after 1066 is strong enough evidence of William's attempt to work within the structure he had inherited, for the archbishop had been an ally of the Godwine family, and was in high disfavour at Rome. Stigand was the wealthiest landowner in England after the greater earls, and his estates were themselves a tempting target. The king gave into temptation in 1070 and Stigand, and his brother Æthelmer, bishop of East Anglia, were deposed with the aid of two visiting cardinal-legates. Stigand was committed to custody in Winchester for the remaining two years of his life. Other deprivations of sees and abbacies followed, 'induced solely by mistrust of losing his newly acquired kingdom', as the Worcester chronicler said. It is not too difficult to link them in with the ransacking of the treasuries of English monasteries that the king had ordered in the preceding Lent, allegedly to search out goods and cash deposited by fleeing and dissident English nobles. The new archbishop of Canterbury was Lanfranc, an eminent scholar, and since 1064 abbot of St Stephen of Caen, an early clerical friend of William's in Normandy. He was an unexceptionable choice in view of the supposed irregular life of his predecessor, and that in itself shows the king was still sensitive to possible criticism. York, vacant due to the death of Ealdred before Christmas, went to Thomas, a canon of Bayeux. New French bishops were provided for Sussex, Winchester, East Anglia and Rochester; a pattern in the Church soon to be duplicated amongst the upper reaches of the aristocracy.

By the end of 1070, when William had returned at last to Normandy, the end game was clear to all but the most wilfully blind of the surviving native magnates. Some may still have cherished hopes. The Danes had not yet left the Humber estuary, and King Swein had himself arrived in the spring of 1070. But discouraged by the mercenary ineptitude of his brother Osbern's campaign, and taken aback by William's grim way with the English, Swein had left again. He withdrew slowly from England, and indeed encouraged and assisted a Fenland rising, based on the Isle of Ely, before he left. But when they had plundered Peterborough, he and his Danes finally cut their losses and left, very much richer than before they had arrived in everything but reputation. Edwin and Morcar, seeing the poor prospects for those of English blood at court, abandoned it later in 1070. Edwin first looked for support on the Welsh March, and then took the usual road north to seek sanctuary at King Malcolm's court, but he did not arrive. He was ambushed and murdered on his travels, allegedly with the complicity of English traitors in his household. His brother, Earl Morcar, with the bishop of Durham, and a number of allied thegns (including the legendary Hereward), gathered at the last pocket of resistance on the Isle of Ely, but soon found themselves surrounded by Norman forces.

William returned for the summer of 1071, and eventually his emissaries persuaded the rebels (with the exception of Hereward) to surrender. Morcar was bundled off to Normandy where he spent the rest of the reign in the custody of a trusted, senior Norman magnate, Roger de Beaumont. His captivity, like that of Wulfnoth son of Godwin, was not apparently too harsh. We find him in Roger's company at the castle of Vatteville on the Seine in January 1086, still being entitled respectfully 'earl' and lending his name as witness to a charter of his Norman host. The king set up new earls in England, with the more limited powers and regional jurisdiction of Norman counts, at Chester and Shrewsbury. He reduced the former Wessex satrapy of William fitz Osbern to Hereford; that of Bishop Odo to Kent; and that of the survivor, Waltheof, to Northampton. Waltheof, married to the Conqueror's niece, Judith, would survive yet for a few years, and after 1072 had his father's earldom of Northumbria added to his responsibilities. It may be that he was William's first attempt to see if he could mould a native magnate into a Norman loyalist. By 1086 Thurkil of Warwick, Edward of Salisbury and Alfred of Marlborough were just such successful political hybrids. Throughout the north and midlands the king was busy creating strategic commanderies based on castles, and reorganising landholding to support them and their lords. Having once made up his mind to a thing, King William never lacked the energy to accomplish it.

King William and the Next Generation

Although five years after the Conquest, 1071 was in fact the watershed year in King William's life. This was not so much because it marked the king's final and decisive moves against the English aristocracy, but because it was at the beginning of the year, in February, that his oldest and closest friend and supporter, William fitz Osbern, was killed while accompanying the army of King Philip of France in its invasion of Flanders. Earl William had been left in Normandy as King William's faithful viceroy the previous year, when it became clear that England would occupy the king for a lot longer than he would have liked. The earl went to Flanders to represent his master in the host of France, which the young King Philip had raised in order to impose his will on the county as it debated the succession to Queen Mathilda's brother, Baldwin VI (who had died in 1070). William fitz Osbern died when the French army was routed in a surprise attack by the Flemings at Cassel. His body was borne back to Normandy for burial, and the grieving king took responsibility for settling the family's affairs. King William's grief and anger are said to explain the poor relations which persisted between the Anglo-Norman realm and Flanders till the 1090s. And it was in settling the inheritance of his old friend's estates that William unexpectedly reached a point of transition in his life.

The king was now in his mid forties. Although in full vigour of mind and body, a new generation of Norman nobles had grown up under him. He and his companions, who had fought the great battles against King Henry and Geoffrey of Anjou, were now the elder generation. This new generation, which included now his own adult sons, Robert and Richard, was to be the enemy of his latter years, not the English or the French. In 1071 the king partitioned William fitz Osbern's inheritance between the earl's two elder sons: William de Breteuil took his great Norman patrimony, while the younger son, Roger, was allotted a portion of his father's English interests, an earldom based on Hereford, with further interests across the Wye in Welsh Gwent (of which Roger called himself 'lord'). Roger proved to be a faithless subject, and the cause of the first major Norman rebellion against William for two decades. The reason why this was so was because he, unlike his father's generation, did not identify with William's ambitions and interests. William, in turn, did not identify with Roger's generation, and very few among them ever penetrated his council, which led to further resentment.

One of the advances in medieval scholarship over the past few decades has been the discovery of this generational rhythm in medieval society, both within families and at court. We have already seen something of it in the clashes between the young William and his uncles after his marriage in 1051; we have seen it also in the way he later redefined the ducal family to exclude their influence. It was not always the case that the younger generation was antagonistic to the elder in the Norman dynasty (as Orderic Vitalis observed). It was a matter of individual disposition. Under Duke Richard II, his elder son Richard, and a number of his younger sons proved loyal and cooperative to their father's will, but the second son, Robert, proved resentful and rebellious. Eleventh-century society possessed a culture of free-living aristocratic youth, a heedless way of life which had the potential to alienate the older generation from the younger: the one was established and in control of the family resources, and the other addicted to an expensive lifestyle but unable to pay for it. The social dangers in this tension were apparent to everyone. A writer from the abbey of St-Benoît-sur-Loire of around this time described Burgundy as being prey to gangs of armed and epicene youths 'full of themselves in their youthful vigour and enterprise' who rode the countryside with musicians at the head of their march, charmingly terrorising the neighbourhood in search of money for their pastimes.[11]

Such violent young vagabonds were following a distinguished trail – as well as prefiguring the aggressive and hedonistic youth culture of the later twentieth century. The latter years of King Robert II of France (died 1031) were plagued by troubles with his sons. The elder, and associate king, Hugh (died 1025) grew up having the title of king from the age of ten, but 'realised that apart from the food and clothing given him from the kingdom over which he had been crowned, he controlled nothing of his own'.[12] So he gathered a band of youths of his own age and pillaged central France until his father came to a compromise. The same story was to be repeated fifty years later in the Anglo-Norman realm in the latter years of King William, and indeed in the next century with the children of King Henry II. William had become a father before the battle of Mortemer finally established him as unchallengeable in northern France. His first child, whom he named Robert after his own father, was born at some time in or soon after 1052, and he was (being close to adulthood) associated with his mother in the government of Normandy in 1066. He had a brother Richard, who was born before 1056, but who never lived to plague his father, for he had died in a hunting accident before 1074. Robert had been conceded the title of count of Maine by his father in 1063, a dignity which in time would have seemed a piece of irony without the power to go with it. By the mid 1070s, Robert was chafing at the constraints his determined father placed on him. By then, a third son, William (certainly born before 1060), would have joined him in his angry need for independence.

The loyalty and stability that had been so characteristic of the Norman aristocracy for two decades first trembled in the autumn of 1074. It began with a marriage alliance between the young Earl Roger of Hereford and another newcomer, Ralph de Gael (son of Earl Ralph the Staller), the new earl in East Anglia. Despite the king's disapproval of the match, Earl Roger married his sister to the new earl. There was an expensive and luxurious wedding festival – celebrations which customarily went on for over a week – at the manor of Exning in Suffolk. Social gatherings of nobles were always places where plots might arise – tournaments were later to be just as notorious as conspiracy-beds. At Exning, with the king safely far away in Normandy, Earl Roger persuaded his guests that they should defy William and extort concessions from him. Earl Waltheof was with the marriage party, and he initially went along with the plot. We know, from the letters which Archbishop Lanfranc wrote to the earl, that the cause of Earl Roger's discontent was the fundamental one that he did not have the same regional power that his father, William fitz Osbern, had exerted. In particular, the king had removed from him the oversight his father had had over the sheriffs of the south west. The king had been made aware of the earl's complaints, and even suspended the sheriffs' jurisdiction over Roger's lands. But promises were not enough, so Earl Roger and his allies rebelled in 1075 as a consequence.

The nature of this rebellion should not be mistaken. When medieval magnates put their castles in defence against their king or lord, it was not generally from the sort of ideological reasons that the modern mind associates with rebellion; it was more of an aristocratic protest riot. In this sort of case, where a magnate felt he was not getting the respect and the privileges he regarded as his right, he was making an armed demonstration to bring home a personal protest. Sometimes this involved 'defying' the king, that is, formally returning his faith to him. If this was done, the magnate was not technically committing treason if the affair led to fighting. What might happen was confrontation, followed by negotiation and submission. Orderic Vitalis in his later account of the rebellion made out that the rebels sought to seize, divide and rule England. But Earl Roger and his allies could have had no thought at the beginning of overturning the king and seizing power; they just wanted their rights. Formal defiance was sent to the king – we know this was done since Archbishop Lanfranc mentions that William sent a reply to the earl offering some concessions. But when Earl Roger persisted, the king became less amenable. He mobilised his English viceroys (Bishop Odo and Bishop Geoffrey of Coutances) against the rebels with the aid of a baron, William de Warenne, and Archbishop Lanfranc laid them under interdict. Earl Roger was deterred from crossing the Severn, and forced back into Gwent, where he took shelter with the king of Glamorgan. Earl Ralph and his large Breton military household were likewise confined to East Anglia by a mixed army of Norman and English loyalists. When no aid came from home or from the Danes to whom he had appealed, Ralph fled the country, leaving his wife under siege in Norwich, and the castle soon surrendered.

Worried by the possibility of a Danish army arriving in England, William returned to his kingdom in autumn 1075 for the first time since the summer of 1072. The Danes, when they came, led by King Swein's son Cnut, settled for looting York and left soon after. The king then sat in judgement on the rebels, many of the lowlier of whom were blinded and emasculated. The king let Earl Ralph's family and household leave to join him in Brittany. Earl Roger gave himself up, but forfeited his lands and liberty (which was the appropriate punishment for a man who had formally 'defied' his lord and become his enemy). Earl Waltheof, however, who had in fact given himself up to Archbishop Lanfranc before the rebellion got serious, was treated with severity. He was tried at Winchester and the court sentenced him to the English penalty for treason, which was beheading. He was executed in May 1076 on a hill outside the capital of Wessex, the last earl of native lineage until the elevation of Patrick fitz Walter fitz Edward to Salisbury around the year

1144. Waltheof's estates were given intact to his widow, the Conqueror's niece. Many writers, French and English, thought that in the end Waltheof did quite well out of his punishment. He was treated by many as a martyr, and his tomb at Crowland abbey became a popular shrine, his miracles proclaiming that God had received him guiltless directly into the company of saints. The next generation of Anglo-Normans reckoned that it was William's remorselessness to Waltheof which deprived his latter years of success and brought continual troubles on him.

Troubles continued to multiply for the king, despite his crushing of the rebellion of 1075. Next to vex him was his own son, Robert. The troubles he stirred up were indirectly related to the troubles stirred up by Earl Roger, because Robert the king's son likewise felt excluded from power. They were also directly related, because the king decided to invade Brittany in autumn 1076, where the exiled Ralph de Gael had based himself in the city of Dol, just across the border, so as to continue his attack on King William. The king moved to try to expel Ralph, but his bad fortune continued when King Philip, still only in his mid twenties, joined with Count Hoël of Brittany, took William unawares and drove him away from Dol with the loss of his army's baggage. William suffered something that looked very like a military defeat, a rarity for him so far in his career; not only that, but he was worsted by the young and relatively inexperienced king of France. So the end of 1076 found William dealing with a revival of the Capetian war that had subsided at the death of King Henry in 1060. Philip – whom his father had named in hope after the great hero-king of Macedon – proved indeed to be a formidable opponent on the battlefield and off. Already in 1075, he had invited Edgar atheling to cross over to France from Scotland and take charge of the important castle of Montreuil between the counties of Ponthieu and Boulogne, to use it as a base to harry William in Normandy. Although the scheme failed, Philip was clearly willing to assist anyone who had a reasonable chance of destabilising the Anglo-Norman realm.

Robert, son of King William, however much his father may have loved him, was a great gift to King Philip, who used him to inaugurate a strategy that was to be used by subsequent generations of Capetians until the fall of Normandy in 1204: supporting the disgruntled heir to England against the reigning king and so weakening both. William was not blind to the strategy being used against him, and turned to diplomacy. He seems to have attempted to neutralise Count Hoël by suggesting a marriage alliance between the count's son, Alan, and his daughter Constance. In 1077 he was able to reach a temporary peace agreement with King Philip. He may have already realised the danger that his eldest son was becoming, for that same year William – with the consent of King Philip – had Robert formally invested with the duchy of Normandy. Robert was labouring at this time under a grievance, although it is hard to say whether frustration with his father or rivalry with his brothers was the source of the problem. At the end of 1077 relations between the king and his son finally collapsed. Orderic Vitalis puts it down to an incident at Laigle on the southern Norman border, as the king was preparing an army to overawe the count of Perche, another new and unwelcome enemy. The king's younger sons, William Rufus and Henry (still only a boy), taunted their elder brother by occupying the upper floor of his lodgings, while he was downstairs. They held a dice party and amused themselves by urinating on their brother and his military household below. A riot ensued as Robert and his men attempted to storm the upper room, which brought the king and his knights to the scene to separate the brothers.

The next day, Robert and his household left the army and attempted to seize Rouen, doubtless as a preliminary to raising his sympathisers in the duchy against his father. When this coup failed, with the king now out against them, Robert, his knights and those barons who had supported him fled for the borders and took refuge at the castle of Châteauneuf-en-Thimerais, in the French March. Open war along the southern and eastern borders of the duchy followed on inevitably. Robert was supported by William fitz Osbern's eldest son, William de Breteuil, a great southern Norman lord, and by the turbulent and charismatic warrior Robert de Bellême, son of Roger de Montgomery. The generational shift within the Norman ruling class can be seen most clearly in the way that the old king's principal friends and supporters produced sons who were his principal adversaries and the allies of his rebel son. Although the king managed to dislodge him from the southern frontier, Robert then resorted to his uncle, the count of Flanders, and was inevitably caught within the net of King Philip of France. Philip gleefully took the opportunity of increasing King William's embarrassment by establishing Robert at the marcher castle of Gerberoy, on the French side of the Norman border opposite Gournay on the Epte. Philip was repeating the strategy he had attempted in 1075 when he had tried to persuade Edgar atheling to harass William from the marcher fortress of Montreuil.

In January 1079, the king was forced to besiege his son in Gerberoy, or suffer a catastrophic loss of face amongst the barons of the Norman March. In the event, what happened was even worse. King Philip moved into the Beauvaisis. When the besieged Normans and the French combined against William in a battle outside the walls, William's army was soundly defeated. Robert Curthose nearly achieved the Freudian ambition of destroying his father. He himself is credited with unhorsing King William and wounding him in the arm; only sparing him when he recognised that the bulky warrior he had brought down was shouting for help with his father's rasping voice. The king's household was cornered and many of them forced to surrender. Some idea of the ferocity of the combat can be found in the Anglo-Saxon Chronicle's report that the English nobleman, Toki son of Wigot of Wallingford, was instantly killed by a crossbow bolt at the king's side as he struggled to bring up a horse on which William could escape. The young William Rufus was wounded alongside his father, but he too was allowed to ride away. King William had to resort in the end to a peace conference at Gerberoy with King Philip in return for his release. Although the terms of their settlement are unknown, it seems likely that he was obliged to undertake to receive back Robert Curthose with a firm undertaking that Robert would have Normandy after his death.

The reconciliation took time to arrange, and may only have been ultimately possible through the intervention – moral and financial – of Queen Mathilda, who seems to have transferred huge sums of her own money to her eldest son. King William was usually patient under his misfortunes, but there is no doubting the fury and humiliation that churned away beneath his pragmatic handling of his defeat. During 1079 the surviving intimates of his generation, his wife, various holy men and even the pope himself, all worked hard to assuage the king's embarrassment and, by their fervent petitioning, to remove some of the sting of concession, by making him appear gracious. At Easter (12 April) 1080, father and son were finally reunited in a spirit of cooperation, and together crossed over once again to England, from which the king had been absent for around four years. As often happened in medieval society, a series of great public events was staged in order to efface the memory of the humiliation. Glittering courts were held in England at the principal ecclesiastical feasts, and in the space between them military manoeuvres were held on the borders of the realm, against opponents who were unlikely to put up much resistance. In the summer of 1080 Robert Curthose and Bishop Odo of Bayeux led a great Anglo-Norman host to intimidate King Malcolm of Scotland and the northern English thegns. In the summer of 1081 the king himself with his son Rufus marched across south Wales as far as St David's, to intimidate and impress the feuding Welsh rulers. The only concrete results seem to have been new Norman castles at Newcastle-upon-Tyne and Cardiff, but it was at least an effective demonstration of the power of the king of England, for those who might have chosen to doubt it.

Rather than demonstrating the undamaged power of William the Conqueror, these campaigns of 1080–81 may have advertised just the opposite: that the internal dissensions within the royal family had undermined the confidence of the realm it ruled. With the king and Robert Curthose uneasily allied, the realm was in reality impregnable to outside aggressors and to would-be dissidents within. But how long would the truce between father and son last; what about when the king died? Robert had demonstrated a real military talent and a political volatility which could only unsettle the whole Anglo-Norman condominium, despite the long and uneventful peace between 1080 and 1084. Some further symptom of perceived weakness may be seen in the sudden demand that came from Rome from Pope Gregory VII that William should acknowledge that he held his crown as a dependency of the see of Rome. The demand seems to have been made by cardinal legates in the aftermath of William's forced reconciliation with his son in the summer of 1080, at a time when the pope and his ambassadors had judged the king to be at a low point. The claim depended on the tribute, called 'Peter's Pence', paid Rome by England since the eighth century, and by the appeal for support for his claims to Pope Alexander II by Duke William in 1066. William flatly rejected the pope's claim, and that was the end of the matter, as Pope Gregory was soon overwhelmed by troubles of his own, but his very claim was revealing about the current perception of William's kingship.

Death, Division and Domesday, 1083–87

The first tremors of renewed internal disturbances in William's kingdom were felt at the end of 1082. Odo, bishop of Bayeux, had been one of his elder half brother's inner circle since his appointment to Bayeux around 1050. With his younger brother, Robert (created count of Mortain around 1060), Odo had been indispensable to William in the conquest and settlement of England. Odo had acquired huge estates in England and the title of earl of Kent. Wax impressions of his double-sided great seal still survive, showing him vested as bishop on the obverse, and on the reverse (just as on the Bayeux Tapestry) mailed and mounted as a count leading his knights. Odo was a gargantuan character: learned, cultivated and a patron of the arts, but ambitious, worldly and enormously wealthy. Like earlier noble Norman bishops, he associated with a concubine and had children: one of them, called John, was to be a chaplain to the royal family. He was the last of the great count-bishops that the Norman ducal family produced – men like Robert and Mauger, archbishops of Rouen but also secular lords of great power. In the reforming church of the 1080s, he must have seemed something like a mammoth in Hyde Park: fearsome and impressive, but somewhat out of place. In the later 1060s and the later 1070s, his brother had chosen him as a suitably loyal and competent viceroy to contain and control England. He lived up to expectations. but it is clear that he used the opportunity ruthlessly to increase his personal wealth and (most unsettlingly) to create a dangerously powerful personal faction within the aristocracy.

The story of his fall given by the chronicles is not universally believed by modern scholars, but it harmonises with what we know of the man's character. Odo had apparently become interested in international church politics. This is not surprising, for he was well known in the wider church as a patron and as a restless intriguer. The growing troubles of the papacy in the early 1080s under the aggressive rule of Gregory VII were seen by him as an opportunity: he decided that he might be able to use his wealth and Norman influence in Italy to secure election as compromise candidate as pope after Gregory's inevitable fall. In the aftermath of Gregory VII's ill-judged attempt in 1080 to get King William to acknowledge the pope as overlord of England, Odo may even have been given some backing by his irritated brother. But Odo became increasingly serious in his ambitions as the Roman Church fell into schism and disorder: he commissioned a grand palace in Rome, dispensed hefty bribes among the cardinals and people, and set up a spy network within the city and papal curia. By 1082 tensions between the king and Bishop Odo had increased, as William made his displeasure with all this expense known. The two men were together in the autumn in Normandy arranging the affairs of the abbey of Grestain, where their mother, Herleve, was buried. William agreed to endow the abbey with the same privileges as a ducal foundation, although it had been set up principally by Robert of Mortain. It was just after this that Odo crossed to England to prepare to travel to Rome (apparently despite the king's prohibition). As Odo was about to embark from the Isle of Wight with a great retinue of adventurers – doubtless intending the long sea voyage round France rather than risk going through his brother's domains) – the king appeared in person to arrest him.

The subsequent trial of Bishop Odo, however inescapable, could not have helped the stability of the Anglo-Norman realm. Many were no doubt happy to see Odo fall, but he was close enough to the king for his fall to be interpreted as dissension within the royal family, which in turn caused the realm itself to tremble. The king brought charges of corruption against Odo, and seems to have been taken aback when the royal court refused to pronounce a judgement against him, whether because he was a churchman or because he was a man whose power was still feared. Odo complicated matters further by taking the amusingly Gregorian stand that as a bishop no lay court could touch him and the pope alone could judge him.[13] The king – with Archbishop Lanfranc (who had suffered much from Odo in Kent) whispering in his ear – retorted that it was not the bishop of Bayeux who was on trial but the earl of Kent. The king himself is said to have taken Odo by the collar and given him to guards to take to the Tower of Rouen, where he was held prisoner until William died.

Soon afterwards, the king was subjected to further family anxieties. Queen Mathilda had accompanied him to England for the arrest of Odo, and returned to the duchy with him early in 1083, but fell sick at the end of the summer. It soon became clear that the illness was mortal, and we glimpse something of her final days in a brief charter she issued allotting a large part of the moveable wealth in her chamber – including her golden crown and sceptre – to the nuns of Holy Trinity at Caen, the abbey she and her husband had founded in June 1066 as a sister house to his abbey of St Stephen in the town. The king was present with her, she made a testament (of which the grant of her moveables was a written part) and was duly confessed before her death. Her body was borne to Caen and laid to rest in the sanctuary of the abbey under a leger stone, which still survives, carved with a Latin epitaph stressing her lineage and her works of mercy. Analysis of her exhumed bones made in 1961 proved her to have been physically a very small woman, of rather less than a metre and a half in height. But small though she was in person, she had filled the demanding role of queen with great dignity and assurance. Domesday Book has numerous references to her viceregal court and to her personal management of her English estates: granting manors to dependents and founding a market at Tewkesbury. She acquired great wealth and deployed it to further her own projects, not least in keeping the peace between her husband and her eldest son. Her influence over her husband and headstrong elder son was acknowledged to be considerable, and she was not afraid to defy William to his face: knowing of her formidable personality, an unnamed Englishwoman commended her estate in Surrey to the queen in return for her protection. Her absence was bound to affect relations between King William and Robert Curthose for the worse.

Within months of the queen's death, probably early in 1084, Robert Curthose had once again left the Anglo-Norman realm for exile in France. In part this may have been the king's fault. It was later believed that he was harsh and sarcastic to his son. Other sources talk of William's deep distress and depression after his queen's death. The couple had married young and formed a close partnership. Since William never acknowledged any illegitimate children, it is probable that he did not form extra-marital relationships, unlike any of the four generations of his male predecessors. He found all the emotional support he needed in Mathilda, and in any case it is likely that he subscribed wholeheartedly to the Church's new teaching on the exclusivity of Christian marriage. This all made the queen's death harder to bear; and as a result those around him doubtless carried the brunt of his distraction. Robert left the court and Normandy, but this time at least he did not turn to warfare and hostile alliances to retaliate against his father. He seems to have learned that such strategies only weakened his dynastic interests.

There are few reports of him in the period 1084–87; the nearest they locate him to Normandy is at Abbeville in Ponthieu, and not Paris. It was assumed by writers of the next generation that Robert allied with King Philip to cause his father trouble, but their inability to say how Robert did this tells against the assumption. In Robert's absence, the king's second son, William Rufus, now in his twenties, assumed the place of trusted intimate and lieutenant that Bishop Odo had once filled.

Because of Robert Curthose's reluctance to make war on his father, William's last years were more peaceful than might have been expected. That said, the king was still deeply committed to the continuing, ex-hausting struggle to maintain the Norman grip on the county of Maine, which he had wrestled from Anjou over two decades before. The claim on England possessed by the king of Denmark was also not forgotten. King Cnut, son of Swein Estrithson, revived it in the summer of 1085 and began the preparation of a fleet. This was enough to make King William return to England in the autumn and take serious stock of his resources in the kingdom. He brought an enormous military force with him, which he needed to retain and pay for into 1086. Perhaps he had been unsatisfied with the response to the levying of a Danegeld early in 1084, and had realised that he had no adequate records of fiscal and military services that he was owed. One survey that he commissioned reported on military service he might expect from the landowners of his kingdom. The other survey, into the actual pattern of landowning and taxation, is more famous because it still survives, as one of the earliest documents in the Public Record Office at Kew.

Both surveys were probably commissioned at the Christmas court at Gloucester in 1085, while William was pondering the Danish threat. There is little reason to doubt that the king himself was the instigator of the project: perhaps he had heard in the readings of the masses he regularly attended of the population survey that the Book of Kings says that the wise King David of Israel commissioned in his realm in his distinguished old age. It was perhaps more likely that he was aware that the pre-conquest English government had conducted similar wide-ranging enquiries, and saw the need to update these. Even though news of the murder of King Cnut, as he worshipped in the abbey of Odense in July 1086, would have removed the urgency of the survey work, King William remained interested in his project. He monitored the work of the commissioners who were quartering his kingdom, recording the evidence of the local juries of English and French landowners. At Salisbury, on the feast of St Peter (1 August 1086), he was ceremoniously presented with piles of parchment returns and received the solemn and exclusive oaths of allegiance of all the major landowners, and their followers too. This great 'survey' (a *descriptio*, as it calls itself in Latin) remains one of the outstanding monuments of William's reign. This is appropriate, for William was well aware in his day of the administrative utility of the written record. He ensured that all his sons had tutors and learned at least the rudiments of reading and the arts, although only Henry showed much real talent. Nonetheless, it would be his other son, William Rufus, who ensured the completion of the project in the course of 1088, after his father's death, when the mass of raw returns were refined and redrafted and bound into the volumes being called, less than a century later, Domesday Book.

King William left England for the last time in autumn 1086. With the ebbing of the threat from Denmark, and the pacification (at enormous expense) of Maine, the king began to look towards Paris. The county of the Vexin, which lay between the Norman frontier of the Epte and the River Oise, had become a new problem in 1077 when its count, Simon of Crépy, entered the religious life and so left a power vacuum between Paris and Rouen. King Philip of France cheerfully took the opportunity to seize the count's former castles of Mantes and Pontoise, and to install royal garrisons and provosts. King William, on the other hand, was able in 1080 to insert a young Norman aristocrat as count of Meulan, between Mantes and Pontoise. It is not surprising that by the summer of 1087 Franco-Norman tensions had wound up to a point where border fighting was going on between the Norman lord, Ascelin Goel, whose lands straddled the frontier, and his opposite numbers, the castellans of Rosny and Mantes. William moved to join the fight. His contribution was a surprise attack on the French plague nest of Mantes, which he clearly intended to cauterise. He had the town burned down, including the large church of the Virgin: anxious for William's reputation, Orderic preferred to think that the French themselves had set light to the town and castle in panic as the Norman army broke in. But such ruthlessness was in William's character, even if only rarely displayed, as at Romsey in 1066 and in west Yorkshire in 1069–70.

It was while he was engaged in this unedifying activity, in the humidity and heat of late July in the Seine valley, as he rode through the acrid smoke of a burning town, that William experienced a sudden debilitating seizure, according to most writers. The spasm was so severe that he slumped forward, and William of Malmesbury repeated one story that it was at that point that he suffered a severe internal wound from his saddle pommel, when his horse skittered over the cinders in the road. In fact, the king's mortal illness had probably been growing on him for some time. Malmesbury also has a story that he had been confined to bed for a while before the Vexin campaign with strict orders from his doctors to lose weight, and this could only be because he was experiencing internal discomfort. King William had grown grossly corpulent over the years, a common result of the aristocratic diet of his day: rich in meat and fish and low in vegetables and dairy products. The result for many was that the excessive protein-rich diet led to liver problems, for others it led to late-onset diabetes. The king seems to have finally succumbed in July 1087 to a serious failure in one or other of his internal organs, which his doctors at Rouen were able to diagnose as fatal, probably because they saw so much of it in the upper classes.

The king languished at Rouen, first in the castle; then, because of the heat and noise of the city, he was tenderly carried to the priory of St-Gervais, on a hill to the west, in the freer air above the river valley. He had the best of medical care, including the services of the learned bishop of Lisieux, Gilbert Maminot, a former chaplain. His decline towards death took six weeks, and his deathbed was managed through the usual medieval stages. Eventually, after what seems to have been a slight recovery, his doctors convinced him of their belief that he was dying, and did what they could to alleviate his symptoms. After that the chief concern was the state of his soul. After some initial reluctance, to which Anselm of Bec attests, the king was brought to confess his sins and make restitution where he could: the church of Mantes did well out of this, as did his political prisoners, who were all released by his sealed writ to their custodians (although he is said to have hesitated before letting Odo of Bayeux loose again). Instructions were given for his burial – although it had been long established that he was to lie in the abbey he had founded in honour of St Stephen at Caen around 1063. Just as his late wife had done, the king bestowed his regalia – his crown, sword and sceptre – on his burial church; he sent his royal cloak to his other foundation at Battle (perhaps remembering that a cloak was a very suitable gift to a church dedicated to St Martin). There were to be disbursements of great sums out of his treasury to the poor – which had been one of his late wife's enthusiasms – and to the minsters and local churches throughout England, for masses for his soul. Following confession and penance, the king received absolution and communion, probably repeated daily while he was able to receive it. As far as his political testament was concerned, he was able to make his views known clearly, although he waited till his last few days on earth before finally committing himself. Robert was to receive Normandy only, while the faithful William Rufus was to have England and the kingship as his share. The youngest son, Henry, would receive the huge cash sum of 5000 pounds. Henry also later claimed that the king had promised him the late Queen Mathilda's estates in Gloucestershire and elsewhere, although he never got them.

William the Conqueror died at the age of fifty-nine just after dawn on Thursday 9 September 1087, as the sound of bells being rung for the office of prime drifted up from the church towers of Rouen below. Orderic tells us that he had lapsed into unconsciousness the previous night, but – as is not uncommon – had come around for the last struggle, and he is supposed to have managed a final commendation to the Virgin, the protector of the dying. There followed some scandalous scenes. No one had expected the king to die quite so suddenly. A couple of days before he had urged William Rufus to leave for England, carrying sealed instructions to Archbishop Lanfranc to deliver the kingdom to him. Henry too had been sent away to secure his cash legacy, so when the king expired there was no one to take charge: Robert Curthose had refused to return to visit his father's deathbed. The nobles and bishops present scattered to protect their homes and possessions, so the un-supervised servants plundered the death chamber and rifled the corpse, tipping it on the floor. It lay there throughout the morning until the archbishop of Rouen rallied the ecclesiastical community of his city and began suitable liturgical commemorations with a great procession through the streets to St-Gervais. The next problem was the preparation of the body. It was left to the piety of a local landowner to take charge of the arrangements for preparing the body and taking it to the port of

Rouen for transport by a small barge to Caen, because so one else was prepared to organise it. William's reception in his own town was not auspicious. While the corpse was being received at the abbey, a great fire broke out in Caen, and the vigil office for the dead had to be abandoned as people rushed out to assist in the firefighting. There was an all too obvious parallel to the late king's coronation at Westminster.

To the delight of a later generation of moralists, the Conqueror's funeral was another scandal. It gave them wonderful material with which to reflect on the vanity of worldly glory. A host of bishops and abbots was present at Caen, but few laymen of any importance. To his credit, according to both Robert de Torigny and William of Malmesbury, the king's son Henry was there, but there was still no sign of Duke Robert Curthose. In fact the senior member of the royal family present was the aged Abbot Nicholas of St-Ouen, son of Duke Richard III and the late king's eldest first cousin. At the end of the funeral mass, when the empty coffin had been lowered into a grave in the sanctuary ready to receive the shrouded body still visible above ground on its bier, the bishop of Evreux mounted the pulpitum of the abbey to address the people and ask their prayers for the departed. He and everyone present were shocked when a citizen of Caen came forward and volubly complained that William had taken the land on which the abbey was built from his father, and had given him no compensation. What was worse, a loud murmur of agreement arose from the Caennois in the church when the protester demanded that the body of the robber should not be buried on what was in effect his land. Rather than face a riot at the funeral, Count Henry, the king's son, made a payment to satisfy the man on the spot and a promise of further compensation. The next embarassment was the burial, when it was found that the royal body was too big for the sarcophagus that had been provided. As the desperate attendants tried to force it in, the inadequate embalming at Rouen gave way, and the corpse opened, spilling out the foulness of the internal decomposition and driving the clergy from the grave's edge. So the funeral of the greatest king of his age ended in confusion and humiliation.

King William's tomb was duly completed, a solemn, classically-inspired epitaph was inscribed on it, and it was richly decorated with precious metals and gems at the expense of his successor as king, William Rufus. William did not rest in peace perpetually surrounded by the masses and prayers of his monks. In Catholic France as much as in England, the tombs of kings were vulnerable to religious revolution and humanistic prying. The macabre curiosity of the sixteenth century led to the opening of his tomb in 1522, and William's mummified corpse was put on view for a while. An artist was commissioned to paint a portrait of the king from the evidence of his remains, a copy of which still survives. The king was found to be a man of above average size, very long in his limbs, which tallies well with contemporary descriptions of a powerful and commanding man, with a harsh voice, fierce in face with a receding hairline. Unfortunately for the scientific curiosity of later ages, the tomb was wrecked and ransacked by Calvinist rebels in 1562, and one thigh bone was all that they overlooked. The sad remnants of the great king were reburied under a suitable altar tomb in 1642 (of which engravings survive) but that too was swept away by the Revolution in 1793. As with Queen Mathilda, his remains were exhumed and examined in 1961, and the thigh bone was estimated to have belonged to a man of some 1.75m in height – over half a metre taller than his tiny wife.

William is the first of his dynasty of whose personality we know a good deal, enough to estimate something of his character. What we discover is a conventional man, although not in his day a conservative one. In fact in matters of personal morality and piety he was very much a new sort of medieval man. He was open to the movement in the church to ecclesiasticise lay life. William de Poitiers was his chaplain for a number of years before his promotion to an archdeaconry in the diocese of Lisieux. His evidence about William's conduct is first hand, and he describes a man whose life, like that of a clerk, was woven around the framework of the church's timetable. He attended part at least of the daily office said by his chapel clerks,[14] or in the greater churches of his realm. To do that to any purpose, he must have had some grasp of spoken Latin, and this is what William of Poitiers implies when he says that the king could follow the set lections. He may even have joined in the recitation of the psalter,[15] as did his great nephew, Charles of Flanders. The households of King William and Queen Mathilda were strongly marked by meticulous observance. Its members either rebelled against it, like his sons, or they were attracted by it. The king's kinsman, the young Count Simon of Crépy, spent some of his youthful years at the English court in the early 1070s. He became the very model of the pious layman

in fasting, observance of the office and in almsgiving. The fact that he did
so can be attributed to the influence of his foster-parents, not his violent
and loose-living father, Count Ralph, except perhaps as a reaction to
paternal oppression. Not surprisingly, Simon ended his days as a monk.

Principally, the king valued attendance at daily mass, and by all
accounts had a thorough theological understanding of its significance.
His undertanding was in some ways mathematical. Domesday Book
preserves some remarkable evidence of his concern that as many possible
masses be said with the intention of his personal safety in life and
salvation after death. He had the three priests occupying royal churches
in the district of Archenfield in Herefordshire so organised that a daily
mass was said for him in one or other of their churches. When permission
was sought from William for the building of a suburban church in
Norwich – probably around 1076 – he granted it providing that the priest
'sings a mass for the king every week and recites also the psalter'.[16]
William was a man profoundly marked by a passion for religious observance, yet without being in any way a *prêtre manqué* or being
considered a candidate for sanctity by his contemporaries. This is what
made him remarkable for his day and age. The source of this passion is
difficult to locate. His guardians appointed a tutor for him as a boy, and
his brother Odo became accomplished as a scholar. Perhaps the main
influence on him was the remarkable personality and intellect of Lanfranc, the scholar and theologian he first made abbot of Caen and then
archbishop of Canterbury. Their relationship began before the duke was
twenty, and Lanfranc is credited with the position of being William's
'spiritual adviser' (as we might say nowadays). Eadmer believed that
Lanfranc moulded the king's spirituality and that together they pursued
a programme for the increase of religious feeling amongst the laity of
England and Normandy.[17] The principal monuments to this endeavour
are now the ruins of Battle abbey, and William's mausoleum church at
Caen. When he decided to fulfil his battlefield vow of October 1066 –
which he seems to have done at the end of the military crisis of 1069–70
– King William concerned himself intimately in what followed. He
rebuked the monks of Marmoutier who presumed to cross him on the
matter of the abbey's site. He wanted the altar erected on the spot where
Harold fell, and was not interested in the monks' objections to the lack
of a water supply on the hilltop. When they objected to the lack of

suitable local stone, he had limestone brought from Normandy. His religious desires had to be carried out according to his imperial will, as closely as were his secular ones. This was made as clear to the monks of Battle as it was also to the numerous councils of the English and Norman churches over which he presided, enthroned as a latter-day Constantine.

William has been condemned as a man of pronounced cruelty on the basis of his devastation of Yorkshire in 1069–70, but that is unfair. His natural tendencies were always towards moderation and mercy. The sophisticated warfare practised in France in his day was organised around threat, feint and quick horseback movement. The ambush of the Angevins on the estuary of the Dives at Varaville in 1057 was the apex of this sort of war. It tended to limit damage and violence to the vicinity of castles, unless the commander was determined to cripple his opponent economically, in which case it was taken out on the rural settlements of his lordship. Aristocratic soldiers in his day tended to die in bed, for defeat led to imprisonment, not butchery. William was criticised by Guibert of Nogent in the next century for his refusal always to ransom captives, but in humanitarian terms that is a mild criticism. William time and again treated political opponents with forbearance: his uncles William of Arques and Archbishop Mauger were exiled on their defeat as rebels, but both were granted handsome incomes on which to live. The pattern was repeated in dealing with Count Walter of Mantes, Earl Morcar and Bishop Odo, all three kept secure but in aristocratic comfort. Edgar atheling spent many years untroubled in England by William, which shows surprising forbearance towards a man who had made war on him and had a better claim to the throne than he did. The execution of Earl Waltheof was the major exception to this; William himself may have regretted it, but it shows that the man could panic and his judgement was as fallible as anyone else's. When forced, William could be as ruthless as any other commander of his day. He terrorised the inhabitants of Alençon into surrender in 1052 by an act of economical and calculated cruelty. In great peril in the winter of 1069–70 he bribed the Danes to go into camp, and then neutralised them as a threat by spreading fire and theft over an entire province. After he had finished his grim work, the Danes could fight no campaign the next year with English support. The people of Mantes in 1087 also saw this sort of calculated ferocity. Since the French practised just the same sort of measured viciousness on the Normans, it could hardly be said to mark out William as an opponent who was more cruel and ruthless than any other ruler of his day.

It is William's determination that registers most strongly with the modern observer, or as David Bates would have it the 'brute force ... of his inner will'. But that did not make him unsympathetic nor did it deny his frailty as a personality. He could be hopelessly optimistic, as he was in the euphoria following the Conquest when – ignoring the racial arrogance of his followers – he vainly hoped to be an absentee king of a kingdom that would carry on its untroubled English way. He could be openly frustrated and exasperated, as he was with his son Robert, who was too selfish to see, as his father could, that he was a trustee in a dynastic enterprise not a joyful winner in the lottery of life. He must have been on occasion terrified, depressed and despairing; but his early experience of mortal danger as a boy in a volatile and treacherous court trained him in the emotional impassivity that was demanded of a ruler. Even so, he could be given to displays of grief and affection, and his capacity to bind his intimate followers closely to him indicates that he could be a very good friend. He could be physically exuberant: his energy and redoubtability on the battlefields of the 1040s and 1050s annoyed his elders. He rejoiced in feats of physical stamina, which he possessed till quite late in his life. He had a whimsical humour at times: pretending to Harold's monastic emissary at Hastings that he was his own steward, and stringing the man along until he confronted him in state as duke. Perhaps the key to his personality was his renowned addiction to the hunt – it was how he whiled away the days of the winter siege of Domfront in 1051, and the protection, management and exploitation of his forests occupied much of his spare time. It is not too fanciful to see here the reflex of a man trapped by duty, by his own inner drive to dominate his world and by the claustrophobia of court life. The forest was a medieval metaphor for escape and alternative living: the fact that William felt so much at home there – and so much drawn to the ecclesiastical round – tells us perhaps, deep inside the prison of his responsibility and duty, was a man who had rather have been in another job.

5

William Rufus

The second King William of England is more of an enigma than his father. The Conqueror was a determined man, who was always closely focused on what was before him. If he had contradictions of personality, and, if he had doubts, he had the ability to strangle them to leave him free to pursue his ambitions and agenda. But in fact the stability of the Conqueror's personality and his supreme self-assurance left little room for doubt and none at all for flightiness. His son and namesake was another matter. He was remorseless, cruel and calculating but also at times facile, ironic and humorous. His political vision and military skill were quite equal to his father's and may even have surpassed him, yet he failed to establish his line. He was as forgetful of his mortality as any twenty-first century man. Unusually for an educated medieval man, his gaze was less directed to the eternal than to the here and now. William the father was deeply and quietly pious, assiduous in his Christian duty; William the son only remembered God when it suited him, and seems to have had something very like contempt for theology and piety. He was generally called 'William Longsword' before he was king, and appears by that name in both the Welsh and Norman chronicles. This dynastic surname was an allusion to the man who was by now regarded as having been the second duke of the Norman dynasty, the son of Rollo. But William was also more commonly known as William Rufus, or in French 'le Rou' from his reddish hair. Reddish-blond hair – a characteristic of the Norman dynasty, which passed by marriage also into the Breton ducal house – was regarded as an unfortunate trait in a person's appearance: a mark of the uncanny, or of wickedness. No one called him 'Red William' to his face.

The younger William was in his late twenties when he became king. He had apparently been at least partly brought up in the household of Archbishop Lanfranc, and had received arms from his patron when he came of age, perhaps around the year 1076. He had been at his father's side during the disastrous battle outside the castle of Gerberoy in 1077, and had been one of his father's principal military commanders since 1081, when we find him independently leading a tough campaign in south Wales against the princes of Gwent. It may have been the first campaign in which he was given an independent command and his early success there would account for his abiding interest in the extension of the Welsh March in his later career. In all things the younger William was loyal to his father, and hostile to his elder brother Robert. If it was William's intention to spend his adult years at court transferring his father's affections to him and away from Robert, he certainly succeeded. When his father lay dying in September 1087, circumstances were very favourable for Rufus. His elder brother Robert was estranged from their father and ignored the summons to return home. William Rufus therefore had uninterrupted access to the dying king's ear, and, like Jacob, received from his father the misdirected blessing of Isaac. He had the nomination to succeed to England. So, carrying with him sealed letters to Archbishop Lanfranc directing his coronation as king, Rufus rode from Rouen to the coast a few days before his father died. While he was awaiting a ship at Bonneville-sur-Touques with his companions, the news followed him that the king was dead.

The Rebellion of 1088

William Rufus was probably twenty-seven when he ascended the throne of England at Westminster abbey. He was the youngest king since the sons of Cnut. His succession was not resisted in England, where he was already well-known as a successful and established warrior-prince. He found Archbishop Lanfranc at Canterbury, apparently already aware that the Conqueror was dead. Lanfranc made no resistance to his former pupil's request that he crown him king, charmed to find William as amenable as any parliamentary candidate to helpful suggestions about his future conduct once he was in power (but unfortunately just as sincere). The coronation took place at Westminster on Sunday 26 September 1087, about a fortnight after his interview with the archbishop. It may have been Lanfranc's influence that caused Rufus to pay promptly from the royal treasury the lavish gifts to the churches of

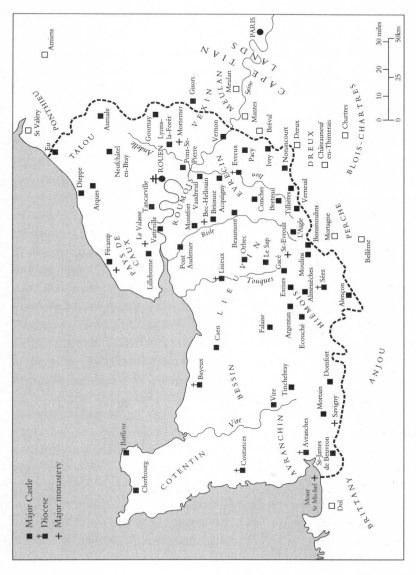

Map 2. Normandy in King Stephen's reign, 1135.

England made by his father for his soul; in fact his elder brother did exactly the same in Normandy, and Rufus would not wished to have seemed meaner to his father's memory than his estranged brother. He did not, however, allow those of his father's prisoners he had brought to England with him to go free, as his father had wished. Earls Morcar and Wulfnoth Godwinson continued to be held under supervision: Wulfnoth lived on for several years in Hampshire and Wiltshire, loosely supervised. He probably died around 1094 in Winchester cathedral priory.[1]

The new king assembled a governing clique around him. Bishops were surprisingly prominent among them, considering their master has a reputation today as something of an eleventh-century freethinker. Archbishop Lanfranc is credited by all commentators as having been very influential with Rufus until his death in May 1089, but the bishops of Durham and Lincoln were also important immediately after the coronation. A few noblemen were taken into immediate favour: William de Warenne and Henry de Beaumont (both of whom acquired earldoms within a year of the king's accession), and Robert and Hamo, sons of Hamo Dentatus, viscount of the Cotentin, were also to be found close to the king. It seems that in each case these men had been intimates of Rufus before he came to the throne and in his first weeks as king he depended heavily on their support. Few other magnates responded, other than Earl Hugh of Chester, who may have resented that his Norman lands had been subordinated by Duke Robert to Count Henry soon after the Conqueror's death, without his agreement.

The first problem for William Rufus was how to expand his support beyond his cronies, only two of whom, William de Warenne and Hugh of Chester, were magnates of any power. It may be because of this that he was even happy to welcome back to court at Westminster at Christmas 1087 his uncle, Bishop Odo of Bayeux, and to restore him to his lands in Kent. Unfortunately for him, Odo was already planning a future for the Anglo-Norman realm that did not include William Rufus. The new Duke Robert II of Normandy had made it known that he did not accept the division of his father's lands. Robert of Mortain and Odo of Bayeux, his uncles, must already have decided by Christmas 1087 to further the interests of Duke Robert against Rufus. Odo was in England principally to create a rebel party. Throughout March and early April he and the count of Mortain secretly and successfully mobilised a formidable body of rebels against the new king. They included the greatest among the Anglo-Norman magnates: Bishop Geoffrey of Coutances and his nephew the earl of Northumbria; Earl Roger of Shrewsbury and his warrior sons; Count Eustace of Boulogne; and the castellans of Leicester and Norwich. Worst of all for Rufus, his intimate friend, Bishop William de St-Carilef of Durham, came to the conclusion that the strength of the dissidents meant that the new king's reign would be short. The bishop listened favourably to the promises of Duke Robert's supporters and joined the conspiracy.

The rebellion against William Rufus was apparently already under way by mid March, when we are told that the king ordered the seizure of the bishop of Durham's lands. It may be that Northumbria had risen in revolt before the rest of the country. The main movement against the king was centred in Kent and Sussex, where the count of Mortain and Bishop Odo took the field, but not until after Easter (16 April 1088). The brothers were intending to act as vanguard in England for the duke their nephew. He was supposed to join them with a great fleet and army to take possession of England. Odo based himself in the north of Kent at Rochester, while Count Robert made his base at his castle of Pevensey in the east of Sussex. This was their fatal mistake, and the salvation of William Rufus's fortunes. Counting on the imminent arrival of Duke Robert, the king's uncles made the error of sitting still in garrison. Perhaps they thought that William Rufus would be unable to rally enough support to attack them, perhaps also they thought their mission was only to organise the rebels already in the field, without moving forward towards London. However, Rufus was not short of counter-strategies. He appealed to the still-powerful constituency of free English landowners, who had little sympathy with the great Anglo-Norman magnates. The English thought naturally of England as their concern and for them Normandy was a matter of indifference. The Anglo-Norman magnates had a selfish desire for a united Anglo-Norman realm; it made the overlordship of their cross-channel possessions less of a problem. Rufus promised the English to lift all sorts of restrictions and financial constraints on them; and, though they had little faith in his promises (as the Anglo-Saxon Chronicle says), still they rallied to him.

With the support of a few magnates and many English soldiers,

William Rufus moved into Kent, ignoring the fact that the north and midlands were in arms behind him. Rufus took his enemies by surprise in first striking hard at the castle of Tonbridge, which lay on the route from Rochester to Pevensey. The castle surrendered swiftly, much to Bishop Odo's alarm, for it now opened for Rufus a route to Canterbury and Dover, where Archbishop Lanfranc was defying the rebels. Odo shows no sign of having any of the military capacity of the rest of his family, and his conduct shows how it was that he had ended up as a bishop. Disconcerted and in a panic, he took to the byways with a small escort and made his way to his brother at Pevensey, leaving behind him at Rochester the count of Boulogne and other French reinforcements whom Duke Robert had finally sent across the Channel (although he did not himself follow them). Hard on his heels came the king who closely besieged his uncles, now he had them trapped together in one castle. After six weeks, supplies at Pevensey ran short and the bishop was forced to negotiate a surrender. He agreed to leave England and to ride first with some royal knights to Rochester and command his men there also to disperse. But the frustrated garrison there, which had in the meantime been raiding fiercely as far away as Canterbury and London, would have none of it. The troops in Rochester took Odo and the king's knights prisoner and obliged Rufus to reduce the city and castle by siege, presumably so that their honour as soldiers was satisfied. Eventually disease broke out in the blockaded city and it surrendered some time early in July. The garrison slouched out resentfully as the trumpets of Rufus's armies blared the king's triumph over their heads. Rufus seems to have decided early on that Rochester's surrender was inevitable, and had been relaxed enough to let its bishop have free passage in and out of the city through his lines.

Once he had mastered the rebel centres in Kent and Sussex, and harried his uncles back to Normandy, William Rufus moved north to subdue what was left of the rest of the outbreaks. But he found little left to do. His father's loyal sheriffs and their English allies had contained the rebels. The earl of Shrewsbury, his principal adversary outside the south east, had withdrawn his support for Odo of Bayeux early on, perhaps intimidated by the loyalism of his neighbour, the earl of Chester, and perhaps worried by the way the Welsh kings had become aggressive as England fell into disorder. The worst trouble had been in the Severn valley where the bishop of Coutances at Bristol and William of Eu at Chepstow had indulged in aimless plundering of royal estates. Leadership here had been lacking, and the saintly bishop of Worcester, Wulfstan II, was able to contain the troubles with the aid only of the local sheriffs and English levies.

The most persistent rebel – presumably because he had the least to hope for – was the king's former intimate, Bishop William de St-Carilef of Durham. He held out stubbornly at Durham, attempting first to maintain that he had always been loyal to the king. Then, when the king's army moved north, he refused to surrender himself unless he was tried according to the law of the Church by ecclesiastical judges. When he finally appeared before the king's court in November 1088 under safe conduct, he found an even more infuriating way of evading judgement – by appealing to Rome. The outrage amongst the barons and bishops of the court at this sort of stonewalling by such a man finally caused Bishop William to lose his nerve. The king was insistent and we hear his raucous voice in a memorial of the trial drawn up by one of the bishop's clerks: 'Believe me, bishop,' he shouted, 'you're not going back to Durham, and your men men aren't going to stay at Durham, and you're not going free, until you release the castle.'[2] In the end, the bishop was confined at Wilton abbey until the castle surrendered, and he eventually took ship into exile in Normandy once Durham was safely in the king's hands. He stayed in exile until 1091, when he was restored to Durham through Duke Robert's intercession. The bishop's treatment, it has to be said, shows some humanity and forbearance on the king's part. His betrayal of William Rufus was blatant, shameless and opportunistic. The king's willingness to treat him firmly but still mercifully seems to reveal a man who had low expectations of his courtiers; he may have come as a young man to disillusionment with human nature.

The Character of the King

William Rufus is a sympathetic character to present-day historians, in that he seems to them detached and ironic in his dealings with his contemporaries (detachment and irony being the principal vices of historians themselves). At first sight Rufus stands a little apart from his own time. His outlook was unusually secular for one of his family, which earns him the sympathy of post-Enlightenment commentators. He seems to them to have been a modern man out of his time. In fact he was very much a man of his own time. In his pronounced secularity and distance from the Church, Rufus was reacting to the intensity of the piety and spiritual discipline of his parents' generation. The Conqueror had been a model layman, as the Church would look at it: devout, observant and respectful. He was generous in his dealings with the Church and heeded his curial bishops, even if he was assertive of his own rights as duke and king. Rufus had less time for the Church and its claims, and his sympathies were enlisted by an alternative – but still contemporary – culture: that of the 'youth', the young warrior elite. Aristocrats in Rufus's lifetime had come to see themselves as a social group with a culture and ideals rooted in the sporting and hedonistic values of horseback warrior life. It was not unusual or unnatural for those who embraced the knightly life to profess contempt for the clergy, and portray them as hypocritical and greedy. Hypocritical and greedy clergy were the sort Rufus usually associated with: perhaps they confirmed his prejudices.

William Rufus was not alone amongst his brothers in rejecting the stifling piety of his parents' courts. His elder brother also took on board the spendthrift and vagabond rival culture of the camp. Despite their other differences, the two brothers had a mutual understanding about this. When in 1091 Robert and William Rufus were encamped on the seashore besieging the island abbey of Mont St-Michel, they amused themselves by sponsoring daily tournaments on the tidal sands between their pickets. Like Robert, William Rufus did not forsake the secular culture of the noble warrior when he came to rule over a realm, although he did not reject his responsibilities as ruler either. It would be going too far to call William Rufus 'anticlerical' as some have done, but throughout the 1090s he showed little engagement with the dominant and emerging piety of his day. He had no apparent devotion to the mass, he founded no religious houses (although he supported the foundation of Cluniac Bermondsey), he patronised no scholars and showed no interest in the Crusade. He was more than willing to exploit the Church shamelessly by deliberately extending the vacancies in sees and abbacies while collecting the rents due to these offices while they were in royal wardship. He was also willing to take payments from candidates for ecclesiastical office, such as Herbert Losinga who bought the abbacy of Ramsey. On the other hand, bishops and abbots were happy to attend his court in great numbers, and the bench of bishops was fully behind him in his punishment of the bishop of Durham. His closest administrative advisers were clerics: Robert Bloet, bishop of Lincoln, and Ranulf Flambard, whom he made bishop of Durham in succession to William de St-Carilef. The pious monk Gundulf, bishop of Rochester, was prized by him as a clerk of works for his military buildings. It was doubtless the secular talents of bishops that interested him most.

William Rufus's court did not earn the approval of the more austere and serious sort of clergyman. It is in his reign that we first hear in England clerical blasts against the luxurious fashions and sexual indulgence of courtiers. The first condemnations of long hair, lavishly cut clothing and pointed shoes amongst Normans come from the time of Rufus. The Conqueror had maintained a conservative line in dress and manners: William de Poitiers spoke for his Norman contemporaries in marvelling at the long-haired and mustachioed English courtiers who arrived back in Normandy with the conquering duke in 1067. The cultural difference is obvious in the design of the Bayeux Tapestry and became legendary. Wace has a little story of English scouts returning to Harold's army in 1066 amazed that the Norman army had apparently more priests than soldiers, never having seen laymen so closely shorn. King Harold – speaking from his international experience – corrected them: 'Normans don't have beards and moustaches as we do!' The Conqueror did not approve of facial hair. An Englishman writing in the next generation in Denmark claims that in 1086 William ordered his English soldiers to shave their beards and dress in the simpler Norman style in order to strengthen the French identity of his army.[3] The Conqueror's sons defied him by adopting fashions calculated to annoy him, if he had ever seen them. In the decades on either side of 1100 English and Norman bishops condemned – in extreme terms – the effeminate hair and dress of courtiers. Anselm of Canterbury in 1102 – after an active eight-year campaign against long hair – took the matter so seriously that he had it proclaimed in the canons of the Council of Westminster that 'men wearing their hair are to have it cut so as to leave part of their ears visible and their eyes not covered'. The same condemnation had been proclaimed in a council at Rouen in 1096, when

Rufus was ruling Normandy. The bishop of Séez in 1106 exploited Henry I's need for church support in Normandy so as to get him to cut his hair short publicly and foreswear the dissolute lifestyle of the day.

The culture of the generation of the Conqueror's sons provoked other luxuriances than in hair. It had a material reflection in the amply-cut gowns, cloaks and sleeves of the late eleventh century: previously a feminine fashion. Embroidered hats came into vogue, commonly the 'Phrygian' type, long preserved as the ornamental headress of the doge of Venice. The new culture also came out in military fashions. The austere and functional armour of the Conqueror's generation began to be adorned with gold and semi-precious jewels on helmet bands, harness, baldrics and shield bosses. Some remorselessly trendy knights even had their iron helmets hammered into the fashionable Phrygian shape of the hats of their day. In the time of Rufus's brothers, after 1100, magnates began to cover their horses with mail and coloured cloths. They began to distinguish their banners and household knights with dynastic symbols, displayed on the new style of triangular shield which first appeared in the later 1120s. Armour was increased, with mail-leggings generally adopted to cover the legs exposed by the smaller new shield. Bright armorial surcoats were worn by some lords in battle to distinguish them from their household company. Young knights at the end of Henry I's reign tied long, coloured strips of leather to their wrists and to the back of their helmets so that they would whip out in the wind, and flap and crack behind them as they rode along. All these cultural changes and affectations were symptoms of a rich society which had found ways of making social distinctions by material means.

William Rufus was believed by hostile clerical writers to have been right in the centre of the dissolute fashion and lifestyle of his generation. William of Malmesbury preserves a portrait of him as stocky and muscular, direct and aggressive in his dealings with people: 'he feared God but little and man not at all'. His voice was harsh and he found it difficult to string words together, so he often asserted himself incoherently and ferociously. In small gatherings of trusted intimates he was somewhat different: facetious and humorous, he was usually open-handed and generous in his treatment of his dependents. With his pot belly and unprepossessing apoplectic face, Rufus looked less than elegant in the flowing robes which he affected, and in his flowing hair, parted severely down the middle. But his clerical critics had more serious offences with which to tax him than bad taste. His court openly sheltered sodomites, they said. There may be an implication that the king himself shared their sexual tastes, although it is sexual debauchery in general for which he was condemned. But the fact that he did not follow his brothers in taking on long-term female sexual partners in his youth or while he was king needs some consideration.

The point that Rufus did not make a formal marriage is neither here nor there: his brother Robert did not marry till he was approaching fifty, after thirteen years as duke. Unlike his brothers, William Rufus had – or acknowledged – no children by concubines before marriage, and yet was still considered dissolute by his critics. Orderic Vitalis is quite explicit in his allegations that homosexual liaisons took place in the rooms of Rufus's palaces, where no lamps burned at night. The choices seem to be that Rufus was either homosexual, bisexual or sterile.[4] He was very close to certain of his courtiers, not least to Robert fitz Hamo, to whom he made the extraordinary gift of the English lands of Queen Mathilda, his mother. But the gift may have been made in 1088 simply to insult the king's brother, Count Henry, who had petitioned for them, rather than because fitz Hamo was his male lover. Fitz Hamo and the king's other close friends were all – or would soon be – married men with children. William Rufus's possible homosexuality will always be a matter of speculation and cannot be resolved, but certainly there is a better case to be made for it than for that of Richard the Lionheart.

Like Duke William of Aquitaine, William Rufus is one of those medieval characters of whom writers preserved funny and risqué stories. The Benedictine historian, William of Malmesbury, was only too happy to retell such stories about both rulers.[5] He had a fascination with the alternative culture of the camp which masqueraded as moral disapproval. Nor could he resist the temptation to shock. The most shocking thing to be said about Rufus was his willingness to trifle with the truths of his faith. He was said to have set up a debate between the scholars of the London Jewry and his bishops, and joked that if the Jews had the better of the argument he would convert. He was also said to have taken money from senior Jews of the community at Rouen to prevail on Jewish converts to return to their faith. Apart from Rufus's love of loose language and money, none of these stories is likely to have been true. Malmesbury derived them from the malicious work of Eadmer,[6] the English secretary of Archbishop Anselm, who had every reason to blacken the king as Anselm's enemy. But Malmesbury was not himself fully convinced of the wickedness of William Rufus, and has much more to say on the magnanimity and generosity of the king. He was willing to pay him the lettered compliment of possessing the soul and talents of Julius Caesar. It is this generosity and valour that later non-monastic writers, like Wace of Bayeux and Geoffrey Gaimar,[7] also highlight. There certainly are grounds for moral disapproval of William Rufus, although they have nothing to do with his sexual behaviour and inappropriate sense of humour. Reasons to be wary of Rufus are hinted at in clerical condemnation of his wild and unconstrained language. He was a king who could lose control of himself, which was contrary to the behaviour expected of him and disturbing to the realm he ruled. He was also possessed by a paranoia that could trigger extreme and brutal behaviour, as we will see below.

Dominating Normandy

Rufus's ambitions were soon fixed on Normandy. He saw no reason why his elder brother should be left in peace in his possession of the duchy, and he cannot be blamed for that. Even though Duke Robert was anything but energetic, he had still managed to demonstrate to his brother the central dynastic problem after 1087. While you could separate the realms of England and Normandy under different rulers, the Conqueror had created a group of influential 'super-magnates' (as they have been called) whose interests straddled the Channel. Such men would not leave well alone. It was to their advantage that England and Normandy should be welded together again, under the weakest and least burdensome ruler. These men had nearly toppled Rufus in 1088, and would try to do so again in 1095. For the sake of self-preservation, William Rufus had to reconstitute his father's realm. It is perhaps to Rufus's credit — and some evidence of his political subtlety — that he chose to insinuate himself into Normandy by stratagem rather than attempt to seize it by war.

It was probably in the aftermath of the death of Archbishop Lanfranc in May 1089 that William Rufus began to piece together a practical strategy for dealing with Duke Robert. In the summer of 1088 he had apparently toyed with the idea of employing Count Henry, their younger brother, as an agent. He also recruited into his camp the young Robert de Bellême, the talented and ferocious son of Earl Roger de Montgomery. Henry had crossed to England to meet him after the defeat of Bishop Odo, and the king dangled the prospect of giving him their mother's extensive west country lands in return for his cooperation. But when Henry and Robert de Bellême went back to Normandy and were arrested at the instigation of Bishop Odo that scheme was shelved, and another use was found for the late Queen Mathilda's dowry. In England, in the meantime, a new star was rising at Rufus's court, a chaplain called Ranulf, the son of a country priest in the diocese of Bayeux who had been around the court in a lowly capacity since the early 1080s. He entered court circles as a clerk of Maurice, the royal chancellor, to whom he became deputy as keeper of the royal seal. It would have been at this time that he had attracted the notice of William Rufus through his liveliness, his ready wit and the blatant secularity of his ambition. It was Ranulf (called 'Flambard' or the 'Torch' because of his irrepressible and incandescent personality) who was to provide him with the means to achieve his Norman ambitions: money, and lots of it.

As early as 1090 Flambard was at his devious and inexhaustible work in the royal treasury, searching out obligations and dues and harassing landowners to meet new tax targets. Churches came in for his particular attention. Whenever senior posts in abbeys and dioceses fell vacant, he installed agents on commission and siphoned off the surplus wealth into his master's coffers, which were soon brimming over with cash. The cash streamed into the purses of anyone willing to further Rufus's interests in Normandy. At the end of 1090 English money had already created a party supporting Rufus in the city of Rouen, and it took to the streets against its duke. The urban rebels were sternly repressed by Count Henry, who had come to understand that he was not included on the king's list of Norman friends, and so had to fight Rufus wherever he could. Rufus's first converts amongst the magnates were in upper Normandy where the count of Aumale and the cross-border lords of Gournay and St-Valéry formed the nucleus of a dangerous party, soon joined by the count of Eu. The counts of Aumale and Eu were close cousins to the royal family, and their support was more useful to the king than just in military terms: they represented dynastic sanction. In February 1091 Rufus was confident enough to move his court from England to the port of Eu, on the border of Normandy and Ponthieu. The pro-Rufus party extended itself further as more subsidies – and a weather eye to their future security – brought the lord of Mortemer and Longueville into the king's camp. The ducal centre of Fécamp was surrendered to the king by the new count of Mortain, William son of Robert.

Duke Robert was in no situation to oppose his brother, despite the attempted intervention of King Philip of France. The two met at Rouen where Rufus spelled out his terms. The party of upper Norman magnates which had defected to the king was to be from now on regarded as a group of Rufus's dependents, not the duke's. Fécamp and Cherbourg were to be surrendered as pledges to Rufus, and formed useful ports of access for him in future. The king settled down to live in royal state in the heart of his brother's realm until the summer. In the interests of Earl Hugh of Chester, the king swept Duke Robert into a joint campaign against their brother Henry, and dispossessed him of the Cotentin and Avranchin, sending him into exile in France. William Rufus left Normandy in August 1091, bringing back Robert Curthose with him. He had accomplished many of his targets. He had erected a powerful Norman party, dedicated to his interests, and he had made his elder brother look like a marginal and powerless figure. In forcing Robert to sit with him in his court – notably at an assize at Caen in July intended to establish the customs of Normandy under their father – Rufus had asserted himself as joint-ruler of the duchy. The assize pointedly referred not to the rights of the 'duke' of Normandy, but to those of its 'lord'. William Rufus clearly did not want his rights over his part of Normandy compromised simply because he was not its duke.

Asserting Kingship in Britain

Once in England, the king and the duke marched north to confront King Malcolm of Scotland, who had spent the early summer plundering the north of England. Malcolm was protesting that Rufus had withheld from him the northern estates conceded to him by the Conqueror. The brothers organised what was to be a spectacular combined-operations force of cavalry and sea-borne infantry to penetrate Lothian and devastate the coastal, flatter and more valuable parts of Malcolm's kingdom. Unfortunately, in the last week of September, a sudden easterly squall sank most of the fleet on the rocks of Coquet Island off the coast of Northumberland, and severe weather inland played havoc with the cavalry columns. In the end, Rufus was forced to negotiate. Duke Robert took the lead, using his exiled friend Edgar atheling as an intermediary at the Scottish court, and in October Malcolm was restored to his property, in return for a formal act of submission to Rufus. Robert got no credit for this act of kindness and fraternal support. In the end, he left England empty-handed – along with Edgar – on 23 December 1091. The 'joint government' suggested by Rufus seems only to have been intended to be effective in Normandy. Rufus spent much of the next year strengthening the fabric of English lordship in the north. He took and refortified Carlisle, and expelled the Anglo-Scottish governor of Cumbria. He established new castle-based lordships in Cumbria and across the Pennines. He even attempted some ethnic adjustment in the north by colonising the Carlisle area with southern English peasants, who were more likely to be loyal than the indigenous British-Scandinavian population. It was a tactic that he would also encourage in south Wales over the next few years.

In 1092–93 William Rufus's priorities shifted to the fringes of his kingdom in Britain, to Northumbria and the Welsh March. Why he abandoned his concern with Normandy at this point is not entirely clear, unless it was that he had been happy with what he had managed to achieve in 1091, and saw the power of Malcolm III of Scotland and the Welsh kings Rhys ap Tewdwr of Deheubarth and Cadwgan ap Bleddyn of Powys as having grown too intrusive to overlook. It is revealing of William Rufus's attitude to England that he had such a concern with its frontiers, taking up where Harold of Wessex had left off nearly thirty years before. It was not something that had much bothered his father. At the beginning of March 1093, Rufus was at the manor of Alveston in Gloucestershire, clearly en route to the Bristol Channel crossing into south Wales. He was mobilising an army to extend Anglo-Norman lordship along the coastal plains of Gwent and Glamorgan. This was to be carried out under the command of his friend, Robert fitz Hamo, lord of Gloucester and Bristol. But in the event, Rufus himself was put out of combat by the onset of a sudden, painful and very severe illness. His household rushed their ailing king up the Severn to Gloucester, and summoned the doctors and clergy, each to offer what support they could to a man who was apparently dying.

The severe illness of 1093 had little permanent effect of William Rufus in terms of the moral amendment hoped for by his bishops, but it was important for the future of the English Church and its relationship with the monarchy. At that time Abbot Anselm of Bec was in England. Anselm was already an ecclesiastical celebrity. A man of great sanctity, theological originality and fearless determination, he had assumed control of the great Benedictine house of Bec-Hellouin in 1078 after the death of its founding abbot, Herluin. He had little affection for William Rufus, but circumstances had brought him into contact with the king's inner circle. In 1090 he had confronted and faced down the king's friend, Robert of Meulan, over his claims to rights over Bec as lord of neighbouring Brionne. Late in 1092, he arrived in England partly at the entreaty of another of the king's friends, the earl of Chester, to found a monastery in his comital city. He had come reluctantly, forced to cross the Channel to set the abbey's English affairs in order by a unanimous resolution of his monastic chapter. When the king fell ill Anselm was travelling in the neighbourhood of the court in the Severn valley, apparently marking time till he could arrange an interview with Rufus over the business of Bec. The king's envoys found him somewhere in Gloucestershire or Wiltshire, and bundled him off to Gloucester to administer the last rites – as a suitably saintly and authoritative figure – to a less than pious king.

Anselm came to the king's bedside on 6 March 1093 promptly and with quiet authority. The royal chaplains had prepared their lord to make the necessary confession which would precede absolution, and even the bishops present willingly made way for the great and famous abbot to administer the rite. Anselm naturally insisted that the king must undertake to make amends for his misdeeds, and Rufus promised much the same amends as his father had done: he ordered writs to be sealed releasing political prisoners, forgave debts and pardoned all his enemies. He also promised that, should he recover, he would much improve his rule of his realm. The clergy and nobles in the crowded bedchamber were much impressed at the king's resolution to make a good end. Pious ejaculations and wholesome suggestions flew in on him from all sides, not least that he should appoint a new archbishop for Canterbury, vacant since the death of Lanfranc, Anselm's old master, in 1089. And the king promptly appointed Anselm, much to the abbot's horror.

Eadmer's description of the turbulent scenes in the crowded and darkened royal bedchamber is vivid. Anselm was rigid with shock while the bishops present were in transports of subdued delight. He was so struck with the stress of the moment that he burst a blood vessel in his nose. When they finally understood that Anselm was refusing the nomination, the bishops knelt before him in entreaty at the king's suggestion. He knelt too in prayer, to deflect the symbolic assent of the Church to his promotion. But he was in the grip of a particularly devious king, who – even though weak and sick – knew how to get what he wanted. Since he wanted to live, and had convinced himself that he was damned to aeons of purgatorial torment if he did not appoint a worthy primate for the English Church, Rufus exploited the anxiety of his bishops that Canterbury should be occupied by a figure of international authority and repute. He got them to implore Anselm, to try to force a pastoral staff into his clenched hand, and finally to manhandle him to the nearby abbey and consecrate him while the archbishop-elect himself shouted: 'It is of no effect! No effect!' (indeed he had to go to church again to be properly consecrated in December). When he returned to the king's bedside, Anselm assured him that he would recover and that, when he did, he had better undo what he had just done.

Anselm had good reason to object, although in March 1093 his objection was to the administrative burdens which would take him from his scholarship. He would have objected even more had he realised that the king had in his devious way succeeded in compromising him. Anselm some years later subscribed to the programme of the late Pope Gregory VII: that the powers of Church and the world be separate, and that the Church should rule its own affairs. One of the things that Gregorians objected to was the investiture of bishops and abbots with the symbols of their office by princes, a practice outlawed by Rome since 1078.[8] Rufus had arranged that this very thing be done to Anselm all unwilling, and followed it up by writing the necessary letters to secure his release from his abbacy and from his obedience to the duke of Normandy. Rufus also appointed his friend Bishop Gundulf of Rochester – a former colleague of Anselm's at Bec, who had been minding the diocese of Canterbury – to supervise the new archbishop's household and daily routine. There was to be no escape for Anselm, but it seems that by August 1093 he had reconciled himself to his new condition. He wrote to his restive chapter at Bec telling them that they had to let him go and elect a new abbot.

The king of course recovered, and as soon as he was in good health he revoked many of the charitable acts of his supposed deathbed. When advised by Bishop Gundulf to reflect on his future life after his escape, the king is supposed to have scoffed: 'By the Holy Face of Lucca you may be sure, bishop, that God will never find me become good in return for the evil he has done me.'[9] We hear in this comment a genuine echo of the pragmatic culture of hall and camp: disinterested moral introspection was for monks and priests, soldiers were loyal only to those who were loyal to them. Holy names were for taking in vain. Rufus immediately set about reclaiming what he could from his generosity when he appointed a new archbishop, by setting Ranulf Flambard in September 1093 to open up expensive lawsuits against Anselm. In the meantime, the situation on the Marches of England improved dramatically in his favour. By the end of 1093 large new areas of Wales were subjected to Anglo-Norman power and Malcolm III had fallen to the sword of Earl Robert of Northumbria in a catastrophic Scottish defeat on the River Alne. Whatever the discontent of his subjects, King William Rufus could reasonably claim to have reclaimed much of the lost authority of the king of England over his wider tributary realm in Britain.

Conspiracy and Crusade

William Rufus was ready now to return to the subject of Normandy. He had parted from his brother on bad terms in 1091, and Norman envoys reached him at his Christmas court at Gloucester in 1093 informing him that Duke Robert had renounced their agreement. Count William of Eu, his cousin, also came to England at that time to confirm the arrangement that Rufus had entered into with his father in 1090, and perhaps also to update the king on Norman affairs. In February 1094 Rufus crossed once again to Normandy seeking a meeting to re-establish his dominance over Duke Robert's council. Rufus met his brother the duke near Rouen, but found him unforthcoming. He also discovered that the neutral guarantors of their 1091 agreement took Robert's part, and laid the blame for the failure wholly on Rufus's shoulders. As a result the king dropped diplomacy, rallied his party and took the castle of Bures from the duke's son-in-law, Count Elias of Arques, as a pragmatic warning to his brother as to where power actually resided in their relationship. Ranulf Flambard sent huge amounts of provisions and cash from England to support his master; necessarily so, because King Philip of France again took the field to assist Duke Robert, although he did not attempt to confront Rufus directly. Philip joined with Duke Robert in a menacing march on Eu during the summer of 1094, but when the time came to commit himself to military action, he found excuses to return to Paris. Rufus stayed put in upper Normandy until the end of the year, secure in the region but perhaps a little unsure of what to do next. Unexpectedly, he found that his brother's fortunes were on the rise. A measure of his bafflement may be that he sent messages to his youngest brother, Henry, then sheltering in Domfront, to join his party. He needed Henry's family support and perhaps also his cunning to pursue his Norman objective; Count Henry was in fact named as Rufus's Norman lieutenant in February 1095, and Henry's rightful possession of the Cotentin was recognised.

On 29 December 1094, Rufus returned to England. There were troubles in the Church, where Archbishop Anselm was agitating for the king to recognise Urban II as pope rather than his rival, Clement III. There had been more serious troubles in Wales after the previous year's campaigns, and it was necessary for Rufus to reassert his military power within the March, which he did early in 1095 in a campaign which was set back by the weather. It was at this point that – most unexpectedly – conspiracy once again appeared amongst the Anglo-Norman aristocracy. The principal conspirators are named in the sources as Earl Robert de Mowbray of Northumbria, a rebel of 1088, and Count William of Eu, who, before he succeeded his father in 1094 had been lord of Chepstow in the Welsh March. Associated with them in the plot were Eudes of Champagne, lord of Holderness, Roger de Lacy of Weobley and Philip de Montgomery. The alleged plan of these men was to murder Rufus and set up as king in his place Count Stephen of Aumale, a nephew of the Conqueror. No source suggests that Count Stephen knew of the plot, but he may well have been nominated by his father, Eudes of Champagne. Unlike the conspiracy of 1088, the conspiracy of 1095 was not devised in the interests of Duke Robert. The only convincing explanation of the conspiracy is given by Robert de Torigny,[10] who says that Earl Robert had a grievance against King William over lands and castles he claimed to be under his authority as earl of Northumbria, and which he had been denied. The Anglo-Saxon chronicle tells us that Earl Robert was already at odds with Rufus at Whitsun (13 May 1095), when he refused to come to court since the king would give him no assurance of safe conduct. The fact that northern and marcher lords were prominent in the conspiracy perhaps confirms that Earl Robert was at the centre of it all: these were men who would sympathise with his grievance against royal high-handedness. For the king's part, the enormous wealth and renowned savagery and aggression of Earl Robert would have been enough to bring him under suspicion.

Rufus took the plot very seriously. Agents had passed information to him about the conspiracy, and indeed contemporary sources tell us that informers were given an all-too-ready hearing by the alarmed king. At the end of May he marched an army rapidly north and took Earl Robert by surprise, trapping his men in various castles in Northumberland. After a close two-month blockade, the king ordered the earl's principal castle of Newcastle to be stormed. Earl Robert meanwhile was besieged further north in his powerful fortress of Bamburgh, which the king did not attempt to attack directly but blockaded with siege works. Probably at some time in August, the earl attempted a break out in the king's absence in the direction of Newcastle, which he hoped to recapture. But he underestimated the strength of the besieging army. He narrowly escaped capture and was pursued as far as Tynemouth priory, which he garrisoned and held desperately for a week, until wounds and lack of men allowed the royalist troops to force an entry. They caught the cornered earl in the priory church and dragged him out. He was sent south to the dungeon of Windsor castle to await the king's justice.

Something of a witch-hunt followed the defeat of Earl Robert, in which a variety of aristocratic scores were paid off. The king was prepared to be brutal. He would have had Robert blinded after his capture had his wife and nephew not surrendered Bamburgh. This nephew, Morel, then turned informer and gave the king the names of those who had sympathised with the revolt; Orderic says that Gilbert de Clare was another plotter who turned on his co-conspirators. Many barons had already been seized, the most significant being Eudes of Champagne. The Anglo-French barons, William of Eu and Ernulf de Hesdin (both formerly powerful in Gloucestershire and the March), were charged at court in the autumn of 1095 with treason and were obliged to defend themselves in a duel. Orderic later tells us that William of Eu's accuser was his own brother-in-law, the earl of Chester, who hated William because he had flaunted his extramarital affairs and completely ignored his sister. The royal officer Geoffrey Baynard, per-haps another conspirator who saved himself by shopping others, was set to fight Count William of Eu, and defeated him in a duel in January 1096 at Salisbury. Rufus ordered his cousin to be blinded and castrated and the count died soon after his mutilation. The count's steward and kinsman, William d'Audrey, was executed by hanging at the same time on the word of an informer. Ernulf de Hesdin's champion was able to defeat his lord's accuser, but Ernulf quit England in disgust at the barbaric and tyrannical proceedings he had witnessed, and joined the Crusade to witness a different sort of barbarism. Earl Robert and Count Eudes were dispossessed of their lands and spent the rest of their lives in prison. Earl Robert survived as a prisoner until around 1125, according to Orderic: he was not released by King Henry on his accession in 1100. The rest of the alleged conspirators were forced to clear themselves by the payment of huge fines.

The year 1095 shows William Rufus in a bad light. The querulous and vengeful part of his nature has been seen earlier in his shabby treatment of his brother Henry in 1087–88 and again in 1091. His treatment of Edgar atheling is also in marked contrast to the more tolerant and friendly way the English prince was tolerated and supported by Robert Curthose and Henry I. The way Rufus terrorised his aristocracy in the summer and autumn of 1095 is a different order of reaction to that of his father over a similar conspiracy twenty years before. His father's strategy had been to identify the principal conspirator and deal with him with severity, but to allow the rest of the main rebels to get off with banishment and confiscation. Rufus was not so moderate and considered. His personal insecurity was the trigger for widespread and vicious terror at court, where he was willing to suspect almost anyone. The trend amongst historians lately has been to rehabilitate Rufus from what is seen as the unreasonable strictures on him by clerical writers annoyed at his unrepentant secularity. He is seen as a secular, chivalrous hero at odds with a narrow-minded Church establishment. What may have been forgotten is that his critics may have had other reasons to attack his moral reputation than those which they openly gave. Rufus had a dark and dangerous side, and it is clear that his clergy were intimidated by him: it was not for nothing that Anselm compared him famously to a rampaging bull. The abbess of Romsey, talking of her feelings about him in 1093, said she feared to meet Rufus, 'who was a young king and untamed and wanted to do immediately whatever came into his head'.[11] The merciless and harrowing scene as William d'Audrey was dragged off protesting his innocence through shocked courtiers to execution was the principal memory of most people of Rufus's court – not its gaiety and luxury. When William of Malmesbury talked of Rufus's resemblance to a Roman emperor, Nero might have been a better comparison than Augustus.

It was perhaps as well that other developments in 1095 overshadowed the dark and tyrannical deeds done at Rufus's court. The West was being mobilised to ride to the aid of the Eastern emperor in his troubles with the Turks, and in November 1095 it was learned that one of the foremost of the campaign's leaders was to be Duke Robert of Normandy. Robert needed a huge amount of money to finance his travels and his military retinue, and the willing supplier of his needs was William Rufus. The cost for the king was to be £6666 13s. 4d. and the security he was offered and agreed in April 1096 was the duchy of Normandy itself until the duke should return, and its succession if he failed to come back. In the grim and fearful mood following the suppression of the Mowbray rebellion, bishops, abbots and nobility dug deep without protest to raise this great sum, passing on the cost to their dependants and peasants, themselves labouring under the difficulties of a bad harvest and fears of famine. In September 1096, the king crossed to Normandy with the barrels of silver pennies that contained the mortgage payment, and formally took control of the duchy from his brother, who left for the south of France and – as it turned out – eternal fame and glory. King and duke seem to have had an amicable meeting before they separated:

Duke Robert left his natural son Richard to his brother to take care of in his absence.

Seated in Rouen in state in September 1096, William Rufus found himself possessed of his father's reunited realm. He stayed in the duchy until the beginning of April 1097, when he returned to England to lead another campaign against the Welsh. He was mostly to be found in Normandy for the remainder of his reign. Chronicles give little detail as to what he did in the duchy. The Norman nobility gave him little trouble, for in uniting kingdom and duchy he had removed a major source of internal problems. Most of the leaders of the aristocracy were already in his pocket before 1096 – notably the dynamic warriors Robert of Meulan and Robert de Bellême – and dangerous dissidents like Odo of Bayeux had left with the duke for Constantinople. Orderic tells us that Rufus occupied himself in reclaiming lands, rights and churches his brother had alienated. The king also allowed his officers to adopt the same harsh measures in pursuit of his advantage as they used in England. The king's main task was to revive his father's strategies for bolstering the frontiers of Normandy. This meant pursuing the Norman claim to control the whole Vexin, and labouring to regain control of Maine, which his brother had been unable to get back from the intruding Angevins and rebel Manceaux. In the case of the Vexin, liberal amounts of English money and fierce raiding convinced many of the local barons to favour Rufus over the now ageing and unpopular King Philip of France. Norman armies raided freely and almost unopposed in 1097 and 1098 into the regions of Paris and the forest of Rambouillet, much to Philip's humiliation.

Rufus had less success in regaining influence in Maine. He was vigorously opposed by many of the Manceaux barons and their lord, Count Elias, none of whom were open to bribery. A major campaign, masterminded by Robert de Bellême, was mounted against Maine early in 1098, which succeeded in capturing Count Elias, who was put in prison at Bayeux. Moving an enormous host to take possession of Le Mans, Rufus was disconcerted to find that Fulk of Anjou had got there before him, with the connivance of the citizens, who wanted no Norman lord. The Angevin army was able to thwart Rufus's attempt to take Le Mans, and the king had no choice but to withdraw, laying waste the county as he went. In the end Count Fulk of Anjou ironed out a deal in which Elias of Maine was released and restored to his castles, but Rufus was to be conceded Le Mans and the castles built in Maine by his father: a deal which the Norman chroniclers proclaimed to be a conquest of the county. Maine did not stay settled, and when Rufus returned to England at Easter (10 April 1099) Count Elias once again took the field against the occupying Norman forces. He had sufficient success to bring the king back across the Channel to recover Le Mans and contain him. William did contain Elias, although he failed to defeat him, and was able to leave Maine to his lieutenants in July 1099. He was once again back in England by the end of September.

The Sad but Unmysterious Death of William Rufus

Although the king's political fortunes reached ever greater heights in the years after his brother's departure, he was dogged by some sort of nemesis. He had come to the end of the road with Archbishop Anselm by the autumn of 1097, and the archbishop took himself off into voluntary exile at Lyon as a protest against Rufus's failure to honour the Church and respect his position. Rufus is reputed to have been unmoved by the archbishop's protest. Yet at the same time as Anselm quit his realm, the king vigorously and defiantly asserted his worldly dominance by ordering the reconstruction of his royal hall at Westminster on a larger scale than any other known royal or imperial palace in Christendom. Forced labour was levied on the home counties in order to further the great work, and Ranulf Flambard grew ever more oppressive in the exactions imposed to enrich his master. His reward was nomination to the vacant see of Durham in the grand ceremony which inaugurated the new hall of Westminster palace on 29 May 1099. The hall was so vast that it was impossible to find enough tiles to cover the pitched roof in time for the ceremony. Instead, the king's officers plundered London's warehouses to find sufficient bales of scarlet cloth to raise a tent roof over the great space.[12] The ceremony involved a state procession of such grandeur and a banquet so huge that it was still being recalled and marvelled at forty years later. Yet Rufus was not satisfied. When asked if the new hall was too big for him, he is said to have replied that it was not half large enough.

The king was dogged by low spirits and unsettling premonitions. In

Maine in July 1099 he was besieging the castle of Mayet, to punish one of the followers of Count Elias. A stone lobbed from the keep plummeted amongst his party while he was inspecting the defences and dashed out the brains of the knight standing next to him. As howls of laughter and whoops of derision echoed after him from the castle, the shaken king ordered a withdrawal to Le Mans. Like some Roman emperors, he could no longer bear to be reminded of his mortality. He returned to England late in September. By this time news would have been filtering back from the East of the astonishing success of the Latin armies in Syria and Judaea several months before. Rufus must have begun to realise that his brother would soon be returning to reclaim Normandy. The fact that he stayed put in England through the winter, spring and summer of 1100 is a little curious in the circumstances. There is no direct evidence as to what Rufus was planning to do about the duchy, but the fact that he awaited his brother's return on the English side of the Channel tends to indicate that he would not have resisted Robert's reclamation of Normandy. He would have heard by the spring of 1100 that his brother was returning with sufficient treasure from Jerusalem and Apulia to repay the pledge, if it was required of him. It was said that he was gathering a fleet to cross to Normandy at the time of his fatal accident, in time to meet his brother perhaps. His plan in 1100 would doubtless have been no different from his strategy of 1091 and 1094: to insinuate his own power into Normandy by buying the loyalty of the greatest of his brother's subjects. There were rumours that Rufus was looking elsewhere: negotiating a similar deal over the county of Poitou to that he had struck over Normandy. Duke William IX of Aquitaine was planning in 1100 to lead his own army to Palestine, and sought English money by mortgaging Poitou to Rufus.

In the meantime, the king was again distressed by the death of another close to him. He had taken his nephew, Richard, illegitimate son of Duke Robert, into his household when the duke left for the East. The young man was popular and the king had supported him handsomely. But in May 1100, hunting in the New Forest, an arrow shot by one of his own household struck Richard in the chest and killed him on the spot. Orderic's account of the incident dwells on the king's rage at the accidental death. It seems that the whole world was conspiring to throw omens at Rufus. At the end of July, the county of Berkshire was astonished when a spring at the village of Hamstead Marshall began bubbling up what appeared to be blood. Since the manor was the possession of a court officer, the news reached the king's ears, and he laughed at what others considered an omen. In the aftermath of his death, many people recalled dreams or uncanny messages which foretold the event. Abbot Serlo of Gloucester and Robert fitz Hamo are both said to have confronted the king with the details of ominous dreams that had been told them. But still he laughed them off.

His end was quick, if not apparently unexpected. On the morning of 2 August 1100 Rufus was in a lodge in the New Forest, perhaps Brockenhurst, and spent the morning planning a deer hunt. The household that morning contained several great nobles: the count of Meulan, William de Breteuil and Count Henry, but it was not otherwise large. The nobles divided into parties and took up stations in various parts of the wood after lunch, waiting for the beaters to drive the deer past them. The king kept a new friend by him, a French nobleman called Walter Tirel, a native of the French Vexin with family connections in Normandy and England. Tirel seems to have been one of those French border magnates who had abandoned King Philip for Rufus during the campaign of 1098. Tirel and the king awaited the running of the deer together, bows drawn, and as one raced between them Tirel incautiously let loose with his bow before checking where the king was. The arrow grazed the back of the beast and buried itself in the king's chest. Rufus stood literally transfixed for a moment. Clutching the arrow in momentary shock he tried to pull it out, but the shaft broke and, as he fell to his knees and slumped on to his face, the arrow was punched deeper in. The king was already senseless when his servants reached him and died soon after without a word. As shouts rang out through the woods and courtiers ran up, Tirel realised his danger, found a horse and rode for his life. He made it to the coast and out of the realm before any pursuit could be organised. The count of Meulan and Count Henry in the meantime were engaged in a hasty conference over the royal corpse. The subject of their conversation had nothing to do with the pursuit of Walter Tirel; it was about making Count Henry king as quickly as possible.

Of course, the sudden and unexpected death of a king caused a good deal of comment. In a society where the divine will was being unfolded in every event, the king's death had to be accounted for: was it by the hand of God or of man that the king fell? In 1100 there were two choices. If Rufus was not a good man, his sudden and unconfessed end was a demonstration of God's disapproval of his fornication, his contempt for the episcopate, or even for the sins of his father and himself in depopulating the New Forest and levelling its churches. If he had been a good man it would have been just as easy to account for his sudden end: he had been murdered by the malice of wicked men who had not stopped short of slaying the Lord's anointed. In 1100 and in the years following, no one suggested that Rufus had been assassinated, which indicates that he was not generally regarded as a good man.

Suggestions that Rufus had been killed in furtherance of factional fights in his realm do not occur till 1895. The genealogist John Horace Round pointed out a fact he considered significant: that Walter Tirel had married into the Clare family before 1086. Members of the Clare family were strong supporters of Henry I after 1100 and did very well out of the connection, well enough to suggest that they might have accelerated William Rufus's departure into eternity: 'I do not say,' said Round, 'that all this points to some secret conspiracy, to which Henry was privy', but he did not need to say it, for the insinuation was enough.[13] Successive generations of twentieth-century historians were quite happy to accept the insinuation as a proven case, and so the murder of William Rufus became common historical currency until 1973, when Warren Hollister demolished Round's insinuations and for good measure pointed out that, for Henry, his brother's death came at the worst possible time.[14] The fact was that hunting could be dangerous, not least hunting with crossbows, and William Rufus was the third casualty of such an accident within his dynasty. The fact that Walter Tirel immediately fled abroad without being pursued proves only that he was prudent and that there was no one at the time with a will to apprehend him. The assertion by some writers that Count Henry left his brother's body dead and unregarded is simply untrue; he attended the funeral at Winchester, when it would have been more pragmatic for him to ride for London at once. If the argument *cui bono* is employed, one can only reply to it that, by that logic, John F. Kennedy must have been assassinated by a cabal of conspiracy theorists. William Rufus died because he played with sharp weapons.

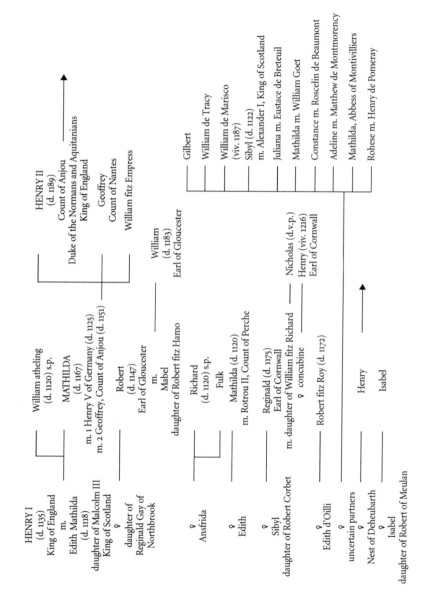

Table 4. Descendants of Henry I of England.

6

Henry I

With Henry I we reach the Norman ruler with whom modern historians have had the most sympathy. Historians brought up in the tradition of constitutional history as it was taught in twentieth-century Oxbridge and in red-brick lecture rooms were fond of him, as to them he was the first recognisable administrator king: the architect of the exchequer and the central judiciary; the king whose name is first attached to a government financial account. Henry was a king who did business. The more heterodox historians of the end of the century liked him because of the complexity of his character: his enormous sexual appetite; his lapses into savagery and morbid mood swings; his remarkable intellect and strategic vision of his own age. Henry was a king who clearly belonged on the analyst's couch. Besides this, Henry's life and works have great appeal to historians simply because of the great amount we know about him: sources become abundant during his life and reign. It was in his reign that we are told that governmental pressure first began to force written records on a medieval society formerly reliant on memory. Some 400 written acts survive of those issued in his father's name as king; but around 2000 royal acts of King Henry survive. Some of the finest historical writers of the middle ages were active in his lifetime: Eadmer, William of Malmesbury, Henry of Huntingdon and Orderic Vitalis to name but the most famous. We know more about Henry as king than any other ruler of his generation, and far more about him than any of his predecessors.

The Outsider

Henry seems a different sort of ruler from his elder brothers and his father. This does not mean that he exercised his kingship in any particularly new way; it may just be the result of his being brought up as a king's son with no particular expectation of ever being a king. The crown descended on his head when he was past thirty years of age, when he had already experienced a long adult life full of insecurity, conspiracy and disappointment. This left its mark: as king he was insecure, suspicious and restless, morbidly protective of his personal dignity. We are given some glimpses of his early youth and the way it affected him later. Even as a child, he knew the value of alliances at court, especially as we know that he was frequently bullied and harassed by his elder brothers to the point of tears. In the incident at Laigle in 1077, the boy Henry was allied with his brother William Rufus against their eldest sibling, Robert Curthose. Like William Rufus, Henry kept in his father's good graces, knowing that his future would be very uncertain when it was at his brothers' disposal. These experiences, and probably many more like them, caused Henry to develop his capacity to manage relationships and situations by staged, public displays of affection. He could be immensely charming – as when he ravished the monks of St-Evroult on his state visit to the abbey in 1113 – but always to a purpose, for he seems soon to have recognised the survival value of attaching people and engaging affections.

As a boy, Henry spent a lot of his time following his father's court. In 1081, for instance, he was with his father at London in February and in May at Winchester. He followed his father back to Normandy and returned with him to England again at the end of 1082.[1] He must also have had a liberal amount of time left to his own devices, especially after his mother's death in 1083, when he was already being credited with the title of 'Count Henry'. We know of an independent visit he made to Oxfordshire in 1084, escorted by Bishop Osmund of Salisbury and Giles Crispin, lord of Wallingford, when he spent Easter (31 March) at Abingdon abbey and stayed at Oxford castle. It was on this visit, or another like it, that he began as a teenager a relationship with an Englishwoman, a daughter of a north Oxfordshire landed family called Gayt, which seems to have had a profound effect on him on several levels.

Henry's sexual life to begin with was not unlike that of his grandfather, Duke Robert I, in that he found a sexual partner from a relatively humble sphere early on, and was a father long before he succeeded to his throne. The difference was that by the end of the eleventh century no child of such a union could be counted in the succession to the kingdom and duchy, and in Henry's case he freely chose to take as concubine a woman of the conquered English. A marginal figure at court, he chose to associate with the marginalised nobility of England. In the southern midlands of England, the young Henry built up his own surrogate (and probably bilingual) family, perhaps settling them at the then minor royal hall of Woodstock. Before 1090, when he would have been only just over twenty, he had a son whom he called Robert, presumably recalling his ducal forbears. His first concubine perhaps died young. Intriguingly, he soon formed a relationship with another young Englishwoman, called Ansfrida, a widow with a small son deprived of their lands by royal dispossession on her husband's death in gaol. She too was from the upper Thames valley region, and when she sought out the young Count Henry to intercede with his brother, they became bed partners and she bore him a second son, Richard. The circumstances seem to fit the later 1090s, after Henry had entered the favour of his brother, King William Rufus. Another early known liaison lasted a number of years. This was with yet another Englishwoman residing in Oxfordshire, Edith, the noble wife of the castellan of Oxford, with whom he had a daughter, Mathilda, and a second son called Robert. By the end of Rufus's reign Count Henry had already fathered several Anglo-Norman children, and formed a ménage in the upper Thames valley, which was perhaps the nearest place to home that he could have named.[2] Significantly for the future, when he chose the site of his expensive Cluniac[3] mausoleum in the 1120s, he fixed on a place in that very area: Reading, on the Thames across from Oxfordshire. We know from his adult treatment of his children – as well as their own testimony – that Henry was a fond and concerned father, and had his eldest son Robert assiduously educated in Latin and elements of philosophy, history and theology in the same way that he himself had been.

Henry was a young man whom women found difficult to resist; perhaps they found him an intriguing mixture of the domineering, the charming and the vulnerable. For all the number of his liaisons, there is no hint that Henry ever forced himself on his sexual partners or threw them carelessly off when he had used them. Whatever the bishops might have said, his personal morality within relationships was notably consistent, if not monogamous. The fact that by 1100 he had already had three notorious affairs with women of English blood explains well enough why, when he married an Anglo-Scottish princess, Edith (or Mathilda, as she was renamed at court), the royal couple were surreptitiously mocked by French courtiers as 'Godric and Godgifu'. Henry's Anglophilia was by then well-known amongst his contemporaries; and, although the French nobility may have looked askance, he traded on it. He and Queen Mathilda named and continued to call their only daughter Æthelic, although she was baptised with the name Mathilda, the name she used for court purposes. Their son William was credited with the English title of 'atheling', like his great-uncle Edgar. The support of the great number of surviving moderately-landed English families was crucial to Henry's taking of the throne in 1100 and his conquest of Normandy in 1106. He was happy to identify with the remnants of the house of Wessex: after 1106 he allowed back to England his ageing cousin, his wife's uncle, Edgar atheling, and supported him in a comfortable rural retirement that lasted at least two decades; and in years to come he promoted his Anglo-Scottish brother-in-law, David of Huntingdon, to the apex of the English nobility. Art historians have noticed a strong revival of English motifs in the art of his reign, and the new generation of historians and hagiographers who wrote in his time were obsessed with the political and spiritual past of England. We see the result of all this in the peacefulness of England in his long reign – remarked upon by all contemporary chroniclers. It must have had much to do with his English subjects' identification of their fortunes with Henry's.

For all Count Henry's Anglophilia, he was nonetheless tightly bound, as all his family was, to northern France. It was here that the Anglo-Norman king needed principally to be, to defend his realm from his many dangerous French rivals. Henry was in France on campaign with his father in the Vexin when the Conqueror was seized by his final illness, and he attended him on his deathbed. Henry had no choice: this was a critical moment for his future. He could not expect succession to one of the components of the Anglo-Norman realm, but he desperately needed some foundation on which to erect the superstructure of a political future. The old king's deathbed extended over six anxious weeks, first in the castle-palace of Rouen, and then in the priory of St-Gervais. A piece of good fortune for Henry was that Robert Curthose was at the time estranged from his father and residing somewhere in France; nor did he seem inclined to return to Rouen while his father was dying. Henry's assiduous attendance on his father secured him a legacy of as much as 5000 pounds in silver in the Conqueror's last will. At his father's insistence, Henry is said to have hastily secured the money from the treasury, had it weighed carefully and confided it to safe custody; it was because he was preoccupied with this that he missed the king's actual death. Henry was not present to prevent the general confusion on 9 September 1087 which left his dead father's body abandoned and plundered, but two contemporary writers confirm that he did have sufficient filial piety to attend the funeral at Caen, from which his elder brothers were absent. It was Henry who used the money in his purse to settle the scandalous claims of Ascelin son of Arthur – which he proclaimed at the graveside in the abbey of St Stephen at Caen – that the Conqueror had stolen from his father the land for the abbey and grave in which he was to lie.

Count Henry's plan in 1087 for his future – which can easily be reconstructed – was to seek a great place at his eldest brother's court in Normandy. It was on the surface a good plan, as he must have been well aware of Duke Robert's pliable and generous disposition, as he would also have been aware of the cleverness and ambition of the new King William Rufus of the English. He could exploit Robert, but the likelihood was that Rufus would exploit him. Henry's mistake in retrospect was in forgetting that he was not the only man who could formulate such a plan: others had made the same assessment of Duke Robert II. His uncle, Bishop Odo of Bayeux, reluctantly released by the Conqueror on his deathbed, promptly took control of Duke Robert's council. Odo and his brother, Robert of Mortain, planned to extend the potential benefits of the rule of Duke Robert by imposing him on England too. The great rebellion in the spring of 1088 failed, as we have seen.[4] Henry was too politic to get involved directly in a fight between his brothers, and instead accepted a commission by Duke Robert to fortify the Breton march, receiving in return for financing this campaign an assignment of the counties of the Avranchin and Cotentin, with control of the cities and bishoprics of Avranches and Coutances and the allegiance of numerous powerful barons. Sources are divided as to whether Duke Robert went so far as to do more than loan this considerable honor to his brother in return for money owed, but the known resistance to him at this time by Bishop Geoffrey of Coutances indicates that some contemporaries thought that Henry held the counties by grant of his brother.

Count Henry had so far done well, but his attempts to play off one brother against the other recoiled on him. He made as much hay as he could while the sun shone. He was at Robert's court through the spring and early summer of 1088, while the duke was preparing an invasion to support Bishop Odo's English insurrection. In the absence of the bishop, Count Henry can be found happily arranging the business of the duchy for his brother and advising him on restitutions to particular monasteries. Henry may even have received the lieutenancy of the Tower of Rouen at this time. Late in the summer of 1088, after he had watched the warfare between his brothers subsiding, he sailed to England to see if he could take advantage of the new king William Rufus, who was now settled on his throne. Henry's aim was to secure a grant of their late mother's dower lands (a very considerable estate, the core of the later earldom of Gloucester) which the Conqueror is said to have assigned him in his will. Since Henry was a man of influence at this point, he found William of a mind to grant his request. After a peaceful stay at his court, Henry returned to Normandy. But he returned to discover that his many rivals in the duchy had been able to make his newly-acquired favour with Rufus look like double-dealing. He had earned the hatred of his uncle, Bishop Odo, who had discovered how Henry had furthered his own interests in Normandy while he had been vainly staking all his English lands on Duke Robert's future.

Count Henry arrived by ship back in Rouen to find the duke's officers waiting on the quay to arrest him. He was taken off to be incarcerated at Rouen for six months, while Bishop Odo did his best to secure his own hold on Normandy. Henry's western Norman appanage must have been taken from him at this time, and on his release in the spring of 1089 he found himself without much choice but to cross back to England. Now a rather desperate and sorry figure, he had to hang around his other brother's court looking for new opportunities to further his fortunes. But he found only vague promises, and discovered that his mother's prized dower lands had in fact been given instead to the king's favourite, Robert fitz Hamo. The grant was likely enough intended as a personal insult to Henry from his triumphant and triumphing brother. Within the year, Henry had given up on Rufus, and was back in Normandy. He was restored to some sort of favour by Duke Robert and enjoyed once again the Cotentin and Avranchin, although the restoration may have been achieved with difficulty and some use of force according to William of Malmesbury. It was during this period that he began grimly consolidating his hold on western Normandy, taking into his retinue a number of local barons and knights who were to serve him long and faithfully: men like Richard de Redvers, Roger de Mandeville, William d'Aubigny, John fitz Waleran, Rhiwallon d'Avranches, Geoffrey de Clinton and Humphrey de Bohun.

Secure and steadily more powerful in the west, Count Henry brooded on the growing influence of his now resented brother, William Rufus, in Normandy and monitored the troubled court of Duke Robert. He had learned the necessity for a serious politician to have a spy network at court. Alerted by his agents, in November 1090 he suddenly appeared at court at Rouen in time to baffle a conspiracy in the city to overturn the duke and declare for Rufus. Hustling his brother to safety across the river, Count Henry rallied the loyalists, cut down the conspirators and drove out Rufus's agents. At the end of a bloody day on the streets of the city, the young count had a chance to demonstrate his classical learning and with a few friends hurled the chief conspirator off the top of the battlements of the riverside ducal castle and into the Seine below, where he drowned. This was the punishment of precipitation, as dealt out by the Romans to traitors off the Tarpeian Rock. The several accounts of the event all dwell on the relish with which the young count made polite and ironic conversation with his terrified victim as he walked him up to the place of execution.

This coup did not in the end do Henry much good. He had moved in the duke's support in order to frustrate Rufus's ambitions to seize the duchy, but he did not find Robert grateful. And as far as Rufus was concerned, Henry had simply demonstrated that he was a dangerous rival to his schemes, and so must be neutralised. In January 1091, King William Rufus arrived in person on the Norman coast at Eu and over-awed his elder brother into conceding him control of most of upper Normandy, where he resided in royal style until August. Count Henry could only expect the worst, and in early spring Rufus and the ever-hapless Duke Robert arrived in the Cotentin, driving Henry back on the

Breton border, where he took his stand at the island-abbey of Mont St-Michel. Later generations remembered the siege as something of a prolonged military fiesta, with daily mounted tournaments on the sands between defenders and besiegers, as the tide went out. Even William Rufus rode into the fray, and Duke Robert contributed to the merriment by sending wine and water across to the island when he heard that Henry's garrison was short of drink. Count Henry was probably not in a festive mood. Grimly surveying the grey seas and his even bleaker prospects, he was blockaded for a fortnight until lack of supplies forced him to negotiate a surrender of all his castles in return for safe conduct out of the duchy. So he departed into exile in France with no more of a household than a knight, a clerk and three servants. He travelled in this humble manner to Paris and the Vexin, where he had a friend in Count Robert of Meulan. Many contemporaries expressed sympathy. A contemporary clerk of Fécamp wrote that Duke Robert and King William 'should have between them promoted and supported him as was proper for a man who was their brother and a king's son, but this they did not do, they strove instead to drive him out of his father's realm!'[5] They were not, however, wholly successful. As the same clerk notes, Henry soon crossed back into the duchy to occupy the border fortress of Domfront, probably in 1092 with the support of a cell of local knights fighting in opposition to Robert de Bellême. There he maintained himself as a continuing irritant to both his brothers, but could not be dislodged.

Count Henry's fortunes did not in fact change much for several years. The circuit of Domfront remained the limit of his terrestrial honor, despite the continuing loyalty to him of a number of barons of the Cotentin peninsula. What did in the end change was his relationship with Rufus, who seemed in fact to relax towards Henry as his ability to interfere with his Norman ambitions was diminished. In 1096, when Rufus had arranged to take charge of Normandy in his brother's absence on Crusade, a reconciliation was staged with Henry, who was invited to join the royal court. Robert de Torigny tells us that King William sealed the new relationship by conceding the Cotentin to Henry and adding to it the Bessin (excluding Bayeux and Caen). For the next few years, Henry was obliged to be the loyal servant of his brother, fighting his battles and propping up his throne. He was not, however, inactive. Henry reactivated an old friendship with the brothers Robert and Henry

de Beaumont, both noblemen of his generation and both close supporters of William Rufus. Robert was count of Meulan and lord of much
of central Normandy; Henry, who was intimate with the king, had
acquired the earldom of Warwick and great estates in England. When,
in August 1100, the fatal bolt pierced William Rufus's chest in the New
Forest, it was with the help of these men, and his old associates from
the Cotentin, that Henry was able to lever himself on to the throne of
England.

Succession and Marriage

The events of 1100 were in many ways a rerun of 1087, with Robert duke
of Normandy – imminently expected in his duchy, but still returning
from the Near East – reappearing in his original role. Henry stood in
for his brother Rufus. In place of Bishop Odo of Bayeux was Bishop
Ranulf Flambard of Durham, who had to provide the strategic vision
and energy that Duke Robert lacked. King William Rufus died in the
afternoon of 2 August 1100, a Thursday. Count Henry was one of a
number of courtiers stationed in various quarters of the wood where
the hunt was being staged. We can imagine how he must have reacted
to the sudden outcry from the neighbouring clearings as the news of
the king's accidental death spread. We can imagine also how he would
have run to inspect the body and verify the fact. He must have taken
immediate charge of the body, as the king's brother, but the fact that
he made no attempt to apprehend the accidental perpetrator of the
death proves not so much his complicity, but that his thoughts were
immediately turned to the awesome opportunity that had descended
upon him without warning.

Henry's first move – maybe decided with his friends in a hasty
conference in the woods over the dead king's body – was to ride to
Winchester and seize the royal treasury. Instructions were left with
servants to follow with the body. Henry revealed a certain amount of
fraternal piety, considering the hurried circumstances, in that he seems
to have insisted that his brother be buried early on the Friday morning
in the cathedral, presumably so that he could hear the mass, witness
the burial and then ride off to London immediately it was over.[6] He
may have reached the city before Saturday morning, and on the Sunday

he was crowned king at Westminster. It was a remarkable feat, assisted by the fact that the court nobility gave him prompt and unanimous support, led by his close friends, the eminent brothers Robert count of Meulan and Earl Henry of Warwick, and the less distinguished brothers Robert and Hamo fitz Hamo. The wonder is how quickly he mobilised the English Church in his support, but we can glimpse something of how he achieved that. Archbishop Anselm of Canterbury was in exile in France, so Henry had to secure consecration as best he could. Anselm's return was deeply desired by the church hierarchy, so Henry had a very useful counter with which to trade. Bishop Maurice of London, the senior bishop of the southern province, was the only prelate available with whom to negotiate. He and Henry quickly agreed a deal that, if the count would repudiate his brother's cynical manipulation of church vacancies and recall Anselm, the bishop would consecrate him king. Irregular though this arrangement was, it was carried out with the help of the bishop of Hereford, on the Sunday morning, and it is clear that Maurice even dared to place a crown on Henry's head. Bishop Maurice had to suffer the wrath of Archbishop Thomas of York, who arrived in haste a few days later from Ripon, claiming that coronation was a rite reserved to him if there was no archbishop of Canterbury available. The new king was worried by this and pleaded the danger of disorder if there had been a delay. Archbishop Thomas – now very old and sick – was finally placated by the privilege of confirming the act by placing the crown on Henry's head at a church council held soon after.

Unlike his father, and his successor Stephen, King Henry showed little inclination to revel in his newly-acquired royalty. It was not in any case his style: he was porphyrogenic; he had been born the son of a king and so royalty had perhaps less mystery for him than for the others. He also had very little time, for he was immersed in the flood of events. His elder brother, Robert, was not yet back in Normandy but was imminently expected. Whatever his opinion of his brother, Henry had to contend with the daunting fact that Duke Robert – whom his brothers must have faintly despised as much as they manipulated him – was now universally hailed as a champion of Christendom, and many said he could have been king of Jerusalem had he wished. This, as much as anything else, obliged Henry to project himself in the summer of 1100 as a friend and protector of the Church. Letters were immediately despatched from the

king, from the 'English Church' (meaning the hierarchy) and from the
'barons of England' (meaning Henry's cronies), begging Anselm to hurry
back to the kingdom. The king's letter begins with an apology for having
organised a coronation without Anselm's presence – and confesses that
it had been done by his suffragans, even though he says he would have
rather been crowned by Anselm than anyone else – but it also declares
firmly that he considered himself king by the election of the Church
and the people of England. Henry ended with friendly advice to the
archbishop to avoid Normandy, and come by way of the county of
Boulogne to Dover, where he would be waiting to receive him. Anselm
eventually arrived back in England on 23 September 1100, but did not
find the king waiting for him as promised; a fact that probably did
not surprise him in the least.

The new king had to charm the people of England too. Just as with
the Church, he had much with which to bargain. On the day of his
coronation Henry and his new council devised and published a state-
ment implicating his late brother as the author of the people's current
problems, and undertaking a programme of reform. He appealed to the
new generation of English-speaking landowners by setting the good
customs of the reign of Edward the Confessor as his benchmark for
civil justice. Henry said he would never extort money in the ruthless
ways his brother had, when estates were inherited or when daughters
were married. To show he was serious, Henry pardoned all debts owed
to his late brother, other than what he had a traditional right to exact.
On the day of his coronation, he gave orders for multiple copies of this
programme to be made, and sent to be read out in all the shire courts
of England, as well as to many of the greater abbeys and churches. There
was to be no mistake that Henry was a new sort of king; and, to show
that he listened to his people, he offered them a living scapegoat to
blame for all the oppressions they had suffered under his dead brother.
The hated bishop of Durham, Ranulf Flambard, was tracked down and
arrested ten days after the coronation, and placed in the Tower of
London. With an eye both to the Church and to the English – whom
he knew better than any other of his family – Henry chose this time
formally to marry. His choice fell on Edith, sister of King Edgar of
Scotland. She had the advantage of youth and of descent from King
Æthelred of England. Their children would therefore possess a direct

blood line from the house of Wessex, a fact that pleased the contemporary English mightily, as we learn from the witness of Ailred of Rievaulx.[7] That Henry was married pleased the bishops, but they were to be disappointed, for his sexual adventuring continued to be as flagrant as it had been before his marriage: for instance, a campaign in Wales in 1109 was the excuse for a notorious fling with a Welsh princess of great beauty and sexual allure, Nest of Deheubarth, which produced another illegitimate son, called Henry. As king Henry was never long away from his ménage at rural Woodstock when he was in England, and his bishops were frustrated in their hopes that marriage would sort him out, and that he would give up his 'chasing after whores', as William of Malmesbury so delicately put it, or 'brainlessly rutting like a mule', as Orderic Vitalis (disgusted of St-Evroult) had it.

On Sunday 11 November 1100, Archbishop Anselm performed the marriage ceremony and conducted Edith's consecration as queen in the abbey of her great-uncle, Edward the Confessor, at Westminster. At this point she took the name of Mathilda, perhaps deliberately to recall King Henry's mother, universally hailed now as a paragon of queenship: 'the second Mathilda' is what several chroniclers called her. She was indeed in the end to eclipse her dead mother-in-law in devotional practice, pious works and political expertise. She was politic or indifferent enough not to resent her husband's mistresses and numerous illegitimate children; she came from a background where such things were accepted and knew well before she married him that her husband already had a surrogate English family. More than that, she succumbed like many others before her to Henry's astonishing capacity for gaining the sympathy of women. Their marriage (bizarrely to modern eyes) was universally held to be loving and successful, and the king undoubtedly mourned her death with sincerity. She became pregnant during the marriage festivities, and, although their first child was stillborn, she and Henry had both a living daughter and son by the end of 1103. Thereafter the couple seem to have lived in separate establishments, with Queen Mathilda residing principally in Westminster and London. She would have regarded her chief activity as the support of the religious life, in which she was very much her sainted mother's daughter, although she was trusted by her husband as an able regent in his long absences in France.

Edith-Mathilda had spent part of her childhood in the 1080s in the royal abbey of Romsey in Hampshire, being educated under the protection of her formidable aunt Christina. Although, before her marriage, she had given evidence to Archbishop Anselm in a hearing at Lambeth that she had never been veiled a nun, and had even resented her confinement to a nunnery, it has to be said that her later piety was egregious. Her household presented an interesting contrast to that of her royal husband, but she seems to have influenced him at least in the matter of seeking regular absolution, for like her he appointed an Augustinian canon as his licensed confessor. He was also influenced by her devotion to the poor, for the abbey he founded at Reading in 1121 after her death was specially charged by him to use its wealth to feed the destitute. Queen Mathilda used some of her London estates to found a large Augustinian priory within the walls at Aldgate around 1107, where she installed as prior an austere and eccentric French scholar called Norman; she valued him particularly as her father confessor. But her practices of austerity went much further. She wore a penitential hair shirt in the season of Lent; she washed the feet of lepers and made a practice of kissing them as representatives on earth of Christ; and she founded a large hospital for them at Holborn. The new queen was devoted to sponsoring with her considerable wealth the endeavours of church and secular poets and musicians, many of whom came seeking her patronage from abroad. A chapel choir of talented clerks supported the sung daily office, which she attended, and her chapel was staffed with notable churchmen, some of whom were promoted to bishoprics.[8] She established a pattern of pious queenship in England. We can see how Mathilda her daughter, empress of Germany, and Mathilda her niece, the queen of Stephen of England, consciously copied her style of regal piety; like her, they both set up their households within the precincts of agreeable monastic houses.

The Conqueror of Normandy

By the time that King Henry had married, his brother had been back in Normandy for at least two months, and by all accounts was very annoyed that Henry had taken the throne of England away from him. Annoyed he may have been, but Duke Robert did little immediately to challenge Henry; he was in any case better off as duke in 1100 than he had been in 1096, as he could seize back the parts of the duchy which his brothers had taken from him before he had left. There was no immediate attempt by Robert to challenge Henry in his possession of England, and perhaps left to himself he would have done nothing; the catalyst for activity was Ranulf Flambard. The bishop had friends on the outside of the Tower of London who, at the beginning of February 1101, smuggled a coiled rope into his cell in a flagon of wine. While his guards were lying around drunk at his expense, he escaped out of a window. He fled at night to a ship which his agents had already loaded with what had been salvaged of his treasure, and apparently also his aged mother. Once in Normandy, Bishop Ranulf was welcomed by the duke and – as an opponent of his brother – he was granted the revenues of the vacant bishopric of Lisieux for his support. In England, in the meantime, the king was furious with the keeper of the Tower, William de Mandeville, whom he suspected of complicity. Henry was beginning to fear that there were many magnates whom he had not won over as securely as he had hoped, and that his position was weakening. Bishop Ranulf knew this too, and energised and guided his new patron, Duke Robert, into taking advantage of the discontent, by preparing an invasion fleet.

Duke Robert in 1101 had temporarily regained the confidence of the Norman aristocracy, notably the central Norman families of Laigle, Montfort, Grandmesnil and Breteuil, all of whom were hostile to their neighbours, the Beaumont brothers, the chief supporters of King Henry. This party was paralleled by a growing faction in England which would rather have had Robert as king. Count William of Mortain, son of the late Count Robert, was bitterly opposed to King Henry, and he was backed by two of the most powerful earls in England: William de Warenne, the earl of Surrey, and Robert de Bellême, earl of Shrewsbury. Ivo de Grandmesnil, lord of Leicester, was influenced against the king by his elder brother, Robert. The king's party was weakened further by the unfortunate illness and death of the great Earl Hugh of Chester, which left King Henry supported only by his former cronies at Rufus's court, the Beaumont and fitz Hamo brothers. Circumstances were as favourable to Duke Robert as they ever would be. Bishop Ranulf began the preparation of a fleet at Le Tréport, the northernmost Norman Channel port around Easter (21 April 1101) and by June all was ready.

An account from Winchester cathedral gives the number of ships at two hundred, perhaps a third of those assembled by the Conqueror at St-Valéry, forty-five years before. King Henry's agents in Normandy kept him informed. Like King Harold before him, he attempted to mobilise an English fleet to meet the invaders off the Channel coast. His naval preparations were as useless as those of 1066, indeed worse than useless. When Duke Robert's fleet sailed on 19 July, it encountered some of the English ships somewhere off the Sussex coast, but the masters were persuaded by Bishop Ranulf to defect to Robert. They helpfully escorted the Norman fleet further down Channel to land in Portsmouth harbour on Saturday, 20 July 1101, outflanking Henry's army which was encamped (with a certain lack of originality) at Pevensey.

The king rallied his army and marched westward along the South Downs into Hampshire and attempted to block his brother's route to London. He had to abandon Winchester. He was in a far worse position than Harold had been forty-five years before, for he was forsaken by most of the aristocracy of his realm and reliant on what help the free English landowners could give and on mercenaries paid for by the bishops – who clearly regarded him as a better hope for Church reform than his brother. But, unlike the late Harold, King Henry was too astute to fight on poor terms, and a finer master of politic evasion even than his father. Just like the Conqueror at Pontefract in 1069, Henry was willing to promise the earth to divide and neutralise powerful and overwhelming opponents:

> It is better to give a small part of the kingdom than to sacrifice victory and life itself to a host of enemies. When with God's help we come safely to the end of this business we will propose practical measures for recovering the demesnes appropriated by rash deserters in a time of war.[9]

Orderic Vitalis put into the mouth of the devious Count Robert of Meulan his understanding of the wary strategy that King Henry adopted in 1101, although the likely author of it was Henry himself. As Duke Robert's forces left the Hampshire coast and marched up the Meon valley to Warnford, the king was already pondering how he could divide his enemies.

The two armies met at Alton, on the road from Winchester to Guildford and thence to London. They encamped at a distance one from the other, but it turned out mercifully that neither side was anxious to proceed to battle. The chroniclers all say that the leading men of each party were reluctant to embark on a fratricidal civil war, although the duke and king were serious in their preparations for battle. It was the petitions of the leading men of each side which brought about a peace conference, we are told. Certainly we can believe that the philosopher saint Archbishop Anselm – personally leading the knightly contingent from his estates and sleeping in tents with them – was anxious for peace for its own sake. We know that he headed a party of bishops (including Gundulf of Rochester) who crossed between the camps looking for common ground. We can be less sure of the others. The probability is that the leaders of the duke's party, particularly Ranulf Flambard – having got their hero as far as they had – were already on the look-out for overtures from his royal brother. Flambard seems at this point to have joined the peacemakers, seeing perhaps the chance to regain Henry's favour.

Duke Robert also deserves some credit for the eventual peace. His career so far had proved him too amiable to pursue war to the death against any opponent other than a Muslim. He accepted a pay off of 2000 pounds a year from Henry to surrender his claim on England. He was seduced also by pledges of joint-government with his brother over the Anglo-Norman realm. Henry made a parade of consulting him; at least one document subsequently survives from Bath abbey which the brothers issued jointly. Duke Robert pottered around England with his brother until the end of September 1101, and then sailed home to Normandy to be with his wife for the birth of their first child in November. So amiable was the duke that he remitted the 2000 pounds he was owed by the king to his sister-in-law, Queen Mathilda, as a wedding gift: with such amenable enemies King Henry hardly needed friends.

Henry revealed a new side to himself in the next few years. His priority was to establish himself as unchallengeable in England. To do so he had first to weed out or convert the unreliable amongst his magnates, and then to follow his late brother's strategy of building up an ascendancy over Normandy and ousting Duke Robert. In this he revealed a remarkable discrimination in selecting those magnates who could be of use to him. It was as if he and his intimate advisers had sat down and

undertaken an audit and analysis of the entire Anglo-Norman aristocracy and classified each individual according to the degree of threat or
promise they exhibited. Such obsessional comprehensiveness was indeed
to be the hallmark of Henry's kingship. The young Earl William de
Warenne of Surrey had impressed him despite choosing the duke's side
in 1101. Although Warenne withdrew to his Norman estates and kept
out of the subsequent troubles, the king used favours and flattery to
talk him over to his side by 1105. Other magnates who were more hostile
were quickly broken; all the more easily because Duke Robert seemed
incapable of understanding what his brother was doing. Count William
of Mortain and Cornwall, for instance, had all too obviously sympathised
with Duke Robert, and in 1101 had made his acquiescence to Henry
dependent on the king's recognition of his claim to his uncle Odo's
earldom of Kent. The king put him off with smiles and promises until
the danger was over, and then in 1102 swamped Count William's claims
on Odo of Bayeux's vast estate in specious law suits and delayed judge-
ments, until William left England in anger and took it out on the king's
Norman possessions. This, of course, gave Henry all the excuse he
needed to confiscate William's English honors. Ivo de Grandmesnil of
Leicester found himself a victim of the same sort of treatment, and his
only escape in the end was to surrender his lands and children in return
for a loan to finance a pilgrimage to Palestine. Ivo's loss was the gain
of Count Robert of Meulan, who took his estate over in pledge, and
never gave it back to his heirs, when Ivo failed to return from Jerusalem.

As King Henry laid low his potential opponents in England, he raised
a new crop of loyal friends. Former allies from his hard days in western
Normandy were found posts at court and estates in the country. One
such man was Geoffrey de Clinton, of Semilly in the Cotentin, and
another was Richard Basset of Montreuil-au-Houlme in the Bessin; both
were men of the same sort as Henry had allied with amongst the English,
men of moderate landed property with an insatiable desire to gain more.
In return for their ceaseless energy, and their ruthless and devoted
service, Henry saw to it that they acquired the wealth and advancement
they desired. They were his 'new men'. Such men were not actually new
in Anglo-Norman politics, but what was new was the way that Henry
deployed so many of them: the first cadre of an increasingly familiar
breed of royal servant. The greatest of them had already been singled

out for advancement before the end of the year 1100. This was a priest
from the diocese of Avranches by the name of Roger. Somehow in the
1090s, perhaps as early as 1091, he had attached himself as a chaplain to
Count Henry's household and impressed his new master; one story says
that it was the speed and elegance with which he said the morning mass.
But the two men were of an age, and mutual sympathy is a more likely
explanation. The most influential link between the two men must have
been Roger's enormous appetite for work, wealth and power. William
of Malmesbury says that Roger was already Count Henry's chief household officer before he became king. In 1100, Roger was immediately
promoted to be the new king's chancellor in succession to William
Giffard, who had been named as the new bishop of Winchester. Perhaps
as early as September 1101, the king had indicated that Roger was to be
the next bishop of Salisbury, and he received the estates of the bishopric
a year later (although he was not consecrated until 1107). Bishop Roger
was to be the engineer who erected the structure of a new and remorseless machinery of kingship around the king, and the man trusted to
be the king's chief justice and representative in his long absences in
France.

Between 1101 and 1106, Henry devoted himself to the duplication of
William Rufus's achievement in securing Normandy. Even Duke Robert
must have realised what Henry's intention was by 1103. The most
powerful of his surviving allies from the 1101 campaign was Earl Robert
de Bellême of Shrewsbury. Robert was not just a powerful marcher earl,
he was lord of Arundel in Sussex; one brother, Earl Arnulf of Montgomery, controlled the bulk of the former Welsh kingdom of
Deheubarth, and another, Roger, controlled the entire north west of
England. Robert was the lord of a great part of southern Normandy,
and could be fairly claimed as the single most powerful Norman after
the royal family. He was also insatiable in his ambitions, skilled in
warfare and singularly cruel in his conduct. In 1102 King Henry summoned both Robert and Arnulf and charged them with offences against
himself and (artfully) against Duke Robert, presumably as joint-rulers
of England. Seeing what was coming, Robert and Arnulf fled the court,
Arnulf going to Wales, in order to ally with the Irish Norse and carry
on the fight. Robert tried for several months to resist the king from
his English castles, but found that he had been outmanoeuvred and

subverted. King Henry cut him off from support from the kings of Powys and also stirred up Duke Robert to attack his Norman lands. By the end of summer, Earl Robert had to surrender himself as castle after castle fell, and, having lost his English lands, he left with his brothers for France. Robert de Bellême was to be the last man ever to take arms against King Henry in England.

The retreat of the Montgomery brothers to Normandy at the end of 1102 assisted King Henry even further because Robert went on to destabilise the entire south of the duchy and take revenge on Duke Robert for siding with the king. With the duke weakened, King Henry was now in a position to begin to undermine him completely. He seized the opportunity of the death in 1103 of the duke's old ally, William de Breteuil, to intervene in Normandy's government. The king married William's illegitimate son, Eustace, to one of his young illegitimate daughters, Juliana. Then, as Eustace's father-in-law, he demanded from the duke the right to intervene and arbitrate in the struggle for Breteuil, and sent as his ambassador his old friend, Count Robert of Meulan. In this way, King Henry gained a powerful ally in the duchy and established unchallenged a right to intervene in its affairs.

Duke Robert finally seems to have recognised the endgame his brother was playing – indeed, he should have recognised it from his earlier experience with William Rufus – and he quickly made peace with Robert de Bellême so as to neutralise one enemy at least. It seems that he even exerted himself so far as to cross over to England in 1103 to intercede with Henry for the magnates whom Henry was victimising. When Henry crossed to Normandy with a great fleet in 1104, it was in very much the same spirit as William Rufus had crossed in 1091. He was there to show the Normans what a great ruler looked like, and to show up his brother's inadequacies with a display of wealth and power. He was also there to assemble an alliance which in the end must corner and overthrow Duke Robert, and by its comprehensiveness make it look as though the Normans themselves wanted him as duke. Orderic Vitalis – who was eager to justify Henry's seizure of power – portrays a supposed interview between king and duke in 1104 as a trial of the duke by his brother on the charges of breaking their agreement and failing in his duty as prince to secure peace and justice. In doing so Orderic passes on to us Henry's party's view of the justice of their support of the king against their

rightful duke and lord. He also passes over the difficulties which Henry
was now experiencing with Archbishop Anselm, who was once more in
exile and residing at Lyon; Anselm was a continuing embarrassment to
Henry's attempt to command the moral heights. The archbishop's supporters were active at this time in heightening the king's embarrassment,
and the pope cooperated by excommunicating the king's friend and
adviser, the count of Meulan.

In the spring of 1105 Henry returned once more to Normandy. His
party had made it increasingly difficult for Duke Robert to maintain
even a semblance of authority. When a party of ducal loyalists based at
Bayeux arrested Robert fitz Hamo, a prominent royal agent who was
being active in Henry's interest in Lower Normandy, this was merely
used as the excuse for the king to step up his campaign. On Easter
Sunday (9 April) the king openly stated in an emotional interview with
the bishop of Séez at Carentan that he considered himself the protector
of the Norman Church, which was in fact also to say that he considered
himself the rightful ruler of Normandy. He then applied himself a little
belatedly to his duties as protector of the English Church, in order to
avoid looking foolish. He sought a rapid settlement in his dispute with
Archbishop Anselm. His sister, the countess of Blois, acted as intermediary, and in July 1105 at Laigle, on the Norman frontier – all charm
and complaisance – the king was reconciled with Anselm. To secure
peace, the king agreed to set aside the ancient royal custom of investing
bishops with their staffs, and asking homage of them. The king knew
when to give ground, especially when the would-be protector of the
Norman Church was reputed to be threatened momentarily with ex-
communication. While they were both at Laigle, Henry made a huge
public show of hanging around his prize archbishop as if he were a
devoted disciple rather than his king, and he returned to England to
take advantage of the public relations triumph. Henry was good at public
relations.

Duke Robert, now very alarmed and supported only by diehard
enemies of Henry like Robert de Bellême and William of Mortain,
attempted rather late in the day to salvage his position. Early in the year
he crossed to England and sought an interview with his brother at
Northampton. He asked the king to withdraw from the duchy but was
met with a blank refusal. Robert had no choice but to return and face

13. A page from Domesday Book. (*Public Record Office*)

14. The seal of William Rufus, dated between August 1091 and May 1092. The king is depicted in military gear, carrying a gonfanon, the mark of a commander or duke. (*Eton College Library*)

15. William Rufus, from British Library, MS Cotton Claudius, B. VI, fol.
124. Thirteenth century. (*British Library*)

16. Henry I is attacked by peasants. From his dream of 1131, as recounted by John of Worcester in about 1140. Corpus Christi College, Oxford, MS 157, fol. 383r. (*Corpus Christi College, Oxford*)

17. Henry I is attacked by knights. Corpus Christi College, Oxford, MS 157, fol. 383r. (*Corpus Christi College, Oxford*)

18. Henry I is attacked by bishops and abbots. Corpus Christi College, Oxford, MS 157, fol. 383v. (*Corpus Christi College, Oxford*)

19. Henry I undergoing a rough crossing of the Channel in 1131. His son and heir William atheling was drowned in the loss of the White Ship in November 1120. Corpus Christi College, Oxford, MS 157, fol. 383v. (*Corpus Christi College, Oxford*)

20. King Stephen, according to George Vertue in the second English edition of Rapin de Thoyras, *History of England* (1736). A small medallion with the image of the Empress Matilda is below him.

21. A battle between knights, from an English life of St Edmund, illustrated in about 1135. Pierpoint Morgan Library, New York, MS 736, fol. 7v. (*Pierpoint Morgan Library*)

22. Westminster Hall, outer walls built by William Rufus in 1098–99, still remains in use. (*A. F. Kersting*)

the inevitable, final confrontation for which Henry was now as prepared as his considerable manipulative abilities allowed him to be. The king crossed once again to the duchy in the spring of 1106, and announced his arrival by avenging the arrest of Robert fitz Hamon on the city of Bayeux, which he burned. In May he met Duke Robert again at Cinteaux, but it is clear that Henry was simply talking in order to appear accessible, not in order to make peace. On the duke's side some contemporaries believed that his cousin, the hawkish young Count William of Mortain, was now in charge. The duke settled with his army at the fortress of Falaise, while the king stationed himself at Caen, and they both awaited the final confrontation, each looking for the advantage. Henry had a final reconciliation with Anselm at the abbey of Bec in August, before packing off the archbishop safely back to Canterbury. After that the king hit on a scheme: he marched west in arms and began to reduce the count of Mortain's castles. It was undoubtedly his intention to weaken the ducal party and demonstrate their ineffectiveness. The count of Mortain had to move in support of his castle of Tinchebray, or appear a poor lord, but to do that was to risk open battle. He and the duke demanded that Henry withdraw, but the king stayed where he was, embracing civil war, as Orderic said 'for the sake of future peace'.[10]

The battle of Tinchebray was fought on Friday 28 September 1106, forty years nearly to the day after the Normans had landed in Sussex under the Conqueror. Now the Conqueror's sons were in arms against each other in rivalry for the realm he had created in 1066. There was no shortage of people who thought this a shocking thing, despite Henry's relentless battery of self-justification and pious posturing. Vitalis, the venerable abbot of the count of Mortain's monastery of Savigny, embraced the role of prophet and to their faces forbade the brothers to fight in God's name. Other churchmen were quite as active in the cause of peace. They even ironed out some sort of compromise proposal by which King Henry would take over the administration of the duchy in return for Robert's receiving of a large annual income. Not surprisingly, Robert and his advisers had doubts as to Henry's sincerity. They rejected the offer, and readied their army for battle.

The battle was very different from Hastings, and in some ways a more usual medieval engagement. It was brief, and the issue was probably resolved in well under an hour. Both sides deployed in dismounted lines in a confined arena near the castle. The king, surrounded by a Praetorian guard of loyal English soldiers, took station in the rear of his line: he was dismounted, in the manner of Julius Caesar, to give his men confidence that he would not abandon them. But the king would not entirely relinquish the advantage of cavalry. He chose to station a force of Manceaux and Breton knights under Count Elias of Maine off to one side, perhaps deliberately concealed. This force proved decisive, for the ducal army was short of horsemen. As the opposing and dismounted lines of the count of Mortain and the royalist viscount of the Bessin met, weight of numbers caused them to grind to a halt. The battlefront was so crowded that movement became difficult as both sides locked shields in a shoving match. At that point, Count Elias saw an exposed flank and charged his knights into the end of the ducal line, which panicked, collapsed and ran. All that was left for the royalists was to round up the defeated, and the duke, the count of Mortain and many other leaders (none of whom were mounted) fell into their hands along with four hundred knights and thousands of foot soldiers. Only Robert de Bellême amongst the ducal leaders escaped. There were very few casualties even on the ducal side; estimated figures of wounded and killed range only between sixty and 225. One account says not a royalist was hurt, although the king's letter written to Anselm after the battle admits a few casualties on his side. The king proclaimed the great victory as a manifest sign of God's approval of his invasion of his brother's lands. In contrast Anselm's supporters declared it was in fact God's reward for making peace with the archbishop.

Reinventing Government

Henry spent some time after Tinchebray prowling his new duchy. He headed first to Falaise and secured its surrender before Robert de Bellême could seize it. Along with the castle and the Norman treasury he acquired the custody of his nephew, William Clito, not yet five years old. Rather than keep the boy in his own household, he cautiously entrusted him to Duke Robert's great friend and son-in-law, Elias de St-Saens, count of Arques. Henry was already nervous of how the world would regard his treatment of his brother's heir, and for him Count Elias was a safe choice, for he had maintained a friendship with him too. From Falaise

the king marched to take possession of Rouen, which he found enthusiastic about his success: Duke Robert's chaotic rule had not been good
for business. Duke Robert made things easy for his brother by commanding his castellans to surrender to Henry and by releasing his men
from their oath of allegiance. By October the king was able to declare
his peace throughout the duchy, resume all alienated ducal estates and
receive the allegiance of his new subjects. William of Mortain and other
leaders were sent back to England to be held in safe custody, as also
was his brother the duke. The duke's captivity was to be comfortable,
with substantial funds allotted to maintain the style of life of a king's
son, but he was never unsupervised until he died at Cardiff in 1134. In
a final move to establish peace, Robert de Bellême sent intermediaries
seeking a settlement, and was given moderate terms. In 1107 the business
of pacification and reconciliation continued. The king met Ranulf Flambard, still living in style and cheerful corruption at Lisieux, and listened
to his overtures about returning to England. The bishop was allowed
to return to Durham, and spent the rest of his days employing his
energies and wealth in building works and improvements in Durham
diocese, until he died in 1129.

Henry returned to England for the Easter court of 14 April 1107 and
celebrated the feast in great style, as a triumphant conqueror. His tireless
friend and counsellor the count of Meulan was rewarded with a second
comital title, Leicester, and great gifts of estates. But the king had
returned not to rest – which would have been out of character – but to
inaugurate a programme of administrative innovation. He had been
taxing the country hard in the years before Tinchebray, and seems to
have found grounds for dissatisfaction with his subordinates and the
system he inherited. So his desire for control of people and events led
to him to attempt unheard of levels of control over the business of his
kingdom. Orderic marvelled at his prodigious memory, his inexhaustible
thirst for the detail of administration, justice and financial resources. He
says too that Henry went out of his way to improve on the gifts with
which nature had endowed him, to the extent of employing a wide
network of agents and informers to feed all sorts of rumour and information into his capacious and retentive mind. Some documentary
remnants of this information revolution survive. A number of thorough
surveys were carried out for the king around this time into the tax

obligations of certain counties: the Lincolnshire and Northamptonshire records still exist. The royal clerk Walter Map,[11] said in the 1180s that he had seen an account that Henry kept of each earl and baron of England, with their individual allowances when attending court noted and described. The contemporary Welsh chronicles too marvel at the wealth and organisation of his court, where the captive King Cadwgan ap Bleddyn of Powys was allotted two shillings daily for his upkeep in 1110.

It may be that it was in this period of residence in England in 1107–8 that he and his inner council – in what must have been something of an exceptional brainstorming session – made a unique breakthrough in the art of government in the west. We can say with some confidence that it was the king, Bishop Roger of Salisbury and Count Robert of Meulan who between them thought up the idea of a central government accounting office.[12] They or their officers were soon calling it the 'exchequer' from the chequered cloth used as a calculating device in its accounting sessions. Twice a year, at Easter and Michaelmas (29 September), a team of royal representatives were to meet face to face with the king's local agents, collect the dues owed the king, issue receipts and, in the second session, compile a record roll of national income and expenditure.

King Henry's intention after Tinchebray was no more than to upgrade the mechanisms for collecting the huge amounts of cash that he needed to maintain his realm. Some of these must have existed before: England had long been a country capable of exacting a national property tax and managing a national coinage. William Rufus had little trouble in raising and squandering vast sums from his subjects. There was a royal treasury at Winchester, where not just money but records too were kept. It was at Winchester that Domesday Book was first kept, and an indeterminate number of other documents and surveys called in the 1110s 'the royal charters at Winchester'.[13] Richard fitz Nigel, Roger of Salisbury's great-nephew, preserved the information that the exchequer had grown out of an earlier body called 'at the tallies'. Since tallies were split hazel sticks used as receipts for cash, this reference indicates that before the exchequer Winchester was used as an authorised place to deposit money owed the king, as and when it became due. Making fiscal records was not a new development either. The administration of the count of Flanders is known to have been making financial accounts well before

1100. The first mention of the exchequer by name is in 1110, a year the king caused much complaint by raising an 'aid' (a sum of money owed by all his tenants) to help in the marrying of his daughter to the emperor. Was this – as one authority has suggested – because this was the year the exchequer first functioned, or was it because it was the year it was first noticed by the written record? [14] The evidence is not there to decide. My grounds for suggesting it was thought up earlier is simply because the institutution seems already suspiciously well-articulated in 1110. In 1111 we find the queen in charge of the exchequer court session, but Richard fitz Nigel tells us that usually it was Bishop Roger. Once it did begin to meet it changed the nature of England. The record it compiled (the 'pipe roll') defined the extent of the realm every Michaelmas and remorselessly dragged officers to a central point from its every corner. In the swarming courtyards of Winchester castle, at the exchequer board and in the city's inns, a new culture of government was instituted. Administrative specialists must for the first time have found a group identity, and established a social ritual and work routine apart from the royal court.

The royal court too was changing. The king disliked the way his brothers had lived. It did not suit his careful and detailed mind that the itinerant royal household should travel the land like an army on campaign. He had a constitution drawn up, with allowances for auth-orised officers and established departments. This not only controlled expenditure, it limited the number of hangers on at court. The king also had his route posted months in advance so that provisions could be made ready and supplicants might gather in advance of his coming. Rather than keeping regular courts at established crown-wearing places, Henry moved more freely around his kingdom. On grounds of expense, he also scaled down the elaborate ritual of the principal court feasts which his father had begun. His favourite place in which to be, Wood-stock in Oxfordshire (the Sandringham of the twelfth century), would not support that sort of state in any case, as it had no major church close by. It was the place he went to be domestic. It may be also that the contemporary intellectual fad of despising the luxury and glory of the world rather appealed to him; he had got by for so long on so little, and was so well-seated in his royal status, that glittering and expensive state occasions probably meant little to him for their own sake.

Another new development in the royal household was the king's expansion of its military department. The royal household was a diverse and multi-functional institution which altered with the king's need. It could be a court of law (the *curia regis*), a council chamber, a place of entertainment or even a school. Under the Norman kings it had always had a military dimension because the aristocrats who composed it were all trained and sometimes enthusiastic soldiers. When the king went to war, so did his household. Henry, however, used his increasing wealth to employ and retain on salary a rather larger body of soldiers than his predecessors had kept about them. These companies of professional soldiers, drawn from all ranks of society, operated under the household constables and marshals as an extension of the household (rather like the Secret Service is a semi–independent office of the US Department of the Treasury). This small and permanent force of knights and mounted archers did not compare in size with modern armies: it was probably never larger than two nineteenth-century cavalry regiments. But it suited both the king's personal insecurity and his political needs to be able to deploy it rapidly in key garrisons and in trouble spots: it formed the core of his army at both Tinchebray and Brémule. This was especially the case because the military household (the *familia*) attracted military specialists in the same way that the exchequer attracted administrative specialists. The royal troops were issued with uniform equipment as part of their stipend. They trained hard and regarded themselves as an elite force. In some respects, Henry's military household even acted as a war college further to propagate its expertise. We find that young aristocrats from surrounding realms, southern France, the Empire – even Welsh princes – were sometimes allowed to learn their military craft there.

In this way the character of the king altered the nature of the kingdom he ruled. But in the environment of the early twelfth century, it just so happened that those changes could not be transitory. King Henry lived in an age in which literacy was changing the nature of administration and perception. His exchequer was founded on a systematically kept written record of debts and obligations, and communicated its wishes by sealed writ. Once set in motion, it had an interior momentum that kept its rolls turning down the decades and generations. His specialist soldiers and administrators slowly developed a culture and common memory that perpetuated their valuable skills from reign to reign. By 1100, schools of all sorts were growing up around individual masters and greater churches, and the supply of their pupils far surpassed the needs of the Church. Literate stewards and reeves were to become a commonplace within a generation of Henry's death, and they were needed precisely because the exchequer and processes of royal justice imposed on the kingdom the need for their skills. The push that King Henry gave to administration in his reign caught a breeze that brought it out on to great waters from which it could never return.

War with King Louis VI of France, 1108–24

The years 1108–10 were significant in ways other than administrative. There had been years of peace between the Capetian and Norman dynasties since the death of the Conqueror. This had a good deal to do with the difficulties which King Philip was experiencing with the Church, his magnates and his own family. After several successes in harassing and humiliating William the Conqueror, King Philip had been able to rest content with the long separation between England and Normandy and turn his mind to other problems. Towards the end of his life, as the power of Henry I was all too obviously increasing, Philip began to realise that the Anglo-Norman realm was again a threat. His estranged son and heir, Louis, took refuge with Henry's court in England at Christmas 1100 and stayed for some months before returning, loaded with gifts, to France. It may be that it was Henry's support which persuaded Philip to give Louis control of the county of the Vexin as an advance on his patrimonial inheritance. This thwarted Henry's chances of playing off the son against the father, and put Louis in the front line of Norman aggression. Philip tried to keep the moral edge over his powerful neighbour. Between 1103 and 1105 Philip corresponded with Anselm of Canterbury, attempting to capitalise on Henry's difficulties with the Church by offering the exiled archbishop his support. But Philip was entirely unable to exploit the war between King Henry and Duke Robert in 1106.

Philip of France died in 1108. For several years already his son and heir, Louis, had been engaged in reducing the power of the disorderly magnates of the Ile de France. By 1109 Louis VI was in a stronger position

than his father had been, and could look to see how he might deal with
the Anglo-Norman threat. There was plenty of evidence that Henry was
seeking to reinvigorate his dynasty's influence around the fringes of
Normandy. He had lost Maine to the power of Anjou with the death
of Count Elias, but Henry saw opportunities upriver towards Paris,
where the count of Meulan exerted great influence, and further south
too, where his nephew Theobald was now powerful as count of Blois-
Chartres. Open conflict began because Henry succeeded in regaining
control of the border fortress of Gisors that his brother had raised to
strengthen the frontier. Louis assembled an enormous host and devastated Count Robert of Meulan's lands, as a warning to the count's
master. A confrontation between the two kings at Gisors led to Louis
challenging Henry to a personal fight to decide who had true claim to
the castle. Certain members of the French army, with an eye to the
increasing weight of the king of England, suggested that they fight on
a nearby rickety bridge, to give their king an advantage. A personal
challenge was the usual way for a French prince to try to put an enemy
at a moral disadvantage: the Conqueror had tried the trick on Harold
before Hastings, although the subtlety had been lost on the English.
Henry is said to have compared Louis's challenge to being kicked in the
shins by a child, and scornfully rejected it, saying he would have his
fight with Louis when they met in the field. As it happened, no battle
occurred in the spring of 1109, despite menacing manoeuvres between
the two great armies, and a truce was concluded. Henry felt confident
enough to return to England at the end of May. It was a classic instance
of the economical and subtle way that medieval French rulers played
out their confrontations with menace, feint and propaganda. The violence was done to the fields, houses and vineyards of the Seine valley.

The confrontation at Gisors inaugurated an extended period of rivalry
between Louis and Henry, which involved both kings in some of their
most dangerous moments. It would not be until 1124 that long-term
peace was re-established. Louis, with the instinct of his dynasty for
finding weaknesses in the Norman camp, was very soon given the chance
of supporting William (called 'Clito' or 'the Young'), the son of the
imprisoned Duke Robert II. King Henry had wisely entrusted the boy
in 1106 to a neutral guardian, Count Elias of Arques, at his castle of
St-Saens, between Dieppe and Rouen. Until he was nearly ten years

of age, the boy had a peaceful aristocratic upbringing in upper Normandy. But as tension between the king and Louis of France increased Henry decided that it was too dangerous to leave the boy on the loose, and sent a ducal officer to take him into custody – most probably on his abrupt return to Normandy in August 1110. Henry miscalculated: Count Elias was affronted that the arrest had been attempted at St-Saens in his absence. His people hustled the boy away and brought him to Elias, who took him across the frontier and into exile. William Clito was to find aid and support in many places where King Henry was feared and his power resented, and it was not long before Louis VI found it politically advantageous to support his claims on Normandy. What was more worrying for Henry was the popularity of the boy's claims with internal dissidents in the duchy. It was very easy for them to throw a virtuous cloak over their rebellion by claiming to be supporting the rightful claims of William Clito.

One of the first to offer aid and comfort to William Clito was Henry's deadly enemy, Robert de Bellême. Robert had remained powerful on the southern frontiers of the duchy, where the growth of Angevin power in Maine also challenged King Henry. It became the king's objective to strengthen his frontier here by building new castles and alliances. Henry was keen to remove Robert altogether. In the autumn of 1112 the king put together charges against him and formally summoned him to appear to answer them. Robert, rather surprisingly, came to meet the king at Bonneville-sur-Touques, where he was arrested and sentenced to imprisonment for life. It may be at that time that Robert thought that he was untouchable as an envoy for the coalition of the Henry's enemies. He had many years in various prisons to repent of that error. His Norman lands were forfeit, and his lordship of Bellême was eventually handed over to Robert's enemy and King Henry's ally, Count Rotrou of Perche. The sudden lurch in the balance of power towards Henry persuaded Count Fulk of Anjou to seek peace in 1113, and the king was willing to compromise so far as to allow the Angevins to occupy Maine, providing his overlordship was acknowledged. King Louis too realised that Henry had outflanked him and sought a truce at Gisors in March 1113. Henry had demonstrated to Louis's discomfort that his resources and the network of his allies and kinsmen had created a line of buffer states around the fringes of Normandy that was going to be difficult for him to penetrate. What Louis had plainly feared and anticipated as early as 1108 was now a reality. The Capetians were being remorselessly marginalised in north-western France, and pressed back into the Parisian heartland of the upper Seine. It was not until 1116 that Louis was able to put together the makings of a counter-strategy, which had less to do with invasion, and more to do with internal subversion within Normandy.

On 1 May 1118 Queen Mathilda died at Westminster, and just over a month later Count Robert of Meulan died, probably also somewhere in England. King Henry was in Normandy at the time, containing renewed aggression from Louis VI in the Seine valley. He therefore missed the queen's elaborate funeral, more elaborate than any previously seen in England, with tens of thousands of masses said for her soul and 67,820 poor fed at royal expense within eight days of her death. The deaths had a direct impact on Henry's fortunes. His late queen and his late friend had been established and valued counsellors. The queen had embodied the loyalty of the English to Henry, a point emphasised by the fact that their son William was known by the English style of 'atheling'. The clerk who wrote the so-called *Chronicle of Hyde Abbey* directly related Henry's subsequent political problems to the fact that Mathilda was no longer in the world to pray for his kingdom.[15] More pragmatically, Count Robert had provided an invaluable military obstacle to Louis VI in the French Vexin, where the castle and county of Meulan blocked communication up and down the Seine and closed the principal bridges at Meulan and Mantes. Their deaths coincided with a period of turbulence in Henry's fortunes, and it was to be several years before he was again in control of events.

Another death in April 1118 was that of Henry's cousin, Count William of Evreux. This event sparked major trouble because Count William's nearest male heir was his nephew, Amaury de Montfort, a loyal baron of Louis VI with castles and lordships south of Meulan and along the Norman border. Naturally, the succession of this compromised French-man was blocked by King Henry. Unfortunately for Henry, he forgot that a royal mandate was not always enough to command the obedience of the Normans, and the knights of the county of Evreux rebelled in Amaury's favour. He had already seriously antagonised the nobility of Normandy by abruptly arresting the count of Eu and Hugh de Gournay, who had come peacefully to his court because he had information that they were intriguing with the count of Flanders. This harsh act motivated many recruits to join Amaury de Montfort's rebellion, including the count of Aumale, the count of Eu's neighbour.

Quite suddenly, in the autumn of 1118, King Henry's border strategy collapsed. King Louis found to his delight that, with Meulan neutralised and Amaury de Montfort fighting for control of the county of Evreux, the whole March of Normandy had become unstable. All the dissidents – who included Henry's son-in-law Eustace de Breteuil – embraced the rival cause of William Clito as a way of escaping Henry's remorseless rule. Count Baldwin VII of Flanders also mobilised against Henry and in favour of the western Norman rebels and William Clito. With the help of the counts of Aumale and Eu, Henry's own cousins, he marched an army deep into Normandy, as far as Dieppe. On the southern frontier, Count Fulk of Anjou marched north through Maine in July and seized Norman outposts. By the beginning of autumn, Henry had lost control of large parts of his duchy. His enemies were threatening Rouen from the east, and the border region towards France had been lost. Then, to cap the disasters, at the end of November, the town of Alençon rose in revolt and opened its gates to the army of Fulk of Anjou.

Louis VI had not immediately joined in the assault on Normandy, although his younger brothers Philip and Florus and other French knights had enlisted in Amaury de Montfort's invasion force. King Louis was distracted by inopportune internal troubles of his own in the Ile-de-France, and he may well have thought that with luck the duchy would collapse into the hands of William Clito with no need for him to intervene. But King Henry's doggedness, the support of Theobald of Blois and the loyalty of the magnates of the west and centre of the duchy allowed him to survive the winter of 1118–19. Henry was also able to drive a wedge between his enemies. He bought off Fulk of Anjou by arranging a marriage between his son and heir and Fulk's daughter (a girl of about twelve) in June 1119, and by agreeing to his demands to restore the son of Robert de Bellême to his southern Norman lands. Count Baldwin of Flanders was incapacitated by a head wound in a tournament at Eu and chose to withdraw to convalesce in the county of Ponthieu, but died of an illness contracted at Abbeville. Henry also secured numerous reinforcements of English and Breton mercenary

knights, and deployed them in an elaborate and sustained campaign of
siege warfare against the dissident magnates of the border. When Louis
finally did move a French army into the Vexin in August 1119, the rebel
strength was beginning to soak away into the sand, and his intervention
seems to have been an attempt to restart the bandwagon.

While King Henry was preoccupied with the reduction of the castle
and fortress of Evreux, Louis put pressure on the line of strongpoints
William Rufus had erected along the River Epte, and punched a hole
through. This breakthrough brought Henry and the Anglo-Norman
army to the valley of the River Andelle, the last defensible line before
an enemy came to the walls of Rouen. On 20 August Henry took the
Roman road out towards Gisors, but, as he was watching his troops
foraging food from the fields of the Vexin, pickets reported that they
could see the standards and glittering helmets of another army which
was moving further south parallel to them: Louis was making his bid
to breach the line of the Andelle and open the way to take Rouen. The
armies wheeled and came face-to-face on an open plain called Brémule
where the Roman road to Rouen crossed west of a village called Ecouis.
It is a measure of the desperation of both kings at this point that they
so readily listened to advisers in each of their armies who urged them
to take the chance of battle. The Hyde account actually says that Henry
was bullied into fighting by his barons. The armies were about equal in
strength, around five hundred knights. William Clito, now in his eight-
eenth year, was with Louis riding against his uncle. The Anglo-Norman
army chose to dismount, and the king took his stand in the front line
with his guard and an English lord, Edward of Salisbury, as his banner-
bearer. As at Tinchebray, he kept a mounted squadron in reserve. The
French launched a fierce charge against the Anglo-Norman line, but it
was undisciplined and badly supported. Despite breaking through the
first ranks, it was held by the disciplined shield wall of the household
guards. Although there were some desperate attempts at rallying, the
battle rapidly ended as the wings of the Anglo-Norman line began to
encircle the French. Realising that they would be trapped, many ran.
The victory was not without its dangers for King Henry. The leading
enemy company of William Crispin, a baron of the Vexin, made a very
determined attack. Crispin was able to push himself as far through the
ranks as King Henry, and struck the king two hard blows on the head,

before being thrown down and captured. Nothing can better illustrate the fact that kings in the twelfth century put their lives as well as fortunes on the line when they risked battle under a banner that told everyone precisely where they were.

Brémule was a catastrophe for French arms. Louis's army was probably scattered in less than an hour. As was usual when most of the troops were knights in full armour, there were few fatalities (sources agree on only three) but many were taken captive. King Louis was separated from his guards in the flight from the field. There seems to have been an assault by the Anglo-Norman mounted reserve troops on his company, which was honourably covering the French retreat; it was overwhelmed and the royal standard captured. In the retreat Louis lost his horse and ended up on foot in a wood somewhere north of Les Andelys. He had to talk a sympathetic passing peasant into guiding him back to his camp on the Seine. William Clito also escaped on foot. In a noble but inexpensive gesture, King Henry and his son, William atheling, returned their captured horses to Louis and Clito the next day. Only one Anglo-Norman was taken prisoner, a young knight who got quite carried away and pursued the French so hard that he rode right into their camp at Les Andelys. Louis had no choice but to abandon his invasion of Normandy and return to Paris. Things got worse when on 17 September 1119 he attempted a counter-stroke against the border town of Breteuil in order to salvage some prestige. The resistance of the town and the approach of King Henry forced another embarrassing withdrawal across the border, which was followed by the abrupt collapse of the Norman rebellion on the southern frontier.

In the wake of these reverses, the sweet breath of peace suddenly pervaded the air of northern France. Henry must have been happy to have survived some very dangerous moments, and keen to let the wheel of fortune come to rest. Louis, in contrast, must have been disappointed in his Franco-Norman allies, and the fact that Henry had been able to outmanoeuvre him even when he was at his weakest. The more astute of the former rebels found ways to make their peace. Richer de L'Aigle and the men of Breteuil found friends and relatives who would intercede with the king, who was happy to see them desert William Clito. By the end of October, Amaury de Montfort too was looking for peace through the good offices of Count Theobald of Blois, the king's nephew. Count

Stephen of Aumale, left alone against the king, swiftly capitulated. Everybody was treated with politic generosity: Henry did not want to leave soil in which for future support for William Clito would grow.

In October a great opportunity to put triumphant pinnacles on the edifice of peace-making presented itself when Pope Calixtus II arrived in north-eastern France and held a council at Reims at which the English episcopate was much in evidence. Also present were William Clito with King Louis, who took the opportunity to charge Henry with the violent dispossession of Duke Robert. When the archbishop of Rouen and bishop of Evreux attempted to intervene, they were shouted down. The pope, however, was not there to take sides. He planned to bring about a settlement that would add to the credit of his visit, and he could hardly do so by condemning Henry, whose assistance he needed against the antipope, Gregory VIII. At the conclusion of the council of Reims, Pope Calixtus ventured further north than any previous pontiff and came to the very borders of Normandy at war-stricken Gisors for a meeting with Henry. It was a very great occasion, with the pope and his cardinals lodging at the French fortress of Chaumont-en-Vexin, 6 km from Gisors. Henry greeted the pope with deep reverence, when they met at a country church on the road between Gisors and Chaumont, and prostrated himself at Calixtus's feet. In return he was welcomed warmly by the pope as a kinsman, for both men were great-grandchildren of Richard II of Normandy. Calixtus, before his election, had been Guy, archbishop of Vienne, a member of the dynasty of the counts of Burgundy which had allied with the Norman dynasty a century before. The claims of William Clito were discussed. Henry presented his case to rule Normandy on the basis of the incapacity of his elder brother, and declared himself surprised that William Clito had fled his power and had ignored his repeated invitations to return, especially as he had offered the young man three counties to support him in England. Calixtus doubtless realised that he had done as much as he could, and ended the interview by urging Henry to make peace with Louis. A witness to the interview reports that Henry concluded the subject by saying with a degree of ambiguity: 'I am sorry about the quarrel, I want peace; nor have I any reason to avoid willingly doing whatever the duke of Normandy owes to the king of France.' [16]

The peace between Henry and Louis was ratified by the performance of homage for Normandy to Louis by William atheling at some time

early in 1120. William had now passed the age of majority (if it was
calculated as sixteen). The rest of the year was a time of reconstruction
and discreet triumph, as Henry re-established his grip on the shattered
Norman aristocracy. There is little apparent sign that he was preparing
to weed out the unreliable magnates in the duchy, in the way that he
had done in England in 1101–3. Had he planned such a purge, the events
at the end of 1120 would have halted it. On 25 November, Henry
embarked for a late autumn crossing to England from the port of
Barfleur in the Cotentin. Just after sunset, on a peaceful and calm
evening without a moon, the royal fleet rowed out of the harbour and
into the dark of the Channel night, expecting to catch the turning tide
and the land breeze and be taken away from the shore and so land in
England the next morning. The great royal *esnecca* called the 'White
Ship' followed on later, with the younger elements of the court on board
in partying mood. William atheling, his half-siblings, Richard and
Mathilda of Perche, and several other magnates were having a fine time,
urging the master to race the king's ships across the Channel, while
offering the crew handsome rations of wine. But the darkness, their late
start and the receding tide led to tragedy. As the White Ship cleared the
rocky coast and turned north towards Southampton the master mis-
judged the state of the tide and the space needed to clear the reef called
the Raz de Barfleur. A tidal rock submerged and invisible just beneath
the placid surface stove in the bottom of the ship. The ship capsized,
turning out its passengers and crew into the sea. Only one man survived
the cold November sea and the long, frosty night under the stars by
clinging to a spar, to be picked up by a fishing boat at dawn. Although
the wreck was salvaged the next day at low tide and the king's treasure
recovered, no bodies were found in or near the boat.

The unexpected death of William atheling was a personal and national
catastrophe. The young man had established himself at least in England
as the most desirable heir to his father. Writers accepted that he rein-
troduced through his mother the lineage of Alfred the Great into the
Norman royal dynasty, and therefore blunted any criticism of his right
to the throne as opposed to that of his cousin, William Clito. The award
to William of the title of 'atheling' seems to have been very much a
decision which rose from the people, and tells us how much the lesser
English aristocracy pinned their hopes on him. For his father, his birth

had resolved many dynastic and personal issues, and gave him his best weapon against William Clito's claims. The shock of the sudden bereavement, as much as its implications, struck the king down for many days. The fact that the boy's body was never recovered (although a few bodies – notably that of the young Earl Richard of Chester – were later found thrown up on the shores of the Bay of the Seine) meant there could be no burial or tomb. This would doubtless have prolonged the king's mental agonies, and the contemporary Anglo-Saxon Chronicle says as much. If the loss of his heir was not enough, one of Henry's elder natural sons, Richard (born in Oxfordshire before he was king) had died too. Richard had already been deployed in Normandy as a commander and potential magnate: he had been awarded in marriage the heiress to the great honor of Breteuil. Richard and his sister Mathilda seem to have befriended their legitimate half-brother, so a large part of Henry's affective family went down with the White Ship.

The northern French princes were as aware of the consequences of the dynastic disaster as was King Henry. The fortunes of William Clito rose accordingly. Many now were clearly calculating that Henry would eventually have to accept his nephew's right to the Anglo-Norman realm. The count of Anjou had married his daughter Mathilda to William atheling in June 1119, but the boy's death had now cancelled that alliance. Henry hung on to the girl in England, not so much perhaps from affection but out of a plan that he might one day marry her to an obliging magnate and seek to control the county of Maine – her dowry – through her. Count Fulk of Anjou returned from Jerusalem early in 1121 and demanded the girl back, well aware of Henry's strategy, and was profoundly annoyed when the king refused. It was probably this that pushed Fulk into a new pro-Clito alliance in northern France. The king's magnates and counsellors pondered the choices. Finding the king still set against the idea of Clito's succession, they persuaded him that the best option was remarriage with the hope of further legitimate sons. The king consented to this scheme early in January 1121, and within a month a bride had already been found in the young Adeliza, daughter of Godfrey, count of Louvain and duke of Brabant. The king, now around fifty-three years of age, married his teenage bride at Windsor on 2 February 1121.

The new queen seems to have been a confident and politically alert young woman. This was not surprising as Flanders and northern France at the time would have provided her with a number of role models of politically powerful women. Adeliza proved to have a good understanding of the way that her predecessor had developed the role of queen, and adopted her literary and charitable causes. Henry's usual generosity left her very wealthy, with free control over the revenues of Rutland, Shropshire and a large district of London, with possession of the city of Chichester and the castle and lordship of Arundel, so she was well able to exert herself politically. She financed a distinguished household chapel and a number of her chaplains were promoted high in the church; her chaplain Simon, who had accompanied her from Brabant, was nominated bishop of Worcester in 1125. An interesting development in her relationship with Henry was her appearance with him at Woodstock in 1123. Despite appearing often with her husband when he was in England, the late Queen Mathilda seems never to have ventured to – or been permitted to – enter that particular resort. Queen Adeliza was there frequently.[17] It seems likely that the catastrophe of 1120 had provoked a change in the ageing king's domestic habits, and he no longer felt the need to support an alternative household and family to which to retreat. The Woodstock ménage was dismantled and his new and attractive wife was allowed to take her seat in the domestic heart of his life where the serious and demure Mathilda seems never to have reigned. Henry's children from the English concubines of his youth and young manhood were in any case now grown up and mostly independent, so Woodstock was free to be reinvented as a royal palace. His ménage of concubines and children was replaced with a menagerie of exotic animals, including a porcupine he had somehow acquired. This does not mean that Henry had yet given up extramarital sex. He had a few short-lived later affairs, including a notable one with Isabel, the teenage daughter of his late friend, Robert of Meulan, which produced a daughter. It may be that, like many ageing and powerful men of our own day, he was irresistibly attracted to nubile girls and found some at court willing to take advantage of his weakness, or pushed by their families to cooperate with the king's lust.

The problem for Henry and Adeliza was that no children followed on from their marriage. The fact that the young queen discussed this misfortune with a sympathetic correspondent, Bishop Hildebert de

Lavardin of Le Mans, tells us that she felt that it had affected her relationship with the king. Since she went on to have several sons and daughters with her second husband, the fault may not have been hers. Continuing good relations between Henry and Adeliza, despite their childlessness, indicates that the king did not blame her but another agency, physical or supernatural. Every year that passed with no child being born from the union strengthened the party of William Clito. By the end of 1122, a party was already re-forming to promote his claim to Normandy. It focused on a surprising new entrant into the high political game. When Robert, the great count of Meulan, had died in 1118, he had left as heirs identical twin sons. The elder of these was named Waleran, after the eleventh-century founder of the French county he inherited. The younger was called Robert and took his father's English county of Leicester. Waleran in 1122 was of age although only barely eighteen; he had been knighted by the king in 1120. He ruled the largest part of central Normandy and his father's lands in the Vexin and Paris. For some reason – which may have to do with a baffled ambition to be as important at court as his famous father had been – Waleran opened secret communications with William Clito. Orderic Vitalis blamed Amaury de Montfort for turning Waleran's head, but this may be unfair: in the descriptions of events, it is the young Waleran who always appears to be taking the initiative.

Waleran deployed his wealth and influence, and the marriages of his younger sisters, to put himself at the head a formidable party of Anglo-French barons. By September 1123, he was ready to move and a final meeting had been convened at his castle of La Croix St-Leuffroy to agree the details. Unfortunately for the plotters, the king's agents had long been in on the conspiracy. Henry knew exactly what was going on and had been in the duchy watching the plot develop since June. As the meeting at La Croix St-Leuffroy broke up, the king rode south with a powerful force of his military household which he had assembled at Rouen. The king took the conspirators by surprise. He arrived at the central Norman castle of Montfort-sur-Risle and demanded its surrender. Hugh, its lord, barely escaped to ride off and warn Waleran and his other allies. Waleran's plans were now badly dislocated. The fighting had begun before the French mercenaries he had earlier hired had arrived. King Henry had grabbed the initiative and the rebels were caught completely out of field. Some of Waleran's Norman tenants refused to join him; a particular blow being the defection to the king of the lord of Harcourt, his principal baron. Waleran carried on regardless, although one after another of the rebel castles fell, including his own chief fortress of Pont Audemer in December 1123.

The rebels were only able to recapture the initiative when the king sent his household and the Breton mercenaries he had hired for the campaign into winter quarters in strong points and siege works around the surviving rebel centres. The king himself marched reinforcements to Gisors, which had come under threat from the French. Amaury de Montfort had once again incited the barons of the French Vexin to make an attempt on Gisors, and came close to succeeding before the king's approach drove him off. Amaury's energy in all this was remarkable. He had been busy too at the court of Anjou and had persuaded Count Fulk to agree to a marriage between Sibyl, another of his daughters, and William Clito. Once again the county of Maine was deployed as a marriage-portion. The threat to King Henry of placing Clito in charge of it was unmistakable. The strategic vision evident in all this, and the military resources available to the Norman rebels from the Capetian realm, more than reveals that Louis VI was promoting Amaury's manoeuvres. King Henry could hardly have missed that deduction, and moved some pieces of his own to intimidate Louis in turn. He motivated his son-in-law, Emperor Henry V, to march with a great host south as far as Metz from his imperial estates in the Low Countries. The reason the emperor was so keen to help was that, if Henry had no further sons, he was the husband of the next heir. He had married the king's only other legitimate child, Mathilda, so he too was in direct rivalry with William Clito.

The Norman revolt flared up again in March 1124, when Waleran and Amaury decided on a raid from his headquarters of Beaumont-le-Roger to take the pressure off Waleran's beseiged castle at Vatteville on the Seine. Although the raid was a success, the rebel force found its return south to Beaumont hampered by a company of the royal guard which had anticipated its movements and blocked their road across fields near the small town of Bourgtheroulde south of Rouen. The royal troops numbered three hundred disciplined professionals under their commander, an otherwise obscure constable called Odo Borleng, and a few loyal

Norman barons who were riding with them. Waleran's force of local knights and French adventurers was somewhat larger, and with the advantage in numbers he decided that the risk of battle was worthwhile. Amaury de Montfort, who knew all too well the capabilities of King Henry's household, advised against this, but Waleran was young, had read too much heroic history and heard too many songs of valour to care for pragmatism. The royal force had dismounted and deployed bowmen – it made an irritatingly plebeian target for a young mounted nobleman with high ideals of knighthood and little judgement. Waleran rallied his own tenants for a charge across the fields but they were predictably mowed down as the royal archers brought down their horses under them. Waleran fell with the others and was seized by the king's chamberlain, William de Tancarville, along with several other rebel leaders. Amaury had hung back, then, seeing his rebellion swept away by a shower of arrows, he rode off with several knights in pursuit. Fortunately for him, he was apprehended by one of the more aristocratic members of the royal *familia*, William de Grandcourt, son of the count of Eu. Rather than take Amaury prisoner, he chose instead to assist so noble and high a count to escape, and rode off with him to France. When King Henry at Caen heard the news of his household's victory, he was so taken aback at his luck that he said he wouldn't believe it till he saw the evidence with his own eyes.

The capture of Waleran of Meulan more or less ended the rebellion in Normandy, for the king had only to order the intimidated young man to command his fortresses to surrender and the fighting was over. Henry made a few fearsome executions and mutilations of captured rebels, put Waleran and his friends in prison, and the last serious challenge to his rule over Normandy was done with. It may be that Henry did not quite realise at the time that his victory was quite so final, but 1124 was to be the last attempt of his Norman aristocracy to replace him. Thereafter the only question would be who was to succeed him, a question on which there remained many opinions.

The Succession Debate

Henry I's only biographer to date, the late C. Warren Hollister, has demonstrated how Anglo-Norman court politics between 1125 and 1135 was fixated on the succession to the king. One very important event at the beginning of that period was the death of the Emperor Henry V, King Henry's son-in-law. The emperor had been looking more and more closely at English affairs since the death of William atheling in 1120. It may be significant that when he had married Adeliza of Louvain, King Henry had married the daughter of one of the closest of the emperor's associates, Duke Godfrey of Brabant. A child from the marriage would at least have continued imperial involvement in England. From 1122, following the settlement of his differences with the papacy, Emperor Henry V was increasingly drawn to the Low Countries and the North Sea coast, and Utrecht became something of a western base for him. In 1124 the emperor had mobilised an army to intervene in the affairs of northern France and support King Henry by distracting Louis VI. The emperor's marriage to Mathilda of England had by 1125 proved childless, although there is a rumour that the empress had produced a stillborn son. The emperor's succession to England seems, however, to have been accepted as a likely event on both sides of the North Sea until his death from cancer at Utrecht on 23 May 1125. Mathilda left Germany by the end of the year and joined her father in Normandy.

Until William Clito died unexpectedly, and without leaving children, near Aalst at the end of July 1128, the eyes of the Normans had always been on him, despite the return of the Empress Mathilda to add her claims to the succession debate. It was probably Clito's continuing threat to the borders that kept King Henry in Normandy for much of the period after 1124. The king's agents and informers followed his progress, and Henry had mobilised Count Stephen of Mortain and Boulogne, a favoured nephew, to coordinate opposition to Clito within Flanders in 1127. Stephen was an effective agent, channelling English money into the support of successive claimants, first William of Ypres, then, after his capture, Thierry of Alsace. William Clito's death must have been a great relief to Henry, and the fact that no source mentions that he financed any commemoration for his noble and dispossessed nephew may say something about his attitude to him. King Henry was usually more generous than that, making grants for the souls of both his dead brothers. Orderic reports that the dying count had dictated a letter to King Henry, asking his pardon for the wrongs he did him – doubtless the consequence of his deathbed confession and penance – and asking

the king to pardon his adherents. Henry is said to have done what his
nephew required of him, but no more apparently.

Even before William Clito's death, Henry had made his own choice
as successor uncomfortably clear to his magnates. When his daughter
returned to him in 1126, he seems to have come to the conclusion that
he had but one legitimate child left and God was apparently denying
him further children. Therefore he began moves to clear Mathilda's way
to the throne. Henry still had great faith in an Angevin alliance. He had
been working towards it since arranging with Count Fulk a marriage
between his son, William, and Fulk's daughter, Mathilda, in 1119. Henry's
idea was not a bad one. By uniting Normandy and Anjou in an alliance,
the power of Louis VI to challenge the Anglo-Norman realm would
have been diminished. For this reason, Henry mobilised all his resources
of cunning and influence to thwart a marriage between William Clito
and Sibyl of Anjou in 1124. When Henry was considering what to do
about ensuring Mathilda's succession, he had to give due consideration
to the idea of a husband who could deploy sufficient military and
political weight to assist her. There was no shortage of candidates
presenting themselves in 1126. William of Malmesbury talks of a number
of princes and magnates of the empire who followed the king from
Normandy to England in September and made overtures to Henry for
his daughter's hand. But the king seems already to have decided that a
marriage with the ruler of Anjou held out more prospects for his
daughter and his realm. The bridegroom to be was a teenage boy,
Geoffrey, son of Count Fulk. Fulk himself was on the brink of returning
to Jerusalem to marry the heir to the crown of the Crusading kingdom.

The historian Warren Hollister locates the point when Henry made
his decision about his daughter at the end of 1126, when he switched
many of his political prisoners around in England, removing Duke
Robert from the custody of Bishop Roger of Salisbury and into that of
Earl Robert of Gloucester, the king's eldest son. Since this was said to
have been done on the advice of his daughter and her uncle, David of
Scotland, the move might well be seen as a shift of power within the
court and the appearance of a new group of supporters around Mathilda's
candidature for succession. In midwinter a protracted ceremony was
staged when the magnates and bishops of England were required to take
an oath to support Mathilda's succession when her father died. The new

party at court had then to accept the king's choice of a husband for Mathilda, and we at least know that Earl Robert of Gloucester and Brian fitz Count were asked for their advice. In May 1127 the former empress returned to Rouen and was betrothed to Geoffrey. A year later Geoffrey appeared in person at Rouen, and King Henry himself presented him with arms on his coming of age in a ceremony whose sumptuousness was still being recalled with wonder a generation later. The marriage followed on 17 June at Le Mans. If King Henry was resolved on his daughter's succession to England and Normandy, then Count Geoffrey might well look forward in due course to the rim of a crown descending on his brows at Westminster. Henry of Huntingdon tells us that this was his expectation when his father-in-law eventually did die.

Unfortunately for Henry's plan for his daughter's succession, its most persuasive point was that he wished it to be so. In the winter of 1128 there was no one able to tell him face-to-face that it would not work. One of the main obstacles was Mathilda herself, and that for two reasons. First, the idea of a woman succeeding to the throne was an untried innovation in England. There was certainly no reason why it should not happen; had there been Henry himself would not have suggested it, and people such as King David of Scotland would not have been willing to support her. But the newness of the idea certainly did not help her cause. The other problem was the state of her marriage, which began unhappily and worsened rapidly. By the summer of 1129 relations between the young husband and the more mature wife were so cold that Mathilda packed up in haste and returned to Rouen. It seems that King Henry blamed his son-in-law for the differences, and he allowed Mathilda to live quietly apart from him in Normandy. It seems likely that it was not until his excursion outside Normandy to meet the new pope, Innocent II, at Chartres in January 1131 that Henry turned his mind to the problem of the separated couple. In the three-day festival at Chartres where the pope placed a royal crown on Henry's head after he had prostrated himself – rather as Pope Stephen had crowned Charlemagne – it would have been surprising had the subject of the Angevin marriage not been discussed.[18] In September 1131, at a council at Northampton, Mathilda was formally asked to return to Geoffrey. A significant point is that the same council was asked to swear faith to Mathilda as heir to her father; it was not asked to include Geoffrey of Anjou in that oath.

A contrite Waleran of Meulan was released from prison in order to swear the oath and so put the weight of his powerful family behind it. The precautions taken more than hint that one of Geoffrey's complaints against Mathilda and her father was that the marriage promised him too little. Mathilda's dower estates and castles on the southern Norman border had not been handed over to him, and – against all normal practice – King Henry clearly intended that they should stay under his control until he died.

Henry became a grandfather of a legitimate child when Geoffrey and Mathilda's first son was born in March 1133 at Le Mans (the king's eldest son, Robert of Gloucester, had presented him with a first grandson called Richard, also illegitimate, perhaps as early as 1105). At the baptism of the baby at the cathedral on the liturgically very appropriate eve of Easter, it was King Henry who lifted the baby from the font and gave him his own name. Mathilda's second son, Geoffrey, was born at Rouen in June 1134. With now two legitimate male grandsons, the succession through Mathilda looked more assured. Anyone who objected to Geoffrey or his wife could fix their hopes on the succession of another King Henry in the future. As it turned out, there were to be problems with this optimistic outlook. The dower castles in Normandy which Geoffrey wanted handed over to him were still withheld, and he was in a mood to quarrel with the king about them. This time Mathilda joined with her husband and the disagreement led to a long separation between Henry and her, whether because she took her husband's part or not. The other problem for Henry's planned settlement of his realm was that he was mortal and he was not given the time to repair its defects.

The great huntsman of humanity caught up with Henry as he was himself starting a hunting expedition with his court at the ducal forest of Lyon where he had moved on Monday 25 November 1135, at a time when he and his daughter were still estranged. He had planned to go hunting on the Tuesday morning, but a sudden onset of severe illness woke his attendants in the night. He decided on the Tuesday that he was dying, and his chaplains were called to his chamber to hear his confession. Messengers flew to Rouen to summon the archbishop. On his arrival in company with the bishop of Evreux late on Thursday or on Friday, the king confessed to him again. He confessed and was absolved daily till he died. He also insisted that the archbishop impose an oath on his courtiers not to leave his corpse but to accompany it in proper state to its burial. In his last days, the disgraceful conduct of his father's death and burial were clearly in Henry's mind. For several days the king lingered on, attended by his eldest son, Robert of Gloucester, and a number of other important counts and barons. Earl Robert was given instruction to draw 60,000 pounds from the Norman treasury at Falaise to pay the king's debts, distribute alms to the poor and pay off his retainers. Henry is said to have been lucid and alert for much of the time, and discussed the problems of his succession with those who were at his bedside. The best interpretation of the accounts that survive is that at the end he chose not to endorse his estranged daughter's succession, but declared that he released his men from the oath he had forced on them, and left them free to decide who to support. This was the account of his last instructions on the succession which was presented to the archbishop of Canterbury the next week by two witnesses from the royal household, and their account was not contradicted later by the archbishop of Rouen, who had been present. Henry sank into unconsciousness on the Sunday, by which time he had received anointing and his last communion, and he died as the sun went down on 1 December 1135.

On the morning after Henry's death, his body was borne on the shoulders of his magnates to Rouen, attended by the knights of his household and great crowds. The corpse was taken directly to the cathedral and, in a corner of the building, embalmers were put to work to try their skill at staving off decay, for the king had requested burial in England at the Cluniac abbey he had founded in 1121 at Reading. The king's internal organs were boxed and sent for burial across the Seine at the priory of Notre-Dame-du-Pré, a dependency of Bec-Hellouin, which he had patronised in his lifetime. The rest of the body was appropriately wrapped and attended, and escorted by a company of his household by road to Caen, to rest in the choir of the abbey of St Stephen until the weather permitted its carriage across the Channel. This took four weeks. After Christmas the monks of Caen attended the bier to the quay and a party of them accompanied it across the Channel. His successor, Stephen, and the new court met the body on the coast as it landed, and the new king himself was one of those who put his shoulder to the bier as it was taken to Reading, where it arrived probably

in the evening of Sunday 4 January 1136. The funeral and the burial of
the body before the high altar occurred on the next day. As well as King
Stephen, Henry's widow Adeliza was present too. How many more of
the king's extensive family was present is unknown. Robert of Gloucester
was certainly still in Normandy, but at least one of the king's several
sons is noted as present at the funeral by the Anglo-Saxon Chronicle.
Queen Adeliza travelled up from Arundel to Reading abbey the next
year too, in order to inaugurate the perpetual anniversary mass for
Henry's soul appropriately. In 1151 she made her final journey to the
abbey when her body was laid beside King Henry in the abbey choir.
Their bodies lay there together until the Reformation carried away
Reading abbey. Henry's descendant and seventh namesake on the throne
of England signally failed to honour his memory by taking measures to
preserve his ancestor's burial place.

Such was the end of one of England's more remarkable kings. The
many chroniclers of his reign generally speak well of him, although it
has been suggested that they dared not do otherwise. But there is no
doubt that the peace he maintained in England and brought to Normandy was deeply appreciated, even though the cost was the imposition
of a new administrative elite. He was certainly less heedlessly rapacious
than his elder brother, Rufus. Condemnation of his extramarital pecca-
dilloes was the concern of a few radical clergy and a matter of
indifference to lay society, which recognised as yet no exclusive sexual
union in marriage. Henry, for all his exceptional administrative and
military talents, was in some ways a conventional enough medieval man.
He was obliging and generous to his friends and remorseless and, on
occasion, singularly cruel to those he identified as his enemies. The
tenants of Waleran of Meulan captured at Bourgtheroulde in 1124 were
mutilated, although the mores of the time excused them as simply
following their lord's orders. Henry made out that some of them were
also royal tenants and had them blinded and castrated anyway. As a
young soldier he was willing to carry out his own death sentences: he
had personally hurled a man to his death at Rouen in 1090. As with the
rest of his contemporaries, his preferred form of warfare was economic
– which was hard on the peasants and townsfolk of the borderlands he
devastated. But the abiding impressions of Henry are not of an unrestrained and hypocritical sadist. He invested heavily in the emotional

life of his official and unofficial families, and extravagantly furthered the fortunes of his children, nephews and grandchildren, who clearly loved him. His generosity even extended to his enemies: the fate of his captive brother was not in the end an unhappy one, unless enforced boredom is unhappiness. He went out of his way to discharge his pious obligations to his father, brothers and nephew. Moreover, King Henry was – unlike either of his brothers – a subscriber to the new twelfth-century culture of moral self-examination through regular sacramental confession. Although this was his first wife's obsession, Henry came to share in it and maintained the discipline after her death, until his own. Such a man could be no monster, just a human as flawed as any other; his flaws the more noticeable because of the huge canvas on which his life was painted and the outstanding proportions of his talents.

7

Robert Curthose and William Clito

The complications of succession in the Norman period, and the lack of hard and fast rules – as they were understood in the later middle ages – meant that it was often possible to contest the possession of the throne. After the death of the Conqueror there were three serious contenders for the throne of England who spent years arguing and fighting for what they considered their rights. The first of the three was Robert Curthose, duke of Normandy from 1087 to 1106, who saw himself as deprived of his father's crown by his younger brothers, and who made two serious attempts to assert his rights. Following his capture and enforced retirement in 1106, Robert's claims were asserted and pursued by his son, William Clito, the Young Pretender of the twelfth century. Between 1087 and 1128 father and son posed a serious problem for successive kings of England, and offered would-be rebels a banner and rallying point for their dissatisfaction. Lastly there was the Empress Mathilda, who had been promised the succession to the throne by her father, Henry I, but found that on his death those promises meant little. The Empress Mathilda has perhaps the best claim to be considered the last of the Normans, but it was her fate to be considered more as the originator of the royal claims of the Angevin dynasty.

It is worth saying something about how succession actually occurred in the Norman period. The fact that only one person at a time could exert princely power over a recognised Christian realm had been established in the land of the Western Franks before the arrival of the Seine Vikings at the beginning of the tenth century. Once Normandy had been established as a Christian principality there was never in all its history an attempt to partition it between competing heirs, as if it were the simple estate of a baron, or a conglomerate principality like Blois-Chartres-Champagne. Similarly, the unified kingdom of England had become an indivisible political unit by the end of the tenth century, despite attempts at co-rulership such as that which happened between the rivals Cnut and Edmund Ironside in 1016. Succession to both realms was ideally from father to eldest adult son, but this did not always happen. Richard III of Normandy had a young son, Nicholas, but he was in fact succeeded by his ambitious and domineering brother, Robert I. The fate of a child on the premature death of a father depended on the ambitions of the senior males of the dynasty. Robert I of Normandy was himself succeeded by his small son, despite there being a number of uncles who might have brushed the boy aside but who chose not to do so. The regular succession of male children to their fathers was not an issue that was ever resolved in the central middle ages. John became duke of Normandy and king of England in 1199 despite the claims of Arthur, the under-age son of his elder brother, Geoffrey.

The seizure of the throne by Harold Godwinson in 1066 was a dramatic coup inspired by personal ambition, but it shows how a man with barely a shred of blood connection to the royal house could still attempt to establish himself as king in this period. Harold based his claim on the nomination of his predecessor and the acclamation of the English people. When Stephen laid claim to England and Normandy in 1135 he asserted exactly the same rights, although he could at least back them up by the fact that he was a grandson of the Conqueror. Still, in the view of Mathilda and her descendants, Stephen was a usurper. She was the lawful child of Henry and had on more than one occasion been confirmed publicly as his heir, even if father and daughter were estranged at the time of the old king's death. Lack of a hard-edged custom of succession in the central middle ages therefore meant that here was plenty of scope for rivals and pretenders to trouble the kingdoms and principalities of north-west Europe. This is nowhere more clear than in the way that Robert Curthose was on two occasions sidelined over the right to the throne of England. The newness of the Anglo-Norman realm meant that it could not be regarded as a single and indivisible political unit, as England and Normandy severally were. There was plenty of scope for division of his lands when William the Conqueror died, and schemes of division were continually being proposed throughout the twelfth century. Robert Curthose lost out over England to his younger brother, William Rufus, in 1087, and to his youngest brother, Henry, in 1100.

The Protracted and Quarrelsome Youth of Robert Curthose

Robert was born well before his father's conquest of England, perhaps around 1052. By one account he was left in nominal control of Normandy when William sailed for Sussex in 1066, although real power rested with his mother and a council of senior magnates. Relations between himself and his father were to be a matter of some importance in the subsequent years. Although they are regarded as having usually been at loggerheads, it is much more likely that tension between father and son – however passionate – was episodic, late and brief. Robert grew into a remarkably easy-going man for a medieval prince, and the idea of him sustaining burning resentment against his father is difficult to square with what we know of his behaviour once he was duke of Normandy. If Robert did indeed maintain a grudge against the Conqueror for as long as the chroniclers suggest, he must have had more provocation than they tell us about; either that or there were unknown men stoking his anger behind the scenes. There are only a few glimpses of the young Robert in the chronicles. Since they are mediated through the hostile prose of the writers of Henry I's reign, we cannot entirely trust them. Orderic Vitalis made much of the poor relationship between father and son, and he takes the Conqueror's side because he blamed Robert for the damage his abbey had sustained in the period before 1106. It is from these writers that we learn that Robert's nicknames of 'Gambaron' or 'Curthose' ('Little Fat Legs' or 'Little Breeches') were bestowed on him by his father when he was a child and stuck. The rough affection of a caring father might well have given rise to such a name, so it can hardly be the basis of a lasting hatred based on childhood humiliation that some have suggested. If there is evidence of childhood tension it is to be found between Robert and his lively, arrogant and highly intelligent younger brothers. We know from the account of their violent quarrel at Laigle in 1077 that they were as unpleasant as brothers can sometimes be when together.

The roots of the major quarrel that divided King William from his son lay in Robert's concerns about what it was he was in the end to inherit and where he stood in the meantime. The king recognised early on that something had to be done to exalt his eldest son above the counts and magnates of his realm. His solution was to give Robert the title of count of Maine, the border principality that William had first invaded in 1062 when he was dominant in northern France after the deaths of King Henry and Count Geoffrey of Anjou. William had been able to intimidate the then count of Maine into betrothing his sister to Robert, then only around ten. The marriage had not taken place, but William maintained his ascendancy in the county by military force for most of his subsequent reign and Robert is credited with the title of count of Maine as early as 1063 (he continued to use it till at least 1096). Robert stayed in Normandy during the entire period of the Conquest, as far as can be told, and the expedition gave his father the opportunity to nominate him formally as his heir as duke. William did so before he left for England in 1066. The nomination was given some real weight when Robert was left as regent of Normandy when his mother went to England in 1068, by which time he was probably considered as being of age.

If there were any problems between the king and Robert in the years from 1068 to 1077 we have no word of it, other than in the work of chroniclers of the next generation. According to Orderic, Robert began agitating for his father to give up the rule of Normandy and Maine even before he was of age. This is not entirely convincing, as it was more than any reasonable child would have dared demand from his father at the time. It is just as likely that the problem that erupted in 1077 was of recent origin, and related more to Robert's brothers than his father. The problem may not have been that Robert was anxious to rule some part of his inheritance before his father died, but that he wanted to be sure that the full inheritance would be his. As a younger son with no automatic right to inherit anything, William Rufus, abetted by Henry, was by this time devoting all his considerable talents to wheedling some sort of promise of a future inheritance out of his father. The younger element in the royal court may have polarised around the rival brothers, and the father was caught in 1077 in the middle of an ugly family feud. Robert's anger led him to demand the impossible: direct rule of the duchy. If he had that, none of his brothers could expect any share of their patrimony. By Orderic's account King William tried to reason and conciliate but simply worsened things, and Robert stormed out of the court. Since Robert apparently then tried to seize Rouen, it would seem that he was intent on furthering the demand that he be given Normandy.

On his failure, all that was left to him and his companions was to ride to the frontiers at Châteauneuf-en-Thimerais and into exile.

After a while, needing support, Robert headed for the court of Count Robert of Flanders, his mother's brother. He was received in friendly fashion and, for Queen Mathilda's sake (and perhaps with her financial aid), was handsomely treated. When he travelled further afield, to the western regions of the empire and across northern France, he was met with some enthusiasm, nowhere more so than at the court of King Philip of France, to whom Robert Curthose's secession from his father's realm was a considerable opportunity. Philip had been working hard to secure what he could of the French half of the county of the Vexin since Count Simon of Amiens, Valois and the Vexin had retired. By the end of 1078 Robert had been enlisted in King Philip's campaign against Norman influence in the Vexin. It was a very ill-judged thing to do. It brought Robert into direct conflict with his father and disrupted the political fabric of his homeland as with him in France were some of the more distinguished of the heirs to the great Norman baronies. Understandable or not, it was a warning of the poverty of Robert's political judgement. King Philip allowed Robert to take up quarters in the French castle of Gerberoy, opposite the Norman fortress of Gournay. When early in January 1079 his father led an army to beseige Gerberoy, Robert compounded his misjudgement not simply by attacking his father's force outside the castle walls but by soundly defeating it. He nearly succeeded in killing his father before he recognised William's voice shouting for aid.

This Oedipan act of folly led in the end to negotiation, and in the winter of 1079–80 King William received his son back, solemnly repeating his investiture with the duchy of Normandy. There were consequences, however. The father could not forgive the son for the humiliation he had inflicted on him. Success in war had been the source of William's reputation and strength. Robert had undermined his father's reputation in as personal and as drastic a way as could have been arranged, and after 1079 the Anglo-Norman realm was the more insecure as a result. It may well be that Robert realised the consequences of what he had done. Difficulties with his father continued after 1080; but, although Robert went into exile again in the last year or two of his father's reign, there is no convincing evidence that he allied with his father's external enemies this time. As far as can be told, Robert simply travelled expensively and ceaselessly with his entourage of free spirits. In the course of his travels in France he formed at least one protracted sexual liaison and by 1100 had two adult sons and a daughter. This profligacy had a long-term and unfortunate effect on him; he found that he enjoyed the life of a wealthy vagabond and prince without responsibilities. The customs of the time allowed him plenty of scope for an expensive and itinerant life. There was no shortage of French and imperial princes who were all too happy to entertain a young man of such celebrity. The late eleventh-century 'cult of youth' laid no expectations on him that he should be better and more usefully employed. He could visit notable places of pilgrimage whenever he felt like travelling respectably, and he could also attend the growing number of informal gatherings of knights in northern France for mock fighting and military games.

The cause of Robert's final abandonment of his father's realm was most likely the death of his mother in November 1083. She was close to her eldest son and it was well known that she had defied her husband when he caught her sending abroad money and sympathetic messages to Robert in 1079. It is a fair assumption that she had kept the peace between William and Robert in the aftermath of the reconciliation of 1080. It was not easy to do, as King William could not resist insulting his son in public when they were together, and Robert treated him with indifference as a result. It is difficult to say precisely when the final breakdown occurred. Orderic gives two different accounts of its timing, saying in one place it happened soon after the reconciliation of 1080 and in another that Robert had left Normandy just before his father's death in 1087. In exile, Robert is said to have associated with his father's enemies, notably King Philip of France, and most modern accounts of this period – including that of David Douglas – characterise him as 'in revolt'. Orderic in fact only states that Robert went off to the king of France before his father's death; it is William of Malmesbury who says that he was at war with his native country in 1087. These are, however, hostile accounts written in the next generation by men who ran together the events of 1079–80 and 1087. Contemporary chroniclers are silent on the subject. The only other writer who has anything to say is Robert de Torigny who states that Robert and his troublesome and expensive

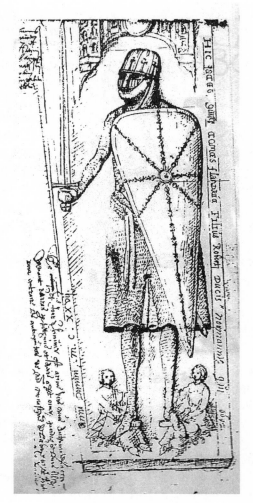

The Tomb of William Clito.

following of young nobles was housed at Abbeville in the county of
Ponthieu when his father was on his deathbed, a place which was far
from the war zone of the Vexin and well outside the effective realm of
King Philip.

Duke Robert, Normandy and William Rufus, 1087–95

Robert did not return to see his father die at Rouen, although he was
notified by a messenger of high rank that his father wished to see him,
nor did he return for the funeral at Caen, where the family was represented by his uncle, Bishop Odo, his eldest first cousin, Abbot Nicholas
of St-Ouen, and his younger brother Henry. This behaviour was hardly
commendable by either modern or medieval standards, but once back
Robert is at least said to have carried out his father's wishes that money
should be distributed to the poor and to the abbeys and churches of
the duchy for his soul, and he is credited with having done so handsomely. The new Duke Robert II also released some of the younger
political prisoners his father had held in Normandy: notably the young
Ulf, illegitimate son of the late King Harold Godwinson, and Duncan,
son of King Malcolm III of Scotland. He is even supposed to have
entertained them and personally bestowed arms on them before they
left the duchy.

The new ducal court did not lose the character of the playboy entourage that had accompanied Robert while he was the dissident heir
to the Anglo-Norman realm: Robert continued to support near him
men who could not be counted on for sage advice in difficult circumstances. He had expected that he would succeed effortlessly to his father's
lands on both sides of the Channel. When he found that William Rufus
had promptly taken England with their father's blessing he was at a loss.
He was a man for war, but only providing someone else worked out
the strategy and logistics. The actions of his contemporaries indicate
that they well recognised Robert's limitations, and the possibilities that
went with them. There was a race between a few ambitious political
heavyweights in his family to elbow aside the useless drones and calculating hangers on who customarily leeched off his good nature, and get
to Robert's ear. First to buttonhole the new duke was his youngest
brother Henry, who was on the scene when Robert arrived in Rouen

and was able to secure from him a grant of the counties of the Avranchin and the Cotentin in return for a large loan out of Henry's cash inheritance. Next in the race came Robert's uncles, Bishop Odo of Bayeux and Count Robert of Mortain. They intended to sharpen Robert's vague resolve to mount an invasion of England. Their own aim was to restore Odo himself to the pre-eminence he had enjoyed before his fall in 1082. Whoever they were, the duke's would-be advisers all had their own interests in mind. All clearly expected Duke Robert to fall in with them, and none were disappointed in his good-natured acquiescence.

Between them, the duke's uncles persuaded him to raise a fleet, an army and allies. Before Christmas 1087, they sailed for England to prepare the way covertly for his invasion force. Duke Robert was left behind to carry on building up the resources to reinforce their rebellion, when it broke out. The two brothers peacefully obtained their lands from an unusually trusting William Rufus, and then got busy undermining him by raising an aristocratic party against him. Encouraged by this evidence of energy and activity, numerous magnates resident in England had embraced the cause of Duke Robert, notably the earls of Shrewsbury and Northumbria. But King William Rufus proved rather more resilient than Bishop Odo and Robert of Mortain had expected. He appealed over the heads of his barons for the assistance of the still numerous group of lesser landowners of English blood. With a modest but loyal force, the king took the war to his enemies and marched into Kent and Sussex, where the invaders had split their forces before going into garrison at Arundel, Pevensey and Rochester. The king seized the strategic strongpoint of Tonbridge, in a fierce but brief siege. Unwisely at this critical point in the campaign, the Norman invaders sat tight in garrison rather than retaliate. It was their calculation that Duke Robert would arrive with an overwhelming force and oblige William Rufus to capitulate, or fight a battle at a disadvantage. This was a mistake because the duke had in fact not got round to organising a second fleet, and was perhaps even beguiled by the influence of Count Henry, his brother, into staying put in the duchy. While warfare raged throughout England, King William Rufus concentrated untroubled on the siege of Pevensey, where he had trapped his uncles. As we have already seen,[1] the hopes of the rebels were eventually in vain, and by July 1088 the duke still had not stirred himself. After a period of turmoil, first Pevensey and then

Rochester surrendered and the rebellion spluttered out like a damp firework. A measure of their humiliating ineffectuality is that the king in the end allowed the rebel leaders to go free and leave England.

On his angry return to Normandy, Bishop Odo re-established himself again at the court of his nephew, where he was to remain influential until the time of the First Crusade. He decided that his other nephew, Count Henry, was a dangerous rival, and maybe also was to blame for the failure of reinforcements to arrive to save the rebellion. Anger will always find a victim. So much is clear from the fact that when Henry reappeared in Normandy in autumn 1088, after a suspicious trip across the Channel, Odo arranged for his arrest and imprisonment in Rouen. Once he had returned, Odo set about addressing the problems of the duchy so far as he could. Like the Conqueror, he saw the danger of letting the county of Maine escape Norman control, and persuaded Duke Robert to undertake a campaign against both Maine and the Bellême family in August-September 1088. Robert started his campaign well, seizing the Manceaux fortress of Ballon and the Bellême castle of St-Céneri. By such prompt action he succeeded in bringing Alençon and Bellême to the brink of surrender. At this point, the duke was supported by some formidable barons of central Normandy, notably William de Breteuil, the son of the late Earl William fitz Osbern, and Ralph de Tosny, lord of Conches. Severe measures were taken against captured rebels, and for a while it looked as though the duchy would be brought to heel. At the approach of winter, however, Duke Robert decided to offer his enemies terms, and ended the southern campaign before he had brought it to any decisive conclusion: doubtless he thought he had done enough to convince his magnates that he had to be treated with caution. In the same spirit he released Count Henry, his brother, and let him resume control over the western provinces of Normandy.

Duke Robert's actions in the crucial period of 1088–89 are symptomatic of his entire career as duke: fitful action not followed through, mingled with uncalculated acts of generosity and long periods of inactivity. He was not an incompetent: he could be trusted to seize castles and win battles. Robert simply lacked much capacity for reading people and situations. Medieval rulers who had no apparent appreciation or understanding of their own situations are a problem to historians. They infuriate us because in the medieval period it is only by working back from people's actions that we can try to appreciate the strategy that may have lain behind them, but Duke Robert is unfortunately resistant to this form of analysis. Irritating or not, historians have to admit that there were such people. Contemporary writers usually had no such problems. For them, faced with someone like Robert, it was enough to say – as Orderic Vitalis said of him – that he was simply a weak duke of whom people took shameless advantage.[2] Duke Robert is more of an enigma to us today than any other leading member of his family. Even with a so-called 'weak king' like Stephen, we can usually work out that he had plans and objectives, even if they were not successful. With Robert we are confronted with a man who at times appears to have been living a rudderless and aimless life which only found direction when a stronger mind (such as his brother Henry or Odo of Bayeux or Ranulf Flambard; or, on Crusade, Raymond of Toulouse) took him in tow for a while. In so far as we can analyse it, his life seems to me to have been a matter of adopting roles and other people's expectations. Before 1087 he buried himself happily in the role of young, free-spirited warrior at large in the world. He had a mistress, fought with his brothers, plagued his father, caused his mother grief, and poured out money like water. He was good at that role, and in an odd sort of way he freely adapted it later to present himself as the warrior and defender of Christendom. This meant that he could surrender his will to Providence and distinguish himself simply by going on long journey and fighting successfully and courageously when he got to the end of it. Crusade involved as little independent effort as any other part of his life.

In 1090 the ducal court's domination by an established aristocratic clique became clear. Its principal members were Bishop Odo, Count Robert of Mortain and William de Breteuil. This group was ruthless with its rivals, as Count Henry had already discovered. In 1090 the clique moved against another perceived rival, Count Robert of Meulan. The count of Meulan was roughly the same age as Duke Robert and had an friendly relationship with him. The count also managed to be quite as amicable with William Rufus, and was the only man who had the political skill to bridge both Anglo-Norman courts in the late 1080s. The Conqueror had given Count Robert control of the key border fortress of Ivry, a castle which provided him with a secure link between Normandy and his French county of Meulan in the Seine valley west of Paris. In 1090, the count of Meulan's rival, William de Breteuil, got the duke to agree to hand Ivry over to him. The agreeable Duke Robert did so but, sensing a problem for once (or being alerted to it by his clique), attempted some compensation. The duke had at his disposal the castle of Brionne, and hoped to defuse tension by giving it to the count of Meulan's aged father, Roger de Beaumont. But although Brionne would be a useful – indeed handsome – addition to the count's family's lands in central Normandy, it was less useful to the count himself, since his aged father, Roger de Beaumont, was still in control of the patrimony.

A visit to the castle of Brionne and a tour of its neighbourhood convinced Count Robert of Meulan that the exchange of Ivry for Brionne was a bad one; we have a description of an especially unpleasant interview he had at the nearby abbey of Bec-Hellouin, where the monks repudiated him as their patron. When Robert confronted the duke and protested loudly at the exchange to which he had not agreed, his enemies in the court – named by the Bec source as William de Breteuil, William Crispin and representatives of the Clare family – had all the excuse they needed to persuade the duke to arrest and imprison him, and take back Brionne. It was left to the count's aged but cunning father, Roger de Beaumont, to get his son out of prison by bribery and flattery. Duke Robert agreed to restore Brionne to the Beaumonts, but to do so had to first lay siege to it, because Robert de Bienfaite – to whom it had been given in custody in the meantime – claimed the castle as his hereditary right.

Such was the unrestrained nature of the politics of Duke Robert's faction-ridden court. Because the duke could not manage his magnates at court, their rivalries spilled out into the country, discrediting his authority and standing. The Brionne problem was only one of the faction fights in 1090. The count of Evreux caused further problems in the autumn by commencing a private war against the neighbouring lord of Conches, Ralph de Tosny. Since Ralph had been one of Duke Robert's early supporters and intimates, he expected help – which was maybe why he had gone so far as to defy the powerful count of Evreux. When he got only vague promises, Ralph followed the same route as Robert of Meulan, and appealed to King William Rufus, who was only too happy to assist. As it transpired, the king's response was subtle and

long-term. Determined to avoid the accusation of crudely seeking to
conquer Normandy and dispossess his brother, he seems to have resolved on a slow and patient insinuation of his power into the duchy.
Instead of a face-to-face once and for all confrontation, Duke Robert
was to be undermined, sidelined and confused. Considering Robert's
personality, William Rufus's plan was extraordinarily clever.

Rufus arrived in eastern Normandy in ostentatious royal state around
the feast of Candlemas (2 February) 1091. He came determined to portray
in his own person the very ruler Duke Robert should have been but
was not. Rufus had in fact been preparing his arrival for some months.
English money and English agents had been entering Normandy since
at least the summer of 1090. Rufus's men were politically creative. By
bribing a faction in the city of Rouen, they had almost been able to
cause a revolt against the duke in November. Fortunately for Robert,
his brother Henry had seen what was coming and arrived in the city
with a force of soldiers and a ruthlessness sufficient to crush the conspiracy. Rufus's money was more effective elsewhere in the duchy. Bribes
secured the support of the count of Aumale and the cross-border lord
of St-Valéry. It may have been encouragement from Rufus that caused
the enterprising French freebooter, Ascelin Goel, to kidnap Duke
Robert's chief supporter and friend, William de Breteuil, in February
1091. Ascelin kept William in prison and safely away from the duke
throughout the crisis period of Rufus's low-key invasion of the duchy.

As with the situation at Rouen, Duke Robert's advisers – perhaps Odo
of Bayeux in particular – were not unaware of what was happening and
attempted to mobilise King Philip of France to assist their man. The
king indeed came and threatened Rufus's base with a sizeable force, but
English bribes bought him off too and the French army returned home.
King Philip's support was always equivocal. On the southern frontier
he was busily helping the duke's enemies to destabilise the frontier
around Ivry. When he arrived, King William set up his court at Eu,
Normandy's easternmost seaport, and confidently opened negotiations.
The result was that king and duke met at Rouen, and came to an
agreement about their future relationship, witnessed by the greater
Anglo-Norman magnates. Duke Robert was obliged to give up to his
brother the ports of Cherbourg and Fécamp and the allegiance of the
eastern counties of Eu and Aumale. He also had to promise not to allow

any punitive action against Rufus's open supporters in Normandy. In
return, the king had only to promise to restore the English lands of
those who supported Robert in 1088; that and to join his brother in a
campaign to regain control of Maine.

In fact, Duke Robert and King William Rufus ignored Maine and
made their brother, Count Henry, their next target, driving him out of
Normandy.[3] The agreement made at Rouen was intended to be hostile
to Henry. Part of the reason for the hostility was that neither duke nor
king had a legitimate heir, and they had to make some decision about
the future. The decision was that they had no intention of letting Henry
benefit from the situation. Each made the other his heir; Count Henry's
claims on the succession were firmly ignored. Duke Robert readily
followed William Rufus's lead in the persecution of Henry, but, on the
success of the siege, it is said that he softened and let Henry ride out
unopposed into exile. Robert followed the king back to England in
August 1091 and made himself useful in the Scottish border war of that
summer, not least in acting as intermediary along with Edgar atheling
in arranging the peace settlement with Malcolm III. Robert hung on
amiably at Rufus's court until within two days of Christmas. By then
he had discovered that Rufus had no intention of honouring his agreement to restore Robert's former supporters to their lands in England.

Despite disappointment in England, Duke Robert nonetheless honoured his part of the bargain, and for a while there was relative peace
in Normandy, despite the continuing depredations of dissidents in the
southern border region (including the activities of his brother, Henry,
now at Domfront). The peace was mainly due not to the duke's strength
but to the long absence of his brother, the king, in England. It was not
until 1094 that William Rufus was able once again to take up his
ambitions to exert control over Normandy. He arrived again at Eu in
mid March, in response to an angry demand from his brother that he
honour the terms of their agreement. Robert and the king met and
talked near Rouen, but got nowhere, if indeed either of them had any
real objective other than tussling for as much control of Normandy as
each could obtain. William Rufus was still spreading money around the
duchy to strengthen his already strong party amongst the magnates.
Duke Robert was still hoping for Philip of France to come to his rescue.
When the brothers came to blows in the summer, King Philip used the

conflict as an excuse to move into southern Normandy. A French army seized Argentan and Philip, then assisted Duke Robert to defeat rebels in central Normandy. The duke's position was now strong enough for him to move with the French to attack Rufus's base at Eu; even though the attack was abandoned at King Philip's request, Rufus was for once on the defensive. It seems that he had moved too fast and had raised the suspicions of King Philip. Late in 1094 he sent instructions to England to disband a huge force of mercenaries that had been collected on the south coast and send money instead. He returned to England himself just after Christmas 1094, having this time achieved very little.

Duke Robert was riding high in 1095, and it was partly because his brother had been ill-judged enough to give Robert the chance to do what he did best – lead armies in the field. Rufus had an even worse time that year as he fought his way through serious domestic difficulties in England. Rufus delegated the pursuit of his Norman ambitions now to one man whose self-interest he could trust, his brother, Count Henry, and he gave him money and a free rein to keep up the pressure on Robert. In the meantime, however, the Norman situation was resolved by circumstances set in train far from the Anglo-Norman realm. The French pope, Urban II, crossed the Alps and travelled to a great synod he had summoned to meet at Clermont in the Auvergne on 18 November 1095. At the conclusion of the council he made a momentous address to the assembled bishops. He dwelt on the perilous state of Christianity on its borders, and he called on the lay magnates of the West to take up their cross and fight to turn back the tide of Turkish aggression that was threatening to overcome the Christian empire in the East. One of the first of the leading princes to answer his call was Duke Robert II of Normandy.

The Hero of Christendom

In the aftermath of the success of the First Crusade, an Anglo-Norman writer wrote of Duke Robert's decision to go that he went 'as much because he had no choice as out of religious feeling'. His view was that Robert's attempts to gain England had failed and his barons were in arms against him, so he had no choice but to take the 'limitless silver and gold' offered by Rufus and try his luck in Palestine.[4] There may be some truth in this piece of twelfth-century cynicism, but there were reasons why Duke Robert should be seduced by the idea of Crusade. It offered him a respectable way out of the restrictions and tedium of rulership, and a return to the open road that he seems to have enjoyed in his youth. Many of his relatives were going: his first cousins, Robert of Flanders and Stephen of Aumale; his brother-in-law, Count Stephen of Blois-Chartres; and – perhaps most influential – his uncle, Bishop Odo of Bayeux. Bishop Odo and several other Norman bishops had been at Clermont, and Odo may well be one of those 'men of religion' who Orderic says inspired the duke to take the cross. Another such influence on him was the abbot of St-Bénigne of Dijon, the papal legate, who in April 1096 undertook a mission to England to agree terms for Robert's surrender of Normandy to his brother for the duration of the expedition. Robert could, it seems, be inspired by religious enthusiasm; there is no doubt that in his own way he shared the piety of the rest of his dynasty. The duke left for southern France and then Italy in September 1096, having fitted out a large military entourage from the payment of ten thousand silver marks (£6666 13s. 4d.) which he received from William Rufus as a pledge for his rule of Normandy in Robert's absence. His departure from Normandy was not without scandal. Some of his less disciplined followers rioted in the Jewish quarter of Rouen and attacked a synagogue, killing Jews of all ages and sexes until ducal household knights intervened.

Duke Robert travelled south in company with the counts of Flanders, Blois-Chartres and Vermandois. Theirs would have been an impressive and well-equipped military array, somewhat better organised and armed than the many other miscellaneous and undisciplined companies travelling the same road, or travelling down the Danube and along the Dalmatian coast into the lands of the eastern empire. Duke Robert and his companions crossed the Alps and he and his uncle, Bishop Odo, had an interview with the pope at Lucca. They spent the winter in Calabria, as guests of the Norman dukes of those part. Bishop Odo died in February 1097 on a side trip to Palermo, where he was buried. In the early spring of 1097 the Crusaders sailed across the Adriatic from Brindisi to Durazzo and took the Roman road into Macedonia, where they joined with the southern Norman commander Bohemond, who had preceded them into Greece and found himself at war with imperial mercenary Turks and heretical Christian groups in what was already a complicated region. Together, this formidable army moved on to Constantinople. On 1 April 1097, the Wednesday of Holy Week, Robert became the second Norman duke of that name to gaze at the massive curtain walls, the palaces, basilicas and columns of the imperial city, still undimmed in its ancient and golden glory. The French newcomers found the Crusade in complete disarray: the earliest companies to arrive had been urged by the Greeks to cross the Bosphorus. Ill-supplied and poorly led, they had been massacred by the Turks occupying Anatolia. The French also found the Emperor Alexius to be deeply suspicious of the westerners who had arrived in response to his appeal. He had wanted professional warriors; he was getting far too many vagabonds and zealots.

Duke Robert and Count Stephen, his brother-in-law, seem to have spent some time in and around Constantinople – perhaps as tourists – and did not immediately join the rest of the French as they crossed the Bosphorus to proceed to the siege of Nicaea, the Turkish capital, in May 1097. They turned up with their companies when the great siege was already well-advanced under Bohemond's direction. The siege had a certain family point for Duke Robert, as his grandfather and namesake was buried in the besieged city. By the time Robert arrived the siege had settled into a blockade. The Crusaders were able to bring the blockade to a conclusion at the end of June when – with the help of imperial troops – they sealed the water route to Nicaea, at which the Turks surrendered the city on terms for fear of starvation. The French leaders decided after this major victory to press on through the Turkish kingdom of Rum towards Syria. It may be that this decision had a lot to do with good imperial intelligence of the internal discord and infighting amongst the Turks and their various subject populations. When the ruler of Rum, Qilij Arslan, attempted to block the Crusaders' route by ambushing Duke Robert's column on the plains of Dorylaeum, a decisive French victory ended any resistance to their progress. Duke Robert played a full part in rallying the Crusaders in his column and leading the great cavalry attack that came up just in time and swept the Turks and their allies aside, leading his company on the left of the French line.

The subsequent march into Syria across the desert plains of Anatolia, a place of blinding white limestone dust and little water, was an epic of endurance. In part the French owed their success to the military skills that their peculiar political system fostered. Thirsty and stricken by heat exhaustion, they still put out cavalry screens and collected intelligence, and knew when to strike hard. It was because of such tactics that they were able to seize the Armenian city of Heraclea (or Eregli) and its supplies from the Turks, just at the point when they were approaching the formidable heights of the bare Ante-Taurus mountains. Duke Robert stayed with the main army, which left Heraclea seeking a way to Antioch through the Armenian lands, rather than joining Bohemond on his invasion of Cilicia. He took the hard way through the mountains and came down with his men into the green valley of the Orontes in October 1097.

The siege of Antioch, which lasted from 21 October 1097 to 3 June 1098, was a defining event in Duke Robert's career, as it was for several of his princely colleagues. The hardships of the siege, the lack of supplies and delayed support from Emperor Alexius made cowards of many. It has been suggested that its tedium caused Robert himself to withdraw to the coast at Latakia at one point. But he did not go so far down the road to disillusionment as his brother-in-law, Stephen of Blois-Chartres, who became sick and depressed during the winter and then abandoned the siege in the crucial days of May 1098 when the besiegers were themselves besieged within the walls of Antioch by a Turkish army. Count Stephen fled to the emperor's army in Armenia. Robert of Normandy was instead one of those commanders – such as Godfrey de Bouillon and Robert of Flanders – whose resolve kept his force of Manceaux, Normans, Bretons and English together. He and his colleagues overbore the relieving army, and eventually forced the Turkish garrison of the citadel of Antioch to ask for terms on 28 June 1098. Robert seems to have been personally indifferent to the discord that then paralysed his colleagues as to what to do next, and certainly is not named as one of those who manoeuvred to secure control over a principality based on Antioch or one of the surrounding cities. He was one of the small group of prestigious leaders to whom in November the Crusaders entrusted the decision as to what route the march must take. It was a recognition by the Crusaders that Robert was there for the sake of principle alone, not to create a principality for himself.

The march into Palestine was not resumed till November, the reason being given out that the late autumn was a better and cooler season for the campaigning that would take the Christians into the mountains of Judaea. The march south up the Orontes valley met its first obstacle in the Saracen city of Marra on 28 November 1098, but the skills of the Christian army in siege warfare led to its seizure within a fortnight. Here the Crusaders demonstrated the ruthlessness customary in their French warfare, where garrisons which failed to surrender at summons were massacred when their fortifications were breached. The same fate had fallen upon Antioch that summer, although there the sheer size of the city meant that many if not most of the people were able to escape through its many exits. The Greeks and the Turks were not so ruthless, preferring to sell captives as slaves. Robert of Normandy missed this act of butchery, staying behind in Antioch with a few other leaders as guardians of the disputed city. The act was brutal, but it had its intended effect in intimidating the surrounding Arab and Saracen magnates into ask for treaties of peace with the French. Duke Robert joined the count of Toulouse in urging a resumption of the march and stayed at Marra into January, walking barefoot south with a group of protesters amongst the poorer Crusaders to embarrass the less eager leaders into moving.

The march south continued, despite the hesitation of the other leaders, and by mid February the army was in the north of Lebanon. The march stalled at a protracted and unsuccessful siege of the fortress of Arqua for three months, but on Friday 13 May 1099, after divisive quarrels and high tensions in their camp, the Crusaders abandoned it. Robert of Normandy was one among the leaders who urged the need to continue, and was helped along by the Arab prince of Tripoli, who offered an alliance against the Egyptian Fatimid sultan, who had seized control of Jerusalem and southern Palestine the previous year while the attention of the sultan of the Turks had been distracted by the siege of Antioch. The march was now very rapid, for the Holy Land is compact. Tancred son of Ottobon, nephew of Bohemond, was able to reach Christian Bethlehem, kilometres south of the holy city, before the rest of the army had reached their main target. The Crusaders came upon Egyptian-held Jerusalem unopposed on 6 June 1099, having covered from Tripoli a distance equivalent only to a march from London to Lincoln. The emotion in the army at the sight of the holy city sprawled across its ancient hill in the beautiful light characteristic of that mountain region reduced men to tears. Duke Robert's division took station in the siege to the north of the New City of Jerusalem outside the dilapidated Byzantine wall next to the basilica of St Stephen the protomartyr, camping in tents in the parched fields. There were several assaults on the walls, all fiercely repulsed, but the breakthrough came on 15 July, when a siege tower was brought up to the eastern walls, north of the deep and narrow Kidron valley and the Temple mount. The penetration of a few Crusaders onto the ramparts from Duke Godfrey's tower caused a panic amongst the defenders, who fled the walls for their lives.

As some of the city towers – notably the Fatimid citadel on the hill called 'Zion' south west of the Temple – surrendered, bloody carnage began in the streets on the east of the city. Many Muslim inhabitants were caught fleeing to the Temple mount where the surviving defenders held out on the roof of the Al'Aqsar mosque on the south of the Temple plain. Duke Robert and his men would have been able to swarm south through the narrow streets of the New City while this was going on. It may be that they chose not to join in the butchery happening in the east of the city. In parts of the city both Jews and Muslims were apprehended and escorted unharmed out of the city, while their houses and their contents were confiscated. Duke Robert and his men did not fail to take advantage of the opportunities for pillaging the abandoned city, and this may have delayed Robert in reaching first what was the Crusaders' principal objective: the basilica of the Holy Sepulchre, where the remaining Armenians and other Christians of the city were sheltering. Duke Robert was actually well-placed to achieve this, but for whatever reason it was an honour that went instead to the Apulian Norman, Tancred son of Ottobon, who stumbled on the great church – as people still do – when he emerged out of the climbing maze of Jerusalem's streets at the head of his men. Two weeks later, however, the duke of Normandy had the pleasure of witnessing the enthronement, under the magnificent Byzantine rotunda that sheltered the shrine of Christ's tomb, of his chancellor, Arnulf of Chocques, as first Latin patriarch of Jerusalem.

Duke Robert and the Anglo-Norman contingent remained for many months in the holy city. By at least one account of a contemporary Robert was a strong candidate amongst those discussed for the position of Latin king of Jerusalem, but he refused the nomination 'because it was too much trouble'.[5] The duke was, however, one of the joint-commanders, with his friend Raymond count of Toulouse, in the subsequent battle on the coastal plain at Ascalon (12 August 1099) which drove off the attempted Egyptian counter-attack against the French holding Jerusalem. The duke in fact distinguished himself by leading the charge of the centre of the Christian line, himself killing the standard-bearer of the commanding Egyptian emir. After the battle he bought the standard from the knight who had picked it up for twenty marks and presented it to his friend, the patriarch. (Master Wace says he later retrieved it, brought it home and gave it to the abbey of Holy Trinity in Caen, where his mother was buried.) The victory was somewhat clouded by the dispute to which it gave rise between the count of Toulouse and Duke Godfrey, the newly-elected advocate of the Holy Places, over the city of Ascalon. Duke Robert supported his friend against Godfrey, and it may have been this dispute which decided both men to leave for home the next month.

Losing Normandy

The astonishing events of 1099 transformed Duke Robert's standing in the Christian world. As one of the conquerors of Jerusalem and a prop of Christendom, he could no longer be considered quite the feckless buffoon that his hostile contemporaries had tried to portray. To Wace – writing in the next generation and in a good position to know – Robert 'had obtained great celebrity and distinction and the whole world talked about his deeds'. The way a contemporary Welsh annalist (writing in 1100 at remote Llanbadarn Fawr) heard the story was that Robert had been the leader of the whole successful enterprise.[6] He had indeed earned imperishable fame, even though it was not by calculation. Indeed – personal bravery aside – he earned it largely by following the direction of more formidable men. Duke Robert travelled home with the counts of Toulouse and Flanders, his closest companions on the journey to Jerusalem. They travelled back up the coast to Antioch, where Bohemond was vigorously etablishing a Latin principality for himself. From there they crossed back to Constantinople, where apparently Robert was honoured by great gifts from the Emperor Alexius, who was anxious to

help the westerners on their way and out of his hair, now that they had
achieved what he had wanted of them. When he returned to Italy, Robert
found that he and his men were celebrities: they were lavishly entertained
by the great count of Sicily, and a marriage was arranged for the duke
with Sibyl of Conversano, great-niece of the famous Robert Guiscard
and first cousin of Bohemond of Antioch. With this much-admired
beauty Robert received a large dower of money and treasure to allow
him to redeem Normandy from his brother, William Rufus.

Robert began his journey back through Italy to France in the spring
of 1100. He was unaware as he slowly travelled back that two men close
to him were meeting their end in the New Forest in Hampshire. In May
1100 Duke Robert's own elder illegitimate son, Richard – then living at
his royal uncle's court in England – was killed in a hunting accident
when a knight of his own following carelessly loosed a crossbow at a
deer and missed. The knight fled for sanctuary at Lewes priory and
escaped King William Rufus's vengeance for his nephew by taking vows
as a monk. This accident was all very ominous, for on 2 August 1100
almost precisely the same fate befell the king himself. As we have seen,
Count Henry was on hand and ready to seize the throne in the continued
absence of Duke Robert. When he finally returned to his realm at the
beginning of September Robert found himself confronted by personal
tragedy in the recent loss of a son, by cause for war with his remaining
brother, and by the good luck of being able effortlessly to reclaim
Normandy without spending a single coin of the treasure he had brought
back from Apulia and Jerusalem.

Yet the circumstances of 1087–8 were duplicated in 1100–1. Although
reportedly outraged that yet another of his brothers had ignored his
claims to the kingship of England, Duke Robert failed to move quickly
or resolutely to assert himself. As we have seen,[7] he allowed himself to
be manipulated by men with their own agenda (notably his cousin,
Count William of Mortain, and Bishop Ranulf Flambard) and was
outmanoeuvred by his calculating brother. Henry remained king and
Robert retired back to Normandy after an invasion which began well
but petered out when there was a need for ruthless and decisive action.
The end of 1101 found Duke Robert back once more in Normandy, faced
with restive magnates and a brother whose ambitions were not satisfied
by securing England. Robert could at least be consoled in the birth of

a daughter in November 1101, to be followed by a son and heir the next year, called William and surnamed 'Clito' (the Young).

The relentless progress from 1101 to 1106 of King Henry's schemes to conquer Normandy and dispossess his brother have been described elsewhere.[8] Robert's difficulties in reasserting himself in the duchy were not inconsiderable. He tried to assert himself but seems to have come to the conclusion quite early that any success depended on cooperation with Henry. He had returned as unable to manage his magnates as he had been before he left, but if Henry and he could find a working arrangement then much of this handicap would be mitigated. Unfortunately, it was not King Henry's nature to wish to share power. Robert's eminence in wider Christendom made Henry cautious as to how he went about eliminating him. He devoted great efforts to secure the consent of the Norman bishops for his actions, and, in the run-up to the decisive battle of Tinchebray, was apparently seriously suggesting that Robert remain duke in name but live in a well-upholstered and supervised retirement. This apparent reasonableness masked a certain insecurity over how to deal with a heroic Crusader duke. It may be that he sensed that Robert was not entirely averse to the suggestion. In the event, it seems that people's memories were short, and little protest greeted Henry's decision to incarcerate his elder brother for life. Certainly the Normans – who had suffered most from his inadequacies – made little immediate protest. When they had some experience of what the rulership of Henry I involved, they changed their minds, but by then Duke Robert had been replaced in people's heads as alternative ruler by his son, William.

Robert's final disappearance into supervised retirement in 1106 seems peculiar. Later medieval writers had some difficulty in believing that Robert did not attempt escape, and put down his passivity to his having been blinded by his brother. But no contemporary writer accused Henry of such brutality, however much they disliked him, so it seems highly unlikely that Robert was badly treated. Robert's passivity was not unprecedented. Another hero of the First Crusade, Edgar atheling, went into retreat at much the same time. The effect of the Crusade on the status of one who returned successfully from the Holy City might have been regarded as equivocal in relation to the world. At various times in the twelfth century, it was suggested that certain sorts of problematic people ought naturally to go to Jerusalem, either that or into a monastery. Deposed kings and men who had been anointed at the point of death and then recovered provided examples. Urban II proclaimed that those who went on Crusade went with what was in effect a deathbed indulgence for their sins. For the many who were to die on the road or in battle this was a consolation. For those who returned, it marked them out starkly from their neighbours. Retirement from the world's affairs was an option that several eventually took. Count Eustace of Boulogne, one of Duke Robert's colleagues on Crusade, took to the cloister in 1125 well before he died. By quitting the world of affairs under compulsion, Robert may simply have seen himself as doing what he always should have done: his misfortunes between Jerusalem and Tinchebray simply underlined his mistake in re-entering high politics.

Robert was well supervised in his retirement. His first place of detention was the castle-palace of Rouen, but he was quickly moved across the Channel to the castle of Wareham in Dorset, being held there briefly before being escorted to Devizes and put into the custody of Bishop Roger of Salisbury. He stayed in Wiltshire until 1126, when, because of a shift in the balance of factions at Henry's court, his custody was entrusted to Earl Robert of Gloucester, Duke Robert's own eldest nephew. The earl moved him into new quarters first at Bristol and then across the Severn to his great castle of Cardiff. His 'captivity' was not by any means onerous, and if John of Salisbury is to be believed he went about in public and may even have received visitors; at least when he was being kept in Wiltshire. Certainly there are records in the 1130 pipe roll of large payments being made for suitable clothing and furnishings for his use. Robert's ducal status in captivity was not queried by his brother: in 1130 the government records themselves call him 'count of Normandy'.

King Henry did not himself attempt to lay claim to the title of 'duke of Normandy', but appears to have pretended to rule Normandy almost as his brother's vicegerent, in the manner of the terms discussed before his capture. In the view reported by Orderic, King Henry saw himself as having taken up the reins of power in the duchy because his brother was inadequate to the protection of the Church in Normandy and because he needed protecting from himself. The words put in the king's mouth in reply to complaints of the duke's treatment voiced by the pope in 1119 may actually be quite close to the truth:

I have not kept my brother in fetters like a captured enemy, but have placed him as a noble pilgrim (*peregrinus*) worn out with many hardships, in a royal castle, and have kept him well supplied with abundance of food and other comforts and furnishings of all kinds. [9]

Henry's initial provision for the boy William Clito also indicates that, in his mind, his brother and his family were to be treated as favoured members of his royal court, so long as they respected the status quo and his family primacy was respected.

Robert Curthose was in his early fifties when he was captured at Tinchebray, and died at Cardiff in February 1134 when he was around the age of eighty-two, having seen his son and heir predecease him in 1128 – a sad fate he shared with his royal brother and captor. The king ordered the duke's funeral to be appropriately conducted, and he was laid to rest before the high altar of Gloucester abbey: a former Mercian royal abbey and site of ceremonial crown-wearings. Henry arranged things with his usual generosity and (as well as the annual commemorative mass) gave an endowment for a perpetual light to burn at his brother's tomb. Robert's reputation grew after his death, and the Norman vernacular historians of the reign of Stephen picture him as the heroic leader of the First Crusade, not just one of its stalwarts. Ten years or so after Robert died, Abbot Suger had an image of the duke at the battle of Ascalon worked into the stained glass at his abbey of St-Denis. The romance literature of the second half of the century expanded fantastically on Robert's Crusading prowess, and he ascended to a place not far below the Arthurian pantheon in his Christian heroism. The abbey of Gloucester much prized its Crusading hero-duke and in the next century paid for a suitable effigy to be placed over the stone cover of his tomb to mark the site for interested visitors and to dignify the solemn anniversary mass. Although damaged, it still survives, which is ironic in that King Henry's tomb and abbey church of Reading have long passed into oblivion.

William Clito

William was born on 25 October 1102, the second legitimate child of his father Duke Robert. He was the duke's third son, however, for Robert had two much older illegitimate sons from a long-term liaison in the late 1070s or early 1080s with a young French woman (allegedly the former sexual partner of an aged priest, whom the young duke cuckolded). William was fated to be the tragic hero of twelfth-century Normandy. His mother, Sybil of Conversano, died a few months after his birth, possibly because of complications caused by the delivery, although contemporary gossip alleges that she was poisoned by a group of envious Norman noblewomen. Little is known of the boy's early life, until he appears in the sources in the aftermath of his father's final defeat at Tinchebray in 1106. Then a boy of four, he came into the hands of his uncle, King Henry. The king, in something of a quandary, decided to give custody of the boy to Duke Robert's elder illegitimate daughter, the countess of Arques, and her husband, Count Elias de St-Saens, formerly a pillar of the cause of the duke, and the principal magnate of the Norman region of Talou. It may be that the king was in fact doing no more than confirming a family arrangement made by Duke Robert after his wife died, when his daughter (whose name is unknown) was asked to take charge of her baby brother.

For his first ten years, the boy William Clito had a standard aristocratic upbringing in upper Normandy, where his guardian controlled the castles of St-Saens and Bures. It was a good time for the boy, whose sister and her husband clearly regarded him with great love and affection. But in the fourth year after the battle of Tinchebray, the security abruptly ceased. King Henry became nervous about the use to which dissident Norman nobles and French agents might put the boy, and soon after August 1110 sent agents to take custody of William. Henry had taken care to choose a time when Count Elias was away from home, calculating on catching the St-Saens household by surprise. But for once the king was outflanked, since Count Elias understood him all too well. His people were on alert and hustled William Clito away into hiding and then brought him to Elias secretly. The count would not give up his charge, seeing it perhaps as a sacred duty to his imprisoned lord, Duke Robert. Leaving his wife and possessions, he smuggled William Clito over the frontier and into perpetual exile. King Henry immediately confiscated St-Saens and gave it to his new crony, the earl of Surrey; the immediate fate of Elias's wife and children is unknown, although a daughter, Mathilda, appears in England under royal protection in the reign of Stephen, by the end of which time Count Elias's son and namesake had recovered his father's patrimony in Normandy. It seems likely that it was the noble King Stephen who restored the family's possessions after 1135.

For the next eighteen years, William Clito wandered north-western Europe in company with his guardian and brother-in-law, who acted first as his tutor and protector, later as his friend and military chief. Their wanderings can be reconstructed to some degree: which is testimony to the public interest of people of the time in the exile and sad fate of the young prince. One of his first hosts was the dissident border magnate, Earl Robert de Bellême, who offered immediate support and assistance against the hated tyrant, Henry. Earl Robert was at the time working closely with King Louis VI in attempting to undermine King Henry in the duchy, so an immediate link was made between William Clito's cause and the agenda of the Capetian kings. Count Elias and Robert de Bellême apparently began their moral campaign with the issue of letters to the princes surrounding Normandy, stating William Clito's case and asking for all sorts of aid, moral, financial and military. This was ominous for King Henry. In Duke Robert he had been dealing with an opponent of fitful energy and little political imagination. Robert's son and his advisers were more acute, opportunistic and had the energy of desperation. They devised a difficult case for the king to answer: they said Henry was excluding William Clito from his rightful inheritance, and holding prisoner his heroic Crusading brother – who was also his lord. William Clito's case was attractive to King Henry's rivals, for the boy could be used to justify any action against the king as an act of charity and justice. When Robert de Bellême was captured and imprisoned by Henry in 1112, Clito and his small entourage were welcomed in turn by his cousin, the young Count Baldwin VII of Flanders, son of his father's friend and companion on Crusade. Baldwin provided William with a home and ample support, and knighted him in 1116 at the early age of fourteen.

As William Clito came to manhood in Flanders, the king his uncle alienated more and more Norman magnates by the decisiveness of his exercise of rule in the duchy. A strong party grew up in Clito's support in Normandy. Chroniclers of the time make much of the boy's alleged poverty and insecurity as he grew up. It is likely enough that he was shadowed and pursued by King Henry's agents wherever he was, but it is also unlikely that his chief sponsors, King Louis VI and Count Baldwin, would have allowed their principal weapon against Henry to lose its edge. The tales of poverty and fear come from William Clito's camp: it was a powerful way of embarrassing the king who was persecuting him, and another way of eliciting sympathy. It was certainly effective propaganda. The Clito party was able to earn the sympathy even of Orderic Vitalis, a professed admirer of King Henry. Orderic had heard that the boy preferred exile and poverty to the offer from his uncle of three counties to rule over in England. It is hardly surprising therefore that, when Amaury de Montfort laid claim to the county of Evreux in 1118, Amaury and his Norman supporters assisted and expanded their cause by rallying around the rebel banner of William Clito.

The Norman rebellion of 1118–19 was not in the end a success for William Clito's cause. It started well, with Count Baldwin leading an army into upper Normandy, powerfully helped by the counts of Eu and Aumale, Clito's kinsmen. The army of the counts was too powerful for King Henry to withstand in the field. It marched to assault the key fortresses of Arques and Bures along the line of the little River Béthune, perhaps with the intention of restoring them both to Count Elias (to whom they had belonged), but in September 1118 Baldwin of Flanders was wounded in the siege of Arques and was put out of action. The army of the counts regretfully pulled back to the border; but what was worse for William was that Count Baldwin's wound had serious long-term consequences, eventually killing him in June 1119. Before Baldwin's death, William Clito had already moved (or was sent) to join the court of King Louis, who was planning his own invasion of Normandy down the Seine valley. Clito was in the king's company when the French army met the Anglo-Norman defenders of the duchy at Brémule on 20 August 1119, and rode as a *bacheler* (that is, a retained young knight) in King Louis's guard. He barely escaped capture in the ensuing catastrophe, which ended his chances of freeing his father and winning Normandy for the time being. He may not have appreciated the generosity of his cousin and rival, William atheling, who sent him back the horse he had lost in the battle, with other gifts of 'necessities'. It only rubbed in the message that Clito was needy.

Following the death of Count Baldwin and the defeat at Brémule, King Louis did not give up the struggle. He continued to take responsibility for William Clito and his cause. Louis was very alert to the potential for embarrassing Henry with his nephew's plight. In October 1119 he brought William with him to his meeting with Pope Calixtus at Reims. Pale, tall and heavily-built, the king made an eloquent and powerful plea against Henry of England before the papal throne at the great door of the cathedral of Reims, his voice echoing back from the west front. Supported by many of the French princes, and with the handsome and youthful figure of the Clito at hand, Louis accused Henry of invading his realm, seizing the duchy of Normandy, imprisoning its duke and exiling and dispossessing its heir. When the archbishop of Rouen and the Norman prelates who were present stood up and attempted to intervene on Henry's behalf, they were shouted down. It was a most satisfactory coup for the French king, whether or not it achieved anything for young William. When King Henry met the pope in person the next month on the Norman frontier, he could only protest at the injuries done to him and repeat the offer he had made to William Clito: to treat him as if he were his son and endow him with suitable lands and honors. Naturally enough William ignored the bait, and the pope could do no more for him.

The Norman rebellion of 1123–24 also had for its rationale the restoration of William Clito. The young Norman conspirators behind the rebellion wanted the young pretender as their duke; they were as uninterested in William's septuagenarian father as they were in his uncle, King Henry. With Henry now without a male heir, the cause of Clito was advancing strongly within his realm. On King Louis's part Amaury de Montfort worked hard (if not selflessly) in William's interest, not least in his scheme in 1123 to secure a marriage alliance for William with a daughter of Count Fulk of Anjou. The girl was to bring with her to William the county of Maine, which Fulk had abstracted from Norman control. It would be a perfect base for operations against King Henry. Fulk seems to have lavished money and troops in his prospective son-in-law's interest, seeing the downfall of an Anglo-Norman realm united under Henry as imminent. The marriage took place but unfortunately fell victim to Henry's astute appeal to canon law, which forbade the marriage of cousins within the degrees which William Clito and Sibyl of Anjou enjoyed. Calixtus II annulled the marriage in August 1124 just after the collapse of the rebellion. The rebellion's failure seems to have made Fulk philosophical about the loss of his new son-in-law, and William returned wifeless to Louis VI's court to await his next opportunity.

Louis VI was once again nothing if not loyal to William, and he was prepared to make real and important sacrifices in his support. With great generosity, in January 1127 Louis bestowed his own county of the Vexin on William, with all its castles and demesne, a magnificent base with which to threaten Normandy and foment future revolts. This was probably the occasion when Queen Adela of France married the young prince to her own half-sister. Even more was offered to William Clito when the county of Flanders became vacant on the childless death of Count Charles on 2 March 1127. Louis VI marched promptly into Flanders and set up his headquarters in the south of the county at Arras on 13 March, with William Clito in his entourage. A week later he summoned the barons of Flanders to meet him to discuss the future of the county. He had already rejected one possible candidate, William of Ypres, an illegitimate son of Count Robert II's younger brother who was known to have the support of King Henry of England. On 30 March 1127 the barons of Flanders assented to the nomination of William Clito as count by King Louis, and elected him unanimously. After a formal act of investiture, the king wrote to all the cities of Flanders giving as his reasons that William 'formerly grew up among you from infancy to boyhood and then to strong young manhood. It is well known that he has always had good habits and you will be able to direct him so that he will observe good customs and be gentle and docile as you see fit'.[10]

King Louis's intentions in nominating William Clito as count of Flanders were less altruistic than he claimed. He had created a major new player in northern French politics. William was now claiming one of the wealthiest and most populous of the French principalities, with claims and influence which spread to the northern Norman border. It would be suprising indeed if, as soon as he was in full control of his new realm, he did not use it to assail Normandy and reclaim his patrimony. That was undoubtedly what Louis wanted, and what King Henry feared. But first, of course, William had to get a firm grip on Flanders, and that was something which Henry was going to do his utmost to prevent. Henry was already involved in the succession contest by the time Louis crossed into Flanders, and had sent money to his own favoured candidate, William of Ypres. At that time Henry could not have imagined how dangerous the situation was about to become for him – his plan was simply to keep the county in turmoil and promote a harmless candidate of his own. As soon as William Clito's election was known to him (he is said to have heard the news in Easter week at Woodstock), Henry sent his trusted nephew and aide, Count Stephen of Mortain and Boulogne, to take control of a military and diplomatic campaign to oppose him.

William and King Louis rode north through Flanders, by way of Béthune, Therouanne and Lille, and were received in procession by the city of Bruges on 5 April. This was a good start to his rule, and he issued his first charters as count to that city and its church. But conditions remained dangerous and uncertain, especially in the west of the county, where William of Ypres was still in arms. William Clito found that his progress towards the key city of St-Omer was fraught with danger; indeed many of the conspirators who had murdered Count Charles were still on the loose. It was not until 16 April that he reached St-Omer in the west of his new realm. But he was in very good humour. An account survives of the young count's reception outside the city by an armed company of grinning boys with whom he playfully scuffled, making himself their captain by seizing their banner. So to smiles and cheers he rode into the city in procession with the city elders and clergy. In the meantime French forces were moving to corner his rival, the count of Ypres, in western Flanders. The count was trapped in the streets of his own city, when the townsfolk betrayed him to the French on 26 April.

In less than a month, Count William Clito had established his authority over the cities and barons of most of Flanders, which was a heavy blow to his uncle. But once King Louis left the county, early in May 1127, William's problems began in earnest. Count Stephen of Boulogne, his first cousin, had arrived from England with a great sum of money and was at work putting together an anti-Clito coalition. A writer in the thick of the troubles, Walter of Therouanne, reported a rumour that King Henry was claiming Flanders as his own inheritance rather than let William Clito get it unopposed. Henry attempted to gain the assistance of Godfrey, duke of Brabant, his father-in-law, although with no success. He had more luck in buying the support of dissident northern Flemish barons and powerful factions in the Flemish cities which favoured England for the sake of trade. Realising where the source of all the trouble was, Count William assembled an army to move against Boulogne and Count Stephen. Count Elias de St-Saens was still at his side, and one of William's first acts was to bestow on his faithful friend the lordship of Montreuil-sur-Mer on the southern borders of Boulogne as a springboard into enemy territory. In August 1127 William Clito crossed into Boulogne with fire and sword and attempted to intimidate Stephen into submission.

Unfortunately, while Count William was fighting on the Channel coast, Henry's tactics began to come to fruition in Flanders. Lille had rebelled against Count William's officers at the beginning of August and, although he suppressed the rising, other cities began to distrust him and the dispossessed Norman mercenaries he brought in to increase his army. Troubles brought him back to the northern cities in September and forced him to conclude a three year truce with Stephen of Boulogne. Other dissident lords were also conspiring against him in favour of his most serious rival for Flanders, Thierry, son of Duke Simon of Alsace, and, like the late Count Charles, a grandson of Robert I of Flanders. In February 1128 William was defied first by St-Omer and then by Ghent, and it is clear that English influence and money was behind the trouble, as the cities did not like the embargo King Henry had laid on trade with Flanders. By the beginning of March the situation was fast deteriorating for William Clito. The critical moment came when Thierry of Alsace appeared at Ghent on 11 March and was accepted by the people as the rival count of Flanders. By now only the southern towns and a few barons were loyal to William; the major cities of north and west were supporting a variety of rivals and contenders. William marched on St-Omer and subdued it on 21 March, and then turned on Ypres; but, while he was marching across southern Flanders, Bruges too accepted Thierry within the city walls and acclaimed him as count of Flanders.

The crisis in William Clito's fortunes as count of Flanders now came fast upon him. He gathered his army of loyal Flemings and Normans at Courtrai in the centre of Flanders, as he pondered a march on the northern cities and on his rival, Thierry. He had William of Ypres released on condition that he joined his army and added his support to his cause. Letters had also flown to Paris to King Louis, who sent a sheaf of warnings to the Flemish cities announcing his impending arrival in the county and his intention to settle their differences with his nominee. William Clito rode south to meet the king at Compiègne at the end of April, but in his absence Thierry struck out towards Lille and secured its obedience, thus hemming William's area of control down to the very fringe of the southern march. On 6 May 1128 the king reached Arras and moved north to try to oust Thierry from Lille, while William Clito dug in further north at Ypres, laying waste all the region as far north of Bruges, which he attempted to blockade. But Louis's attempted siege of Lille failed and, fearing that he would himself be encircled, he evacuated his troops and retreated in confusion across the Flemish frontier. This left Count William isolated and desperate.

On 21 June at Axspoele, south of Bruges, William Clito took the ultimate medieval gamble of a pitched battle with Thierry and his Flemish and German allies. Before battle he had all his knights cut off their long hair, cast off their rich garments and do penance for their sins, as if they were expecting death. The battle was fought on horseback, with William in the front rank of his knights, fighting as if he intended to conquer or die. In the event, his rival's line was the one that collapsed when Count William withdrew in a feigned retreat and his second echelon caught Thierry's men in an ambush. The better training of the Normans paid off, and William's enemies were pursued to the gates of Bruges. William's cause was now beginning to look up and Bruges was under serious threat. The duke of Brabant realised this. With a mass of imperial auxiliaries, Duke Godfrey opportunistically crossed into eastern Flanders to join William and, on 12 July 1128, laid siege to the castle of Aalst, with an eye to the seizure of Ghent immediately Aalst fell. William Clito rode to meet Godfrey with a large force of knights. He was very active in prosecuting the siege, but one day (possibly 22 July) he was engaged in repelling an attempt to relieve the castle when he was pushed from his horse. He grappled with a foot soldier, struggling to wrench the man's spear from him. The blade sliced his lower arm and, losing blood, he was hustled away by his men. The wound became inflamed and soon it was clear that it was gangrenous.

As the young count lay in great pain and in a high fever in his tent,

tended to the end by Count Elias, the siege continued and eventually
Aalst surrendered. By then, William had realised that his death was on
him. He made his confession and had letters written to King Henry
which expressed sorrow for the differences between them and asked his
pardon, and pardon also for the Normans who had supported him. He
sought admission into the Benedictine community of St-Bertin of St-
Omer, and on 28 July 1128 he died at the age of twenty-five. There was
one family member at his deathbed; this was John, a clerical son of
Bishop Odo of Bayeux, and therefore William Clito's cousin. He seems
to have attached himself to the young count as chaplain. King Henry
received back into favour many of the exiles, but the fate of Count Elias
is unknown. He may have been one of those supporters of Clito who
left for Palestine and did not return. Count William's body was carried
to the abbey of St-Bertin at St-Omer and buried there with due honour,
an honour which seems to have increased as the legend of William's
tragedy and chivalry grew. Either the abbey, or later counts of Flanders,
paid in the 1180s for the grave to be covered with a remarkable carved
military effigy, one of the first ever to be set up within a church; a
suitable monument to one of the twelfth century's more remarkable
and famous errant knights. Like his father, who is said to have had a
vision of his son's death while in confinement in Cardiff castle, William
Clito experienced great misfortunes and reverses in his own lifetime,
but after their deaths both men were suitably rewarded by becoming
the objects of a cult of knightliness: secular saints in niches above the
political altar on which their lives were sacrificed.

8

Stephen

When Stephen was born, in or around the year 1096, the world had long accepted as an enduring fact the great power of the Anglo-Norman realm. It dominated the political world in which he grew up, although he did not pass its borders until he came of age in 1112. Like most outsiders, on the edge of something powerful and great, he doubtless wished he could be part of it. But in a sense, he was himself a product of the Norman kings' universal impact on the politics of northern France. His father, after whom he was named, was count of Blois, but his chief city was Chartres (as a result of which historians call his realm 'Blois-Chartres'). Count Stephen was in turn named after the last independent count of Champagne, whose rich and extensive realm to the east of Paris was added to the great complex of family estates in 1027. He is also called Stephen-Henry, probably because his godfather was King Henry of France. It was not infrequent for godsons to take the name of the godfather who lifted them from the baptismal font. The family lands had come intact to Stephen-Henry's father, Theobald III in 1066. When he died in 1089, Theobald used the Blois-Chartres portion to provide for Stephen, but when his elder brother Eudes died, in 1093, Stephen-Henry inherited the lot. At first sight then, Stephen, the future king of England, grew up in a world somewhat removed from the Anglo-Norman realm: a central French world close to the court of France, where Theobald his grandfather, and Hugh his uncle, held the ancient and very distinguished title of 'count palatine'. But his father's marriage to Adela, daughter of the Conqueror (made between 1080 and 1084), provided a new orientation to Blois-Chartres.

Although important, Blois-Chartres was not quite a first-rank power in the politics of northern France at the end of the eleventh century. There was a time – when Richard I was count of Rouen – when Blois dominated the Loire valley, included the city of Tours, and exercised

overlordship over faraway Rennes in Brittany. It had often threatened
the nascent principality of Normandy. But the growing power of Anjou
had forced the counts back on Chartres in the early eleventh century,
and into the arms of the kings of France, to whom they had been obliged
to become loyal and important allies. But Theobald III's realm still
approached quite close to Normandy, and Chartres was within easy
sacking distance of Norman armies (Rollo had allegedly sacked it in
Normandy's earliest days). In the aftermath of the revolt of Robert
Curthose in 1077–79, it was a great coup for the Conqueror to marry
his younger daughter to the heir to Blois. It added Blois to that network
of satellite states which lay like a cordon between Normandy, France
and Anjou and promoted the duchy's security. The match was a great
one too for the young Stephen-Henry of Blois, for Adela was the
daughter of a king (she may well have been born after William's coronation). There were other family links to the Anglo-Norman realm.
Count Stephen-Henry's first cousin, Eudes of Champagne, had partici-
pated in the Conquest and had married (as her third husband) King
William's sister, Adelaide, and so obtained the county of Aumale in
Normandy and later Holderness in Yorkshire.

It was not to be the young Stephen's fate to know his father well.
Stephen-Henry decided to respond to the call to defend Christendom
from the Turks in 1096, along with his brother-in-law, Robert II of
Normandy. Although things started out well, Stephen-Henry fell into
disgrace when he panicked and fled the Crusading army besieged in
Antioch in 1098, which he was supposed to be leading, fearing the fall
of the city. Under cover of a pretended illness, he retreated to Alexan-
dretta, and, too daunted to attempt Antioch's relief, he abandoned the
Crusade and left his men to their fate. He looked extremely foolish
when in his absence the Crusaders defeated the Turks and scored a great
triumph. On arriving home, Stephen-Henry found that his unwelcome
reputation had come back with him. Rather than live with it, he chose
to return to Palestine and there he died at the battle of Ramlah in May
1102. As a result, his acquaintance with the toddler who was his younger
son and namesake could not have lasted much more than the year 1100.
That they were together at least once is proved by Stephen's presence
as an infant witness with his brothers to a charter of their father to
Chartres cathedral.

A much more important person in Stephen's life was the pious, wealthy and cultivated princess who was his mother. She assumed the rule of Blois-Chartres in her husband's absence and after his death, a duty she discharged with great confidence and ability. Unusually for a young medieval aristocrat, Stephen lived in his mother's household till he came of age, and there she had him educated in his letters: we know the name of his tutor, 'William the Norman'. The choice of a Norman for his tutor may indicate that plans for a future in the Anglo-Norman realm had been made very early in his life. Growing up in a realm ruled by such a distinguished woman might very well account for the way he was quite happy in due course to delegate much of his royal power to his own wife, Mathilda. But the chief influence of his mother on his upbringing was her decision what to do with him. Stephen was one of four brothers (a fifth, Eudo, did not survive childhood). When the succession to their father was eventually decided in 1107, the eldest son, deferentially named William, was eliminated from consideration as the new count. This was an honour which went to Theobald IV, his younger brother, who secured the family support of his senior uncle, Hugh, count of Troyes, who had brought up Theobald in his household. William ended up as count of the lesser lordship of Sully. This left the two youngest boys, Stephen and the last-comer Henry (born as a result of their parents' passionate reunion in 1099) to be provided for elsewhere.

Early in 1113 Stephen's intended destiny became clear. At that time he appeared with his brother Count Theobald at the court in Normandy of his uncle, King Henry, on the occasion of a royal visit to the abbey of St-Evroult. Stephen had by then passed his sixteenth birthday, and we can be confident that he had been sent to his uncle for the ceremonies associated with coming of age. Quite likely he experienced his rite of passage alongside another distinguished foreigner, David of Scotland, Queen Mathilda's younger brother, who appeared at court at the same time. Like David, Stephen was given a handsome welcome to his uncle's court in the shape of a county to rule: David was granted Huntingdon, and Stephen got Mortain, the now ancient appanage of the ducal house, vacant since 1106 with the imprisonment of Count William, Stephen's first cousin. Along with Mortain the king gave him great estates in Suffolk and the north west of England. It was probably in the summer of 1113 that Stephen crossed the Channel and saw the kingdom of England for the first time. For the next twenty-two years, over half his adult life, Stephen was one of the leaders of Anglo-Norman court life, trusted by his uncle and never anything other than loyal to his benefactor.

The court of Henry I was one of the cultural and political centres of the Europe of his day. It was a place of great spiritual and literary endeavour, but it was not renowned for sexual morality. Stephen was not exceptional as a young courtier, and found a young woman of the London region with whom he established a long-term sexual relationship, having a son, whom they called Gervase, and also a daughter. His mistress's name – perhaps his nickname for her – was 'Damette' (little lady). Stephen followed custom and set her aside when he married, but he may well have arranged a respectable marriage for her, as she had other later-born sons who are called Gervase's brothers: Amaury and Ralph. She was clearly a woman of means and reputation when we meet her in 1138 receiving a preferential lease of the rich manor of Chelsea from her son Gervase, by then abbot of Westminster.

Stephen established himself early on as a capable soldier. He first appears in command of a force when, still only in his early twenties, he was sent in 1118 by his brother to Champagne to defend the county from Louis VI. The same year saw King Henry invest even more heavily in the Blois connection. He granted to Count Theobald the former lordships of the Montgomery family around Séez and Alençon, on the understanding that Theobald would grant them on to Stephen. The idea was that, by this grant, Stephen would give up any claims he might have put forward to their father's lands. But another motive behind the idea was King Henry's. With the complex of estates of the Montgomery-Belleme family partitioned now between the family of the counts of Blois and their minions, the counts of Perche, the power of Count Theobald would now include the southern Norman March, and make him a more effective barrier to the Angevins in the west. The Angevins were allied with the surviving members of the Montgomery lineage, the king's enemies. Good plan though it was, it failed. The people of Alençon would not accept the arrangement and soon rebelled, with the willing assistance of the count of Anjou. In the ensuing fight, the Anglo-Norman army was defeated, and in the peace settlement that followed the original plan was dropped and the Montgomery family

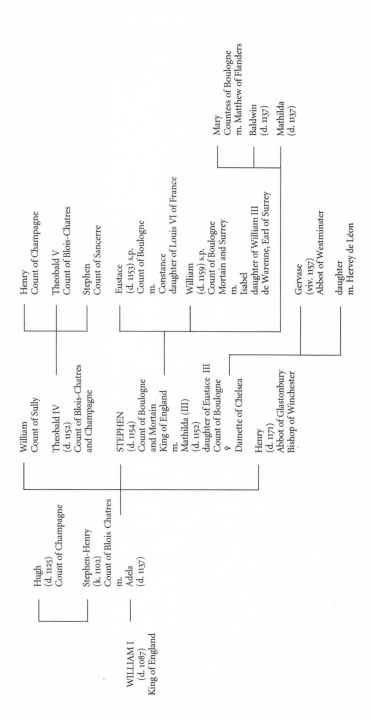

Table 5. The connections of King Stephen.

were reinstated. Despite Orderic's belief that Stephen was in some way to blame for provoking the rebellion at Alençon, Stephen was simply the victim of the local loyalty to the Montgomerys, which he never had the chance to counteract.

In the end, Stephen was compensated more than handsomely for the loss of the Montgomery-Belleme lands. After stalwart service to his uncle during his several years of confrontation with Louis VI of France, he was chosen as husband for Mathilda, heiress to the county of Boulogne, in 1125. Boulogne, and its associated county of Lens further east, were not domains subject to the king of England: the counts of Flanders actually claimed to be suzerain over Boulogne. But even before 1066, the count of Boulogne, as one of those minor princes of the Channel coast north of Normandy, was a person of interest to the dukes. After 1066, with the Channel a Norman lake, Boulogne could not ignore the power of the king-duke. Eustace III was a major Essex landowner as well as count of Boulogne, which further cemented the Norman-Boulonnais relationship. When he decided in 1125 to become a Cluniac monk, Count Eustace consulted with King Henry about a suitable husband for his daughter, and the king suggested Stephen. Such seems to have been the way that Stephen acquired Boulogne, and became one of the wealthiest magnates within his uncle's realm, for the Boulogne estates in England increased his grip on Suffolk and Essex. But Stephen also gained considerable degree of status from the match: his wife's uncles had been the first rulers of the kingdom of Jerusalem, and her father had been a distinguished Crusader in his younger days. The marriage went some way to cancelling out his own family's unfortunate Crusading record. Stephen and Mathilda, as a couple, seem to have thought a lot about the Holy Land; they were great supporters of the Templars and in 1141 Queen Mathilda made the suggestion that his captors release Stephen to her so that they could turn their back on the Anglo-Norman realm and emigrate to Palestine.

The Boulogne marriage brought the thirty-year-old Stephen bodily into the front line of the dynastic struggle between his royal uncle and the dispossessed William Clito. We have already seen how in March 1127 William Clito was elected count of Flanders. By the beginning of April, Stephen and William were already at war, and Stephen was busy orchestrating an opposition party in Flanders on his uncle's behalf. This led to a Flemish invasion of Boulogne in August 1127, which damaged the county, but which Stephen successfully resisted and which led in the end to a three-year truce between the cousins. William Clito's sudden death in July 1128 and the succession of Thierry of Alsace, King Henry's favoured candidate, brought peace to Boulogne. Stephen duly did homage to the new count of Flanders. In the aftermath of all this war and high politics, Stephen had a chance to lean on his sword and take stock. When he did so he would have seen a transformed political landscape. The king his uncle was now sixty years old, and his only recognised heir was the widowed Empress Mathilda, his daughter. But there was resistance to Mathilda, not just because she was a woman, but because the king had married her in 1128 to the young count of Anjou, an untried and alien youth who could in the course of time claim the kingship through her. Stephen and Count Theobald, his brother, cannot have been happy about this match. For Theobald, the main point of the Anglo-Norman alliance was to gain support against Anjou, but after 1128 he had to calculate on the likelihood that Geoffrey of Anjou would one day rule the Anglo-Norman realm. Then Blois-Chartres would be caught between an Angevin empire and the Capetian realm and have to surrender its independence to one or the other. The brothers must have agreed at some point that the only way around this was for Theobald, as the king's nephew, to claim England on Henry's death. We know that they corresponded, for Andrew de Baudemont, Theobald's seneschal, is found on occasion in Count Stephen's travelling retinue.

Becoming King

News reached Stephen that his uncle was on his deathbed while he was residing in the county of Boulogne, perhaps on Wednesday 27 November 1135. It must have taken him aback. Although the old king was now sixty-seven, he had been well and vigorous till that week, on a hunting holiday in the forest of Lyons. Stephen had probably last seen him a month or two previously, when he joined the king patrolling the southern marches of Normandy with his military household. The fact that Stephen was in Boulogne when he heard that the king was dying explains what happened next. There is every reason to believe that Theobald and

Stephen had already agreed a strategy to seize the throne on Henry's death. But when it came to the crunch, Theobald was in central France and Stephen was in an excellent position to move on England. Even more luckily, Stephen was at liberty to move, unlike many of his colleagues at court, who were bound by a solemn oath to stay in Normandy till the king was appropriately buried. The king died during the evening of Advent Sunday, 1 December, and the all-important news may have reached Stephen during Monday, if teams of horses brought the message by relay.

If Stephen had taken ship on Monday afternoon from the port of Wissant, he would have been in Kent with favourable weather as early as 3 December. It is unlikely, however, that he did move that fast, for news had reached England of the king's death before Stephen arrived with it. Knowing what we do of Stephen's intense piety, it is quite likely that, before he crossed the Channel, he would have thought it decent first to organise appropriate commemoration and alms for his departed uncle and benefactor's soul. Dover shut its gates against him; it had been forewarned from Normandy by its lord, Robert of Gloucester, who attempted to close the Channel ports. Stephen landed nonetheless, and, although he found the gates of the city of Canterbury also closed against travellers, rode on to London, where he found a very different welcome. The city was in a tumult over the old king's death: a royal succession was an uncertain time and bad for business. Stephen arrived there at the right time. He was known by the city fathers and popular with the people. A party already existed in the country at large which looked to Stephen and Theobald as lords, as contemporaries tell us – and it was nowhere stronger than in the capital. Count Stephen, the king's nephew, was often in the city, was patron of two of its great churches, St Martin-le-Grand and Aldgate priory, and his mother-in-law was buried at Cluniac Bermondsey, just down the river from the city.[1] So he found the ground for his succession already well prepared. His brother Theobald was hardly known to the English. So rather than proclaim Theobald the rightful king, Stephen rode the moment and answered the popular mood by nominating himself for the succession. The city responded with enthusiasm and its leaders and people were the first to hail him as king.

But Stephen was not yet king; he had a way to go yet before he could sit on his late uncle's throne. In England, from the time of the Conqueror till the time of King John, kingship ceased on the death of the old king, and there was a gap till the new king was formally inaugurated by anointing and coronation. Stephen as yet needed to get himself anointed, and so put his status beyond dispute. Fortunately for him the means were ready to hand in the agency of his younger brother, Henry. Henry of Blois was four or five years younger than Stephen: named not after his uncle but more probably his father, Stephen-Henry of Blois. His mother had arranged for his reception as a boy in the great abbey of Cluny in Burgundy, and there he was educated and professed in what was then the very centre of western monasticism. But in the end, when his uncle offered him the abbacy of Glastonbury in 1126, he followed Stephen into a career in the Anglo-Norman realm. Three years later, when he reached the canonical age of thirty, Henry was nominated to the rich and distinguished see of Winchester, a senior bishopric which he held in conjunction with Glastonbury abbey. He was a singularly princely and political bishop – although no one has ever questioned his dedication to his vows as monk, priest and bishop. By the time King Henry died, he dominated the bench of English bishops with his intellect, authority and self-assurance.

Bishop Henry soon joined his brother in London, and with him came another invaluable adviser, Bishop Roger of Salisbury, the head of the administration of the kingdom. The two bishops got to work. They went into conference with the archbishop of Canterbury, who had doubts about the propriety of setting aside the oath to support Mathilda's succession that Henry I had imposed on the bishops, abbots and magnates of England in 1127. They argued that the king had done wrong in imposing such an oath on his unwilling subjects; and that he had done it only to keep the realm together. Finally – their trump card – they produced the royal steward, Hugh Bigod, who had attended Henry's deathbed and was willing to swear that the king had released his barons from the oath as he was dying, and at the end was not insistent that they accepted his daughter as ruling queen. In the meantime they were urging on the archbishop that the unsettled state of the kingdom would soon cause internal collapse unless he consented to anoint a king: and who was more suitable than Stephen, by lineage and by his military capacity? The archbishop wearily consented, and on the third Sunday of Advent, 22 December 1135, Stephen was crowned king in Westminster abbey. It was a sparsely attended event, since most of the great magnates were still in Normandy, and the coronation banquet was also less than splendid, but the point was that the deed was done, and England had a king. It remained as yet to see whether he would be challenged as king.

The main source of dissent was likely to be in Normandy, where the great magnates of the court had begun their deliberations as to the proper successor while the dead king's body was being embalmed in Rouen. A series of conferences led in the second week of December to an invitation being issued to Theobald of Blois to assume the rule of Normandy, as might have been expected. But all was thrown into confusion when, in the middle of Theobald's first court with his future subjects, a monk brought news from England that London had already accepted Stephen as king. Rather than start a fraternal civil war, Theobald withdrew to Chartres; annoyed, as the sources say – although if so, his annoyance was only temporary. For him, the most important thing was that the count of Anjou was excluded from the succession. For their part, the count of Anjou and the empress had seized several border fortresses north of Maine on news of King Henry's death, but that was all they accomplished. The bulk of the Normans simply refused to accept them, and so, when Stephen was crowned, he was already accepted (*faute de mieux*) as duke of Normandy.

King Stephen's advisers, with the remorseless energy that is characteristic now of a presidential campaign team, ploughed onwards. Bishop Henry masterminded an international offensive against the empress and her claims. During the Christmas season, a brief was prepared for the papal curia, and testimonials collected not just from the bishops of England and Normandy but from northern French courts. Louis VI of France and Count Theobald of Blois both obliged, happy to see Anjou excluded from the succession. A high-powered embassy was despatched to Rome to present the dossier and seek the endorsement of Pope Innocent II. Its members were somewhat discomfited when an Angevin ambassador, the bishop of Le Mans, turned up to dispute their case, but in the end the pope was persuaded by Stephen's advocates, and his cardinals no doubt by English money. A papal letter was sent back to Stephen accepting his claims.[2] The pope asserted his own God-given right to judge such claims and make kings if he wished, and recited what he had been told of the circumstance of Stephen's succession. He deplored the civil anarchy into which he understood England had fallen before Stephen's prompt action recalled it to peace, and he noted Stephen's claims of close kinship to the late Henry and his promises to honour the Church and St Peter in particular. For all these reasons, Pope Innocent accepted Stephen's claims and confirmed him as king. The king's advisers prudently circulated dozens of copies of the letter throughout England (and doubtless Normandy too). The reason we know of it is because one was sent as far north as Hexham, whose prior was a man of literary tastes and copied it into his historical notes.

Another thing that the letter established, which would in the end be to King Stephen's disadvantage, was the idea that public order in England tottered on Henry I's death. Stephen's advisers presented their man to the pope and to England as the public order candidate, a man strong on aristocratic disorder: another King Henry, in other words. Stephen was just the sort of man who could continue the good old Anglo-Norman tradition of strong, administrative kingship. As Stephen would find out, 'zero tolerance' of public disorder is a brittle weapon in the hands of a politician. In fact, there had been insecurity when Henry died, but no widespread disorder other than one nasty murder of one of the late king's nastier servants in Pontefract. Stephen pardoned the murderers on the apparent grounds that he had not been king when the assassination had been carried out, so his majesty could not have been offended by it. Henry's kingship had been rather more subtle than 'zero tolerance', and he specialised in trade offs and bribery in order to keep people quiet and happy. Stephen had to continue to operate that venal system, and he would continue to be challenged by discontented magnates, but he had saddled himself now with a public position that would make any sort of compromise in the affairs of state look like weakness.

King Stephen's episcopal advisers stage-managed an effortless first six months as king for their master. He met the late King's Henry's funeral cortège as it landed in Hampshire, and on 4 January 1136 he was at Reading to witness the elaborate and sumptuous funeral. He put his royal shoulder to the bier of the dead king on its procession into the abbey. Stephen then moved north, gathering troops and support as he went to confront his wife's uncle, King David of Scotland, who had occupied Cumberland and Northumberland in support of the empress, his other niece. David, however, proved amenable when Stephen entered the north with an impressive army funded from the bottomless royal treasury, and a fortnight's conference at Durham between the monarchs in February 1136 settled their differences for the time being. The next item on his advisers' agenda was a fitting court at Easter to make good the paltry support on the day of his coronation and at his first Christmas court. The court began at Westminster on 22 March with the coronation of Queen Mathilda, who had arrived from Boulogne after the birth of their latest child. There was a great banquet with king and queen wearing their gold crowns, the giving of gifts and high festivities as the glittering and densely populated court moved up the Thames to Oxford. But not too many gifts were given. Under the tutelage of his advisers, and being already unquestionably king, Stephen could be more economical with his patronage than his uncle had been in 1100. Some courtiers were annoyed at this. The marcher baron, Richard de Clare, left Oxford muttering darkly about the king's parsimony, and was so intent on his grievance that he blundered into a Welsh ambush in the hills and was murdered. Others were content simply to be confirmed in what Henry had given them. Others again were relieved to get blanket pardons for any misdeeds done in the late king's service. Few got much in the way of new lands or acquisitions.

It was not just the barons who were treated economically. They had been wooed earlier in the year by talk of abolishing the Danegeld and limiting forest pleas; all things the aristocracy of Henry I's reign found onerous – at least those who lacked the king's direct favour. After the papal confirmation arrived in time for Easter, such talk was dropped. Stephen (and the bishops who were advising him) was not quite so cavalier with the Church. He issued a general confirmation of its liberties and relieved it of some of the forest dues imposed on it in the last reign. He also promised to show more respect to churches experiencing a vacancy than his uncle had; he would exact no fees from appointees to bishoprics and abbeys. But Stephen was not too cavalier with his magnates. We know of at least one edict that seems to have come out of his court at this time, which answered an aristocratic concern. He allowed that when in future a baron left several daughters as heirs, his estates could be divided up among them. This allowed a baron to provide for all his daughters, and increased the amount of profitable marriages available for the upwardly mobile.

Failing the Test, 1136–38

So far so good, but after April 1136 troubles began to gather around the head of the new king, which was perhaps no more than any new king should have expected. They were not troubles as serious as had confronted King Henry between 1100 and 1103. But, ominously, they proved difficult for Stephen and his episcopal advisers to resolve, and demonstrated rather too publicly that as a king he had limitations. Discontented barons were the first to challenge him. In May 1136, Stephen heard that two west country magnates – Robert of Bampton and Baldwin de Redvers – had put their castles in defence and defied him. Both were men with a grievance. Robert had been discriminated against by the king in a land dispute with Bishop Henry of Winchester; Baldwin believed that the sheriffdom of Devon and control of Exeter castle were his by right. Neither man apparently declared himself a supporter of the empress, although Robert had an unfortunate and close connection with David of Scotland's household which may not have endeared him to the king. King Stephen knew that he had been put on his mettle, and he was going to rise to the challenge: 'zero tolerance' of disorder was his policy. So he gathered a mighty army, headed west, and drove Robert out of Bampton and into a Scottish exile. Then on to Exeter, but here Baldwin proved very stubborn, and a long siege followed which lasted through the summer of 1136. Stephen now found himself trapped by his initial manifesto as king – he must curb disorder. His advisers were not much help: Bishop Henry urged him to stick to the task until Baldwin was a captive. But summer had passed before the rebel was brought to heel in Hampshire and triumphantly exiled. By then Stephen had made a dreadful mistake in the organisation of his priorities.

During the siege of Exeter a party of alarmed barons had urged the king again and again that he was missing something and was in the wrong place. What he was missing was the fact that in the Welsh Marches the dominant power of the English marcher barons and royal border sheriffs had in May 1136 been suddenly challenged and overthrown by an alliance of Welsh kings. By August 1136 marcher power was everywhere in retreat. When Richard de Clare was killed near Talgarth on 15 April, it had set in motion a train of events which led to the extinction of the Anglo-Norman lordships established in Ceredigion, Dyfed, Glamorgan and Gwent in the 1090s. A new generation of Welsh leaders, using new tactics and strategies, led their war bands against the English and overthrew them. These new young kings, Morgan ab Owain of Glamorgan and Owain ap Gruffudd of Gwynedd, knew all too well how to use castles, and how to penetrate them. While Stephen was pounding the fortifications of Exeter, the English position in the March was being set back to what it had been before the Conqueror died. Stephen did not ignore this developing disaster, but his only response was to send a minor baron of the southern March, Robert of Ewyas, with money and mercenaries to stem the Welsh advance in the south. He sent Baldwin, brother of Richard de Clare, to try to do the same in mid Wales. Neither made much headway, and the king seems to have insisted on the major barons of the March (notably Robert of Gloucester) staying with him at Exeter.

Stephen's problems were compounded by the fact that he had not followed through what seems to have been his original plan to go to Normandy after Pentecost 1136. At the beginning of May he had been expected in the duchy to repeat there the triumphal progress he had made through England. Rumours of the death of Bishop Roger offered a flimsy justification for Stephen to cancel his crossing, and the rebellions in the south west soon entangled him. As with Wales, Stephen knew that something should be done. He had sent Count Waleran of Meulan in advance to Rouen to begin the work just after Easter 1136. Waleran was now the king's son-in-law, having been betrothed to Stephen's two-year-old daughter, Mathilda, so he was a reliable choice. But when the king did not appear in the duchy when he said he would, Waleran found the whole task of pacifying Normandy and containing Angevin aggression fell on him alone. A nobleman of great wealth and very grand connections, a cousin of King Louis VI, Waleran allied with Count Theobald of Blois and Count Alan of Brittany, and was able to restore a precarious peace to the duchy. In September 1136 Count Geoffrey of Anjou attempted to extend his enclave northwards towards Lisieux, but his campaign failed to attract Norman sympathisers, and turned into an embarrassing retreat, with Geoffrey sustaining a serious leg wound. Stephen was fortunate in the skills and determination of his lieutenant in this case, but clearly Normandy would not wait for him forever.

In December 1136 the bishop of Winchester crossed the Channel to prepare the ground for his brother, who had set a new date for his arrival in the duchy. The bishop got busy preparing a diplomatic offensive which would complement Stephen's progress through the duchy, particularly looking to arrange a face-to-face conference between Stephen and Louis VI. The king crossed the Channel early in March 1137 and landed in the west of the duchy. He headed east to overawe the last magnate of any consequence who was opposing him, the lord of Tancarville on the Seine. Tancarville quickly submitted and thereafter the king's march became a more peaceful progress to receive the loyalty of the Normans. Easter was celebrated in style at the ducal city of Evreux, where the king had a formal meeting with his brother, Theobald, and his court. Rich gifts in land and rents were offered to the count; he was also given items from the superb treasury of precious plate that King Henry had built up, including: 'two gold basins of huge weight and marvellous workmanship, in which were set most precious gems. which King Henry of England, his uncle, used to have placed on the table before him at his crown-wearings to show off his wealth and glory'.[3] Nothing was spared in making the Evreux meeting a feast of fraternal affection. This was followed up by the conference with King Louis VI on the frontier, which Bishop Henry had apparently arranged. Here the king's heir, Eustace, a boy of around ten years of age, performed homage for Normandy to Louis, and sealed formal Capetian support for the succession of Stephen to England and Normandy. It may have been subsequent to this that Stephen was formally invested with the duchy.

All was going well with Stephen in Normandy at this time, and we can quite clearly see the familiar hand of Bishop Henry, his brother, in orchestrating a careful mix of diplomacy, military threat and sumptuous ceremony by which the Normans submitted to their new lord. Yet the royal progress did not end quite so happily as it began. The fault may have been Bishop Henry's in part. During the spring a considerable force of Flemish knights arrived in Normandy to join the king's military household under the command of William of Ypres, who had been a claimant to the county of Flanders in 1127. The sequence of events resembles what happened in England in February 1136, when great cash sums were spent on hiring a big mercenary army to overawe David of Scotland. The target this time was Geoffrey of Anjou and the empress, for the king had to make some sort of border demonstration to force the Angevins to negotiate or withdraw. What the cosmopolitan bishop may have forgotten was how much Normans despised foreigners, and how their appearance in positions of trust close to the king could be used to undermine him. A riot was provoked within the royal camp, almost certainly by magnates who were hostile to Stephen; the name of Hugh de Gournay is mentioned by two chroniclers as chiefly responsible. But Earl Robert of Gloucester was also in the army, and he is said to have had a hostile encounter with William of Ypres at this time. So the crucial campaign failed, as a number of Norman barons packed up and went home rather than be slighted in favour of a bunch of Flemings. In the end, the king was only able to achieve a three-year truce with the Angevins, beginning on 24 June 1137; which was far less satisfactory than crushing them.

The final and most serious failures in Normandy in 1137 were the alienation of Robert of Gloucester from Stephen's court and the fall from grace of Bishop Henry. Earl Robert does not seem ever to have taken to Stephen as king and the distaste may have been mutual; the two were regarded as rivals even before Stephen was crowned. But, like him or not, Stephen still needed his support. Robert, however, saw himself as threatened by the growing dominance of Count Waleran at court; a dominance all the more obvious as Bishop Henry was himself squeezed out of influence following the military failure that summer. As Waleran's influence strengthened, the king began more and more to turn to direct military action to futher his ends, which was never the sort of policy that Bishop Henry would have suggested. Earl Robert did not accompany the king back to England at the end of November 1137, but Count Waleran did, even though his job in Normandy was not yet finished. Earl Robert stayed in the duchy pondering on the best way to express his opposition to the king, and in the new year resolved on defiance and rebellion.

The king should not have left Normandy in 1137. He should have learned by his uncle's example that the key to security of the entire Anglo-Norman realm lay in Normandy, not England. If he had stayed in Normandy, his enemies would have had to meet him there, and while he was there they could not challenge him in England with any ease. But Stephen returned to England nonetheless, feeling insecure perhaps about Bishop Roger, and that insecurity was fed by Count Waleran and his family and friends, anxious to take advantage of the fruits of favour in England. There may also have been more personal and pressing reasons that lured the king back across the Channel. Two of his infant children, a boy, Baldwin, and the girl Mathilda who had been betrothed and married to Count Waleran, had died in his absence, and been buried in Aldgate priory in London during 1137. It was also the year that the Countess Adela, his mother, had died in the Cluniac nunnery of Marcigny-sur-Loire. Bereaved and perhaps exhausted by now, Stephen may well have wanted to be with his queen for a while.

The Battle of Lincoln

While the king was in England, Earl Robert of Gloucester had all the time he needed in Normandy to decide how to adapt to the new and hostile regime at court. His choice was not to adapt but to resist, and late in May 1138 sent emissaries to the king to 'defy' him; to return that faith he had sworn to him and explain his reasons. According to William of Malmesbury, one of Robert's reasons was his belief that the king had conspired to have him murdered, which was a reason sufficient alone to cancel out any oath of fealty he had sworn. His friends and allies in England had already realised that the earl was going to rebel, and those in Kent, the March and west country put their castles in defence soon after Easter (3 April) before the earl's messengers actually reached the king. Now the king was faced with more than just armed protest; a significant party in England were openly embracing the empress's cause and civil war was looming.

The king reacted admirably; it was almost as if he was relieved that the pussy-footing of diplomacy and court factions was over and it was down to simple fighting. He seems to have visualised four zones of command: Waleran and William of Ypres were sent to deal with Normandy; he himself took the midlands and the March; the north and the danger of Scotland was confided to Archbishop Thurstan; and Kent was left to the queen to deal with. In every zone, the rebels were crushed.

In Normandy Count Waleran outmanoeuvred Geoffrey of Anjou and humiliated Earl Robert, when he drove him back on Caen. In the north the Scottish invasion was annihilated at the Battle of the Standard near Northallerton. In the March of Wales, Stephen first recovered Hereford by a determined siege, and, when it fell on 15 June, harried and drove Earl Robert's supporters from castle to castle until they were penned within the fortifications of Bristol. Then he turned back and wiped out the rebel strongholds in the middle March, finally storming Shrewsbury castle and putting its garrison to the sword. As news of the Scottish defeat and the rout of the rebels in the March was brought to Kent, Dover castle too surrendered to the queen. It had taken Stephen and the royalist party only four months of 1138 to wipe out the most serious rebellion in the Anglo-Norman realm since 1101. It was a military achievement of the first rank, and outmatched the campaigns of all of Stephen's predecessors since the Conqueror's great wars of the 1070s.

But 1138 did not see the end of the rebellion in England. Bristol did not fall to the king, nor was the king able to find the time and resources to move into the southern March of Wales, the heart of the earl of Gloucester's power. Stephen and his new aristocratic advisers spent much of the next year tinkering with local government measures, and plotting against internal rivals. The year also saw progress towards the marriage of the king's son, Eustace, to Constance, sister of Louis VII of France, with Waleran acting as ambassador to Paris in the spring of 1139. The marriage eventually took place in February 1140, with the town of Cambridge as Constance's dower possession. Bishop Roger of Salisbury and his family fell in June 1139 to a court conspiracy sponsored by Waleran of Meulan, but this event did not at the time contribute to the furtherance of the rebel party's aims. Yet 1139 did see the renewal of the rebellion, and the extension of civil war. The rebels for most of the year had been humiliated, imprisoned, exiled and marginalised, but they were not entirely eliminated, and Earl Robert remained in Normandy, biding his time. Eventually, in September, his frustrations got the better of him and, at the very end of the month, he assembled a small fleet of ships and took ship in western Normandy with his half-sister, the empress, his wife and a body of knights, including some of the previously unacceptable Flemish mercenaries. Taking the long crossing of the Channel, they arrived off Sussex and landed near Arundel on Saturday 30 September. The crossing was perilous in other ways, for Stephen's agents in Normandy had warned the king of what Earl Robert and the empress were planning, and he had closed the south coast ports. However, the earl and the empress knew that Arundel would welcome them, for its owner was the dowager queen Adeliza, and she had been in correspondence with her step-daughter, apparently offering her services as a mediator with King Stephen.

Once the empress had set foot in England, the marginalised rebellion burst out again with far greater violence. Now that a rival claimant was actually in England, all the discontented and dispossessed had an alternative court to which to appeal and at which they could attend. At the end of 1139, rebellion became civil war, as two rival centres of power vied and competed for England. The king was in Dorset when the empress landed, having been distracted (probably intentionally) by a coastal raid of her supporters under Baldwin de Redvers, returned from exile. Stephen reacted rapidly, leading his force eastward in haste to blockade Arundel, but he was still not quick enough to prevent Earl Robert slipping out and taking the back lanes of Hampshire and Wiltshire to reach Gloucestershire and rally his supporters. Once he was present there, his former colleague, Miles of Gloucester, and many of the barons of Herefordshire and the southern March, who had hung back from the rebellion of the previous year but had since promised aid, joined his party with their knights. Meanwhile the king was encamped with a large force outside the formidable fortifications of Arundel, within which the empress was sheltering with Queen Adeliza. Although it might look from this as though the civil war was over before it began, the king was in a difficult situation. Stephen did not make war on women, as he had already demonstrated the previous year by refusing to attack Ludlow, which was commanded by Sybil de Lacy. But Arundel was a greater problem than that. Adeliza was actually a firm supporter of his, and she had recently consented to marry Stephen's friend, the loyalist earl, William d'Aubigné. The king had paid the new couple a friendly visit only the previous year. How could he now burn her castle over her head?

At this point, Bishop Henry, his brother and now papal legate in England, arrived at Arundel and got busy negotiating. The eventual arrangement was that the empress and Countess Mabel of Gloucester (who had been left with her) should be released. The bishop and Count

Waleran agreed to escort them and their entourage safely to Bristol, which was done, much to the amazement of contemporaries (some of whom thought Stephen should have ruthlessly taken and imprisoned the women, as his ancestors would supposedly have done). In the meantime, the civil war had gathered pace. The lower Severn valley was lost to Stephen and strategic castles in the north of Wiltshire, notably Marlborough and Malmesbury, were defying him too. Hereford was once more under seige, and on 7 November 1139 Earl Robert sent a force to sack Count Waleran's city of Worcester: a brutal pay-back for the count's ravaging of his Norman lands the previous year. This brought the king and Waleran into the middle Severn valley, and Waleran retaliated viciously by pillaging and burning Sudeley, the castle of his own cousin, John fitz Harold, now one of Earl Robert's allies.

So commenced what historians once called the 'Anarchy'; meaning a time of unbridled political and social chaos when the barons of England fought out their private feuds and ambitions across the kingdom. This view of the period is mistaken, although what happened after September 1139 was bad enough. King Stephen in fact never lost control of much of his kingdom, as Gloucestershire, Herefordshire and Somerset remained the core of the rebellion (with Devon and Cornwall added to it after 1141). In the rest of the realm – even in Northumberland and Cumberland, which David of Scotland secured as the price of his compliance in 1139 – Stephen's kingship remained a reality, and in the south east he was unchallengeable. Nevertheless, a war zone opened up in 1140 along the Cotswolds, on the Wiltshire downs and in the upper Thames valley, a zone which fluctuated but persisted until the final settlement of the civil war in 1153. Here the war was fiercest while Earl Robert of Gloucester headed the Angevin party in England, and with the backing of his Flemish and Welsh mercenary armies he could not be easily dislodged. The campaigns of 1140 demonstrated to the king and Count Waleran that the Angevin party was deeply dug in. They could damage and contain the rebels, but the king was unable to prevent Miles of Gloucester fulfilling his ambition of controlling Hereford.

The king seems to have become frustrated as a result of his failure to close with the Angevin party. This becomes apparent in two ways. At the end of the summer of 1140 Bishop Henry was allowed by his brother to do what he did best and convene a peace conference at Bath – a royalist outpost in Somerset. There the queen and the new archbishop of Canterbury, Theobald of Bec, sat across a table from Earl Robert of Gloucester and his chief supporters for over a week and actually found some common ground. Possible conditions for peace were thrashed out and taken back, not just to the empress and the king, but even conveyed overseas by Bishop Henry in September to King Louis and Count Theobald. But by November the king had lost interest in the proposals, whatever they were. The second indication of the king's frustration is military: on campaign in Devon early in 1140, commentators believed that he was openly seeking a pitched battle with Earl Robert's field army, something prudent commanders generally tried to avoid but which would have instantly solved Stephen's English problems, if he had been successful in the field.

This is perhaps the root of the recklessness which led to the central catastrophe of Stephen's reign: the battle of Lincoln. The episode began with the seizure of Lincoln castle by Earl Ranulf of Chester, a powerful magnate of the north midlands who had been until then a supporter of the king, although he was married to Earl Robert of Gloucester's daughter. Ranulf had ambitions to extend his power in Lincolnshire and reckoned that he had claims to Lincoln castle itself. He was clearly frustrated that they were being ignored. Before Christmas 1140, the king travelled north to reason with him, and the meeting ended in a written settlement very favourable to the earl of Chester, leaving him in possession of the castle and much else besides, most notably the town and castle of Derby. When Stephen returned to Westminster he found his advisers in a state of astonishment at what he had done. When messengers arrived from the bishop of Lincoln early in January 1141, saying that Earl Ranulf and his brother and their wives were happily keeping Christmas in the city, and that they were without a strong garrison, Stephen was urged to take advantage of the earl's weakness and seize Lincoln back. So the king marched north again, taking with him most of the earls of the court for a swift strike at Earl Ranulf, which was so unexpected that the earl of Chester was besieged before he knew what had happened. Ranulf himself slipped out of the walls in the night, and, on surrender of the castle, his brother and their wives were allowed to follow after him.

It was at this point, as he retreated on Derby, that Earl Ranulf

remembered who his father-in-law was. Urgent messengers brought
Robert of Gloucester, his principal associates and a small host of Welsh
mercenaries into Ranulf's camp at Barrow-on-Soar in Leicestershire by
the end of January. On 1 February 1141, Earl Ranulf and Earl Robert and
their army approached Lincoln again from the south west, up the Fosse
Way. Early in the morning of 2 February, the feast of the Purification
or Candlemas, they forced their way across the River Witham upstream
of the city and offered battle. Stephen was all too keen to accept the
chance to destroy his enemies, even though his own army was outnumbered; so, despite both dissent in his council and unsettling omens, he
marched out of the city and accepted the offer of battle. His army
included his own household, a number of his most considerable earls
and their military households, and a force of Flemish knights under
William of Ypres, but there was not much more than the city militia
of Lincoln to act as infantry. The rebel force was much stronger in
infantry, and a credible interpretation of what happened next is that in
the battle on the river meadows the royalist cavalry charge meant to
scatter the Welsh infantry failed. While the earls and their knights
hesitated and rallied, the rebel knights followed up by the English
infantry launched themselves on the king and the main force, which
had dismounted. They were quickly surrounded and beleaguered. The
earls found themselves separated from the king, and gave up the fight,
riding off the field. The king and his bodyguard made a stand, but in
the end they were all killed or captured. The king was one of the last
down, defying the onset of the earl of Gloucester's knights and laying
about with an axe, a gift from the city of Lincoln, until it broke. He
swept out his sword and carried on the fight almost alone. In the
end he was stunned by a rock hurled at his helmet and William de
Cahaignes, a Dorset knight, grabbed him round the neck shouting: 'Here
everybody! Here! I've got the king!' As with most medieval battles, the
issue was decided within an hour. In this case, the verdict was grim in
its implications.

The Two Mathildas

King Stephen was now the captive of his enemies. After spending a night
under guard in Lincoln castle, while the city outside was plundered and

sacked, he was sent south to be kept in prison in Gloucester castle, where, a week after the battle, he met the exultant empress. She committed him to the earl of Gloucester's keeping at Bristol castle, where he was ordered to be kept in chains. With Stephen her prisoner, Mathilda doubtless expected swift progress towards her recognition as queen over her late father's realm. The new situation, however, was not to be quite so straightforward. There was still her cousin, Queen Mathilda, to deal with, and she had gathered around her the many survivors who had fled the field of Lincoln. Surprisingly, few of them were of a mind as yet to abandon the king's cause. Some doubtless were awaiting favourable overtures from the empress, but many were clearly determined to stand by the queen and her children in their sudden adversity. In some ways, this continued resistance is a warm, and often overlooked, tribute to Stephen's capacity to inspire loyalty in his intimates. With Waleran of Meulan based at Worcester, William Martel, the king's steward, at Sherborne, and the queen and William of Ypres at London, the empress and Earl Robert found they were still more or less confined to their original Angevin enclave. Neither Ranulf of Chester nor David of Scotland as yet appeared to add their forces to those of the empress.

It is at this point that we need to consider the two women called Mathilda who had such an impact on the reign. Stephen's wife and his dynastic rival had more in common than their name. They were both, for instance, nieces of King David of Scotland. Mathilda the empress was his niece through his sister, Queen Mathilda II of England. Mathilda of Boulogne, Stephen's wife, was David's niece through his other sister, Mary, who had married Count Eustace III of Boulogne. The two Mathildas were equal in lineage. Both had a line of descent from King Æthelred II of England. The empress's Norman ducal lineage was equalled by the distinguished Boulonnais connections of the other Mathilda: her father and uncle Godfrey had been eminent crusaders, and Godfrey had been acclaimed king in Jerusalem. Mathilda, the daughter of Henry I, had only the advantage of having once been married to an emperor, and a number of writers have remarked on how pointedly she played on her imperial status. It almost seems that she was compensating for an unaccountable insecurity in her view of herself and her claims to deference.

The Empress Mathilda was in a difficult position in England in 1141,

even after the battle of Lincoln, although the reasons why that should
be are not immediately apparent. The political community of England,
the bishops and magnates, did not dispute and indeed never disputed
that she might have been crowned queen. Gender roles in the twelfth
century did not exclude women from the exercise of power and royal
authority. Mathilda I and Mathilda II, the empress's grandmother and
mother, had both held royal power in England in the absence of their
husbands, and not as figureheads. They had initiated policy and justice,
and Mathilda II had presided at the exchequer court. She had her own
clientele of royal justices, such as Gilbert sheriff of Surrey (d. 1126), to
whom she was reputedly a second mother and whose career and
interests she furthered. Henry I well may have mourned such a soul-
mate. The empress therefore had a number of distinguished
predecessors as a potential queen regnant. Yet she was insecure. In
part this may be explained by her almost exclusive dependence on one
noble faction, her late father's administrative cronies. She was continually distancing herself from them. In 1139 she would not settle at
Robert of Gloucester's capital fortress of Bristol, but moved on to
Gloucester, an ancient royal seat. From there, where she found herself
under the shadow of Miles of Gloucester, she moved on to reside at
the castle of Devizes, a royal castle where she could hold her court
without being beholden to anyone.

The most infamous alleged cause for the empress's problems in 1141
was the insecurity she inspired in others. Pro-Angevin and anti-Angevin
sources alike say that her personal demeanour caused problems at her
court. Courage and determination count for a lot, but only if allied with
judgement and flexibility. This was lacking in the spring and summer
of 1141, when she must have decided she was unassailable. The empress
was a woman who could forget the conventions of accepted royal
behaviour, as they were understood in her day. She openly lost her
temper at court, she threatened men who ought not to have been
threatened, and she lacked magnanimity. It did not impress onlookers
that when she had the upper hand she was prepared to chain and confine
her captured rival, which her grandfather and father had avoided doing
to their captives. It rankled that she was more intransigent towards
provision for Eustace, Stephen's son, than her father had been to William
Clito. Her final misjudgement was to turn a hard face towards the

patricians of London, forgetting how precarious was the support for her party in the city and forgetting what her experience as regent of Italy under her imperial husband should have taught her: cities are turbulent, rich and dangerous places. This was the misjudgement that was to lose her the throne.

It has naturally been suggested by several writers that the Empress Mathilda was criticised simply for being a woman in power in an age when women were supposed to be docile and subordinate. But medieval expectations of gender were not quite as crude as was once suggested. The conclusive argument against such an interpretation of events is the way the sources treat the empress's rival, the other Mathilda, the third queen of England of that name. The queen rallied her captive husband's cause with a determination equal to the empress's, but without alienating the magnates loyal to her cause. Even in the desperate month of June 1141, when the earls of Suffolk and Essex defected and she had to retreat from London, she kept up her party's confidence and was alert for any opportunity. She played on the divisions among the Londoners and the disaffection of Bishop Henry of Winchester. She waged a successful propaganda war with the Angevins, playing on her son's rights, her husband's problematical status as a king in chains, and the discomfort of the English bishops with their position. It should not be unthinkingly assumed that the campaigns fought in her name in Kent in 1138 and in the south east in 1141 were fought without her active involvement. She did not apparently wear armour and ride with her troops, as a few twelfth-century female magnates did, but successful generals do not necessarily have to fight with their soldiers.

The campaign that was fought in 1141 without Stephen was therefore dictated by the differing capacities of two women. Earl Robert of Gloucester was the unfortunate magnate who had to steer the empress safely towards her coronation, and bear the brunt of her impatience. He knew that he must proceed with caution. It was not till a month after Lincoln that he was ready to venture out of the south west and accept the surrender of the first major Angevin gain. Bishop Henry, the king's brother, was willing to submit to the empress and offered the surrender of the city of Winchester; he later said that he did so because he wanted to be in a better position to help his brother. The empress made a stately processional entrance into the city, and in the ensuing

court pushed the limits of the bishops' patience by stating her view that
she was now queen of England. She issued at least one known charter
with that title. She stayed in Hampshire and Wiltshire for most of the
next month (apart from spending Easter at Oxford). Early in March she
received the archbishop of Canterbury in residence at the abbey of
Wilton, where she had taken up quarters. It was probably then that she
learned that her bishops were unhappy that she had assumed the title
of queen in advance of anointing, and later at the council of Winchester
(7–9 April 1141) she was persuaded instead to use the title 'Lady of
England and Normandy' until she was crowned. When that was to be
remained uncertain. Archbishop Theobald had insisted that he should
be able to visit the imprisoned king, and take with him under his
protection some of the king's party. This was allowed. They found him
at Bristol very brave and cheerful, and he gave them permission to
submit to the empress if they wished.

The empress next needed to move on London, but that was not easy.
Queen Mathilda still resided in the Tower and was backed by a large
army. The patrician elite of London was divided over whether to stay
loyal to the queen or to accept the empress. Many were apprehensive
that the empress had not yet forgotten that it was London that had
helped make Stephen's seizure of the throne possible, but others were
keen to push forward and accept the new order. When a delegation
appeared at Winchester on 8 April, the royalist faction was aggressive,
asking for the king's release and bringing Queen Mathilda's emissary,
who argued the case for release. It was another two months before the
Londoners would agree to submission. This finally occurred in mid
June, when the empress's army had moved as close to the city as St
Albans, and then at last she was able to occupy the palace of Westminster. Queen Mathilda and her army evacuated the city and moved south
into Kent. In residence in Westminster the empress received her first
major defectors: Stephen's earl of Essex and two other East Anglian
barons, Aubrey de Vere and Hugh Bigod. All now seemed set for the
coronation, but no coronation took place. The empress was acting
imperiously to all around her, and many had been offended and alienated from her court, not least Bishop Henry, who found that she was
less interested in following his advice than his brother had been – he
had tried to get her to agree that his nephew Eustace should be allowed

the estates Stephen had held as count. Sitting in state at Westminster, she high-handedly and threateningly dismissed the delegation from London which had come expecting civil treatment on the eve of her coronation as queen regnant of England. She played right into the hands of the royalist faction, which on 24 June 1141 raised an armed mob by the ringing of the city's bells, inviting the queen and her troops back across the river. As the Londoners marched on the palace, the empress and her court had no option but to flee, humiliating though it was. They rode dejectedly back down the Oxford road.

The Failure of the Empress, 1141–48

The Angevin reverse in London should not much have helped King Stephen in chains at Bristol castle, but somehow it did. The magnates who had gone over to the empress were not impressed by their reception at her court, and many would no doubt soon be ready to do as Bishop Henry had done. He did not return to her side after the disaster at Westminster. The empress and her closest allies could not but notice this defection, and late in July they assembled as large and as sumptuous a court as they could at Oxford, to try to reassert her prestige. Here she and the leaders of her council resolved to humble the legate, as a lesson to others, and an army was summoned to march on Winchester. The empress awaited it at Devizes in Wiltshire, and was pleased and delighted to find that Count Waleran of Meulan, Stephen's former mainstay and lieutenant, had come to her as a humble suppliant. The count's Norman lands had been seized by her husband, Count Geoffrey, in his slow campaign of conquest in the duchy. Rather than lose what he had in Normandy, Count Waleran chose to seek a peace with the Angevin party. Having been gloated over by his delightful adversary, he sailed back home. This was probably the one of the last moments of satisfaction the empress was to enjoy in England, for when, in August 1141, her army moved to confront Bishop Henry in his fortified palace of Wolvesey in Winchester, she found him intransigent. Within days, she set her troops to begin a siege of the palace, and immediately lost the Church's support. She also opened the way to her own military disaster, for she had overreached herself and taken up an untenable military position. Queen Mathilda and William of Ypres skilfully moved their own army to cut off the empress's force in Winchester, and on Sunday 14 September she and Earl Robert unexpectedly found themselves trapped, as her fair-weather supporters (Ranulf of Chester among them) bolted for safety.

With the city of Winchester in panic and her army disintegrating, and with the garrison of Wolvesey sallying out into the streets in pursuit, the empress and her bodyguard attempted to make a break for freedom out of the city gates before the trap closed. Although the empress made it, it was at the cost of the capture of Earl Robert, who defended the causeway over the River Test at Stockbridge to give her time to escape. He was taken prisoner by the young and gallant Earl William de Warenne of Surrey. Earl Robert was taken to Rochester castle in Kent for safe custody. The empress and her party had no other choice but to negotiate for his release, and the only bargaining lever they had was the king. Some attempt was made to revive ideas of a peace settlement: Countess Mabel of Gloucester apparently proposed to Queen Mathilda that one solution would be that the king resumed his throne, but that the government should be entrusted to her husband. If that was suggested, it was not accepted, and in the end a simple exchange was arranged, with elaborate safeguards and the delivery of hostages. On 1 November 1141 the crossover was managed at Winchester. King and earl had time for a few polite words as the hostages were handed over, and Earl Robert is recorded as explaining to Stephen that his opposition to him was nothing personal but a stand on principle.

Stephen was once more king in other than name. His brother the legate arranged a church council in London in December to reassert Stephen's kingship in a public forum; for good measure, and to show he was back, he excommunicated the entire Angevin party, apart from the empress herself. The king then moved on to loyal Canterbury where he held his Christmas court and reappeared with his queen in state, enthroned and wearing golden crowns placed on their heads by Archbishop Theobald. But it was not quite so easy to erase the effects of the best part of a year in captivity. Devon and Cornwall, and most of Normandy, had fallen to the Angevins, and could not be easily recovered. Stephen had suffered an intolerable strain: a chained prisoner, but still a king who was obliged to appear affable and poised before others. This had its effects in what seems to have been a long period of nervous prostration which began soon after Christmas. In the new year he did little campaigning, although he began preparations for the assembly of a powerful army in the north. But on 7 June 1142 he suffered a total collapse in health, and stayed ill and listless in Northampton till the end of August. His enemies were much in hopes of his death. At the end of summer, however, Stephen was well again, and had found some new direction. First he appeared suddenly in Dorset, where he seized the Angevin party's chief port of Wareham, cutting a major link with France. He then swung north, coming upon the outer defences of Oxford from an unexpected direction, and on 26 September 1142 burst through the town defences and drove the garrison into the castle. His speed was such that there was no chance to hustle the empress away, and she was trapped in Oxford castle, which was closely blockaded.

King Stephen could hardly believe his luck; the symmetry of events could not be bettered. There was no possibility of relief for Oxford castle, and the king had no longer any compunction about taking the empress prisoner. Earl Robert of Gloucester was abroad in Normandy, and no other sympathetic magnate had the authority (or apparently the inclination) to break the blockade. Meanwhile the king and his forces camped safely within the heavily fortified borough to the east of the castle, and drew a tight cordon around it. The siege lasted for over three months. Even when Earl Robert reappeared on the south coast at the end of October, he was unable to find the resources to break it. Yet the empress escaped – with the aid of sympathisers in the royal army, some said. She slipped out of Oxford castle on a night in mid December when snow was heavy on the ground and the river courses west of the castle were frozen solid. With an escort of a few knights, all wrapped in white cloaks, they found the Abingdon road and refuge in the abbey, from which they headed south to friendly Wallingford castle the next day. When King Stephen heard that his chance to capture his rival was gone, he philosophically allowed the castle to surrender on easy terms. He was a man of real nobility, as even the twenty-first century understands it.

The civil war limped on. If the king ended 1142 on a height of prestige, the next year saw him plunged back into the depths. Having secured Oxford, and thrown back the Angevin cause across the Cotswolds once again, the king planned to restore his control over Dorset and Wiltshire and link up with his surviving supporters in Somerset. He was busy setting up a campaign headquarters at the nunnery of Wilton in the early summer before unleashing a major assault on Salisbury. As the sun was setting on 1 July 1143 and the royal household troops were settling into their bivouacs, the king's men were surprised by a pre-emptive assault. King Stephen and Bishop Henry were hustled away by their guards and escaped in the dusk, but the king's friend, William Martel, was captured as he covered his master's flight. The royal army was scattered and its supplies seized. It was a more serious blow to Stephen than might appear at first sight. To secure his friend's release, the king had to surrender his principal fortress west of the River Test, Sherborne. His barons refused to support a further campaign west of Hampshire, and so the whole region was perforce conceded to the earl of Gloucester. Surviving royalists in the south west sought a truce, and the king did not return to the region until the last years of his reign, after the war was over.

Wilton was not the sum of Stephen's problems in 1143; he compounded it with a serious political misjudgement. At the end of September at St Albans, he bowed to pressure from an envious court faction and arrested the earl of Essex, Geoffrey de Mandeville. Earl Geoffrey was an unexceptional royal servant, with a wide network of political and family connections, who had been Stephen's principal agent in the government of Essex, Middlesex and Hertfordshire since the beginning of the reign. He had been well rewarded with an earldom and many privileges. Although he had temporised with the empress when she finally reached Westminster in 1141, he had abandoned her before Winchester and joined Queen Mathilda's army. The charges against him were that he was plotting with the king's enemies, and he was seized on these specious grounds and not released till he handed over his castles. As soon as he was free again, he gathered his friends and allies and began a private war on the king. He did not – and this is noticeable – declare for the empress; he clearly saw no point in that. Until August 1144, Geoffrey excluded the king from the fenland areas of Huntingdonshire and Cambridgeshire. He used this debatable land as a secure base for raising funds on surrounding villages and monasteries, and for attacking the possessions of his enemies at court, until he was struck down by an arrow while blockading a castle near Newmarket. He died a month later, on 26 September 1144.

King Stephen was by 1144 in a situation of political and military stalemate. Many of his greatest earls were alienated from him, and from relying too much on the support of a single noble faction (Count Waleran and his allies till 1141) he had veered towards relying too much on the support and advice of a clique of greedy household servants. He was unable to raise sufficient support for major campaigns, and for several years after 1143 he was forced to scale down his military activity to annual initiatives intended to force a route into the vale of Gloucester, and so threaten the central Angevin fortress of Gloucester itself. Securing Gloucester would force a wedge between the two principal Angevin-inclined earls of Gloucester and Hereford (Miles of Gloucester had secured the earldom in 1141). Earl Robert, for his part, was even shorter of support and resources, and was forced back gradually on the defensive. In 1145 even his family turned against him, when his son Philip defected to the king. The civil war was now being fought in a narrow cockpit of the upper Thames valley. Elsewhere, local concordats had begun to eliminate military activity and brigandage. However, constant and dogged pressure brought the king some advantage. By 1146 he had edged forward to within striking distance of Gloucester, which was a significant accomplishment given his circumstances. As a result, the Angevin party agreed to a peace conference, at which the empress was represented by another of her half-brothers, Earl Reginald of Cornwall. Nothing came of it, but it is significant that it happened.

The beginning of the end of the civil war occurred in 1147. It was a curious year. Henry, the son of the empress, now aged fourteen, arrived unannounced in England in March with a small force of mercenaries which he had duped into following him. After an incompetent few weeks of campaigning in the north of Wiltshire, the young man found his men mutinous and his mother and uncle unwilling to lend him money to pay them. So Henry asked the king, his cousin and his enemy, for the cash, and (it is said) King Stephen sent him funds to pay off his men and go back home. Other than that, the desultory campaigning in the Thames valley continued. It was in building up yet another offensive in October 1147 that Earl Robert fell ill and, on the last day of the month, died at Bristol in his late fifties. The empress did not stay in England for longer than four months after Earl Robert's death. There was no one of sufficient authority and commitment to fill his place of leadership.

In mid February 1148, the Empress Mathilda gave up her ambition to be queen, and it seems informed all her former partisans that they should instead support her eldest son, Henry. It is the measure of her failure that her departure was not noticed by any contemporary chronicler. When she went, the civil war effectively ended.

The empress did not disappear into obscurity. She retired to Normandy to be reunited with her husband after nearly a decade of separation; medieval political marriages were punctuated by such absences. By 1149 she had made her permanent home outside Rouen on the left bank of the Seine, at the palace-priory her father had constructed at Notre-Dame-du-Pré. It was a residence comparable to King Henry's other palace-priory at Dunstable, a royal place of retreat from London. Like her mother at Westminster and the other Mathilda, Stephen's queen, at Canterbury, the empress lived in gracious and respectable seclusion. She was withdrawn from court life, yet at the same time in close contact with it. Messengers and suppliants passed to and from the city and her own establishment. She assisted them by sponsoring the building of the first stone bridge across the Seine at Rouen, the 'Pont Mathilde'. From Notre-Dame-du-Pré she monitored the great events of her day: her son's succession to Normandy; his acquisition of Aquitaine by marriage; the settlement of the succession of England; and the first years of a new royal dynasty. She was perfectly capable of asserting herself in the new Angevin world, and her son is said to have consulted her regularly. She issued a writ from Normandy to the sheriff of Hereford to protect the lands of her father's abbey of Reading, for instance. She was particularly active in Norman affairs, where her son seems to have conceded her the right to oversee the duchy's administration. She sat as justice in a number of known cases. She maintained her own court with clerks and knights, and the outer court of her palace at Notre-Dame-du-Pré must have been as busy a place as that of any prince.

The empress remained active politically to the end, but took care to prepare her own memorial and departure from the world, so it is likely she developed a long-term illness that turned her mind to her mortality. She died on 10 September 1167, and was buried with sumptuous ceremony before the high altar of the Benedictine abbey church of Le Bec-Hellouin, in its gentle and wooded valley south of Rouen. Bec was the mother house of the priory of Notre-Dame-du-Pré, and she had made her intention to be buried there know as early as 1134. Her tomb received the famous, if toadying, epitaph:

> Great by birth, greater by marriage, greatest in her offspring,
> Here lies the daughter, wife and mother of Henry.

Her tomb was damaged by a fire which swept through the abbey in 1263, and smashed (ironically) by English soldiers invading Normandy in 1421. Her body was rediscovered in 1684, then lost when Bec's abbey church was levelled by the Revolution. It was rediscovered again in 1846. Her remains now lie in the cathedral of Rouen, which was the place her father had selected for her burial when she was apparently near to death in 1134. The final resting place of the last of the Norman line is therefore where the first of the Normans was also laid. The symmetry of this was not lost on the nineteenth-century Norman historians who lobbied for her to lie there, rather than amongst the French kings at St-Denis.

The End of the Reign

As far as the king was concerned, the last six years of Stephen's reign were a protracted struggle to continue his dynasty in his son, Eustace. The war had died down, and, although an Angevin party continued to exist and the south west of England and the southern March remained closed to royal government, hostilities more or less ceased. There was no longer a pretender to the crown in England to stimulate conflict. The king, for his part, had a different sort of struggle on his mind, more diplomatic than military. Eustace probably came of age in the summer of 1147 when he was twenty-one (the age which was to become the customary age of majority in England later in the century). His father knighted him and invested him formally with the county of Boulogne, no doubt with his mother's approval. Eustace was a promising young man, bearing some comparison with William atheling, son of Henry I. He was fully devoted to his father's interests, and a capable military lieutenant: he was already being used as the king's alter ego in his campaigns of 1148. He was not reluctant to confront some of the more experienced and formidable captains of his day, older men like the earls of Chester and Hereford.

Eustace grew to manhood knowing that his succession to the throne of England was never going to be assured. The only way for him to increase his chances was to confront, and preferably to slay, his chief rival, Henry fitz Empress. Eustace had his first chance in 1149, when Henry arrived once again in England. Henry had not in fact come to fight. In 1149 he was sixteen years of age, and his father Geoffrey, now duke of Normandy, wanted to declare him an adult. So he was sent to his future kingdom, to seek out the senior male of his lineage – King David of Scotland – who would perform the ceremony of the delivery of arms in appropriate style. From the west country, Henry rode north in a company of other young male aristocrats. It was the custom for a prince to receive arms along with other boys, who would receive gifts from the president of the ceremony, add to the lustre of the occasion and participate afterwards in military games which would show off their prowess. Henry rode in peace to Carlisle to meet his great-uncle, and a magnificent festival ensued in which Henry took the title 'duke of Normandy'. It was doubtless his intention to ride back peacefully too, but Count Eustace had got wind of his route. Near Dursley in the Cotswolds he and his knights laid an ambush for Henry and his escort, which the young duke narrowly evaded. Having failed in what seems to have been an assassination bid, Eustace collected his forces and ranged across northern Wiltshire and the Thames valley, seeking to draw Duke Henry into a battle in which he might be killed, humiliated or captured. Henry would not take the bait, but he was lucky enough later to catch Eustace attempting to seize Devizes and drive him away. Contemporaries were well aware of what was happening. John of Hexham noted in this year 'there was a contest of arms between [Henry] and Eustace, the son of King Stephen, for they were rivals for the same crown'.[4]

Stephen knew of measures he could take to increase Eustace's chances of securing England. One option was to seek to get Eustace crowned king while he himself was still on the throne. It was a strategy which had been employed several times over the centuries in France. The current king, Louis VII, had in fact been first crowned in 1131, six years before his father died and days after the accidental death of his elder brother, Philip, who had also been crowned in his father's lifetime. In the previous century King Henry of France (and his elder brother Hugh) had both also been crowned before their father, Robert II, had died in

1031. But this French practice was unknown in England, where it had been the custom before 1066 to designate an heir out of a group of male candidates, or athelings. Custom or no, there was nothing which stood in the way of an English king having a son crowned before he died; indeed Henry II of England would do just this in 1170, with the coronation of his eldest son, Henry the Young King. To secure a crown for King Eustace of England was a realistic dream for Stephen, but a nightmare for his rivals.

It can be deduced that King Stephen first broached the subject of the coronation of Eustace in the aftermath of the 1149 campaign against Duke Henry in the west country. This is some evidence of how seriously the king took the problem which Henry represented. He may first have sounded out Archbishop Theobald, but found no support there. The papacy had cooled considerably to Stephen since Innocent II's endorsement of his kingship early in 1136. Late in 1143 or early in 1144, the then pope, Celestine II, wrote to Archbishop Theobald saying that he considered the succession to England in 1135 to have been irregular and still under dispute, and that he wanted no 'innovation' in relations between king and church. This pronouncement was still in force in 1150, and the archbishop probably backed up his refusal to crown Eustace with its authority. Since Theobald had acquired a legateship over England, there was nothing else preventing his compliance with the king's request. In April 1151 representations were being made at Rome over Eustace's rights. Although Pope Eugenius III was willing to recognise that Eustace was Stephen's heir, the acknowledgement was deeply ambiguous, and certainly did not sanction his coronation. When Stephen insisted to Archbishop Theobald later, at the Council of London (30 March 1152), that he crown Eustace, the archbishop again cited Pope Celestine's letter and proved intransigent, and was even prepared to go into a brief exile in Flanders rather than comply.

Another plan that Stephen could pursue was to finance campaigns against the Angevins in Normandy. Late in 1149, Bishop Henry and the queen were in northern France, and the bishop was in consultation with the French court. An alliance against the Angevins was sought by King Stephen, although he was frustrated in his plans by the harsh winter of 1149–50 and the subsequent famine. But in 1151 an Anglo-French invasion of Normandy was agreed. Count Eustace gathered his forces in the county of Ponthieu while Louis prepared a strike down the River Seine. Their armies would head towards Rouen and besiege the Norman capital; even if they failed to capture the city, a battle with Duke Henry and his father would do just as well. As it turned out in August 1151, Count Eustace succeeded in striking deep into the duchy, seizing the citadel of Neufchâtel-en-Bray, just over 30 kilometres north east of Rouen. But at this point, the offensive went off the rails as news reached the count that King Louis had fallen ill in Paris and his army had been dismissed. A hasty truce led to Eustace's withdrawal once more to the borders of Normandy. Duke Henry was clearly disconcerted by the new alliance, and in September began assembling a force to lead across the Channel to England. If he was there, and his father was holding Normandy, then Stephen and Eustace would have to split resources and the danger would be lessened.

As it happened death took a hand with a vengeance in 1151. An epidemiologist or a pathologist with historical tastes would do well to look at aristocratic mortality in the period 1151–53, for death's hand lay heavy on the Anglo-French nobility in those years. It may in part have something to do with the catastrophic famine that devastated England and northern France in 1150, killing many thousands of the poor and not-so-poor by starvation and its associated diseases. Famine visited the land again in 1151, perhaps because there was too little seed corn left in 1150 to produce a big enough crop the next year. A weakened populace was easy prey to diseases, not all of which the aristocracy could escape. From the number of magnates who rapidly died or fell seriously ill as a result of eating (Ranulf of Chester, Simon of Northampton and Count Eustace himself), it would seem that diseases associated with weakened populations in the aftermath of famine (such as typhus, dysentery and influenza) were rife. King Louis himself may have been one of the first victims in August 1151, and, early in September, Geoffrey of Anjou died within a few days of developing a sudden illness. As a result of Geoffrey's death, Duke Henry could not leave France; his new Angevin-Norman realm had too many internal and external enemies to take the risk of leaving it. The death of King Louis's minister, Abbot Suger, further complicated things, as he had been a brake on hostilities.

The death of Geoffrey of Anjou meant that King Stephen and Eustace had a chance to try their Norman strategy once more, but further deaths brought further delays. Eustace's uncle, Count Theobald IV of Blois-Chartres-Champagne, died early in 1152 – perhaps a victim of his own pious predilection for associating with the poor and sick. This was a major blow to King Stephen's fortunes in France. An even greater blow was the death of his wife, Queen Mathilda, at Castle Hedingham in Essex on 3 May 1152. She had caught a debilitating fever and died within a week. Eustace was in England at the time, assisting his father in one last bid for a coronation, and attended the deathbed. It was not until July 1152 that the Norman campaign was resumed, and Eustace was involved in a second siege of Neufchâtel-en-Bray, but again he was let down by King Louis. The king had begun his march down the Seine, and then circled south through the Montfort lordships in the forest of Yvelines and came to the Norman frontier at Pacy-sur-Eure. But he had been second-guessed by Duke Henry who moved quickly against his army, alarming Louis into withdrawing. The Normans followed the king over the frontier and marched along the borders of the county of Dreux pillaging as they went. Eustace was unable to proceed further, and, when King Louis sought a truce in autumn 1152, he found himself abandoned in Normandy once again by his allies.

In the second week of January 1153 Duke Henry cut free of distractions and sailed for England, no doubt hoping that Eustace would have to follow him. If this was his reasoning, he was correct in his assessment. This was Eustace's last chance of the crown, and he probably knew it. When Duke Henry successfully revived the Angevin party and raised a large field army in the west country, the war of succession in England was renewed in a more dangerous form. The king had been making progress in north Wiltshire and the Thames valley in his campaigns in the second half of 1152, but the duke was able to confront him at Malmesbury in January 1153 when King Stephen had the unpleasant experience of finding that the barons in his army were unwilling to fight the duke. Some indeed were suspected of opening communication with him. The armies withdrew into quarters, and Duke Henry may have taken possession of, and garrisoned, Southampton at this time. In April Bishop Henry was once more involved in diplomacy between the parties, and seems to have negotiated a truce by which king and duke agreed to keep each to his area of England. So Henry celebrated Easter (19 April) at Gloucester and Pentecost (7 June) with his new ally, Earl Robert of

Leicester in the earl's own town. He did not attempt to lead his army directly against the king until August, when he moved to the relief of the stubborn Angevin outpost of Wallingford.

What happened at Wallingford was decisive in ending the chances of Stephen continuing his dynasty. The encounter began well for the king. As the rival armies manoeuvred around the castle seeking advantage, Stephen was eventually successful in trapping the duke in a position where he was outnumbered. He only needed to close in to administer the *coup de grâce* – but his weapon broke in his hands. The royalist army refused to fight, and immediately opened negotiations with their colleagues and cousins in the Angevin army. The civil war had gone on too long, and both parties had long now regarded it as a futile dynastic squabble whose bad effects needed to be mitigated. It was no longer an idealistic struggle about inheritance and loyalty which roused passions and commitment. The king and the duke were annoyed to find themselves bypassed by their supporters, and required to commission a final peace conference. Count Eustace was more than annoyed. He removed himself and his military household from the king's camp and rode in anger to his castle of Cambridge, intending no doubt to find a way of making the war his own. One of his first moves was to try to raise funds. He marched to Bury St Edmunds and on 10 August levied a forced payment on the abbey. On his return to Cambridge, sitting down to a dinner reluctantly provided by the monks of Bury, he was seized by one of the same diseases which were striking down many of his colleagues, and died within a week. Many concluded that this was as decisive a demonstration as there could be that God desired the end of his lineage's control of England.

Peace came to England in November 1153 with the conclusion of a conference at Winchester between the king and the duke, in which the bereaved Stephen recognised Henry as his adopted son and heir, and in which the duke conceded to him a life tenure on the throne. Then their joint court travelled to Westminster by way of Windsor, to celebrate Christmas together and put their seals to the final accord. King Stephen had other legitimate children than the late Count Eustace. He had a second son, William, in his late teens. The Westminster document went into great detail about how young William's political and social position was to be protected. He was to have all that his father had possessed before he became king in 1135: the counties of Boulogne and Mortain, and the honors of Eye and Lancashire. He was also confirmed in his marriage to one of the greatest heiresses in England and Normandy: Isabel de Warenne, countess of Surrey, who controlled great estates in Sussex and Norfolk, besides the honors of Bellencombre and Mortemer in Upper Normandy. The duke was willing to concede William also the castle and rents of Norwich (which would consolidate his control over Norfolk) and the honor of Pevensey (which would increase his hold on Sussex). The result was to create in Count William of Boulogne an even more magnified version of what his father had been in Henry I's reign. Unmentioned in the settlement was Stephen's surviving legitimate daughter, Mary, who was entrusted to a nunnery at this point, or who had been put in one earlier.

Stephen's last year as king seems to have been a surprising success, in view of the years of warfare and national angst that had preceded it. Relations with Duke Henry remained good while he stayed in England (he left from the port of London in March 1154). Thereafter the king had the comforting experience of finding his kingship an undisputed fact in England. There was no longer a rival to whom dissidents could appeal, and the duke had even taken Earl Reginald of Cornwall – his nominated attorney in the monitoring of his rights over England – to Normandy with him. Stephen's writ began to run once again in the west country, and the former Angevin earls and barons began once again to pay in accounts at his exchequer in Westminster. England remained a little nervous, which is hardly surprising. Before Duke Henry left, there were rumours of a conspiracy to assassinate him as he passed through Kent. The rumours implicated Count William, the king's son, who was supposed to have recruited Flemish agents to ambush him. The plot was supposedly abandoned when the count fell off his horse and broke his leg. The rumours tell us more about the anxieties of a people who had only just reclaimed domestic tranquillity than about Count William's state of mind.

The king, for his part, began to busy himself with further reconstruction of his realm, an agenda he must have agreed with Duke Henry before he left. A military progress to the north and the holding of a great court at York signalled to the northern and north midlands barons that they must forget the semi–independence some of them had assumed in the days of Ranulf of Chester. At the end of the year, in October, Stephen travelled peacefully into Kent and met Count Thierry of Flanders, who had sailed over to Dover to meet him for a conference. They seem to have discussed the repatriation of those Flemish soldiers who had immigrated to England in the years of civil war; perhaps they looked most pressingly at the case of the aged and now blind William of Ypres, the king's now retired mercenary general, who was living in Kent and who needed to be sent home on advantageous terms. King Stephen was staying at Dover priory when he fell suddenly ill with an internal affliction, which from the brief description given may have been dysentery. The archbishop of Canterbury was summoned, as was the king's Augustinian father confessor, Ralph, prior of Holy Trinity, Aldgate. Stephen lived out his last days and died around the age of fifty-eight at Dover on Monday 25 October 1154, confiding the kingdom at the last to Archbishop Theobald as regent until Duke Henry arrived to take the kingship, which he did not do until December.

The king's body was taken in procession to the Cluniac abbey of Faversham six miles west of Canterbury, which he and his late wife had begun as a joint project in 1148. It had always been his intention to be buried in a Cluniac monastery. Like his uncle, he valued the elaborate liturgy of commemorative masses for their dead founders' souls in Purgatory, which Cluny had pioneered. Queen Mathilda and his son, Eustace, were already lying in the unfinished choir of the abbey which the royal couple had financed. The abbey – which was never fully completed – and its tombs have now long disappeared under the grass, but a Flemish clerk who visited it in 1216 has left us a brief description of the site of the royal burial: the king and queen lying together in the choir in front of the high altar, each under a separate ledger stone.[5] They lay there at peace in the heart of the community of Faversham for nearly four hundred years, with the monks performing daily masses and an annual repetition of the funeral obsequies for their souls until Henry VIII's commissioners closed the abbey in 1539. Then, as seventeenth-century rumour has it, 'for so small a gain as the lead coffin wherein it was wrapped [his body] was taken up and thrown into the next water'.[6] Strangely, the dead king might not have cared to resent that indignity, had he known the eventual fate of his corpse. It was too much like an illustration of the 'contempt for the things of this world' which was so much a feature of the advanced spirituality of his own day.

The Last of the Normans

There is a case to be argued that the last ruler to be reckoned by contemporaries as a member of the Norman dynasty was also the best of them. To argue that, you would have to make the case on two grounds: on spirituality and political integrity. Stephen was a man of the same spiritual stamp as his grandfather, the Conqueror, who lived his life to the rhythm of the ecclesiastical day. Like the elder William, Stephen seems to have made the witness of the mass the anchor of his day, although there is no direct evidence that he also went so far as to attend the chapel offices sung by his clerks. He was discriminating in his choice of clerical associates, preferring his household clerks to be clergy first, rather than administrators. Even so, very few of them found promotion to the hierarchy; the sort of bishops Stephen seems to have liked were learned and spiritual men, not politicians and administrators in mitres. Like his uncle Henry I, Stephen cultivated a personal peniten- tial regime, with an Augustinian father confessor licensed to hear him by the archbishop of Canterbury. But his character was more religious than that of his uncle; a quality he shared with his brother Count Theobald, commemorated by one writer as 'a prince of great sanctity and of deep generosity to the poor', a man who became regarded almost as a saint by the next generation. This quality was what – apart from his misfortunes – distinguished him in the memory of the next gener- ation. Writers of the later twelfth century frequently refer to him (and to no other English king) as *rex piissimus*: 'most pious king'. Religious observance and seriousness of life were what distinguished him from his forbears and from his immediate successor in the perceptions of contemporaries.

There was a wide streak of moral introspection in his character, and it came out in his political behaviour at times. In 1138 he avoided besieging Ludlow, which was commanded by a woman. The next year he would not take advantage of the empress and the countess of Glou- cester's entrapment at Arundel, partly to spare the embarrassment of Queen Adeliza. Having trapped the wives of the earls of Chester and

Lincoln in the castle of Lincoln in 1141, he let them go. This seems to have been the result of his meditation on his coronation promises to protect the weak and powerless. The moral scrupulosity comes out most strongly in the marvellous memoir of his behaviour in front of Newbury castle in 1152, when he had the cheerful and attractive five-year-old son of its lord, John Marshal, at his mercy as a hostage. Although urged by his barons to intimidate the garrison by killing the boy in several dramatic fashions – as was indeed his right – he refused, and instead took him on as a page. The boy later remembered games of toy knights he played with the venerable old king on the flower-strewn floor of his royal pavilion over the following months.

Stephen can be criticised for poor judgement, and more particularly for trusting men whose advice was self-interested and questionable. The silliest decisions of his career were made under the influence of others. The arrest of Bishop Roger of Salisbury and his family in 1139 was carried out because Roger was seen as an obstacle to the ambitions of leading lay courtiers. Although Stephen and his advisers came out of the affair richer in possessions and patronage, it was at the cost of the trust of his senior clergy. Geoffrey de Mandeville was likewise sacrificed by Stephen in 1143 to the greed of a clique of royal administrators. When Geoffrey fought back savagely, the king was severely punished for his decision. It has to be said that the arrests carried out at Stephen's court had a number of precedents in Henry I's reign. The reason that Stephen's reputation was more damaged by them than that of his uncle is because the prestige of his kingship was undermined by the civil unrest of his reign in England.

Stephen is the first king of England who fits the model of a chivalric king. There was no doubting his success as a military commander and leader of men in battle, as successful as any of his predecessors; he had all their courage, vigour and coolness of purpose. But he belonged also to an age when a theory of military virtue was beginning to fix itself in military minds. Its origins we have seen as far back as the time of William Longsword, count of Rouen, who was memorialised by his elegaist as 'maker and lover of peace; comforter and defender of the poor; maintainer of widows and orphans'. It was the prescription for the conduct of a Christian prince that the Church had devised for Carolingian royalty. Stephen was the first (and last) of the Normans consciously to approach the realisation of this ecclesiastical manifesto in his life. Except in one case, he forbore to kill any opponents who surrendered. The only time he did so (at Shrewsbury in 1138) he was well within his rights, for the garrison had refused the summons to surrender. He was more likely to let honourable enemies go into exile, or even to go free; as he let Geoffrey de Mandeville go free in 1143, despite the risks that he would take the field against him. This preference for being merciful and for scrutinising the morality of his own case was perhaps his legacy to later medieval kings of England. Stephen cannot be linked to the 'bad' kings of English history, for as a king he was not bad in any of the multiple senses of that adjective.

His physical successors did not survive him for long. Count William of Boulogne, his surviving son, lived on as the most splendid magnate of the Anglo-Norman realm until October 1159. William's relationship with the new king, Henry II, was not entirely happy, as could have been predicted. In 1157 the king decided to renegotiate the terms of 1153 with the count. William, who seems to have been a reasonable man, surrendered his rights in Norwich and Pevensey, and even put up with King Henry's hostile demand that he surrender his castles in England and Normandy to royal castellans, although he did complain to the pope (perhaps about the king's abrogation of a solemn pact sworn before God) and pay out the large sum of 700 marks to facilitate the case at Rome. But the next year, the king and he were on good enough terms for Henry to have knighted him at Carlisle on 24 June, when William must have been well past the customary ages of delivery of arms. Count William loyally stood by the king in his campaign to recover the overlordship of Toulouse in 1159, and it was in October of that year that he died (apparently of the dysentery which had killed his royal father) on campaign. William's heir was his sister, Mary. She was in 1159 the young abbess of Romsey, a royal monastery in Hampshire long favoured by royal ladies. King Henry II would not leave her there, surprisingly. He was prepared to let the blood line she inherited loose, although she was harmless to him in the situation in which she was on her brother's death.

Mary was the indisputable heir to the county of Boulogne. All her father's lands were denied her, but her mother's inheritance could not be gainsaid, as it was outside the Anglo-Norman realm. It would seem that negotiations over her future must have begun as soon as her brother was dead, and the approaches almost certainly came from the count of Flanders, Thierry. Thierry had a younger son, Matthew, and for him to secure Boulogne for Matthew would be a magnificent coup. His scheme was to negotiate Mary's release from Romsey and to marry her to Matthew, thus tying Boulogne into closer alliance with Flanders. The marriage was sucessfully arranged for the early summer of 1160, despite Archbishop Becket's vociferous objections to the release of a professed nun from her vows. She died in 1182 without issue, arguably the last of the Norman dynasty, in that she was the last surviving child of a Norman king of England; although perhaps Alice, countess of Eu who died in 1246, last descendant of the cadet line of counts which descended from Duke Richard I, may be considered a rival to that inconsequential dynastic claim.

9

The Norman Dynasty

The idea of the 'dynasty' was already important at the time of the early Normans, even before they developed ambitions to conquer England. Early medieval people had a powerful sense of the past, a sense they applied to families, kings and kingdoms, and this sense of history created family identities. They began doing this in western Europe, according to some recent work, around the beginning of the seventh century, when established and powerful families began to take up names for themselves. Where great families and their areas of political power became linked in people's minds, the idea of the dynasty eventually appeared, although 'dynasty' was not a word they used: Latin writers trawled the Bible and the Classics for terms like *stirps* (stock), *genus* or *domus* (family) and *origo* (descent). But when it came to ennumerating the generations of a dynasty they were able to use the Greek loan-word word 'genealogy', which was there to be borrowed from St Jerome's chapter headings for the Latin Gospels.

'Dynasty' and 'family' are not quite the same concepts. A dynasty is a type of family, an exalted family which wields hereditary power over a realm. But in some ways a dynasty is no different from any other family: it has a structure of generations and a network of kinship which is comprehended by the medieval term 'lineage'. Indeed the medieval French word *lignage* can be translated into English as 'family'. But 'lineage' as it is used today is interpreted as the vertical dimension of family looked at through time, down the generations. The idea of the structure of a family at any one point in time was conveyed by a different medieval French word, *parage*. When we deal with the Norman ducal and English royal family that we call the 'Normans' all these aspects of family need to be borne in mind. But for the most part, the principal concern in this book have been its dynastic and lineal elements.

The Idea of the Dynasty and its Consequences

For a distinguished Franco-German historian, the early medieval idea
of a dynasty arose out of the Merovingian family's success in imposing
the recognition of their exclusive royal power (*principatus*) over the
Franks and the provinces of Gaul.[1] Like the former Roman emperors,
the Frankish kings established that a ruler must succeed another in his
political power, and so the idea of the state and the dynasty grew hand
in hand. Once the Merovingians had established this very desirable
mechanism of political power, other powerful families took to the idea.
The Agilolfings of Bavaria established this same sort of identity between
family and principality in the early seventh century. Other attitudes
reinforced this lineal trend. Early royal families, like the Merovingians,
looked back to a heroic forebear to establish the root of their family's
glamour and charisma; an idea that the former barbarian peoples
grafted onto the Roman notion of public power and pre-eminence of
the ruler.

Writers on early kings and kingship in the British Isles long ago made
the point that, since descent from a hero or a deity was important in
the recognition of a person's royal charisma (for the English as much
as the Britons), society in general was very conscious of family lineage
and identity. The earliest surviving writings from amongst the newly-
Christianised English include detailed genealogies for the major royal
lines. But in England the coming together of the linked ideas of royal
dynasties, peoples and territories came later than on the Continent. In
England, it was the intervention of the Church which ultimately led to
the formulation of the idea of the dynasty of the kings of England. Right
from the sixth century, the Roman Church had adopted the miscon-
ception that there was one English people, who might be ministered to
by an English church under one metropolitan archbishop. By the eighth
century, the Mercian rulers had adopted this idea and postured as
emperors of all the English, an ideology inherited by the West Saxon
dynasty in the ninth century. It was the West Saxon kings who finally
succeeded in uniting theory with political practice, and so the first royal
dynasty of England emerged in the mid tenth century.

It was perfectly natural for the people of the eighth century to think
in terms of royal dynasties. By the time Rollo the Viking landed on the

Seine estuary, it was accepted that there were families holding titles less than that of king who might be regarded as dynasties too. Where a prince wielded hereditary power over a distinct region of France with its own identity, even though he was not a king, his family might be regarded as exalted enough for a father to hand on the *principatus* he wielded to his son, as if he were a king. By the mid tenth century, there were such non-royal dynasties established in the ancient regions of Aquitaine, Brittany and Burgundy, and the newer Marches of Neustria and Flanders. More would soon join them. It was in this environment that it became possible for Rollo and his descendants to establish their identity as the princely dynasty of the Normans, a process that had been consummated before the death of Duke Richard I in 996.

The regional power of such dynasties could be corrosive of royal power, and competitive with it. Much of the civil discord in the tenth century was caused by troubles between these hereditary princes and the Carolingian royal family. Successive tenth-century kings of France handled these new tensions so poorly that royal power was weakened and subverted in France for nearly two centuries, until the Capetian dynasty under Philip II Augustus (d. 1223) began in turn to subvert princely power. In England, under its West Saxon kings, such princely dynasties did not arise because – although there were powerful ealdormen and earls – there never was before 1066 that narrow conjunction between family, lineage and region that produced the French sovereign dukes and counts. The Vikings had more or less eliminated those lesser royal dynasties that might have had the capacity to transform themselves into regional princes under the West Saxon kings. After 1066, only Cheshire and the Welsh Marches produced anything resembling dynastic principalities to trouble the Norman kings.

Inventing the Norman Lineage

For a medieval person, the right sort of ancestry brought dignity and status. Dignity and status could be earned by labour and by luck, but the quality of the people from whom a man was descended and with whom he was connected gave him a head start along the road to public recognition, at the end of which he became what they called a *preudhomme*, a 'man of consequence', a man respected for his prowess in

war and for his good judgement and prestige in civil matters. In more
than one way, medieval literature was soaked in blood, and its importance. In a romance that was being circulated in northern France when
Henry I was king of England, a hero was offered the flattery: 'Your
lineage contains very distinguished people – everyone talks of your
triumphs!'[2]

The French historian Georges Duby went a long way towards defining
the ways that princely lineages invented themselves in the middle ages.[3]
An important way was the commissioning of a genealogical tract, to
demonstrate the lineage's succession and advertise its great deeds. For
this reason Duke Richard II of Normandy (d. 1026) commissioned
around 1020 a Picard clerk and associate of his called Dudo to provide
a Latin panegyric on his predecessors, proving them all to be distinguished Christian princes; as distinguished as, and more honourable
than, any of their Frankish princely rivals. The Normans were by no
means the first to do this, although the work of Dudo in the 1020s is
an early example of this sort of commission. But seventy years before
Dudo began work, Arnulf I, count of Flanders, had commissioned a
written genealogy of his lineage (called *The Sacred Descent of the Lord
Count Arnulf*) from a clerk of Compiègne. As far as his male forebears
was concerned it was a brief tract, going back only to his grandfather,
but it was padded out by the fact that Arnulf's grandfather had married
a Carolingian princess, and that was used to extend the lineage back in
time by including the Frankish kings and emperors. Dudo could not
adopt a similar strategy, but he implied that Rollo of Rouen was of a
distinguished and noble ancestry, even if he could not give details of it,
or even the name of Rollo's father.

Forty years or so before the conquest of England, the Norman ducal
house was already very well aware of the need to have a distinguished
lineage. Perhaps they were more aware than most, knowing as they did
that they did not have to go back too many generations to find a
bloodthirsty, pagan pirate sitting at the roots of their family tree: Rollo,
or Hrólfr the Viking, and no one really knew where he had come from.
William de Jumièges claimed to know a genealogy of Rollo – which he
could have obtained from northern sources – but refused to copy it into
his work, as it did not offer 'a model of what is honourable or edifying'.[4]
Dudo overcame the problem of Rollo's obscurity – or notoriety – by

hinting delicately that he was of very noble Danish blood, unjustly driven
from his homeland by a tyrannical king. Dudo was not, however, re-
sponding to any ideal of historical truth here, but the pressing need of
his Norman patron: the identity and accomplishments of the originator
of the line (*li chiés de lignage*) remained important for his descendants.
Only a score or so years later, the existence of the Norman dynasty was
agreeably acknowledged by the Burgundian historian Ralph Glaber as 'a
succession of most excellent dukes'. He tactfully passed over the problem
of Rollo by beginning his list of dukes with Rollo's son, William.[5]

Richard II of Normandy was already a man rich in connections and
lineage. His sister was the queen of England, the count of Blois and the
Breton count of Nantes were his brothers-in-law, and the duke of
Aquitaine was his close cousin. A century later his descendants were
much more magnificent. His great-great grandaughter Mathilda – who
was arguably the last of his line – was married as a child in 1110 to the
Holy Roman Emperor. Hugh, monk and historian of Fleury, addressed
an obsequious letter to this very grand little girl asking for her literary
patronage for his history of the recent kings of France. He chose the
topic of her descent (*prosapia*) by which to flatter her. Being very much
a Frenchman, it was her Norman lineage that he praised. Dudo's work
had come now to its full fruition and Hugh of Fleury was not embarrassed to say that 'the nobility of her line' began with Rollo 'from whose
blood you have come'. The savage exploits of Rollo were not in the
least avoided now – in fact they fill pages of his work; the cities he
plundered and the rivers along which he raided. Hugh even had Rollo
raiding inland to Fleury itself – a rather odd way of recommending his
abbey to the empress. None of this mattered, for once Rollo was baptised
he became 'the most faithful devotee of Christ, whose most vicious
persecutor he previously was' (a shamelessly flattering allusion to St
Paul). Then Hugh continues the empress's *genealogia* in biblical fashion:
William Longsword and his son Richard I, Richard II who succeeded
him, and Robert son of Richard II who produced William, king of
England whose heir and son was King Henry I 'your magnificent father'.[6]
But Frenchman or not, Hugh of Fleury knew where the danger lay in
constructing the Empress Mathilda's genealogy. Reciting her generations
meant that he could avoid mentioning Duke Richard III, allegedly
murdered by his younger brother Robert I. He could avoid mentioning

the fact that William the Conqueror had other heirs and sons than Henry I, notably Robert II of Normandy, who was cheated of England in turn by his younger brothers, William Rufus and Henry. In 1110 it was very important not to mention Robert II, held then in prison by King Henry at Sherborne, and Robert's son, William Clito, kept in supervised seclusion in Normandy, a boy closer to the head of the lineage than his cousin, Mathilda the empress.

There were other dangers in genealogies, as the empress's father came to appreciate a few years later, around 1113. King Henry proposed to marry one of his many illegitimate daughters to Hugh son of Gervase de Châteauneuf, the young lord of a great honor across the southern boundary of Normandy. The king's plan was to neutralise Hugh and detach him from the coalition of his enemies. The diplomacy was successful and the couple were formally betrothed, and at that point genealogy got in the way. The bishop of Hugh's diocese was Ivo of Chartres (d. 1115). Ivo was a redoubtable and fearless supporter of the hard line that the Church had been fitfully attempting to impose on marriage for some decades. The line was first drawn firmly in the collection of canons of Burchard, bishop of Worms (1000–25). He prohibited marriage between kinsfolk with a common ancestor up to the seventh generation, and Burchard had great influence on the German clergy who were dominant in the eleventh-century papal court. The Norman dynasty had first learned of this prohibition when the papacy attempted to forbid the Conqueror's marriage to Mathilda of Flanders, so Bishop Ivo's intervention in the dynastic policy of Henry I could not have been a complete surprise. Ivo had a wide and inconvenient grasp of French aristocratic family history. He was able to trace back accurately the king's generations to his great-great-grandmother, Gunnor, the wife of Duke Richard I. He knew Gunnor had a sister, Seufria, and he could demonstrate that Seufria was the great-great-great grandmother of Hugh, lord of Châteauneuf. The bishop wagged his spiritual finger at the king:

> This is no figment of my imagination; I have in front of me a genealogical chart compiled from the evidence of Hugh's own relations. These men were quite happy to appear before church lawyers under my protection, to calculate the genealogy and satisfy the law as to its truth. I attach to this letter a copy of the relevant part of it, describing the calculations of

the generations of the pair, so that you can see the truth of the matter
and by good advice prevent them from contracting an unlawful union.[7]

The marriage did not happen, and some years later Hugh married
another woman, allying with the king's deadly enemies and waging war
on him. King Henry, as it happened, may have seen this reverse in a
positive light. He was able to use the Church's own prohibitions on the
marriage of cousins to frustrate a planned and dangerous dynastic
marriage of his nephew and rival, William Clito, in 1124. Genealogy was
a serious business by the twelfth century, and much depended on it. It
could be used to monitor dynastic marriages and to shape the entire
destiny of a nation.

Early in 1154, another writer took up the subject of the empress's
lineage. By now she was a mother of adult sons by her second husband,
the count of Anjou. The eldest surviving of these was Henry, duke of
Normandy and Aquitaine, and adopted heir to King Stephen of England.
Mathilda was by now retired to the palace-priory of Notre-Dame du
Pré, which her father had constructed across the Seine from the dynastic
seat of Rouen, and the hopes of the future lay in her son, who was all
too obviously not a Norman but a proud member of another lineage,
that of the Angevins. The writer who had to take account of these high
matters was Ailred, abbot of Rievaulx (d. 1167), already an eminent
Cistercian scholar, himself born in the year that Hugh of Fleury wrote
his genealogy of the empress. Ailred's own descent was impeccably and
unapologetically English. He was the most distinguished member of a
northern ecclesiastical family, and had been brought up in the community of the Anglo-Saxon minster of Hexham. He had spent his youth
as an intimate of the household of King David of Scotland, brother of
the empress's mother. Ailred was not interested in the empress's Norman
lineage. What interested him was the fact that she and David were
descended from Æthelred II, king of England, and through him from
the ancient royal house of Wessex.

In 1154 Stephen, 'fourth king of the Norman line' as Orderic Vitalis
called him in earlier, happier days,[8] was sharing power with Henry of
Anjou, duke of Normandy and Aquitaine, whom he had adopted as his
heir. When Stephen died, in October of that year, Ailred of Rievaulx
well knew that the new Angevin lineage would take the throne of
England, as it had already invaded and subjected Normandy. He wrote

in uncertain times, and the new heir would rule a very different world than that in which Ailred had grown up. Henry was 'the glory of the Angevins, the protector of the Normans, the hope of the English and the ornament of the Aquitanians'. For Ailred, his genealogical tract had to point out to the young prince that it was not his Norman but his English lineage that was important, and he described it for Henry in great detail back to Woden and Adam. England gave him majesty and royalty, and the future monarch must value it accordingly. Therefore Ailred edited out any Norman ducal succession in his genealogy: William the Conqueror arrives in the story as the cousin of Edward the Confessor, not the son of Duke Robert. It was not the empress's father so much as her mother, the descendant of Alfred the Great, who was the more important. As the political world changed, so did the contemporary perspective on lineage and who was its *chiés*. In 1154, for some people, the day of the Norman dynasty was already done, even while Stephen still sat on the throne.[9]

As we have seen, it was the blood line that remained the defining feature of the dynasty still by 1154. For this reason, Orderic was so keen to portray Stephen as a king of the Norman line in 1135, not a Frenchman from Blois. It was not that Stephen's own line lacked nobility, it was that his kingship had to be justified by linking him closer to the Norman lineage than was strictly accurate. It is a sort of genealogical sleight of hand that we find a lot of in the twelfth century. When in 1160 Hamelin, the illegitimate brother of Henry II, married the countess of Warenne, he arranged it so that their children took the name of Warenne. When Mathilda Ridel married Richard Basset in Henry I's reign and Richard eventually acquired her substantial inheritance, their elder son took the Ridel name in anticipation of taking over his mother's lands. This insistence on name and lineage had much to do with the fact that as yet there was by 1100 little else to distinguish a family. The Norman dynasty developed no single dynastic church in which to house its dead members. Westminster did not become the royal burial church till the end of the thirteenth century. There was a notion current that particular churches had strong dynastic associations. The cathedral of Rouen was certainly regarded in that way in the twelfth century. Henry I tried in 1134 to insist that his seriously-ill daughter accept her future burial there with the heads of their lineage, Rollo and William Longsword, although her preference was to lie in the abbey of Bec-Hellouin. Henry himself was buried at Reading, a Cluniac abbey specifically built for the purpose, as his father rested in his own burial church in Caen and as his successor, Stephen, planned a Cluniac burial church at Faversham. It was not until the death of the Young King Henry in 1183 that Rouen got its first royal burial.

Another way of identifying families was the symbolism of heraldry. Some northern French comital dynasties, notably Vermandois, St-Pol and Boulogne, had developed symbols alluding to their descent by 1100. Although we hear of (and occasionally see) banners which identified Norman kings and dukes, we get no hint that they carried a specific and inheritable symbol on them identifying their owners as Norman. The closest we get is the reference in Crusading chronicles to the distinctive gold banner borne by Robert II of Normandy. All that proves, however, is that Robert had a banner which identified him personally, and it need not have contained a family symbol – in which case it would have been like the 'fighting man' banner of King Harold of England. The reign of Henry I contains some hints that the Norman kings were developing a symbol which was seen as particularly associated with them: this was the golden lion. Certainly the view of the court of Henry II in the 1170s, as reported by the poet Benoît de St-Maure, was that William the Conqueror had landed in England bearing a blue banner decorated with gold lions. But since Henry's father is depicted clothed in a robe and bearing a shield of blue, sprinkled with gold lions, and Henry's brothers all took a lion device, the inspiration for the lions credited to the Conqueror may be Angevin rather than Norman. Those who would identify the origin of the gold lions of England with the time of Henry I point out that Geoffrey of Monmouth refers elliptically to King Henry as the 'lion of justice'. Although that might be no more than to say that Henry was like Solomon, whose judgement seat was carved with lions, coins minted for his son, Robert of Gloucester, found in Wiltshire in 1994, were marked unmistakably with a lion. The case for a Norman dynastic symbol remains therefore tantalisingly open.

Propagating the Myth of Norman Origins

The Normans were already distinguishable as a European people and a sub-group of the French by the year 1000, and as generation succeeded generation their princely lineage gathered more and more charisma. The leaders of the Normans laid claim to and secured the title of duke in the early eleventh century, while the conquest of England in 1066 added royal majesty to the dynasty's claims for distinction amongst other Christian princes. As decade followed decade, the grandeur of the dynasty demanded ever more urgently that its beginnings be understood to be equally distinguished. The question of origins was always a matter of dynastic urgency. This had been the case as early as the 1020s, as we have seen. The foundation of the myth of Norman origins was referred by Richard II to Dudo, dean of St-Quentin, a clerk under his patronage. Dudo took Rollo, the *chiés de lignage* of the dynasty and made him a Danish warrior, a nobleman driven from his estates by a wicked king. With a small refugee fleet he raided England and the Frisian coast of Germany, and from England passed into France. A divine vision, and peaceful (if anachronistic) contact with the noble English king Athelstan, had given Rollo an openness to the Christian message that brought him in the end to a new role as a Christian prince. The opportunity for baptism arrived soon, for when he moved from Frisia to France he was acclaimed leader of the Danes then raiding the Seine valley, and a brief career of pillaging and violence across northern France ended with a treaty at St-Clair-sur-Epte ceding what later became Normandy to Rollo, in return for his baptism. Rollo married Gisla, the king's daughter, and settled down into a new life as a regenerate Christian duke, enthusiastically making war on his neighbours, as Christian dukes then did, until age and exhaustion led him to resign his responsibilities to his son, William.

We can see how the approved historical view of Rollo propagated from Rouen, and deriving from Dudo, became standard amongst Norman historians for well over a century after Richard II. It is neatly summarised by another writer, who wrote in the latter years of the reign of Stephen, the last of the Norman kings of England. This is the view given by Robert de Torigny, the Benedictine prior of the great Norman ducal abbey of Bec-Hellouin:

> It happened that the Northmen, descendants of the Trojans, burst out of Lower Scythia under the leadership of one Rollo. Sailing across the ocean, after repeated seaborne, piratical assaults on the shores of Germany and France, they finally invaded France, which Rollo had glimpsed from the

cliffs of Britain. Occupying the French city of Rouen, still to this very day they call those parts 'Normandy' from the name of the Northmen. Charles, known as the Simple, then ruled the French (the *Northmanni* get their name in their outland language as being 'men of the North', as they first came from those parts). Charles, king of the French, having entered into a pact with them, gave his daughter Gisla to Rollo, and conceded that land, now called 'Normandy', to Rollo, giving as a sumptuous addition all of Brittany, anciently called Letivia or Armorica. For the coastal lands, now called Normandy, lay uncultivated by farmers and ploughs and stripped of woodland, due to the daily raids of the pagan folk.[10]

Here we have the portrayal of a notable warrior leader of the Northmen entering France in force; but a monk like Robert did not like the moral implications of this seizure of the land of others by a Christian prince. Therefore Robert implied that the land of Normandy came to Rollo as a dowry with his new wife, which brought some retrospective legitimacy to his piracy. Robert de Torigny went on to describe how Rollo the pagan became Rollo the Christian at the hands of the archbishop of Rouen in an elaborate baptismal liturgy. And it is as a Christian prince he is then proclaimed by Robert de Torigny (anachronistically) as 'first duke of Normandy' and campaigns and plots amongst the other counts and dukes of the Franks in the early tenth century, establishing his line with his son, William, as his lawful successor.

After Dudo, his imaginative work was consumed and regurgitated as true history by a line of distinguished successors apart from Robert de Torigny: a lineage which included William of Jumièges, Orderic Vitalis, Master Wace, Stephen de Rouen and Benoît de St-Maure. We find it being recycled and improved as late as the 1220s, when an anonymous French clerk offered to the public of Picardy and Flanders a French language *History of the Dukes of Normandy and Kings of England*. William, Wace, Stephen and Benoît can be called 'official' historians of Normandy, as each was under the patronage of the ruling duke of his day. As historians of the Norman dukes and the Normans, these writers do their best to exalt the origins of their heroes. They make high claims for Rollo's lineage in their writings. Although Dudo never actually said that his hero was of royal blood (unlike the biographer of Gruffudd) he subscribed to the well-established view that the Danes were descended from ancient refugee Trojans (Latin *Dardanides*) who had wandered far

from the Bosphorus, establishing colonies in Germany amongst the
Goths in 'Upper Scythia'. These were high claims because (according to
the *Aeneid*) Trojans had settled in Italy and so also ultimately founded
Rome. The tenth-century Normans were therefore claiming to be of
the same lineage as Caesar. Not that they could claim any special
priority there, for it was also claimed for the ninth-century Franks that
they were descended from another party of wandering Trojans under
one Franco, who had settled in the Rhineland. So it is that King
Priam of Troy stands at the head of the lineage of the kings of France
in a genealogy compiled in the 1030s.[11] No ancient name was spared
if it brought its ration of status in the lineage game, and the name of
Troy was of unusual power – despite its people being one of history's
losers.

One measure of how influential the Norman version of its own lineage
was is the way it was used by non-Normans. The Norman princely
house had, by the end of the eleventh century, become one that other
princes would boast about, if they could claim a line of kinship with it;
sometimes even a remote link was enough. Around 1150, a northern
Welsh clerk decided to collect materials and write a biography of the
late ruler of north Wales, Gruffudd ap Cynan, king of Gwynedd (d.
1137). Gruffudd, a young political exile in Ireland, had secured Gwynedd
as a result of a military invasion in 1075. He had a chequered career,
but as a client prince to Henry I in the 1120s he secured his dynasty and
expanded his kingdom. He was half Irish and his claim on Gwynedd
was not beyond dispute, so his biographer worked hard to introduce
what distinction he could into Gruffudd's lineage, including using Norse
genealogies trawled from Irish libraries. The following passage was one
of his more brazen claims:

> Be it known that Harald Haarfagr and his two brothers were sons of the
> king of the northlands [*Llychlyn*: a Celtic name comprehending Norway
> and the northern isles] ... The third brother, namely Rodulf, voyaged with
> his fleet to France, where he settled and overcame the Franks through
> warfare, and subdued a large part of France which is now called 'Nor-
> mandy', because the men of Norway inhabit it; and they are a people from
> Scandinavia ... They built many cities there: 'Rodum' (Rouen) from king
> Rodulf its founder, which was named in the same way as Rome takes its
> name from Romulus and Reims from Remus; and many other cities and

castles and strongholds did he build. From him came the Norman kings
who subdued England in battle, namely King William and his two sons
who suceeded him, William Longsword and Henry, and Stephen his
nephew, who were contemporaries of King Gruffudd.[12]

In this way, the biographer hung his hero's name from the gilded
branches of one of Europe's most distinguished family trees. For by
then, over two centuries after he had died, the descendants of the obscure
Scandinavian Hrólfr – or Rollo, as he had become known to the literate
in western Europe – had become the founder of the greatest of lineages,
and Gruffudd's rather more humble dynasty needed the prestige of
cousinship to such great kings. For it so happened that Gruffudd's
mother, Ragnailt, was a daughter of Olaf, king of Dublin, and Olaf
claimed descent from the same King Harald who was allegedly Rollo's
brother.

Like all the best legends, Gruffudd's Norman genealogy had a fair
share of fact mixed in with the fantasy. There really was a King Harald
Harfagyr (Fine-Hair) who was king of Norway and died in 945, and
there was a Rollo. What is probably fictional is the relationship between
them. But it was important in the mid twelfth century for the Welsh
kings of Gwynedd and the Norse kings of Dublin to believe that there
was such a relationship, because it brought them great prestige. Whatever our ignorance of the real Rollo – and we know very little of him
beyond his existence – his supreme historical importance lay in his
descendants. So for our Welsh clerk Rollo was a northern prince, an
adventurer and warrior; a man of royal blood (for obviously only men
of such lineage could accomplish great deeds of conquest), he was a
builder of cities and fortresses, and in every way what the founder of a
realm and a glorious lineage ought to be.

From the beginning of our story we find glorification through myth-
making and the delicate crafting of facts to be an element in the story
of the Norman dynasty. Always aware of the hostility of their neighbours
– especially their French neighbours – and the political fragility of their
realm, the Norman dukes did not need to be told to cultivate their
image of nobility, or find reasons to justify their hold on northern
France. Their resort to the likes of Dudo of St-Quentin and William of
Jumièges is quite understandable, and as well as understandable it was
also cunning and precocious. Why the precocity? It seems that there

was no lack before Dudo's time of writers such as Richer of Reims, who poked fun at the short lineage of the Norman dynasty, calling them 'pirate-dukes'. Even in their glory days in the twelfth century, according to Wace of Bayeux, their rivals scorned the Normans as 'North-Mendicants', beggars from the frozen wastes of Scandinavia. Such comments were intended to subvert the status of the Normans amongst their neighbours. In their need to make their family identity distinguished the early Norman dukes were happy to draw any glowing, mythological comet into the orbit of their dynastic system. Even the alien world of Arthurian myth was dragged away from Wales by the gravitational pull of Norman Westminster to add its illumination to the Norman mythological firmament.

Appendix 1

The Name and Origins of 'Rollo'

The earliest appearance of our Viking hero's name is in 918 when he is 'Rollo' in an act of Charles the Simple. His contemporary, Flodoard, writing at Reims, calls him by the same name. It is as 'Rollo' that later chroniclers and compilers of ducal acts know him. Rollo was clearly a declinable Latinisation of his original Scandinavian name (nom. Rollo; gen. *Rollonis*), but what was that name? In the 1020s, his name was remembered at the church of St-Ouen-de-Rouen differently, for he was commemorated in an act of that ancient church (which rode out the Viking invasions of the province of Rouen) as 'Rolphus'. This is good evidence of the original form of his name: the church of St-Ouen is one of only two churches in Rouen that may have been maintaining an obituary list in the early tenth century, when he died. So the form 'Rolphus', or 'Rolf' may actually reflect a contemporary version of his name. It may be that, when William Longsword's former concubine, Sprota, named her younger son 'Rodulf' in the 940s, she was recalling her partner's father's pre-Christian name. Likewise, the Welsh elegaist of Gruffudd ap Cynan may perhaps have been drawing on an independent genealogy from Dublin when he recalled Rollo as 'Rodulf'. Therefore the Norse name 'Hrólfr', cognate to the Franco-Germanic 'Rodulf' or 'Radulf' would seem to be the name of our hero.

From what part of the Scandinavian realms did 'Hrólfr of Rouen' originally come? Eleventh-century writers, following Dudo, make him Danish in origin. But the description 'Danish' was a very broad one in western European sources, especially in a century when Danish kings had established a hegemony over much of the north of Europe. It may be that French writers saw all Northmen as Danes. Danes certainly came to Normandy: Bernard 'the Dane' was a companion of Count William Longsword in the early 940s. However, the fact that Bernard's origins were remarked upon may mean that he belonged to a minority group within the Northmen of the Seine. Besides this, there is the point (which several writers have made) that any Viking army was liable to be a miscellaneous mercenary force, and precise geographical origins may not have been that important to the Vikings themselves. There is certainly some reason to believe that the early tenth-century Norman settlers included a number of people who might be called 'Anglo-Norse' who were refugees from England: hence the number of Norman villages that carried the name Englescheville ('the Englishman's settlement').

It is worth observing that the known daughter of Hrólfr carried the name 'Gerloc' or 'Geirlaug', which is understood by commentators (after the work of Adigard de Gautries) to be a name of Norwegian origin, but other evidence points too in that direction. Hrólfr of Rouen became a stock character in the Northern saga tradition; or, rather, a stocky character, for he is generally called 'Göngu-Hrólfr'; a name which means 'Walking-Hrólfr', because he was so fat no horse could carry him. In the first three decades of the thirteenth century, 'Göngu-Hrólfr' appears in two Icelandic historical sagas, the *Heimskringla* and the *Orkneyinga Saga*, where he is explicitly identified as the founder of Normandy. By the fourteenth century Hrólfr had a saga all to himself; one of the *Fornaldarsaga* 'sagas of ancient times'.[1] What is interesting is how far back the character of 'Göngu-Hrólfr' can be traced before the thirteenth century, because this would assist any attempt to locate his origins in the Atlantic fringe.

The lost early twelfth-century original of the Icelandic *Landnámabók* may have had something to say about 'Göngu-Hrólfr', for the *Heimskringla* and *Orkneyinga Saga* are known to have trawled it heavily. Unfortunately it is impossible to do more than hypothesise that the later sagas drew their information about him from the *Landnámabók*, a treasury of earlier historical and genealogical information. The literary tradition is such that the existing later recensions of the *Landnámabók* may have been quoting the thirteenth-century sagas rather than the other way around. Evidence other than literary does, however, support the idea that Hrólfr of Rouen (also known as 'Göngu-Hrólfr') was well-known to the twelfth century as an Irish-Norse heroic figure. The mid twelfth-century 'Life of Gruffudd ap Cynan' – a biography of the Irish-Welsh king of Gwynedd, who died in 1137 – drew on Dublin sources to construct a magnificent genealogy for its hero. Since Gruffudd's mother was of the family of the kings of Dublin, the author of the biography carefully researched the Norse-Irish genealogical tradition. According to him, the first king of Dublin was one of three brothers, the youngest of whom was the Hrólfr (Rodulf) who founded Normandy and the lineage of the kings of England. So it was certainly believed at Dublin in the 1150s – when the biography of Gruffudd was composed – that Hrólfr of Rouen was a historical hero of the Atlantic Hiberno-Norse community. The literary evidence and genealogical evidence therefore converges and points back to Hrólfr as being a man of the north Atlantic fringe.

Can we say anything about Hrólfr's family connections? The Dublin genealogy given for Hrólfr in the Welsh-Irish evidence makes him a brother both of the first king of Dublin and of King Haraldr Hárfagr (or 'Finehair') Hálfdanarson, a historical figure who died in 945. The *Heimskringla* and the *Orkneyinga Saga* on the other hand both say that Hrólfr was the younger son of Earl Rögnavald of Moer, founder of the dynasty which ruled the Orkneys. The two genealogical traditions are incompatible (King Haraldr and Earl Rögnavald were enemies) and both are unverifiable. But both do at least place him in the same generation and the same milieu: the turbulent times of Viking exodus out of Haraldr's Norway and into the northern islands of the Atlantic. Professor David Douglas – so keen to dismiss the evidence of tenth-century Richer and eleventh-century Dudo about Rollo's origins – was more than happy to accept the evidence of thirteenth-century sagas about his parentage, and accepted their genealogy for him after only a slight demur. But the Norse saga-genealogical evidence is late and belongs to a time when Norwegian princes would be all too keen to tie the genealogy of the Norman royal dynasty into their own, so it cannot be accepted so uncritically.

Nonetheless, a belief in Rollo's North Atlantic origins seems unobjectionable. His possible association with the Viking army which settled in Brittany in the early tenth century would be one more link which tied his origins into the Hiberno-Norse area (for that army derived in part from Dublin). However, as far as can be determined, the best evidence for Rollo-Hrólfr's parentage denies any obvious link with the earls of Orkney and the Norwegian kings, for Richer of Reims, fifty or so years after Rollo died, gave his father's name as one Ketil (*Catillus*).

Douglas dismissed Richer out of hand as unreliable, and 'Ketil' as a semi-mythical Viking bogeyman of the ninth century, but as an independent and reasonably early tradition, which probably derives from Hrólfr's grandchildren, that is perhaps as near as we will ever get to the man's origins. The name 'Ketil' is profoundly and disappointingly obscure.

Appendix 2

The Letter of Pope Innocent II Confirming Stephen in his Kingship (February x April 1136)

Innocent the bishop, servant of the servants of God, to his most beloved in Christ, Stephen, illustrious king of England, greeting and apostolic blessing. The king of kings and lord of lords, in whose hands reside all power and the disposal of all realms, has of divine provision, when he wishes, the mystical power to transform circumstances and successions. As the prophet says: 'The Most High is sovereign in the kingdom of men; he gives the kingdom to whom he wills.' [Daniel 4:17]. When our son of glorious memory King Henry ruled, trade, a happy peace and real justice flourished in both England and Normandy – King Henry, who excelled all in the integrity which he applied to the affairs of this world. When this man – a friend to those of the church, a promoter of peace and justice, a steady protector of widows and orphans and a dutiful defender of those who were too weak to protect themselves – when he was taken from among us, as was reported to us, the affairs of the church were put into confusion in England; no royal writ was respected; and thievery went unpunished. So that such terrible disorder should not have a chance to increase its grip on God's people, England was moved by the mercy of divine pity at the prayers of godly men, as well as by the increase of such disorders, to choose you as king by the people's acclaim and the general agreement of noblemen and commoners, and so to be consecrated by the bishops of the realm. This I have learned through several means: the letters of our venerable brothers the archbishops and bishops of England and Normandy, and of those lovers of the Holy Roman Church, the glorious king of France [Louis VI] and that noble lord, Count Theobald [of Blois-Chartres], as well also by the investigation of our agents. Since we appreciate the trust of such men in your good character, moved by God's grace, we have agreed to this. This we have done because of certain future consider- ations, as well as because you promised obedience and reverence to St Peter on the day of your consecration, and because you are acknow- ledged to have been a very close relation of the late king. Now we, acknowledging your thanks, receive you into the special fatherly love of St Peter and the Holy Roman Church, and we wish most sincerely to hold you in that same pre-eminence of honour and love in which your predecessor the late king Henry was crowned by us.

Translated from Richard of Hexham, *De Gestis regis Stephani*, in *Chronicles of the Reigns of Stephen, Henry II and King Richard*, ed. R. Howlett, Rolls Series (1886), pp. 147–48.

Glossary

adoubement (dubbing)
A multi-purpose ceremony amongst the northern European aristocracy in the eleventh century. It involved the ceremonious granting of horse, arms and other trappings by one man to another. It was used when inaugurating a relationship of dependence between a greater and lesser lord, or when a lord took a warrior into household service, or as a rite of passage for a boy into manhood. It was not a ceremony exclusively associated with what we nowadays call 'knighting', although in 1086 the Anglo-Saxon Chronicle borrowed the word when it noted that Henry son of the Conqueror was 'dubbede' as a 'ridere' when he came of age.

Angevin
The adjective derived from the Latinised place-name for Anjou (*Andegavia*). The county of Anjou arose out of the wreckage of the tenth-century Neustrian march between the land of the duke of France and the peninsula of Brittany, and by the eleventh century it dominated the middle and lower valley of the great river Loire.

atheling
A pre-Conquest English title meaning 'man of noble/royal descent'. Anyone called 'atheling' by the eleventh century was a member of the royal family close enough to the ruling king to be considered a possible successor. As a result the term is sometimes translated in the modern English sense of 'prince' (i.e. son or grandson of a reigning monarch), although the medieval use of the term was not so exclusive. The term was still in use in its original sense in the early twelfth century, and was employed for William, son of Henry I of England.

ban

An ancient Germanic term which essentially means 'an area of a lord's exclusive authority'. The English words 'ban' and 'banish' still preserves some memory of its meaning of exclusive authority. An area of a 'ban' was called in medieval French a *banlieu* ('ban-place'). The acceptance of a lord's ban was the foundation of the medieval idea of lordship, and was a social mechanism distinct from – and antagonistic to – acceptance of kingship. 'Ban' and 'kingdom' were not always compatible concepts, which is why kings and their barons came into conflict.

Capetians

A noble dynasty that rose to power in West Francia in the middle of the ninth century, when Robert the Strong (d. 866), a count whose orgins lay in Lotharingia, was given control over the Breton March in 862. The family's early generations are called Robertian from him. Robert and his descendants consolidated their power over the Frankish region of Neustria (in modern terms Normandy, Anjou, the Touraine, Blois Chartres and the Ile de France) and eventually contested the throne of West Francia with the Carolingians. The name 'Capetian' comes from Hugh 'Capet' (d. 996) Robert's great-grandson, the fourth Robertian king, and the first whose kingship was uncontested by a Carolingian. Hugh's surname most probably refers to a cloak (*cappa*) he customarily wore.

Carolingians

The dynasty of Pepin the Short, who was anointed king of the Franks in 751. Since his father was called Charles (Martel) and his famous son was Charles (the Great, alias 'Charlemagne') his dynasty is called 'Caro-lingian' from the Latin for Charles (*Carolus*), although some call it a little more accurately the 'Pepinids'. After the division the Frankish empire in 843, and the extinction of the Carolingian lineage in the land of the East Franks (Germany), the dynasty continued in the land of the Western Franks (France) until the death of Louis V in 987, when the throne finally went to the dynasty of the Capetians.

chapel

The royal chapel was not a building but a department of the king or queen's mobile household. It was presided over by the royal chancellor and consisted of numerous subordinate chaplains who attended the king on a rota system. It travelled with portable altars, vestments, relics and books.

Cluniacs

Benedictine monks from an abbey or priory dependent on the great Burgundian abbey of Cluny, noted for the discipline of its life and its elaborate liturgy.

count

An ancient title which derives from the imperial Roman *comes* (or imperial 'companion'). The ancient Roman count was a court and regional officer of high status, but the office was not hereditary. The office was continued at the courts and in the administrations of the succeeding early medieval kingdoms. It did not become a hereditary dignity until the end of the tenth century, although there seems no reason to doubt that counts had been appointed by the Frankish kings and emperors from a few leading families for some time before then.

earl *see* jarl

faldstool

An ancient form of portable chair, a little like the modern director's chair, but constructed of carved wood and valuable fabrics without a back. It often functioned as the chair of state of a ruler or a bishop. The modern French word for armchair (*fauteuil*) is derived from the old Germanic word.

feudalism

A term difficult to understand unless you realise that it is only a 'construct': a historian's attempt to explain what was distinct about medieval society. Since there are many explanations as to what was distinct about western European society between the eighth and fourteenth century, there are many perceptions of what 'feudalism' actually means. This is so much so that many historians do not now use the term, as it causes more confusion than enlightenment. I have used 'feudal' as an adjective, but only in the strict sense favoured by British historians: to describe the rights and customs that revolved around the possession of land designated as a 'knight's fee' (*feodum militis*).

fisc
A term usually applied to a prince's personal landed estates, particularly by historians of Carolingian France. It is used by historians sometimes to distinguish princely estates from the 'demesne' estates of lords, although that was not the contemporary use of the term.

France
The Frankish empire (*Francia*) was permanently separated by the treaty of Verdun in 843. After that the kingship was split between that of the East Franks and the West Franks. The East Franks became the dominant one of the two kingdoms, and since its kings also secured Italy they were customarily called 'kings of the Romans' and many of them were crowned as western emperors. Their Frankish identity was dropped in favour of their identity as Germans. The West Franks retained the idea of being 'Frankish' and their king was always called king of the Franks (*rex Francorum*). As the kingdom fragmented politically into principalities in the tenth century, the geographical term *Francia* began to be applied narrowly to the lands of the Capetians, who took the title 'duke of the Franks' and later claimed the kingship. In the eleventh and twelfth centuries *Francia* signified eastern Neustria, the area around Paris, now called the Ile-de-France.

Gregorianism
An eleventh-century Church reform plan named after Pope Gregory VII (1073–85) but in fact first propagated by his predecessors, notably Leo IX (1048–54). The basic intention was to free the Church from lay control and concerns: this was to be done by discouraging clerical marriage (nicolaitanism), putting a stop to payments for appointments to Church offices (simony), and removing the right of kings and princes to select and invest bishops and abbots with their office. It was the last item that brought Pope Gregory into conflict with the emperor and led to their mutual downfall.

jarl

A Scandinavian term that relates closely to the English word *earl* . Both *jarl* and *eorl* mean 'man of noble birth and/or conduct' and under the Anglo-Scandinavian kings of the tenth and eleventh centuries became a hereditary title across the northern world. 'Earl' in England supplanted the ancient English title of *ealdorman* in the 1020s, and like ealdorman the earl was equated by the English with the continental title of duke. Under the Normans the English 'earl' was demoted to the status of a French count (as a result of this the female equivalent of the earl in modern English is a 'countess').

litany

A set series of sung prayers, addressed to the Trinity, the Virgin and numerous prophets, patriarchs and saints, with set responses, used during solemn masses, and particularly in ordinations and consecrations.

Neustria

One of the ancient divisions of the Frankish empire, the original home-land of the Franks, and one of their later sub-kingdoms. It made up what would be regarded today as France between Brittany, the Channel, the mountains of the Auvergne and the borders of Lotharingia and Burgundy. In the ninth century it fell into the power of the Robertian dynasty. Following the arrival of the Normans, who took over its coastal lands, the term lost its meaning, although eleventh-century Normans liked to think of Neustria as the historical predecessor of their duchy.

pays

A French term deriving from the basic administrative division of the northern parts of the ninth-century Carolingian empire: the *pagus* (pl. *pagi*). Every *pagus* would theoretically have possessed a communal court (*comitatus*) presided over by a count or by his deputy, the viscount. The *pagi* were well-understood and resilient territorial units. They survived the Viking incursions and were basic divisions of local government in Normandy in the eleventh and twelfth centuries. The Normans equated them (with some justification) to the English shires, as a result of which we use the word 'county' as a synonym for shire to this very day.

psalter

The 150 biblical psalms were the basis for devotion in the daily regime of services (or 'office') of monasteries and other large churches. The recitation of all or part of the psalter was particularly important in the religious devotion of deacons, unordained monks and lay people, as a substitute for the offering of the mass, which was reserved to bishops and priests.

Robertian *see* Capetian

Romanesque

An architectural term applied to the stylistic continuation of Roman sculptural and building forms into the middle ages. In England the term 'Norman' used to be applied to post-conquest Romanesque architecture. Romanesque began to give way to the distinct 'Gothic' style in central France from the 1140s onwards.

scarlet (cloth)

Scarlet was not necessarily the colour of cloth in the twelfth century, but its quality. 'Scarlet' was a heavy and closely-woven woollen fabric, rather more expensive than other sorts.

seneschal

An old Frankish word which was applied by kings and later nobles to their chief court officer. An equivalent English word is 'steward'. Historians use the two terms interchangeably.

style

An official and approved form of address adopted by kings, princes and prelates.

thegn

In the eleventh century a recognised grade of nobility in England. Thegns were wealthy landowners who were the dependents of kings or earls, and who had sufficient wealth to support a prestigious hall and retinue of their own dependents.

Triduum

The principal 'Three Days' of the Holy Week that preceded Easter: Maundy Thursday, Good Friday and Holy Saturday.

Truce (or Peace) of God

A mechanism sponsored by the bishops and abbots of France to limit the impact of war in the various provinces of France. It appears to have begun in Aquitaine and Burgundy in the 1020s and spread more generally throughout France in the following decades. It involved the binding of all adult males in a province by a solemn oath not to take up weapons on certain days, and excluded violence from religious precincts. Transgressors were subject to terrifying ecclesiastical penalties.

Vermandois

A Frankish principality established by an offshoot of the Carolingian dynasty in the ninth century. It was centred on Picardy between Flanders and Hainault to the north, the Carolingian fisc at Laon to the east and the Robertian lands around Paris to the south. It was for three centuries a very important northern French principality, and never more so when it was combined with the county of Flanders under Count Philip (1163–91). Following his death it lost its integrity and disappeared from the political map.

Medieval Sources and Authors

Adhémar of Chabannes (d. *c.* 1028)

Adhémar was a monk at Limoges in the county of Poitou, well-placed to write of the Viking devastation of the Loire valley in the ninth and tenth centuries. He wrote a chronicle of the Franks, which became his own independent work at the end of the tenth century, see his *Chronique*, ed. J. Chavanon (Paris, 1897).

Ailred of Rievaulx (d. 1163)

Son of Eilaf, priest of the community of Hexham, and descendant of a dynasty of clergy associated with the community of St Cuthbert, he was born around 1110. Ailred had a career as a courtier of King David of Scotland until *c.* 1134 when he encountered the new Cistercian community at Rievaulx in North Yorkshire. He entered it as a novice and was nominated as first abbot of its colony of Revesby in Lincolnshire in 1143. He returned to become abbot of Rievaulx itself in 1147. Apart from his important theological work, Ailred was a keen historian of the north of England, writing tracts on the history of Hexham and on the Battle of the Standard (1138). One particularly important work he composed was a tract *On the Genealogy of the Kings of England*, composed around the beginning of the year 1154 in honour of the young Duke Henry of Normandy (the future King Henry II) who had just been nominated as heir to King Stephen. The work praises the English (not Norman) lineage of the duke. An (untranslated) text is to be found in *Patrologia cursus completus, series latina*, ed. J-P. Migne, 221 volumes, Paris (1844–1864) vol. 195.

Anglo-Saxon Chronicle

The English-language annal of English history whose entries begin in the year 494, but whose systematic compilation seems to have begun in the reign of King Alfred the Great (871–99). It was kept concurrently at several great churches, but after the Norman Conquest it was maintained in English only at the abbey of Peterborough. The most convenient translation is the Everyman text by G. N. Garmonsway, *The Anglo-Saxon Chronicle* (2nd edn, London, 1954), but a more detailed and scholarly treatment of the later chronicle is *The Peterborough Chronicle, 1070–1154*, ed. C. Clark (2nd edn, Oxford, 1970).

Bayeux Tapestry

An unusual visual source still preserved in the treasury of Bayeux cathedral. The general consensus still seems to be that it was designed and embroidered in Kent probably around the year 1070 on the commission of Bishop Odo of Bayeux. A similar 'tapestry' is known to have been commissioned for Adela, countess of Blois-Chartres, the Conqueror's daughter, although it does not survive.

Brevis relatio de Guillelmo nobilissimo comite Normannorum

This is a short history of the Normans focused principally on the Conqueror and his sons, but including other diverse material. It was written at Battle abbey in Sussex between 1114 and 1120. For text see, *The Brevis relatio de Guillelmo nobilissimo comite Normannorum, written by a Monk of Battle Abbey*, ed. E. M. C. van Houts, in *Chronology, Conquest and Conflict in Medieval England, Camden Miscellany*, 35, Camden Society, fifth series, 10, (1997), pp. 1–48.

Brut y Tywysogyon (Welsh Annals of the Princes)

The Welsh equivalent of the Anglo-Saxon Chronicle, whose entries begin in 680. It was originally a Latin text compiled up to around 1100 in the episcopal community of Mynwy (St Davids) in Pembrokeshire, but thereafter at the Welsh minster church of Llanbadarn Fawr near Aberystwyth. It is very interested in the doings of the Norman kings of England and provides numerous independent insights. It exists nowadays only in several later medieval Welsh translations. For a Welsh text and English translation, *Brut y Tywysogyon, or the Chronicle of the Princes: Red Book of Hergest Version*, ed. and trans. T. Jones (Cardiff, 1955).

Carmen de Hastingae Proelio (Song of the Battle of Hastings)

A long Latin poem on the battle of Hastings which has attracted much debate as to its date of composition and authorship, attributed by Frank Barlow to Bishop Guy of Amiens, writing in 1070. For text and translation, see *The Carmen de Hastingae Proelio of Guy Bishop of Amiens*, ed. and trans. F. Barlow (Oxford, 1999).

Chronicle of Hyde Abbey

A problematical but very useful text. Its author is anonymous but from the text would seem to have been a secular cleric associated with the Warenne family, earls of Surrey and lords of Bellencombre. The author gives a history of what he called the 'Norman-English realm' from the death of Duke Robert I (1035) to 1120. His work is a valuable and independent source for the reigns of William Rufus and Henry I. The brief work is associated with Hyde Abbey (in Winchester) only because of the preservation of the text in its library. An untranslated text is appendix A of *Liber monasterii de Hyda*, ed. E. Edwards, Rolls Series (1866).

Discovery of the Relics of St Wulfram

This anonymous tract originated in the abbey of St-Wandrille in the Seine valley. It was composed in 1053–54 by a monk of the abbey who says that previously he had been a clerk in southern Normandy at Asnebecq. The author had access to older material and gives a number of insights into the family history and identity of an earlier Normandy. Text (but no translation): 'Inventio et miracula sancti Vulfranni', ed. J. Laporte, in, *Mélanges: XIVe série*, Société de l'histoire de Normandie (1938), pp. 21–83.

Dudo of St-Quentin

Dudo was a clerk from Vermandois whose acquaintance with Normandy and its rulers went back to the 980s; he became dean of the collegiate church of St-Quentin in his homeland. In 1025 he was one of the leading chaplains of Duke Richard II and was commissioned by the duke to tell the story of Normandy and its rulers in a way that reflected well on their piety and Frenchness. His version of Norman origins became the master-narrative behind the work of every subsequent generation. For this source, *De moribus et actis primorum Normanniae Ducum*, ed. J. Lair (Caen, 1865), and for a translation, *History of the Normans*, trans. E. Christiansen (Woodbridge, 1998).

Eadmer of Canterbury (d. 1124)

An English monk of the Benedictine cathedral community of Canterbury, who became a constant member of the household of Archbishop Anselm as sacristan of his chapel after his election in 1093 until the archbishop's death in 1109. He followed the archbishop into exile in 1097. He began a biography of Anselm during the archbishop's own lifetime and finished revising it around 1114: see *The Life of St Anselm, Archbishop of Canterbury*, ed. and trans. R. W. Southern (Oxford, 1962). He also wrote a general history of his own times, the *Historia novorum* which in fact covers the period from the Conquest up to 1121 although its value is limited after 1116 and it is obsessed by narrow Canterbury interests. A translation up to 1109 is *Eadmer's History of Recent Events in England*, trans. G. Bosanquet (London, 1964), the Latin text is to be found in *Eadmeri historia novorum in Anglia et opuscula duo de vita sancti Anselmi et quibusdam miraculis eius*, ed. M. Rule, Rolls Series (1884).

Fécamp abbey sources

The abbey of Fécamp had a long association with the ducal house and it is clear that the abbey kept historical notes as well as a set of annals. Fécamp is the likely source for a list of the burial places of the Norman dukes that was copied into the latter sections of the Battle abbey *Brevis relatio* (q.v.) and also for the famous ship list of 1066. See E. M. C. van Houts, 'The Ship List of William the Conqueror', in *Anglo-Norman Studies*, 10, ed. R. A. Brown (Woodbridge, 1988), pp. 165–77.

Flodoard of Reims (d. 996)

Flodoard was a canon of the episcopal community of Reims and set himself to draw up an annalistic history of the Western Franks from 919. He writes several contemporary notices of the developing principality of Rollo and his immediate descendants. Text is in *Les annales de Flodoard*, ed. P. Lauer, Collections des textes pour servir à l'étude et à l'enseignement de l'histoire, 39 (Paris, 1905). Flodoard also wrote a history of his great church, see *Historia Remesensis ecclesiae*, ed. M. Stratmann, *Monumenta Germaniae Historiae, Scriptores*, 39 (1998).

Galbert of Bruges
The murder of Count Charles of Flanders in 1127 at Bruges inspired several writers, of whom the most distinguished was Galbert, a notary of the town of Bruges. Galbert's work is a detailed and journalistic account of the critical and dangerous years 1127–28 in Flanders and has much to say of William Clito. See the translation and commentary, *The Murder of Charles the Good*, trans. J. B. Ross (New York, 1967).

Garnier of Rouen
Garnier was a noted poet and member of the collegiate community of St Stephen of Rouen at the end of the tenth century and is now chiefly famous for his satirical and scurrilous attack on his Irish neighbour, Moriuht, for which see *Moriuht*, ed. and trans. C. J. McDonough (Toronto, 1995).

Geoffrey Gaimar
A Lincolnshire clergyman who wrote a rhyming French 'History of the English' in the late 1140s, which he dedicated to the countess of Lincoln. Original though it is, the work has little information in it that is unique, although it is markedly more sympathetic to King William Rufus than the Latin monastic sources. The text (but no translation) is published as *L'estoire des Engleis*, ed. A. Bell (Anglo-Norman Text Society, 1960).

Gesta Stephani (The Deeds of King Stephen)
An anonymous history of the reign of Stephen, whose authorship was ascribed by Ralph Davis to Bishop Robert of Bath (1136–66). If it was not written by the bishop, it was certainly written by a senior cleric quite close to him. It was begun around 1147 when it seemed that Stephen would soon win the dynastic struggle with Mathilda, but by 1150 the author had decided the future lay with Duke Henry. It was revised probably soon after Stephen's death. See *Gesta Stephani*, ed. and trans. K. R. Potter and R. H. C. Davis (Oxford, 1976).

Henry of Huntingdon (d. c. 1157)

Son and successor of Nicholas, archdeacon of Huntingdon, Henry took up his office around 1110 and held it for nearly fifty years. He wrote several notable works, principally his *Historia Anglorum*, ed. and trans. D. Greenway (Oxford, 1996), a history of the English which becomes his independent work in the 1120s and carried on till the succession of Henry II. Although his chronicle is regrettably concise, Henry was one of only two historians who worked throughout Stephen's reign. He also wrote a satire on his times, *De contemptu mundi*, which is informative about leading men and women of the reign of Henry I. See Greenway edition for text and translation.

Hermann of Tournai (d. 1147)

Hermann was a senior monk and former abbot of Tournai in Flanders, and in 1142–43, while kicking his heels at the papal curia, wrote a history of his abbey. It is racy and chatty and contains a good deal of material relating to Normandy and England. A translation is *The Restoration of the Monastery of Saint Martin of Tournai*, trans. L. H. Nelson (Washington, DC, 1996).

John of Worcester

The Worcester chronicle compiled by the monk John up till 1141 is mostly a Latin translation of the lost version of the Anglo-Saxon Chronicle kept at Worcester until as late as 1120; however, from 1067 onwards, the work becomes more expansive and varied. John began collating his work in the 1120s and relied a lot on Eadmer's *Historia novorum* for the previous decades, but also trawled other local sources, notably a lost chronicle of Gloucester abbey. John's independent value is greatest in the 1130s. See the text and translation, *The Chronicle of John of Worcester*, ed. and trans. R. R. Darlington and P. McGurk, 3 vols (Oxford, 1995–98).

Orderic Vitalis (d. c. 1141)

Orderic was sent by his Anglo-Norman parents as a child oblate to the Benedictine abbey of St-Evroult in southern Normandy in 1085 at the age of ten, after a Shropshire childhood. He became a senior monk of the community, noted for his literary abilities. Inspired by the historical work of Bede, he began work on an 'ecclesiastical history' of the Norman church around 1114 and continued to work on it until his death in or soon after 1141. In fact it is a history of the Norman people and its rulers. His work on the earlier period is dependent on Dudo, William de Jumièges and William de Poitiers, but also incorporates his genealogical research on the early Norman families of the south of the duchy. For further details and a text, *The Ecclesiastical History*, ed. and trans. M. Chibnall, 6 volumes (Oxford, 1969–80). Orderic also annotated and expanded the work of William de Jumièges, for which see *The Gesta Normannorum Ducum of William of Jumièges, Orderic Vitalis and Robert of Torigni*, ed. and trans. E. M. C. van Houts, 2 vols (Oxford, 1992–5).

Planctus (Lament) for William Longsword
This poetic lament on the murder of the second Viking count of Rouen was written at the abbey of Jumièges soon after the event itself. The most accessible text and commentary is to be found in the site created by Robert Helmerichs: *http://www.ukans.edu/carrie/Planctus*.

Ralph Glaber (d. *c.* 1046)
Ralph was a Cluniac monk associated principally with the distinguished community of St-Bénigne of Dijon in Burgundy. This abbey had links with Normandy, and Ralph's abbot and patron at Dijon, St William (d. 1031) travelled to the duchy to reform the abbey of Fécamp, who died there. Not surprisingly, Ralph makes a number of useful references to Normandy and its rulers. His *Histories* and *Life of St William* are both to be found in *Rodulfus Glaber: Opera*, ed. and trans. J. France, N. Bulst and P. Reynolds (Oxford, 1989).

Richer of Reims
Richer was a contemporary of Flodoard at Reims, but his annals from 966 onwards are based on his independent memories, and continue into 998. Like Flodoard, he has independent material on the Normans and their activities in northern France and has a distinctly hostile attitude to Richard I of Rouen. See *Histoire de France*, ed. R. Latouche, 2 vols (Paris, 1937).

Robert de Torigny (d. 1186)

Robert was monk and prior of the Norman community of Bec-Hellouin and began his historical work early in the 1130s. He was elected abbot of Mont St-Michel in 1154, but continued work on his *Chronicles*, which are a major source for Norman history from the 1120s onwards. The untranslated Latin text is in *Chronicles of the Reigns of Stephen, Henry II and Richard I*, ed. R. Howlett, iv, Rolls Series (1889). Robert also made copious annotations on the work of William de Jumièges, for which see *The Gesta Normannorum Ducum of William of Jumièges, Orderic Vitalis and Robert of Torigni*, ed. and trans. E. M. C. van Houts, 2 vols (Oxford, 1992–95).

Symeon of Durham (d. 1129)

Symeon was precentor of the Benedictine cathedral comunity of Durham and a major literary figure in the north of England in his lifetime. A number of works are credited to his authorship, the principal being his *History of the Kings* – a chronicle of the kings of the English which continues through to 1129. His work is a key source for post-Conquest northern history, but is also (unexpectedly) very informative on Norman events in the 1120s, A text is in the second volume of *Symeonis monachi opera omnia*, ed. T. Arnold, 2 vols (Rolls Series, 1885).

Wace of Bayeux

Wace was already active as canon of Bayeux before 1135, for he says that he owed his promotion there to Henry I. His literary career lasted until the 1160s, and he produced two major vernacular works. His *Roman de Brut* is a French version of Geoffrey of Monmouth's legendary history of Britain. In the 1160s Wace was commissioned by Henry II to write the history of the Norman dynasty, his *Roman de Rou* ('Rou' being 'Rollo'). The work is largely a rehash in French of the work of previous Latin historians, although it includes some legendary material and Norman local history which is unique, and has an unusually positive outlook on King William Rufus. It ends with the aftermath of the battle of Tinchebray. The untranslated text is *Le Roman de Rou*, ed. A. J. Holden, 3 volumes, Société des anciens textes français (1970–73).

Walter Map (d. 1209/10)

A royal clerk of the reign of Henry II whose origins lay in Herefordshire. Famous as the author of a chatty scrap-book of stories for courtiers, called the *De nugis curialium* ('courtiers' trifles'), Map included in his book a number of unique stories going back to the reign of Henry I. His career brought him considerable promotion, including the chancellorship of Lincoln cathedral and archdeaconry of Oxford. See *De Nugis Curialium: Courtiers' Trifles*, ed. and trans. M. R. James, revised C. N. L. Brooke and R. A. B. Mynors (Oxford, 1983).

William de Jumièges (d. c. 1071)

After Dudo, William was the most influential early historian of Normandy. He was a monk of the abbey of Jumièges on the Seine, near Rouen, and was making historical notes there as early as 1026. In the 1050s he began his labours on a revision and continuation of Dudo, which he called 'The Deeds of the Dukes of the Normans'. He ended his work at the year 1069. See *The Gesta Normannorum Ducum of William of Jumièges, Orderic Vitalis and Robert of Torigni*, ed. and trans. E. M. C. van Houts, 2 vols, Oxford (1992–95).

William de Poitiers (d. c. 1080)

William was from a noble Norman family, which some reckon to have been that of the Conqueror's adviser, Roger de Beaumont, lord of Pont Audemer and Beaumont-le-Roger. After a warlike youth in the 1030s, he entered the clerical life, going to study at Poitiers. He returned to Normandy in the 1050s to take up a post as a chaplain of Duke William, and was given promotion to an archdeaconry in the diocese of Lisieux in the 1060s. In the aftermath of the Norman Conquest of England he began a account of the life and times of King William, of which an incomplete manuscript (up to 1076) survives. The missing books up to 1079 are preserved in part by Orderic Vitalis's extensive use of them. See *The Gesta Guillelmi of William of Poitiers*, ed. and trans. R. H. C. Davis and M. Chibnall (Oxford, 1998).

William of Malmesbury (d. c. 1143)

William was the most prolific and (some would say) distinguished of the Anglo-Norman historians. His clear and ironic Latin style has made him many friends down the ages. He was librarian of Malmesbury abbey, and a compulsive traveller and researcher. His first major historical works were produced in the 1120s, a paired secular and ecclesiastical history of England: the *De gestis regum Anglorum*, ed. and trans. R. A. B. Mynors, M. W. Thompson and M. Winterbottom, 2 vols (Oxford, 1998–99), and the as yet untranslated, *De gestis pontificum Anglorum*, ed. N. E. S. A. Hamilton, Rolls Series (1870). After some years of indifference to history writing, perhaps caused by the poor reception of his work, William returned to the history of England with his 'History of Recent Events' commissioned by Earl Robert of Gloucester, which tells the story of the latter years of Henry I and the early years of Stephen, up till the year 1143, when William must have died. See now *Historia novella*, ed. and trans. E. King (Oxford, 2000).

Witgar, priest of Compiègne

Between 951 and 959 Witgar composed a brief genealogical essay on the 'holy forbears' of Count Arnulf I of Flanders, the murderer of William Longsword. See *Genealogiae comitum Flandriae*, ed. L. C. Bethmann, in *Monumenta Historiae Germaniae, Scriptores*, 9, pp. 302ff.

Notes

Notes to Chapter 1: The Counts of Rouen

1. For 'jarl' p. 307.
2. See p. 305.
3. See p. 307.
4. See p. 308.
5. See p. 304.
6. Foe Dudo p. 313.
7. See p. 314.
8. See p. 317.
9. See p. 307.
10. See p. 311.
11. See p. 317.
12. See p. 309.
13. See p. 306.
14. Several writers have doubted the existence of this Gisla, but Witgar of Compiègne's genealogy of Count Arnulf of Flanders (compiled in the late 950s) mentions a daughter of Charles the Simple who was called by that name, *Genealogiae comitum Flandriae*, ed. L. C. Berthmann, in *MGH, Scriptores*, ix, p. 303.
15. See p. 10.

Notes to Chapter 2: Richard II and his Sons

1. See p. 315.
2. See p. 313.
3. See pp. 311–12.
4. *Rodulfus Glaber: Opera*, ed. and trans. J. France, N. Bulst and P. Reynolds (Oxford, 1989), p. 56.
5. See p. 309.
6. See p. 307.

7. See p. 308.

8. See p. 312.

9. See p. 308.

10. *Brevis relatio de Guillelmo nobilissimo comite Normannorum*, ed. E. M. C. van Houts, in *Camden Miscellany*, 34, Camden Society, fifth series, 10 (1997), p. 46.

11. See p. 307.

12. Wace, *Le Roman de Rou*, ed. A. J. Holden, 3 vols, Société des anciens textes français (1970–73), lines 1178–85.

13. D. R. Bates, *Normandy before 1066* (London, 1982), p. 33.

14. See p. 303.

15. Archives départementales de la Seine Maritime, 14 H 255, quoted in Bates, *Normandy before 1066*, p. 144.

16. The exception being William I, count of Eu (d. *c.* 1040), who fell out with his brother over the possession of Exmes early in his reign and was captured and imprisoned. See *Gesta Normannorum Ducum*, ii, pp. 8–9.

17. *Recueil des actes des ducs de Normandie de 911 à 1066*, ed. M. Fauroux (Caen, 1961), no. 74.

18. See pp. 316–17.

19. Orderic Vitalis, *The Ecclesiastical History*, ed. M. Chibnall (6 vols, Oxford, 1969–80), ii, pp. 24, 56.

20. See p. 303.

21. When the duke issued a charter at Fécamp in January 1035 the translation of the dating clause can be read in one version as 'the eighth year of our reign *and the fourth* in which I have sought of God and his saints an opportunity to go and seek Jerusalem', *Recueil des actes des ducs de Normandie de 911 à 1066*, no. 90.

22. E. M. C. van Houts, 'The Origins of Herleva, Mother of William the Conqueror', *English Historical Review*, 101 (1986), pp. 399–404.

23. Ibid., no. 60.

24. See p. 309.

25. See p. 313.

26. Ibid., no. 11.

27. Ibid., no. 58.

28. Ibid., nos 66, 68. The description *nutricius* 'fosterbrother', is often confused with *nutritor* 'foster-father'. There is a comparable example from the 1130s, when Roger earl of Warwick similarly endowed his foster-brother (*nutricius*) Gilbert with rents in the town of Warwick, where Gilbert's family was clearly prominent.

29. Ibid., no. 35.

Notes to Chapter 3: William of Normandy

1. When Orderic Vitalis dealt in the 1120s with the rebellion of William of Arques in 1052 he could only understand it as William being denounced and dispossessed by his uncle as a bastard (*nothus*). Orderic fails to note that William of Arques was also *nothus*. See *The Ecclesiastical History*, ed. M. Chibnall (6 vols, Oxford, 1969–80), iv, p. 84.
2. No impression of William's seal before 1066 survives, although we know he did use one. It is, however, probable that the ducal face of his two-sided seal after 1066 perpetuated the original design of the ducal great seal.
3. See p. 319.
4. *Recueil des actes des ducs de Normandie de 911 à 1066*, ed. M. Fauroux (Caen, 1961), no. 107, finds all these young men in attendance on the duke in an act datable to 1046–47.
5. See p. 36.
6. See p. 309.
7. *Recueil des actes*, no. 147.
8. See p. 305.
9. The vexed matter of this oath and grant is carefully considered by S. Keynes, 'The Æthelings in Normandy', in *Anglo-Norman Studies*, 13, ed. M. Chibnall (Woodbridge, 1991), pp. 177–81.
10. F. Barlow, *Edward the Confessor* (London, 1970), p. 109.
11. See p. 303.
12. See p. 303.

Notes to Chapter 4: The Conqueror of England

1. There were some dissidents, for we know that the prominent elder baron Roger de Beaumont would not join the expedition or (initially) receive the spoils of England; Roger did, however, allow his eldest son, Robert, to lead a company of troops, as his deputy.
2. See p. 313.
3. See p. 308.
4. The comment is part of an aside on effective generalship to be found in the *Roman de Thèbes*, ed. F. Mora-Lebrun (Paris, 1995), lines 7553–62 (a work of *c*. 1150 x 54).
5. See pp. 316–17.
6. See p. 307.
7. Hermann of Tournai, *The Restoration of the Monastery of Saint Martin of Tournai*, trans. L. H. Nelson (Washington, DC, 1996), p. 29.

8. *The Gesta Guillelmi of William of Poitiers*, ed. and trans. R. H. C. Davis and M. Chibnall (Oxford, 1998), p. 74; *The Letters of Lanfranc, Archbishop of Canterbury*, ed. H. Clover and M. Gibson (Oxford, 1979), p. 124.

9. D. R. Bates, *William the Conqueror* (London, 1989), p. 79.

10. Orderic Vitalis, ii, p. 232.

11. *Les miracles de Saint Benoît*, ed. E. de Certain, Société des historiens de France (Paris, 1858), pp. 336–37.

12. Ralph Glaber, *Histories*, p. 152.

13. See p. 306.

14. See pp. 304–5.

15. See p. 308.

16. *Domesday Book seu liber censualis Willelmi primi regis*, ed. A. Farley and others, 4 vols (London, 1783–1816), i, fol. 179r. The church of St Nicholas of Humbleyard hundred in Norfolk (possibly the church of St Nicholas outside the city gate of Norwich) was built with the king's consent before 1085 and there the priest 'cantat missam unaquaque ebdomada et psalterium pro rege', ibid., ii, fol. 263v.

17. See p. 314.

Notes to Chapter 5: William Rufus

1. See the discussion of Wulfnoth's fate in F. Barlow, *William Rufus* (London, 1983), p. 65n.

2. *De iniusta vexacione Willelmi episcopi primi per Willelmum regem filium Willelmi magni regis*, ed. H. S. Offler and revised by A. J. Piper and A. I. Doyle, *Camden Miscellany*, 34, Camden Society, fifth series (1997), p. 89; translation by Barlow, *William Rufus*, p. 89.

3. *The Gesta Guillelmi of William of Poitiers*, ed. and trans. R. H. C. Davis and M. Chibnall (Oxford, 1998), p. 178; *Le Roman de Rou*, ed. A. J. Holden, 3 vols, Société des anciens textes français (1970–73) ii, pt 3, lines 7095–10; Ælnoth of Canterbury, *Gesta Sweno magni regis et filiorum eius et passio gloriossimi Canuti regis et martyris* ed. M. C. Gertz, in *Vitae sanctorum Danorum*, 3 vols (Copenhagen, 1908–12), i, p. 99, quoted in R. Bartlett, *England under the Norman and Angevin Kings, 1075–1225* (Oxford, 2000), p. 573.

4. Barlow, *William Rufus*, pp. 108–10.

5. See p. 319.

6. See p. 314.

7. See pp. 315, 318.

8. See p. 306.

9. Eadmer, *History of Recent Events in England*, trans. G. Bosanquet (London, 1964), p. 40.

10. See p. 318.

11. Her words are from a deposition to Archbishop Anselm quoted by Hermann, abbot of Tournai, some years later. See *The Restoration of the Monastery of Saint Martin of Tournai*, trans. L. H. Nelson (Washington, DC, 1996), p. 32; see also Barlow, *William Rufus*, p. 311.

12. See p. 308.

13. J. H. Round, 'Walter Tirel and his Wife', in *Feudal England* (repr. London, 1964), pp. 355–63.

14. C. Warren Hollister, 'The Strange Death of William Rufus', *Speculum*, 48 (1973), pp. 637–53.

Notes to Chapter 6: Henry I

1. Movements reconstructed from, *Regesta Regum Anglo-Normannorum: The Acta of William I (1066–1087)*, ed. D. Bates (Oxford, 1998), nos 35, 49, 59, 193, 253.

2. This section on Henry's early life is based on D. Crouch, 'Robert of Gloucester's Mother and Sexual Politics in Norman Oxfordshire', *Historical Research*, 72 (1999), pp. 323–33.

3. See p. 305.

4. See pp. 130–35.

5. 'The *Brevis Relatio de Guillelmo nobilissimo comite Normannorum*', ed. E. M. C. van Houts, in *Camden Miscellany*, 35, Camden Society, fifth series, 10 (1997), p. 36.

6. Ibid., p. 37, is good and contemporary evidence that Henry did indeed supervise his brother's burial.

7. See p. 311.

8. See pp. 304–5.

9. *The Ecclesiastical History*, ed. M. Chibnall (6 vols, Oxford, 1969–80), v, p. 316.

10. Ibid., vi, p. 84.

11. See p. 319.

12. The leading men who devised the exchequer can be pinpointed. We have his great-nephew's word for it that Bishop Roger devised and administered its routine. But Count Robert must also have been closely involved, because he was operating an exchequer on his own estates before he died in 1118. This indicates that he had been involved in the planning stage and deployed the idea also for his own personal profit.

13. The phrase is used in an agreement drawn up between William d'Aubigné of Buckenham and St Albans abbey in or soon after 1107, to be kept with 'regiis cartiis Wintonie': Public Record Office, LR14/249.

14. J. A. Green, *The Government of England under Henry I* (Cambridge, 1986), pp. 41–42.

15. See p. 313.

16. Hugh the Chantor, *The History of the Church of York, 1066–1127*, ed. C. Johnson (London, 1961), p. 77.

17. I owe this observation to Professor Lois Hunneycutt.

18. The incident of the papal coronation at Chartres was alluded to by Innocent II in his letter to Stephen of 1136 (see Appendix 2). Innocent makes much of it, as giving him a right to assert himself in the English succession.

Notes to Chapter 7: Robert Curthose and William Clito

1. See pp. 130–35.

2. Cf. the comments in, Orderic Vitalis, *The Ecclesiastical History*, ed. M. Chibnall (6 vols, Oxford, 1969–80), iv, p. 162.

3. See pp. 163–64.

4. *Liber monasterii de Hyda*, ed. E. Edwards, Rolls Series (1866), p. 300.

5. The basis for his refusal of the kingship *causa laboris* is by Henry of Huntingdon, *Historia Anglorum*, ed. E. Edwards, Rolls Series (1866), p. 229. Henry reckoned that the refusal led to God's subsequent disfavour towards the duke, because he had preferred the ease of Normandy to labouring for his faith in the holy city (ibid., p. 236).

6. *Le Roman de Rou de Wace*, ed. A. J. Holden, 3 vols, Société des anciens textes français (Paris, 1970–73) ii, pt. 3, lines 9697–98; *Brut y Tywysogyon: Red Book of Hergest Version*, ed. T. Jones (Cardiff, 1955), *sub anno* 1100.

7. See pp. 169–72.

8. See pp. 174–78.

9. Orderic, vi, p. 286. The same story is given by a well-informed Flemish clergyman writing in the early 1140s: 'Henry commanded that Robert was to be supplied and provided with whatever was necessary in creature comforts as if they were for himself.' Herman of Tournai, *The Restoration of the Monastery of St Martin of Tournai*, trans. L. H. Nelson (Washington, DC, 1996), p. 30.

10. Galbert of Bruges, *The Murder of Charles the Good*, trans. J. B. Ross (repr. Toronto, 1982), p. 196.

Notes to Chapter 8: Stephen

1. See p. 305.
2. See translation in Appendix 2.
3. Ernald, abbot of Bonneval, *Vita sancti Bernardi: liber secundus*, in, *Patrologia Latina*, vol. 185, cols 301–2.
4. *Symeonis historia regum continuata per Johannem Hagustaldensem*, in *Historia regum*, ed. T. Arnold, Rolls Series (1885), p. 323.
5. *Histoire des ducs de Normandie et des rois d'Angleterre*, ed. F. Michel (Paris, 1840), pp. 80–81.
6. F. Sandford and S. Stebbing, *A Genealogical History of the Kings and Queens of England and Monarchs of Great Britain etc* (2nd edn, London, 1707), pp. 41–42.

Notes to Chapter 9: The Norman Dynasty

1. K.-F. Werner, *Naissance de la noblesse: l'essor des élites politiques en Europe* (2nd edn, Paris, 1998), esp. pp. 415–21.
2. *Le couronnement de Louis*, ed. E. Langlois, Classiques français du moyen âge (Paris, 1984), lines 859–60.
3. G. Duby, 'Remarques sur la littérature généalogique en France aux XIe et XIIe siècles', trans. C. Postan, as 'French Genealogical Literature: The Eleventh and Twelfth Centuries', in *The Chivalrous Society* (London, 1977), pp. 149–57.
4. *The Gesta Normannorum Ducum of William of Jumièges, Orderic Vitalis and Robert of Torigni*, ed. and trans. E. M. C. van Houts (2 vols, Oxford, 1992–5), i, p. 6.
5. *Rodulfus Glaber opera*, ed. J. France, N. Bulst and P. Reynolds (Oxford, 1989), p. 36 (my translation).
6. Hugh of Fleury, *Liber qui modernorum regum Francorum continet actus*, ed. G. D. Waitz, in *Monumenta Germaniae Historicae: Scriptores*, 9, pp. 376–81.
7. *Ivonis Carnotensis episcopi epistolae*, in, *Patrologia Latina: cursus completus*, ed. J-P. Migne (221 vols, Paris, 1844–64), vol. 162, no. 112, cols 265–66.
8. Orderic Vitalis, *The Ecclesiastical History*, ed. M. Chibnall (6 vols, Oxford, 1969–80), vi, p. 454 (my translation)
9. Ailred of Rievaulx, *Genealogia regum Anglorum*, in *Patrologia Latina: cursus completus*, ed. J-P. Migne (221 vols, Paris, 1844–64), vol. 195, cols 711–38.
10. Robert de Torigny, *Chronica*, in *Chronicles of the Reigns of Stephen, Henry II and Richard I*, ed. R. Howlett, 4 vols, Rolls Series (1884–89), iv, p. 10.

11. *Genealogia breves regum Francorum*, in *MGH Scriptores*, xiii, pp. 250–51.

12. *A Medieval Prince of Wales: The Life of Gruffudd ap Cynan*, ed. and trans. D. Simon Evans (Llanerch, 1990), pp. 24–25, 56.

Notes to Appendix I: The Name and Origins of 'Rollo'

1. *Fornaldar Sögur Norurlanda*, ed. G. Jónsson, 3 (Akureyri, 1954), translated as *Göngu-Hrólf's Saga: A Viking Romance*, trans. H. Pálsson and P. Edwards (Edinburgh, 1980).

Further Reading

Early Normandy

The most comprehensive and stimulating work in print in English is David Bates's *Normandy before 1066* (London, 1982) which was revolutionary in the way it integrated the Normans and Normandy into their French milieu: no longer were Normans born purely to conquer England. Eleanor Searle's *Predatory Kinship and the Creation of Norman Power, 840–1066* (Berkeley, CA, 1988) projects a different, more Scandinavian Normandy. On the growth of Norman identity, R. H. C. Davis, *The Normans and their Myth* (London, 1976) is not merely stimulating but also well-illustrated.

There have been a number of recent studies of the early ecclesiastical history of Normandy, two worthy of note being Felice Lifshitz, *The Norman Conquest of Pious Neustria* (Toronto, 1995), and Cassandra Potts, *Monastic Revival and Regional Identity in Early Normandy* (Woodbridge, 1997).

For the whole Norman achievement two worthwhile studies are John Le Patourel *The Norman Empire* (Oxford, 1976) and Charles Homer Haskins, *Norman Institutions* (Cambridge, Massachusetts, 1918). Detailed thematic studies can be found in *Normandy and England in the Middle Ages*, ed. David Bates and Anne Curry (London, 1994).

William the Conqueror

There have been many biographies of this singular monarch. The two which command the field now are David Douglas, *William the Conqueror* (London, 1964) and David Bates, *William the Conqueror* (London, 1989).

Robert Curthose

The only published study of the duke is Charles Wendell David, *Robert Curthose* (Cambridge, Mass, 1920), but Judith Green has recently published a reassessment of his reign in, 'Robert Curthose Reassessed', *Anglo-Norman Studies*, 22, ed. C. Harper-Bill (Woodbridge, 1999), pp. 95–116.

William Rufus

There is no competition to Frank Barlow, *William Rufus* (London, 1983).

Henry I

Until very recently there was no comprehensive study dedicated to the life of this outstanding king. The posthumous publication of C. Warren Hollister, *Henry I* (London, 2000) changed this. His administrative achievement however is amply commemorated by Judith Green, *The Government of Henry I* (Cambridge, 1986). Very much worth reading still are Warren Hollister's collected essays: *Monarchy, Magnates and Institutions in the Anglo-Norman World* (London, 1986).

Stephen

There are as many studies dedicated to Stephen and his reign as to that of the Conqueror: brief and stimulating introductions are R. H. C. Davis, *King Stephen* (3rd edn, London, 1990) and K. Stringer, *The Reign of Stephen* (London, 1993). The Empress Mathilda, Stephen's rival, is now elegantly memorialised by Marjorie Chibnall's *The Empress Matilda* (Oxford, 1991). The whole reign is most comprehensively treated by David Crouch, *The Reign of King Stephen, 1135–1154* (London, 2000). For a military history of the reign, see Jim Bradbury, *Stephen and Matilda: The Civil War of 1139–53* (Stroud, 1996). For a recent commentary on its historiography D. Matthew, *King Stephen* (London, 2002). Detailed thematic treatments of aspects of the reign are to be found in *The Anarchy of King Stephen's Reign*, ed. Edmund King (Oxford, 1994).

Index

The index covers the main text and appendixes, but not the glossaries. Persons bearing the same first name are indexed in the following order: clergy, royalty, dukes, counts and earls, viscounts and sheriffs, and the rest.